The Best American Sports Writing 2014

GUEST EDITORS OF
THE BEST AMERICAN SPORTS WRITING

1991 DAVID HALBERSTAM
1992 THOMAS MCGUANE
1993 FRANK DEFORD
1994 TOM BOSWELL
1995 DAN JENKINS
1996 JOHN FEINSTEIN
1997 GEORGE PLIMPTON
1998 BILL LITTLEFIELD
1999 RICHARD FORD
2000 DICK SCHAAP
2001 BUD COLLINS
2002 RICK REILLY
2003 BUZZ BISSINGER
2004 RICHARD BEN CRAMER
2005 MIKE LUPICA
2006 MICHAEL LEWIS
2007 DAVID MARANISS
2008 WILLIAM NACK
2009 LEIGH MONTVILLE
2010 PETER GAMMONS
2011 JANE LEAVY
2012 MICHAEL WILBON
2013 J. R. MOEHRINGER
2014 CHRISTOPHER MCDOUGALL

The Best AMERICAN SPORTS WRITING™ 2014

Edited and with an Introduction
by Christopher McDougall

Glenn Stout, *Series Editor*

A Mariner Original

HOUGHTON MIFFLIN HARCOURT

BOSTON • NEW YORK 2014

www.hmhco.com

ISSN 1056-8034
ISBN 978-0-544-14700-3

Printed in the United States of America
DOC 10 9 8 7 6 5 4 3 2 1

Contents

Foreword

THERE ARE MANY WAYS to measure the impact or success of a book. In these metric-driven times, the temptation is to reduce everything to data—sales figures, "starred" reviews, Facebook shares, etc. Even the fact that this is the 24th edition since the series launched in 1991 says something about its value.

Still, for this book, a collection of stories, perhaps the best measure is the stories inspired by *The Best American Sports Writing* itself. For me at least, that measure helps justify the work that goes into putting it together every year.

To be clear, I am not referring to the *writing* the book has inspired, although it is certainly true that it has done so, serving as some motivation for a generation of sportswriters. I mean instead the stories that contributors and readers have told me about the book, the personal stories about the role it has come to play in their lives.

In addition to my duties as series editor of this annual collection and as the author of the occasional book, for the past few years I have also served as editor of the longform journalism page for SBNation.com. As I acquire and then edit stories for the site, I have had the opportunity to talk writing and work with hundreds of writers; I find these interactions incredibly rewarding and gratifying—as much so at times as I find writing myself. At some point, most of these writers tell me what this book has meant to their career or to their development as a writer. It's something that is always nice to hear, and when I speak with the contributors to this book, they often tell me the same thing.

Given that I've been doing this since 1991, I am older than many contributors and almost all the writers I work with. I have become accustomed to hearing someone say, "I've been reading this book my whole life." Until recently, however, that statement was usually hyperbole.

Not anymore. Earlier this year, as I discussed a story with a younger writer, he blurted out that he found working with me "surreal." I laughed aloud and asked him why. In all seriousness, he told me that he had been reading this book his entire life. I paused, then asked him his age. When he told me, I did the math—not only was he correct, but in fact the first edition of this book predated his appearance on the planet by several years. In fact, I suspect that when he was first old enough to read this book, he was already 12 or 15 years behind. Reality, it seems, has more than caught up with flattery.

I also occasionally correspond on a variety of other matters with writers, including many *BASW* contributors. In one email exchange with a writer whom I've been happy to include in these pages more than once, he told me that the first thing anyone sees when they enter his house is his collection of *The Best American Sports Writing*. I think I responded with some quick quip—my series collection is in the basement, buried on a shelf in my terminally messy office under other books. He soon sent me another email with the subject line "What It Means."

Attached was a photograph. I clicked it open, and sure enough, on a set of shelves that appeared custom-made, was a complete stack of *The Best American Sports Writing*, 1991 through 2013, flanked by the books of writing legends such as Frank DeFord and Jim Murray.

But it's not just what books mean to my colleagues and other writers that matters. There's also the way books can connect readers and bring people together. My only disappointment with the growing trend to read books and stories on tablets and phones is that it is no longer possible to eavesdrop on what people are reading in public places, to find kindred minds by way of a book or magazine cover.

Years ago, I once traveled the country by train, a nearly month-long trip that took me from Boston south through New York and Washington to New Orleans, then up to St. Louis to visit family before heading southwest and up the West Coast to Los Angeles and San Francisco, where I pillaged the bookstores. I returned by way of Portland and Seattle before heading east—a marathon journey home after a more meandering start. But I had a bag full of new books, and as the Rockies gave way to the Great Plains and then the Great North Woods, I read my way back across the country.

Somewhere north of Chicago, on the fourth day since my last shower, someone tapped me on the back. Another passenger had seen what I was reading and wanted to talk. By the time we reached Boston a day and a half later, we were already friends, probably the most memorable part of an 8,000-mile journey across some 30 states.

A onetime *BASW* contributor told me a similar story about this book and the role it played in a friendship of his. He and his best friend from college had something of a mercurial relationship. A few years after graduating, they had a falling-out, stopped talking, and lost touch with each other. One day his former friend was killing time at a bookstore, not really looking for anything but just browsing, and he picked up a copy of this book. He absently thumbed through the pages, and when his eyes landed on the contributor's name, he yelled out in surprise, "Hey, I know this guy!" He was so surprised and excited that he grabbed several strangers and just had to show them that he knew one of the contributors: "My best friend from college wrote this!!!"

That gave him an excuse to reconnect. He called the contributor, told him about finding his story in this book, and they started talking again. They have remained close ever since, a friendship saved by the power and reach of words—and a little help from *The Best American Sports Writing.*

Then there was the time I accepted an invitation to speak. When I arrived and met the man who had invited me, we started chatting. He was a teacher, he said, and knew of me primarily from this book. He told me that when he got the book each fall he would set it aside without even cracking it open, waiting for a snow day. Then, on that special day in the late fall or early winter when he would get the call informing him that school was canceled, he knew it was time. As the snow fell he would settle into a comfortable chair, open the book, and spend his unscheduled holiday sinking into its pages. Now, when the phone rings in my house with news of a snow day or I sit as the snow falls reading through submissions, I think of him.

I could go on, but of all the stories this book has inspired I do have a favorite. A longtime reader of this title was on a bus—or perhaps a subway train, I can't recall—when a young person saw him carrying this book and struck up a conversation. As they chatted this reader mentioned that he was a sportswriter. The younger person, as yet undecided on a career, liked to write, liked sports, and grew curious. So he asked the sportswriter how one becomes a working writer, what courses to take and what to read—all the things young writers worry about. The sportswriter did his best to answer, but they soon arrived at the next stop. It was time to part ways, and he knew he had not answered all the young man's questions.

Then he remembered that he was carrying this book. As they parted he simply handed the young writer-to-be his copy of *The Best American Sports Writing*. "Just read this," he said.

I like to think it helped a young writer get off to a good start. One day I hope to hear the rest of that story, perhaps even in this book.

Each year I read every issue of hundreds of sports and general interest magazines in search of writing that might merit inclusion in *The Best American Sports Writing*. I also write or email the editors of many hundreds of newspapers and magazines and request submissions, and I send email notices to hundreds of readers and writers whose addresses I have accumulated over the years. I search for writing all over the Internet and make regular stops at online sources like Sportsdesk.org, Gangrey.com, Byliner.com, Longreads.com, Longform.org, Nieman.org, and other sites where notable sports writing is highlighted or discussed. Still, I also encourage everyone—readers and writers, friends and family, editors and enemies—to send me stories they believe should appear in this volume. Writers in particular are encouraged to submit—do not be shy about sending me either your own work or the work of those you admire.

Each submission to the upcoming edition must be made according to the following criteria. Each story

- must be column-length or longer.
- must have been published in 2014.
- must not be a reprint or book excerpt.
- must have been published in the United States or Canada.
- must be received by February 1, 2015.

All submissions from either print or online publications must be made in hard copy and should include the name of the author, the date of publication, and the publication name and address. Photocopies, tear sheets, or clean copies are fine. Readable reductions to 8½-by-11 are preferred. Newspaper stories should be submitted with either the original newspaper copy of the piece or a photocopy of the piece as originally published—not a printout of the web version. Individuals and publications should please use common sense when submitting multiple stories. I receive a heavy volume of material, so no submissions can be returned or acknowledged; it is also inappropriate for me to comment on or critique any submission. Magazines that want to be absolutely certain their contributions are considered are advised to provide a complimentary subscription to the address listed below. Those that already do so should extend the subscription for another year.

All submissions must be made by U.S. mail—weather conditions in midwinter here at *BASW* headquarters often keep me from receiving UPS or FedEx submissions. Electronic submissions by any means, whether email or Twitter or URLs, and pdfs or other electronic documents are not acceptable. Only some form of hard copy, please. The February 1 deadline is real, and work received after that date may not be considered.

Please submit either an original or a clear paper copy of each story, including publication name, author, and the date the story appeared, to:

Glenn Stout
PO Box 549
Alburgh, VT 05440

All submissions from me to the guest editor are made blindly, not identified by source or author.

Those with questions or comments may contact me at basw editor@yahoo.com. Copies of previous editions of this book can be ordered through most bookstores or online book dealers. An index of stories that have appeared in this series can be found at my website, glennstout.net, as can full instructions on how to submit a story. For updated information, readers and writers are also encouraged to join the *Best American Sports Writing* group on Facebook or to follow me on Twitter @GlennStout.

Thanks to guest editor Christopher McDougall for his attentiveness, to Michael Everett, Joel Reese, Wright Thompson, and Jon Gold for sharing their *BASW* stories with me, and to everyone at Houghton Mifflin Harcourt for supporting this book. My thanks also go to Siobhan and Saorla for stumbling over the occasional carton of submissions and not complaining too much. And to the writers collected within, I hope this book helps you find more stories.

GLENN STOUT
Alburgh, Vermont

Introduction

DEATH-ROW CELLS have better natural light than the Rite Aid in Lancaster, Pennsylvania, where you can only glimpse the sky through the sad slit of a window above the checkout counter. That's where I was gazing one afternoon when two bodies suddenly sailed past.

These guys had to be six feet in the air, flying by one after the other like they'd been slung out of a catapult. Moments later they reappeared outside the glass doors, this time swinging through the railings of the handicapped ramp. By the time I got to the cash register, I'd watched them hurdle, vault, tightrope-walk, and otherwise wring a crazy amount of movement out of those blue bars. I hurried outside to catch them, but they weren't leaving any time soon. "You start practicing parkour," one told me, "and whole nights disappear."

Technically, he was talking about *l'art du deplacement,* more universally known by the funkified version of its other name, *parcours*—French for "obstacle course." Parkour was born in the late 1980s, when a band of mixed-race kids living on the outskirts of Paris got tired of being roughed up by bullies. Together, they created their own "training method for warriors," as cofounder David Belle would explain. The original parkour tribe didn't mind mentoring other true believers who were willing to submit to their punishing tutorials, but otherwise they had just about zero interest in sharing their skill with the rest of the world. They detested the idea of competition and produced no training videos or instruction books. Until very recently, you had only two choices if you wanted to learn parkour: go to France or try your luck with YouTube.

Not surprisingly, the two guys I met in the Rite Aid parking lot got their start on the YouTube route. They studied videos of other self-taught parkour disciples and broke down lightning-quick sequences, frame by frame, into individual moves. Like the original parkour crew, they were using their own bodies to discover the most animal-efficient way to fly over, around, and under the hard edges of the city landscape the way monkeys tumble through the trees.

"I got into it because I was so fat," Neal Schaeffer told me. He'd begun partying after high school and by age 20 had bloated up from 175 pounds to 240. One afternoon he was in the park watching some strangers "Kong-vault" picnic tables—they'd charge a table, plant their hands, and shoot both feet through their arms like gorillas and fly off the other side—and Neal was talked into giving it a try. Neal was shocked to discover that even out of shape, once he got over his fear he could master skills that at first looked impossible.

Well, maybe not *master.* "You're on this endless trajectory where you're always getting better, but it's never good enough," Neal explained. "That's what's so exciting. As soon as you land one jump, you can't wait to try it again. You're always looking for ways to make it cleaner, stronger, flow into your next move." Neal became a member of a local parkour tribe that likes to train after midnight, when the city is all theirs. Whenever a police car prowls by, they drop to the ground and bang out push-ups. "No matter what time it is, no one bothers you when you're exercising." Within a year, Neal was so fit and trim he was able to scramble to the roof of a three-story building and hang off the flagpole like Spider-Man. *You're back,* he told himself.

Neal still doesn't rank his skills on the level of Andy Keller, a recent college grad who returned to Lancaster to rejoin his local parkour homies. You can tell within about 90 seconds of meeting Andy that he'd probably be superb at any sport he tried. He's strong and graceful, with a swimmer's broad back and enough bad-assery, as I witnessed firsthand the day we met, to bust out a back flip in the middle of a crowded coffee shop because his buddy dared him. I'd come to see him because of a theory I was looking into that the sports that truly evolved from human survival were the ones with the smallest performance gap between men and women. Logically, anything our ancestors relied on to stay alive would be activities that both men and women, old and young alike, would be good at. Endurance sports fit the bill, as 64-year-old Diana Nyad demonstrated when she became the first person to ever swim from Cuba to Florida without a shark cage. And what about parkour? With its emphasis on agility, control, and creativity, was it the tightest link we have in sports to our evolutionary past?

Andy agreed to show me the ropes. Which is how, a few days later, I found myself facing a six-foot-high brick wall outside a bank during the lunch-hour rush on the busiest street in Lancaster. "You've got to learn to shut out distractions," Andy said. "Forget who's watching you. Forget where you are. Just focus, and go." Then he broke into a sprint, hitting the wall full speed. He ran right up the bricks, grabbing for the top and vaulting over. As he trotted back, he was met with applause. An audience had formed, blocking the sidewalk.

"Impressive, isn't he?" I said to the guy beside me.

"I knew he'd make it," the man responded. "I'm waiting to see if *you* do."

Nosy Guy just bugged me at the time, but later—much later, when I was sitting in the middle of dozens of great sports stories from the past year and trying to put my finger on what connected them—I thought back to the way he'd watched me bang the tar out of my knees that afternoon and realized I was kind of glad he'd been there. In his own way, Nosy Guy is what sports writing is all about. Our games are at their best when they're shared, when electricity jumps from the player on the field to the fan in the stands and a connection is sparked between what you see and what you believe you can do yourself.

That's what happened to me when I came across David Merrill's wonderful story "The One-Legged Wrestler Who Conquered His Sport, Then Left It Behind" and Amanda Hess's "You Can Only Hope to Contain Them," her so-smart (and superbly titled) piece on, arguably, the most important breakthrough in athletic equipment of our lifetime: the sports bra. I felt the shock; the spark crackled between my life and two worlds I knew nothing about. I'd never imagined what it would be like to kneel on a mat with one leg and hope I could somehow burst up and around and take down someone with all limbs attached. Deep-diving into that experience through Merrill's reporting made me think that maybe, you know, scuffing myself up on a brick wall to learn parkour wasn't much to whine about after all. And wow! To reach the peak of collegiate wrestling despite that handicap and then suddenly walk away because . . . well, dig in for yourself and find out.

Likewise with breasts. I didn't know Amanda Hess's writing before coming across this piece, but I'm on high alert from now on. What remains with you after you've read it isn't even her light-touch storytelling and ability to pull up just the right tales to bring her point to life, but the gratitude you feel whenever someone opens your eyes so that you see things differently from then on. When I finished reading the stories nominated for this year's collection, I was so blown away I went online to announce, "I'll stack *Best American Sports Writing 2014* against any *Best American* anything of any year." I'd never known I could feel sympathy for such devils as Don King, a criminal cage fighter, and bull sharks. Until Don Van Natta Jr. unearthed secrets from a generation ago, I had no idea that Bobby Riggs loved Billie Jean King. Truly loved her.

Did you? Well, strap in. You have no idea what you're about to discover.

CHRISTOPHER MCDOUGALL

The Best American
Sports Writing
2014

PAUL SOLOTAROFF with RON BORGES

The Gangster in the Huddle

FROM ROLLING STONE

THE FIRST TEXT pinged him around nine that Sunday night: *I'm coming to grab that tonight, you gon b around? I need dat and we could step for a little again.* For Odin Lloyd, this was bang-up news, proof that his luck had turned around. Aaron Hernandez, the Pro Bowl tight end of the New England Patriots, was coming by later to scoop him up for another five-star debauch, just 36 hours after he'd taken Lloyd out for the wildest ride of his life. All night Friday, they'd kicked it at Rumor, popping bottles and pulling models up the steps of the VIP section of the Boston theater district's hottest club. "Shit was crazy," Lloyd told friends the next day at his niece's dance recital. "The girls were off the chain. We smoked that super-duper and Aaron dropped 10 G's like it was nothing. We kept rolling past dawn at his big-ass mansion, then he tossed me the keys to his Suburban."

Big doings for a semipro football player and underemployed landscape helper, though there too fortune smiled on Lloyd, 27. He'd just gotten word that he'd have shifts all week, his first steady hours in some time. And now he was about to burn it down again with Hernandez, the $40 million man with the restless streak and a bottomless taste for chronic. The problem, Lloyd said, was it didn't end there with Hernandez and his how-high crew: "Them boys is into way worse shit than herb."

How much worse? About as bad as it gets, say longtime family friends. In exclusive conversations with *Rolling Stone*, those friends, who insisted they not be named, say Hernandez was using the maniacal drug angel dust, had fallen in with a crew of gangsters and convinced himself that his life was in danger, carrying a gun wherever he went. Sources close to the tight end add that throughout the spring, when players are expected to be preparing themselves for the marathon NFL season, Hernandez had missed workouts and sessions with a rehab trainer and had been told by his head coach, Bill Belichick, that he was one misstep from being cut.

But training camp was six weeks away, and Hernandez wasn't one to heed a warning. He went on hitting the clubs with his boys, including Lloyd, who was dating his fiancée's sister. That Sunday, Lloyd's best friend urged him to stay home, saying he needed his sleep for the week ahead. Lloyd had already been up all weekend—he'd taken his friends clubbing Saturday night in Hernandez's black Suburban. Hernandez wouldn't hear it, though; he kept texting Lloyd. *Aite, where?* Lloyd relented, ignoring his friend. *It don't matter but imma hit you,* said Hernandez at 9:39. *If my phone dies imma hit u when I charge it.*

Tonight, though, wouldn't be anything like Friday. All weekend, Hernandez had been stewing in his 7,000-square-foot mansion 45 minutes outside Boston in North Attleborough, not far from Gillette Stadium, where the Patriots play, fixated on something that happened in the club two nights earlier. Per a close friend of Lloyd's, they'd been getting buzzed in VIP when Lloyd saw two of his cousins downstairs. He went to hug them up and buy them drinks when one of them, a West Indian with dreads, started pointing and mean-mugging Hernandez. "I don't like that nigger, he's one of them funny people," said the cousin. "Stop pointing, that's my boy," said Lloyd of Hernandez. "You're gonna start some shit 'tween me and him." "Well, I don't want you with him, he's a punk," said Lloyd's cousin, jabbing his finger again in Hernandez's direction.

When Lloyd went back upstairs, Hernandez was enraged. Club security cameras allegedly captured the two men squabbling, showing Hernandez, six-two and a rippled 250, facing off with the five-eleven Lloyd. The friends stopped short of throwing punches, though cameras mounted outside the club show the argument resuming in the street.

Most people, even self-important stars blowing thousands on bottle-shaped women, might have simmered down about now. But the 23-year-old Aaron Hernandez wasn't like most people; for ages, he hadn't even been like himself. The sweet, goofy kid from Bristol, Connecticut, with the klieg-light smile and ex-thug dad who'd turned his life around to raise two phenom sons—*that* Aaron Hernandez had barely been heard from in the seven hard years since his father was snatched away, killed in his prime by a medical error that left his boys soul-sick and lost. Once in a great while, the good Aaron would surface, phoning one of his college coaches to tell him he loved him and to talk to the man's kids for hours, or stopping Robert Kraft, the Patriots' owner, to kiss him on the cheek and thank him damply. There was such hunger in that kid for a father's hand, and such greatness itching to get out, that coach after coach had covered for him whenever the bad Aaron showed—the violent, furious kid who was dangerous to all, most particularly, it seems, to his friends.

And so, two days after the spat with Lloyd, he was nursing his rubbed-raw grievance. "You can't trust anyone anymore!" he's heard screaming on the footage of his home-security system. Sometime that night, he reached out to a couple of Bristol goons, Ernest Wallace and Carlos Ortiz—two stumblebum crooks with long sheets of priors and no job or fixed address to lay their heads—and ordered them to take the two-hour drive to Boston on the double, telling one of them, *Hurry ur ass up here, nigga.*

Around 1:10 A.M., Hernandez set off with Wallace and Ortiz in a rented Nissan Altima to pick up Odin Lloyd. Hernandez's security cams show him with what looks like a Glock .45 in hand, pacing in his living room. On the 30-mile drive to Fayston Street, a war-zone block in the Dorchester neighborhood of Boston, where Lloyd lived with his mother and younger sister (he'd been forced to move home after losing his job at the local utility company), the three men stopped to buy a pack of blue cotton-candy Bubblicious and a cheap cigar, the type used to roll blunts. Usually, that was Lloyd's job—Hernandez fondly called him the Bluntmaster. Making do without him, they got to Lloyd's house at 2:33 A.M., where a surveillance camera posted across the street showed Lloyd getting into the backseat of the Nissan. It fast became clear to Lloyd, though, that this wouldn't be a night of hot-sheet fun. He began firing texts off to his sister, sending distress flares every few minutes. *U saw who I'm with . . . Nfl . . . just so u know . . .*

The last one reached her at 3:23 A.M. Minutes later, Lloyd got out of the car in an industrial park in North Attleborough. He seemed to know what was coming, but decided to make a stand:

the driver's side mirror of the Nissan was broken off, a sign that he might have gone down swinging. On a sand-and-gravel patch, Lloyd raised his arms in defense of the first shot, and was then hit in the back twice as he turned away and fell to the ground. The gunman pumped two more rounds into his chest for good measure. The next day, cops lifted tire tracks near the body that matched the Nissan. Tracing the car back to the rental agency, police would eventually recover a .45 shell case and a wad of cotton-candy Bubblicious. And though Hernandez would monkey with his home-security system, getting rid of six hours of key recordings, and smash up the cell phone he'd turn in to cops, he'd neglect to scrub all the data they contained, handing police a honeypot of incriminating evidence.

They'll need every bit of it to convict Hernandez of murder and send him away for life. Both on the field and off, he's been hell to bring down; the man has a genius for breaking loose. According to several experts, he might just do it again, make one last run to daylight around the edge.

There have been 47 arrests of NFL players since the end of the last regular season: bar brawls, cars wrecked, spouses shoved or beaten. Violence travels; it follows these men home, where far too many learn they have no kill switch. But there's the sociopathy of a savage game, and then there's Aaron Hernandez. Since 2007, he's been charged with, or linked to, the shootings of six people in four incidents. Three of the victims were gruesomely murdered. One survivor, a former friend named Alexander Bradley, has had multiple operations and lost his right eye. The other two survivors were shot in their car outside a Gainesville, Florida, bar after an altercation involving Hernandez and two of his teammates his freshman year at the University of Florida. While in Gainesville, he sucker-punched a guy and shattered the fellow's eardrum, and reportedly failed multiple drug tests, though he was suspended only once for those offenses. He posed for selfies in the mirror while (a) wielding a .45 and (b) swathed from head to toe in Bloods regalia, and threatened to "fuck up" Wes Welker, his Pro Bowl teammate, just days after being drafted by the Patriots. (Welker, a veteran, had refused to help the rookie operate the replay machine.) Since high school, he's scourged his skin with a scree of tattoos. Writ large on his left arm: HATE ME NOW. On the meat of his right hand, just above the knuckles: the word BLOOD in bright-red scrawl.

Of all the questions raised by the murder of Lloyd, two enigmas underpin the others: How did a kid so rich in gifts and honors—the most celebrated son in the history of Bristol—grow into such a murderously angry man? And why does Bristol, the town that time forgot, keep landing in the middle of this lurid story?

This city of 60,000 was always a sweet, sleepy place to buy a house, raise children, and send them elsewhere. The locals built firearms and doorbells in the plants here, then car parts and main-springs for clocks. The population spiked in the decades after D-Day—vets moving in to take factory jobs and rent small pillbox homes on the west side of town. No one got rich or stuck around for college, but it was heaven to be a 12-year-old here: manicured ball fields, Boys Club summers, a sky-blue pool in every park.

Aaron's father, Dennis, ruled those fields before his son followed in his footsteps. In the '70s and '80s, Dennis and his twin brother, David, became local sports heroes. Enormous for their age and fast and tough, they took to football straightaway and were happier running through, than around, you. They'd be three-sport stars in high school and draw scouts to their games, though as good as they were at football, they were better in street fights, say friends: nobody fucked with the Hernandez boys.

"They were the roughest kids by far in Guinea Alley," says Eddy Fortier, who went to Bristol Central with them in the '70s and is a former youth counselor. "They had to be tough—they were about the only Puerto Ricans in an Irish-Italian town," says Fortier's brother, Gary, a reformed ex-con who's now a painter and assistant pastor at a Bristol church.

Dennis, in particular, was built for big things. A larger-than-life charmer with a maitre d's flair and a habit of hugging everyone he met, he was called "The King" in his glory days and owned the back pages of the *Bristol Press*. An All-Everything tailback, he was the rare kid from Bristol to get a full-ride offer to the University of Connecticut, the state's only Division I football program. (David, a wide receiver, got one too.) Alas, Dennis was no angel: he loved to drink and get high, and had lousy taste in friends, which did him in. His best buddy was a teammate, Rocco Testa, who fancied himself a mobster-in-training. "Rocco and his uncle did burglaries together, broke into houses here in town," says Detective Sergeant John Sassu of the Bristol Police Department, who also went to high school with the twins. "He got Dennis and David in it before the three of them went to UConn, then more so after they all dropped out."

The twins were pinched for small-change crimes—assault and petty larceny—in the decade after they both left UConn. As late as 1990, Dennis was busted for burglary, though neither brother seems to have done prison time. Friends say they also occasionally smoked crack, beat up dealers for drugs and cash, and bet way over their heads on sports. As for their pal Testa, he was caught in the act while robbing a house with his uncle, who shot and killed a cop while they tried to escape. "The rumor on the street was Dennis and David were there too," says Sassu, "but we couldn't make the case."

Either way, parenthood seemed to scare the twins straight. Both became fathers, found steady work, and had no further truck with Bristol cops. (Neither David nor anyone else in the Hernandez family returned phone calls seeking comment.) Dennis married Terri Valentine, a school secretary in Bristol, and got a job on the custodial staff at the other of the town's two high schools, Bristol Eastern. They bought a small cottage on Greystone Avenue and produced two wildly gifted sons: DJ, now 27 and an assistant football coach at the University of Iowa, and Aaron, three years younger but bigger and faster, the apogee of the family's genetics.

Each surpassed his father, both on the field and off, in part because Dennis took elaborate pains to keep them on the straight and narrow. Dennis built a gym in the family basement, paved a chunk of the backyard over for a half-court and staged three-on-three tourneys there, and peppered the boys with can-do slogans, burning them in through repetition. "Some do, some don't," he was always telling them. "If it is to be, it is up to me," went another. He was bent on getting his sons to do everything right, whether it was making the proper blitz read or handing homework in on time, perhaps because he'd squandered his own chance.

DJ seemed his natural heir—the star passer and guard at Bristol Central who played three years of quarterback at UConn and made the dean's list two years running—until Aaron blew by him on the rail. A huge-for-high-school tight end with wideout speed and a pair of glue-trap hands, he posted the kind of numbers you never see in Northeast states: 1,800 yards and 24 touchdowns in a season, almost 400 yards receiving in a single game, and 12 sacks and three forced fumbles as a part-time blitzer, winning Defensive Player of the Year honors his junior year in 2005. His great asset, besides his hands, which were strong as clamps, was the gift scouts call escapability; he couldn't be brought down after the catch. He was too big and too fast, and he used his free arm well to shed tacklers. You had to gang up or pin him against the sideline, and even then he'd wriggle out for more yards. "Best athlete this city's ever produced, and a more polite, humble kid you couldn't find," says Bob Montgomery, a columnist for the *Press* and the town's official historian. "He'd be in here with his father being interviewed as Athlete of the Week, and there was never any swagger or street stuff from him, just 'Yes, sir,' 'No, sir,' and 'Thank you.'"

"Part of Aaron's problem is, he never got no street sense; Dennis sheltered them from that life with all his might," says Gary Fortier. "He was the perfect dad: he went to every scrimmage, and got 'em up at dawn to work out," says Brandon Beam, an insurance agent in Southington who played against Aaron in practice each day as a cornerback for Bristol Central. A middle-class, mixed-race kid (mom Italian; dad Puerto Rican), Aaron had little trouble fitting into suburban Bristol. "He didn't speak Spanish and had no tattoos," says Jordan Carello, a Bristol football teammate who recently worked at the Doubletree hotel in town. "He was so focused on his body that he barely partied, maybe snuck a little weed here and there. But we all did that, 'cause our parents were always home. If we wanted to drink on weekends, we had to run out to someone's car."

His high school friends describe Aaron as an overgrown goof who was always trolling for laughs. "The guy would do anything to crack us up," says Beam. "Stuff his lunch in his mouth in a single bite, or take a booger that was hanging out and eat that shit." That was Hernandez: physically older than everyone else, but socially about five years younger. Friends say DJ was fiercely protective of his happy-go-lucky lug of a kid brother and taught him what hard work really looked like. They'd be out running suicides in the dead of summer, and rising early to do squats in the basement. "Aaron was driven by DJ, who was like his second dad," says Beam. "He really wanted to make Dennis happy."

It was a very different story with his mother, Terri. "She was good about schoolwork and that sort of stuff," says a friend of the family, "but she brought drama into that house—starting with the bust for taking bets." In 2001, when Aaron was 12, Terri was arrested in a statewide sting for booking bets on sports. The matter was handled quietly and she did no time, but she cast shame on the boys and dug a rift with Aaron that deepened over the next several years. Friends say Terri had begun cheating on Dennis with a physically abusive coke dealer named Jeffrey Cummings, who was married to Dennis's niece, Tanya Cummings.

Terri's relationship with Cummings, whose nickname is Meathead, was a bottomless source of grief for the sons. There was an ugly spectacle in the stands at a UConn game, says a family friend. Terri, on hand to watch DJ play, was angrily confronted by her niece and slapped in the face. The aftermath, says the friend, "hurt Aaron bad and broke his heart."

He might have held it together, or handled the fallout better, if Dennis had been around to see him through it. But in January 2006, Dennis checked himself in for a hernia repair at a local hospital. Something happened on the table, though, and he contracted an infection; two days later, he was dead. He was 49, in otherwise splendid health, and beloved by virtually everyone in town. His funeral, at the Church of St. Matthew, was like an affair of state: 1,500 mourners packed the biggest church in Bristol, and hundreds more waited to view the body. DJ was inconsolable, sobbing over the casket, but Aaron, 16 and shocked beyond tears, sat stone-faced. Friends tried to console him or draw him out; instead, he locked down, going mum. "He'd open up the tiniest bit, then say nothing for weeks, like it was a sign of weakness to be sad," says Beam. "His brother was at college, and the only other person he would really talk to was the one who was taken away."

Heartsick and furious, Aaron seemed to implode. "He would rebel," Terri told USA Today in an interview three years later. "He wasn't the same kid, the way he spoke to me. The shock of losing his dad, there was so much anger." Small wonder there: she moved Cummings into the house she shared with Aaron, and married him when his divorce from Tanya was final.

To no one's great surprise, cops soon fielded phone calls that Cummings was abusing Terri. "We responded to that address on more than one occasion," says Detective Lieutenant Kevin Morrell of the Bristol PD. In June 2010, Cummings got drunk one night and flew into a rage. Grabbing a knife from the kitchen, he slashed Terri's face and body before she fled to her neighbors next door. Cops arrested Cummings in the yard and charged him with assault and sent him to prison for two years. Terri divorced him that year, but took him back, say friends, when he was released in 2012. At last report, they had split for good; she currently lives alone on Greystone Avenue, though she hasn't been seen there much since Lloyd's murder. It bears noting that she's the rare-bird NFL mother whose son didn't buy her a big house when he got drafted.

With Cummings around, Aaron began getting scarce, spending a lot of time with family across town, in a roughneck stretch called Lake Avenue. This was the Bristol version of downward mobility, a hop from the hot plate to the fire. His father's brother-in-law, Uncle Tito, had a house up the block from the projects, where he lived with his grown daughter Tanya—the woman Cummings had ditched to be with Terri. Aaron and Tanya, first cousins bonded by loss, drew close very quickly, friends say. (He has the name of her son—Jano—tattooed on his chest, and has supported them both financially since college.) Among the dubious people hanging around the house were goons like Ernest Wallace and T. L. Singleton, an older-but-not-wiser drug dealer who'd been in and out of prison since the '90s. Singleton would wind up marrying Tanya and siring a child with her after Cummings left. Along with fringe hustlers like Carlos Ortiz, the angel-dust tweaker, they filled the heart-size hole Dennis left, bolstering Aaron with bromides about family love and vowing that they'd always have his back—which is another way of saying they sunk their claws in. Their motives couldn't have been plainer if they'd hung them in neon: here was a kid with can't-miss skills, a malleable man-child who'd be rich one day and fly them out of the hood in his G-5. All they had to do was get him high and gas his head, inflame his sense of grievance at life's unfairness.

From middle school, Hernandez had his sights set on UConn, and committed there as a star at Bristol Central. It had been Dennis's dream to see his boys play there together, having quit the school himself after a couple of years and gone home with his tail between his legs. But then Dennis died, making a jumble of things, and the world came courting his younger son. Enter the University of Florida and the messiah, Urban Meyer, who persuaded Hernandez to renege on UConn and come to Gainesville. It seemed a gift from on high: a championship program in a Bible Belt town with a deeply pious coach and devout assistants. Meyer had a rep for reforming players who'd had trouble elsewhere with the law. And he tried, God knows, to convert Hernandez; did everything short of an exorcism. "But there's only so much you can do in three years," says John Hevesy, Hernandez's position coach with the Gators and now a coach at Mississippi State. "Bristol had him for 17 before he came to us. In the end, I guess, that trumped what we put in."

Hernandez left home in January 2007, taking early graduation to enroll at Florida and be eligible for spring football. But he was miserable and overmatched his first year there and told friends on the phone he wanted to quit. Meyer brought him in for face-to-face meetings, reading Scripture in his office each morning. He assigned Mike and Maurkice Pouncey, twin All-American linemen, to babysit Hernandez, and detailed Tim Tebow, the truest of believers, to be his life instructor. But even Tebow couldn't save him from himself once Hernandez got a few beers in his system. The pair went out that April to a bar near campus, where the underage Hernandez had an argument with a waiter and punched him in the head as he walked away. Michael Taphorn suffered a ruptured eardrum, but didn't press charges on Hernandez, telling the cops he was talking to Florida coaches, according to a police report. The matter seems to have been settled quietly out of court, which was fine with Gainesville cops and the DA. They treated the punchout as a juvie offense, giving Hernandez a deferred prosecution on the hush.

"We didn't hear that story till much, much later—the police didn't file a report," says a local reporter who was covering the team. As a sophomore, Hernandez was benched for the season opener, meaning he'd likely failed drug tests over the summer. But Meyer denied it, saying he "wasn't ready to play," again giving cover for bad behavior. "Meyer kept us at such a distance," says the reporter, "or flat-out lied, that we couldn't verify a pot suspension."

Hernandez would fail other drug tests, according to reports, and should have faced bans for up to half a season, per school regulations. Instead, he didn't miss a single snap, though he was seen hanging out with a crew of thugs at a local bar. One of them was Bristol pal Ernest Wallace, who came down to Florida, says a friend, to be "Aaron's muscle."

"I never saw him with them, but misery attracts misery: there's vultures waiting to swoop," says Coach Hevesy, who did everything he could to protect Hernandez. He brought him home for meals twice a week, took him deep-sea fishing, and treated him like the oldest of his three kids. "He played video games with my son, and my daughter wore his jersey to sleep. But whenever he left campus, he'd come back different. That's when the problems happened."

Those problems didn't hinder his development, however. He was the rare college freshman who outworked upperclassmen, training by himself even before the gym opened, doing kick-flips off the wall of his dorm. As a sophomore, he became a starter and Tebow's third-down outlet, leading the team in catches in the national championship win in 2008, the school's second title in three years. "You see his athleticism and explosiveness, and as an athlete, it's incredible," said Tebow. By 20, Hernandez was a first-team All-American and winner of the 2009 John Mackey Award as the country's top tight end. He could have written his own ticket if he'd kept his nose clean: been a high-first-rounder in the 2010 NFL draft and pulled an eight-figure bonus to sign. Instead, he cemented his don't-touch rep by getting embroiled in a shooting outside a bar. "He was out with the Pounceys and [ex-Gator safety] Reggie Nelson, and some guys tried to snatch a chain off one of the Pounceys," says the local reporter. "The guys drive off, then stop at a light, and someone gets out of a car and shoots into their car through the passenger window. One victim described the shooter as possibly Hispanic or Hawaiian, with lots of tattoos on his arms." The Pounceys were questioned as witnesses to the crime, but Hernandez invoked his right to counsel and never gave a statement, most odd since he was also called as a witness. No charges have ever been filed, and the case is still open. Again, he walked away unscathed: he wasn't even named in the police report. In hindsight, it might have been the worst thing for him. He seems to have concluded, with an abundance of probable cause, that he was untouchable.

In April 2010, a few months before the NFL draft, Hernandez sat down and composed a letter, or had his agent at Athletes First do so for him. (The firm is a top-tier NFL shop, repping Ray Lewis, Aaron Rodgers, and Clay Matthews, among others.) It was a Hail Mary pass to 32 teams, asking them to spike their bad reports and pick a dope-smoking, hair-trigger hothead. "My coaches have told you that nobody worked harder than me," he wrote. "The only X-factor is concerns about my use of recreational drugs. To address that, I am putting my money where my mouth is" by offering to take eight drug tests during the season and to return a portion of his paycheck if found dirty. This was both delusional and an empty vow: the players' union would block even one extra test and any attempt to pay back guaranteed money. After seeing his predraft psychological report, where he received the lowest possible score, 1 out of 10, in the category of "social maturity" and which also noted that he enjoyed "living on the edge of acceptable behavior," a handful of teams pulled him off their boards and 25 others let him sink like a stone on draft day, April 24. Only one team took the bait, burning a midround pick on a guy with "character issues": the stoop-to-conquer Patriots of Bill Belichick.

Time was, the Pats were the Tiffany franchise, a team of such sterling moral repute that they cut a player right after they drafted him, having learned he had a history of assaulting women. But Belichick, the winner of three Super Bowl titles and grand wizard of the greatest show on turf, had decided long before he got to New England that such niceties were beneath him. Over a decade, he'd been aggregating power unto himself, becoming the Chief Decider on personnel matters. He signed so many players bearing red flags they could have marched in Moscow's May Day parade (Randy Moss, Donte Stallworth, et al.), and began drafting kids with hectic pasts, assuming the team's vets would police them. Some of this was arrogance, some of it need: when you're picking from the bottom of the deck each spring, you're apt to shave some corners to land talent.

Hence, Hernandez, who'd make the Pro Bowl one season later on an NFL-minimum salary. Such was his immediate impact, in fact, that the Patriots rewrote the book on tight-end play. In 2011, the tandem of Hernandez and Rob Gronkowski blew away the league marks for most combined yards, catches, and touchdowns at the position, pushing the records far out of reach. It was a wrinkle opponents hadn't seen before and were helpless to defend: two hybrid tight ends who could overpower safeties and outrun any linebacker in coverage. Belichick signed both to big extensions years before their rookie deals expired, giving Hernandez $40 million and Gronkowski $54 million, while stiffing Wes Welker, the slot receiver.

Like most of Belichick's recent gestures, this would come back to burn him—he'd lose Gronkowski and Hernandez to injuries. But the seeds of the fiasco were sown years earlier, when Belichick replaced the Pats' security chief with a tech-smart Brit named Mark Briggs. The NFL and its teams spend millions each year employing a web of former cops and ex-FBI agents to keep an eye on players and their posses. For decades, the Patriots relied on a homegrown crew of retired state troopers to do surveillance. Whenever a player popped up where he didn't belong—a strip joint in Southie or a weed spot in Brockton—Frank Mendes, the team security chief from 1990 to 2003 and a former state trooper himself, would get a call from his cop or statie friends, whether they were on payroll or not. "I'd have known within a half-hour if Hernandez had gotten in trouble with police," he says, "and told Belichick and he'd do whatever." But when Belichick hired Briggs, who'd managed security at London's Wembley Stadium and had limited street associates in the States, the tips from cops and troopers dried up. "The Patriots aren't receptive to those kind of calls," says a law enforcement official who knows the team and dislikes Briggs. "It's not a friendly environment to call over."

In his first remarks after Odin Lloyd's murder, Robert Kraft described himself as "duped" by Hernandez, saying he'd had no knowledge of his troubles. That is arrant nonsense: every team knew him as a badly damaged kid with a circle of dangerous friends and a substance problem. Once a Patriot, Hernandez practically ran up a banner that said STOP ME! I'M OUT OF CONTROL! He'd get high all the time driving away from games, say friends of the family, "smoking three or four blunts" in the ride back to his place. He avoided all contact with teammates after practice, even among the guys in his position group, which is unheard of in the league. Since his arrest, several Patriots have called him a "loner," saying, "No one hung with him." Retired lineman Matt Light went a step further, telling the *Dayton Daily News* that he "never believed in anything Hernandez stood for."

Instead of teammates, Hernandez built a cohort of thugs, bringing stone-cold gangsters over to the house to play pool, smoke chronic, and carouse. "One of his uncles went to Boston to talk to him, and these scary-looking dudes are hanging out in his game room," says a friend. "They wouldn't say hi or shake his hand, and when he brought it up to Aaron, he laughed him off."

There's broad agreement that the problem snowballed once Hernandez signed his megadeal last summer ($40 million over a five-year term, including the largest signing bonus, $12.5 million, ever given to a tight end). In an alleged letter to a supporter from jail, he acknowledged that he "fell off especially after making all that money," though he added, with the diplomacy of a preschool kid, that "all the people who turned on me will feel like crap" when they hear "not guilty."

But even before fixing his name to the deal, Hernandez raised the stakes on bad behavior. Six weeks earlier, at a Boston club called Cure Lounge, he and his crew got into a scrap with some men from Cape Verde, a bar brawl that bred two murders, police suspect. Afterward, a few blocks from the club, a silver Toyota 4Runner with license plates from Rhode Island pulled up beside the sedan carrying the Cape Verdean men. A gun came out the window of the Toyota, spraying the sedan. Safiro Furtado and Daniel Abreu were killed by the barrage. The Toyota sped off and went missing for months, despite a statewide search by Boston cops. It turned up a year later, undriven and caked in dust, in the garage of Hernandez's Uncle Tito back in Bristol.

Hernandez had a dismal season, hobbled by an ankle sprain that cost him six games and about half his yardage from 2011. Then, a week after the Patriots' loss to the Baltimore Ravens in the AFC Championship game, he and a friend named Alexander Bradley were pulled over by a state trooper on Boston's Southeast Expressway, going 105 miles per hour. Bradley, who was behind the wheel, was charged with driving under the influence and speeding, but once again Hernandez (who stuck his head out the window and said, "Trooper, I'm Aaron Hernandez—it's okay") walked away with no summons or team-imposed fine. Weeks later, driving from a strip club in Miami, he allegedly shot Bradley in the face, then dumped him, badly hurt and bleeding but alive, in an alley north of the city. (Bradley, keeping it gangsta, declined to tell cops who had shot him and where. No street code says you can't get paid for it, though; he's filed suit against Hernandez in civil court.) Then, months after that, Hernandez and his crew got in a beef outside a nightclub in Rhode Island. Someone matching Ernest Wallace's description pulled a .22, then ditched it beneath a car. Police traced the piece to a Florida gun shop near Wallace's parents' house, where a second .22 had been purchased that would later turn up in the woods near Hernandez's mansion in the wake of the murder.

By now, even Hernandez seems to have sensed that he was wildly off course. According to a source close to Hernandez, he flew to the NFL Combine in Indianapolis this past February and confided to Belichick that his life was in danger. Hernandez was trying to break away from the gangsters he'd befriended. He worried "they were actually trying to kill him," says the source. Hernandez began arming himself, stashing a rifle in his gym bag and installing a 14-camera security system at his mansion. "He was very paranoid, but was that because of his addictions or because he was trying to leave the gang?"

This past spring he skipped out on team training drills, going to California to rehab an aching shoulder and take a much-needed break from New England. But while out there, according to the source, he blew off sessions with his therapist, Alex Guerrero, and stood up Tom Brady, who was running a camp for Pats receivers. Worse, the police were called out to his Hermosa Beach rental on March 25, summoned by his fiancée, Shayanna Jenkins, after a loud dispute during which Hernandez put his fist through a window. No arrest was made, but word got back to Belichick, who exploded and tendered notice: any more disruptions and he'd be traded or cut at the end of the 2013 season.

Mortified, Hernandez returned to Boston; Belichick, per a close Hernandez associate, had told him to lay low, rent a safe house for a while. In May, he leased a condo in Franklin, Massachusetts, that Carlos Ortiz referred to as the "flophouse," 12 miles from his mansion in North Attleborough. Wallace moved in there, telling neighbors his name was "George," and drove Hernandez to and from team workouts. Neighbors described them as "quiet" or absent, until the day after Lloyd's shooting, when Wallace and Ortiz camped out there before taking off in a rented Chrysler for Bristol, according to a statement Ortiz gave cops.

En route, said Ortiz, Wallace claimed Hernandez had shot and killed Lloyd. Of course, Ortiz also said he'd stayed in the backseat and couldn't say exactly what happened, a contention everyone but his government-appointed lawyer laughs at. The dust-addled Ortiz, the only one of the three men not indicted, is now the star witness in the case against Hernandez, and his account is probably worthless if he takes the stand. Meanwhile, Hernandez is paying a team of strong lawyers to defend him in his first-degree murder and weapons charges, and there's speculation he's paying the legal bills for Wallace, who is being charged as an accessory. It will shock no one if Aaron Hernandez tries to save himself by turning on his friend Ortiz. He and Wallace could tell the same story in court: that it was Ortiz who shot Lloyd out of misplaced panic, and that all they'd meant to do was rough him up.

Whatever went down in that industrial park, Hernandez's motive remains unclear. Had Lloyd, one of the few people Hernandez hung with who wasn't mobbed up or in the drug game, done something else that night to set him off? Did Hernandez mistake Lloyd's West Indian cousins for some of the Cape Verdeans he'd come to blows with? Or did the argument begin as one thing and end as another, broadening into a beef over drugs and money, as was widely conjectured?

"Don't matter what it's about: Aaron's out of his mind," says one friend of the family. "He's been twisted on dust now for more than a year, which is when all of this crazy shit started."

The friend has an intimate knowledge of the player's family and his thug-life cohorts from Bristol. He also knows plenty about angel dust, or phencyclidine, the scourge of the 1970s. Before crack came along in the mid-'80s, dust was the madman's drug of choice. First marketed in the '50s as a surgical anesthetic, it was banned for its psych-ward side effects: mania, delirium, violent hallucinations. Cops shake their heads in awe at the crazy-making powers of dust: "Kids fighting four of us and running naked down the street because their body temp is going through the roof," says Morrell, the Bristol detective. For his department, alas, dust isn't a dead letter; it's still one of the drugs of abuse in Hernandez's hometown. "We have been experiencing a resurgence in the use of angel dust. We deal with it all the time."

As befits a crime studded with gross stupidities—killing Lloyd minutes from Hernandez's house, drawing a bread-crumb trail of texts and calls to the victim's cell, then leaving that phone on the dead man's body for the cops to find—the story ends with an idiot

run by Wallace and Ortiz. They would lead cops back to Uncle Tito's house in Bristol—the very place from which Hernandez's life
vectored off course—leaving evidence out for the cops to bag up.
Ortiz was picked up a week later, while Wallace had the sense to
leave the state, at least, fleeing to Georgia, then Miramar, Florida,
where he was arrested; Tanya Cummings-Singleton bought him a
bus ride with her credit card. She, meanwhile, sits in jail for con-
tempt and accessory charges, having refused to testify to the grand
jury weighing murder charges against Hernandez. Her husband,
T. L., was being sought by cops in connection with the double killing of the Cape Verdean men last July. But before detectives could
come to take him in for questioning, he hopped into his car and
took off with a former girlfriend sitting beside him. Hitting a curve
at high speed, T. L. made no attempt to brake; he jumped the
curb and flew 100 feet into a wall of a country club. The woman
survived, but T. L. was killed on impact—a loose end neatly knot-
ted; an accomplice who'd never flip.

And so here we are now, a year out from trial, and the open-
and-shut case against Aaron Hernandez probably won't be as easy
to prosecute as it seems. Without the gun used in the shooting,
a persuasive motive, or a witness to the crime and its planning,
the state's chances of winning a conviction on murder in the first
will depend entirely on circumstantial evidence. There's no shortage of that, of course, and much of it is compelling: the security
tape seems to show Hernandez with the black .45 the night of the
crime; the videotapes that track his car's movements, from the
time he picked up Lloyd at his house in Boston to the second they
entered the industrial park before the shooting; the shell casing
recovered from the rental car that matched the ones found beside
Lloyd.

To undercut the damning evidence, Hernandez may have to
take the stand and provide an explanation, says Gerry Leone, the
former district attorney of Middlesex County, Massachusetts, who
convicted Richard Reid, the shoe bomber, among other high-profile cases. "You put him on if your defense case hinges on something that can only come from him"—for instance, the claim that
he always carried a gun when leaving the house, protection from
the gangsters who wanted him dead, and that it was Ortiz, not Hernandez, who pulled the trigger after a botched attempt to scare
Lloyd. "If he says he was shocked by the shooting and only agreed

to scare him, that might get him off," says renowned Boston attorney Anthony Cardinale, who repped John Gotti and other mobsters and has taught at Harvard Law School. "It's not a crime to be there if you had no reason to expect that someone would be shot."

A bigger problem for the prosecution is the all-or-nothing charge they've levied against Hernandez. In deciding to try him for murder in the first, they'll be asking jurors to send a young man to prison for the rest of his life, no parole. "In these cases, juries think that reasonable doubt means no doubt at all," says Cardinale. "If the defense can create even the slightest crack, he may walk like George Zimmerman walked—probably guilty, but the DA overcharged."

So call him stupid or sloppy or a menace to society, Hernandez keeps catching the breaks. He's gotten rich running to daylight after being hemmed in, shedding tacklers and accusers to escape. If he eludes pursuit again, there will be blame to go around, but no one can claim they didn't see it coming. He's been getting away with murder, figuratively, if not literally, his whole life.

DAVID MERRILL

The One-Legged Wrestler Who Conquered His Sport, Then Left It Behind

FROM DEADSPIN.COM

THE FIRST MATCH of the last tournament of Anthony Robles's wrestling career began with his dropping to the mat in a tripod—two hands and a knee. There was no other limb to use; Robles had been born without a right leg, and now the bottom of his maroon-and-gold Arizona State University singlet hung shriveled and slack on that side. His opponent in the 125-pound weight class, a Virginia sophomore named Matt Snyder, loomed over him, twice his height, even in a wrestler's crouch.

It was March 2011, and Robles was in Philadelphia for the NCAA Division I championships, college wrestling's preeminent tournament. As a sophomore, he had finished an auspicious fourth; the next year, he had slipped to seventh. Now, as a senior, he was the top seed—a first for a one-legged wrestler. His remarkable achievement had drawn a throng of reporters to the pre-tournament press conference, where, to widespread bewilderment, Robles had announced that he would retire from wrestling at the end of the championships. He would not compete internationally. He would not try out for the London Olympics. He would become a motivational speaker, he had told the baffled reporters and fans before him, and turn his back on wrestling at the moment he had come to dominate it.

Snyder circled. Robles pawed his opponent's head, then shot

forward, viperlike, at Snyder's legs. There was no time to sprawl away. In an instant, Robles took Snyder down and began shifting side to side, looking for an opportunity to lever him onto his back. Seconds later, he found it. Securing Snyder's hands and hips, Robles rolled across his own back, creating such torque that Snyder was forced to give up his position or risk serious injury. Snyder yielded, and Robles flipped him.

The crowd erupted as Robles held his man inverted, watching the referee count off points. Robles let Snyder right himself, then turned him again. And again and again and again. In the second period, with the score 17–1, the ref waved off the match—a technical fall, like a TKO in boxing, saving the loser needless pain and humiliation.

"He just completely dominated me," Snyder said later. "I was like, 'This isn't fair.'"

Something amazing would unfold over the next few days: a one-legged man would climb to the pinnacle of a sport that selects for such anatomical homogeneity that competitors of different weight classes frequently look like Russian nesting dolls of one another. What Robles accomplished that weekend in Philadelphia was unprecedented in his sport, perhaps in any sport. But what he planned to do afterward left everyone just as dumbstruck. Why was he walking away?

The first time I met Anthony Robles—and nearly every time after—he was intercepted by a fan. We had arranged an interview at a Sheraton in St. Louis, where he was in town to provide color commentary for ESPN during the 2012 Division I championships. Robles loped into the hotel lobby on a pair of aluminum crutches—powerfully built with a handsome, gap-toothed grin that faintly recalled a young Mike Tyson.

I turned to greet him, and as I did an enormous man stepped between us. Four-time Super Bowl champion linebacker Matt Millen wanted to introduce himself to Robles and, not surprisingly, I couldn't get around him. Fifteen minutes passed. At last, Robles looked over to his agent, Gary Lewis, who maneuvered me between his client and Millen. Each man, the wrestler and the linebacker, extended a beefy hand in my direction.

It was a daunting decision. Wrestlers are known for their prodigious hand strength. Oklahoma alumnus Danny Hodge can still crush an apple in one hand at the age of 80. But Robles's grip is fearsome even by wrestling standards. Opponents have rarely been able to pry it off with one hand, and only sometimes with two. Many have ended up surrendering to his hold and have focused instead on limiting the damage he could do with it. "I couldn't even think of breaking his lock," one candid victim told me.

I opted for the evil I didn't know and tentatively placed my hand in Millen's massive paw. He squeezed it, hard, and when he finally returned it to me intact, I felt as if I had gotten away with something splendid and improbable, like a deer bolting free of an anaconda's coil. Then I turned to Robles, whose handshake turned out to be restrained, even gentle. I wondered at this as we ducked into the hotel's sticky-floored lounge, which was not due to open for several hours, and where I imagined his fans wouldn't find us.

Twenty minutes later, a middle-aged man with a Negro League baseball jersey peered into the darkened banquette where I was interviewing Robles. He was missing a number of teeth, and he looked like he hadn't been eating well. "Man! Man!" he cried out when he discovered the person he had come looking for, and fell sobbing into Robles's arms. "You're a good brother! You're a good brother!" the man said, over and over again. Robles held him, and they talked for what seemed like a long time.

After the man left, blubbering an apology for interrupting, I asked Robles if he knew who he was. Robles said no. I asked if that kind of thing had happened before. Robles looked at me evenly. "It happens a lot," he said.

Later that day, while Robles, Lewis, and I were walking the concession-stand loop of the stadium, a staffer stopped Lewis to ask if he needed a wheelchair for—pointing at Robles, on his crutches— "that one." Robles demurred so generously that the staffer smiled with the satisfaction of someone who has just discharged an important civic duty.

Wrestling has barely changed since it was practiced in ancient Babylon, and one of the axiomatic truths of the sport is (or was) that success depends on a pair of strong, flexible legs. From my own high school experience, I learned that a wrestler can compensate for minor physical idiosyncrasies—a torso that is too long, say, or arms that don't straighten all the way. But to excel at the Division I level, you need legs like a Clydesdale's.

Yet Robles, in his senior year at ASU, carved through the opposition like Sherman through Georgia. He was so good, in fact, that a contingent of wrestling fans declared his missing leg to be an unfair *advantage*. Most wrestlers outside the Corn Belt train and compete in near-obscurity, but like a gambler who wins too much at the blackjack table, Robles had become too dominant not to be an object of scrutiny and suspicion.

He can carry more muscle in his torso, the brief against him went. *He can get so low you can't shoot under him.* And the ultimate reversal: *It's unfair that he has just one leg for opponents to attack.*

Did Robles win in spite of his one-leggedness, or because of it? It's an ungracious question, but it deserves consideration.

For some differently shaped athletes, the matter is testable. When Oscar Pistorius, the South African double-amputee sprinter now accused of murdering his girlfriend, moved from Paralympic competition to able-bodied races, he underwent intensive biomechanical evaluation to determine whether his artificial legs were inherently faster than flesh-and-blood ones. Treadmills and stopwatches found no advantage, and he was cleared to compete. In his case, the question of fairness was simply a question of physics.

Wrestling is more complex. Where the outcome of a sprint is dictated by a single variable—speed—wrestling matches turn on an interaction of factors, including flexibility, timing, strength, endurance, and countless others.

Robles was at a marked disadvantage on one of the most influential of these dimensions. His balance is awful when he stands without support. A stiff shove sends him toppling like a tower of blocks, hence his dropping into a tripod whenever possible during a match. But wrestling demands a certain amount of time upright. When an opponent stood from the bottom position, Robles had to stand too, to prevent his man from escaping. This left him in the precarious situation of simultaneously leaning on his opponent for support and trying to lift and hurl him back to the mat. When the roles were reversed and Robles began on bottom, it was difficult for him to stand with his opponent clinging to his back. Similarly, the need to keep one leg under him compromised his ability to trip opponents, a common takedown finish.

Strength also figures importantly in a wrestler's likelihood of winning, and is largely a function of his weight. For an ordinary person, one leg takes up about 16 percent of his total body weight, which would give Robles the frame of someone weighing 150 pounds. In fact, he is even stronger than the math would predict, able to bench-press more than 300 pounds and knock out 100 pull-ups in two minutes. A lifetime on crutches has given him tremendous grip strength, which he used in the neutral, or both-men-standing, position to tie up opponents' hands and wrists, preventing them from initiating an attack. Down on the mat, his grip helped him jerk their arms from under them, secure their wrists fast, and wrench them onto their backs. On the occasions that he found himself in the bottom position, he broke the top man's hold and smartly shucked him off.

At five-foot-eight, Robles is also one to three inches taller than most 125-pounders. This gave him a reach advantage and allowed him to create of himself an extended lever arm for "tilts," high-scoring moves that use concentrated torque to briefly expose an opponent's back to the mat.

But perhaps the greatest tactical advantage of Robles's having just one leg was that he had just one leg. This meant, yes, only one leg to defend against attack, but more importantly it meant a profound change in the way other wrestlers related to his body, and consequently the way they experienced the unfolding of a match. They became discombobulated, groping for a part of him that wasn't there. Strangely, they were the ones knocked off balance.

The day Robles entered the world, doctors whisked him from the delivery room, to spare his mother, 16 years old and single, the shock of seeing her one-legged child. He was what's known as a congenital amputee, and the cause of his condition remains unknown. When the doctors finally returned him to his mother, she looked her boy over carefully and predicted that the smooth declivity where his right leg should have been marked the end of her freedom forever.

Three years later, another doctor thought Robles would walk better with a prosthesis and fitted him with a heavy artificial leg. The boy promptly took it off when he got home and hid it behind a piece of furniture. At five, he shinnied 50 feet up a pole outside his house.

But if Robles was willful and assured by nature, a childhood of being stared at and taunted eventually saddled him with terrible self-consciousness. "I wanted to fit in so badly," he later said of his elementary and junior high school years. "For a while I tried to hide . . . to be camouflaged." But the bullies were not put off, and Robles gave up trying to disguise his differences.

And then a new idea began to crystallize along the margins of his awareness. What if, instead of trying to conceal his deformity, Robles were to put it on display? Perhaps by making himself as visible and vulnerable as possible, he could face—and even one day move past—the shame he felt about his body.

So in the ninth grade, about a decade later than most eventual champions, Robles pulled on a singlet and competed in his first wrestling match. He got off to a dismal start. Many of his early outings ended with Robles getting pinned to the jeers of hostile crowds. Worse still were the patronizing, after-match kudos for trying in spite of the obvious. At the end of his first season, Robles was last in the city of Mesa, Arizona, an area not known for great wrestling.

Watching Robles rule the NCAA championships eight years later, many believed that he had always been on an inexorable path to glory. He seemed simply *too good* for it ever to have been otherwise. The problem with this logic, however, is that it only works in hindsight. In the ninth grade, Robles was a miserable wrestler. Virtually nothing about him portended a champion. He was not born into a wrestling dynasty or raised in one of the handful of states where the sport still rivals football in popularity. He was 10 pounds underweight, even in the lightest weight class. He finished half his matches on his back.

What Robles did accomplish in that first season was largely psychological. Standing nearly naked in front of his peers started him, as he had hoped it would, on a long march back to feeling comfortable with his body and his identity, a feeling he had not known since he was a toddler. "Wrestling helped me come out of my shell," Robles has said. "It forced me to say, 'This is who I am.'" If it seems paradoxical that this metamorphosis began with Robles's being repeatedly trounced by his opponents, it may have been that he was learning to substitute the punishments they dispensed for the ones a self-reproving teenager inflicts on himself. Life is full of abuses, Robles knew, even at 14—the trick is to find the ones that offer the promise of redress.

*

After his first year of wrestling, nobody thought Robles stood a chance against most two-legged opponents, except Robles himself, who decided the expedient thing to do was to make the sport *more* difficult for himself. He asked the best wrestler on the team, a 152-pounder named Chris Freije, if they could train together over the summer. Freije agreed, but his interpretation of "training" turned out to be closer to most people's definition of cruelty. With a 50-pound advantage on his new apprentice, Freije pummeled Robles every day, often reducing him to tears. Robles had said he wanted no allowances for his weight, inexperience, or disability, and Freije, with a mix of stewardship and sadism, took him at his word. "He liked to be mean," Robles told me.

Freije smacked Robles in the head and had him push cars over speed bumps in the withering midday Arizona heat. On the mat, he was even more punishing. Robles admired Freije immensely, but he needed to find a way to protect his psyche and his body, fast.

One day, Robles tried a radical change in his stance. Instead of balancing on one leg, he dropped to the mat, on two hands and a knee. Suddenly, with his lowered center of gravity, Freije could barely budge him. And by tucking his leg under his haunches, Robles substantially reduced his exposure to attack.

With his defense transformed, he turned to offense, mastering a series of tilts. By stringing together a few of these, including one he invented himself, Robles discovered he could rack up a dozen points in a single period.

Wrestling offers little room for revolutionary change. There is hardly any equipment to overhaul or reengineer. The principal aim of the modern wrestler is what it's always been, to drive his opponent from his feet to the ground. When a major innovation arrives, as it does maybe once in a generation, one of two things happens. Either a reliable countermove is developed and the innovation is consigned to a footnote in the sport's history, or the innovator catapults his own career, and sometimes those of many others.

There was no countermove for Robles's discoveries. In his sophomore year, his second season of wrestling, he used his lowered stance and his arsenal of tilts to rise from last place in the city of Mesa to sixth in the entire state of Arizona. Then he really started improving. As a junior and senior, Robles went 96–0, crowning his high school career with a national championship.

Becoming a national champion on less than four years' experience is an extraordinary accomplishment, and Robles figured it put him in position to realize a fantasy he had nurtured throughout high school: to wrestle for the University of Iowa, one of the most storied and successful athletic programs anywhere in the NCAA. With two undefeated seasons and a national title behind him, he finally indulged in the conscious belief that he would soon wear Iowa's black and gold.

Only Iowa never called. And neither did Oklahoma State or Columbia, his second and third choices. Only two middling Division I programs offered Robles the scholarship his family needed to afford college: Arizona State and Drexel. Robles was crushed. Rumors circulated that he was considered too small to win at the D1 level; that coaches shrank from the challenge of working with his unusual body and style; and that prospective teammates complained that if they were to train with him, they might become adept at wrestling a one-legged opponent, but ill prepared for the two-legged competition they would face on match days. Robles looked like a gamble at best, a liability at worst. In the end, his mother urged him to go to Drexel because the school's offer covered room and board. Robles chose ASU to stay close to his family and took a night job washing airplanes to make up the scholarship difference.

By the end of his college freshman season, Robles was already one of the best wrestlers on the Arizona State team. The next two years, he won All-American honors by finishing in the top eight at the national tournament. Yet he still wasn't wrestling up to his full potential. Unforeseen events kept him distracted. In his freshman year, the ASU athletic department dropped its wrestling program after the Board of Regents cut the university's budget by $26 million. Robles considered transferring, but didn't know where to go, and the program was eventually reinstated. A year later, his stepfather, Ron Robles, abandoned his mother, Judy, and left for California with another woman.

Ron, Judy, and Anthony had become a family when Anthony was two. Since then, Ron and Judy had had four other children together. Anthony never met his biological father, and always longed to be accepted by Ron, whose last name he'd chosen to take. "I don't call him my stepdad," he told me. "I don't think of him as my stepdad. He's my dad. And I really looked up to him."

Sometimes the elder Robles reciprocated with a queer sort of affection, as when he took the boy to a tattoo parlor so they could get the same guardian angel imprinted on their bodies. It was an ironic choice: there was little Anthony Robles needed more protection from than his stepfather. Both Anthony and Judy told me that Ron criticized his stepson mercilessly, and sometimes physically abused Judy in his presence.

Judy said Ron couldn't forgive her son the color of his skin— Anthony's biological father is black—or forgive her the love she feels for Anthony. For Ron, she believes, these were intolerable, living reminders that he had to share her with other men.

Still, for all the tumult when he was home, Ron's leaving devastated Judy. In addition to losing her husband, she had no income, four children to feed, and a mortgage to pay. She fell into depression and took to her bed. The bank began arrangements to foreclose on her house.

Until then, wrestling had been Anthony's respite from a noxious home life—"my sanctuary," he called it—and even the indignities he suffered in his first season were preferable to the ones his stepfather delivered, because there was always something to be done about the former. Losses, no matter how ugly, could be avenged. Ron Robles could not be made to love.

But Ron's leaving and the gloom that hung over Judy were too much. Even Anthony, unremittingly positive until now, started to despair. He told his mother he couldn't keep his mind on the mat, and he offered to quit college and take a job to help out.

Judy knew her son dreamed of becoming an NCAA champion, and seeing his willingness to give up that possibility inspired her to get out of bed. She told him to stay in school. She sold her blood to get enough money to feed the family. Eventually, she got a job working at ASU.

Anthony returned to wrestling with a ferocious determination to make good on his mother's blessing. Until his senior year of college, few supposed him a real contender for a Division I championship. But in the fall of 2010, he emerged as something wholly different—something redoubtable and unprecedented. Against his first opponent of the season, he reeled off 14 points and a pin in under two minutes. The next he pinned even faster. Robles continued in this fashion from November through January.

Just after the New Year, he assumed the number-two rank in his weight class nationally. He then proceeded to technical fall or shut out his next nine opponents. In February, he became the top-ranked 125-pounder in the NCAA. The ASU Sun Devils ended the season with a road campaign in which they dropped every meet from Nebraska to Stanford. Robles, meanwhile, outscored his opponents 69–2 to close out an undefeated season.

Typically, a wrestling match begins with a series of skirmishes, starting from the neutral position. Grapplers paw and push, cuff and tug one another until one senses he has unbalanced his opponent enough to create an opening, and then lunges at one or both of his legs. The lunged-at wrestler tries to sprawl his legs away or, if he cannot, gives them up and counterattacks with his upper body. This begins the "scramble"—a battle of vectors, inertia, and angular acceleration, alternating between strained counterpoise and flashes of explosive motion, as each wrestler tries for a takedown.

The critical thing about the scramble is that, at the college level and beyond, it is almost entirely reflexive, moving far too fast to be thought through. Scrambling wrestlers rely on muscle memory, developed through extensive repetition and retained for years. (Hence the theatrics in the audience at many wrestling meets, where former competitors jerk their legs, claw the air, and otherwise try to gesticulate their way free of the fracas before them.) Occasionally, a wrestler exerts some conscious control as he scrambles, deliberately trying something new and counter-instinctual. This is usually the point at which he loses the scramble.

Wrestlers scrambling against Robles regularly reached for the leg that wasn't there, the way people who learned to drive on a manual transmission car sometimes grab for a phantom gear stick in an automatic. This was especially true when opponents tried to "turn the corner" clockwise, or slip past Robles's right side to complete a takedown. With no right ankle to catch hold of, they lacked the anchor they needed to finish their attack. A number of other moves were also literally out of reach, including the navy ride, the western ride, and some cradles. One of the most popular and effective maneuvers for the man on top, known simply as "legs," involves lacing one leg through the bottom man's same-side leg and turning it outward at the hip. Needless to say, there is no "legs" without legs.

Whenever an opponent attempted to gain purchase on a part of Robles that does not exist, muscle memory failed him. It was a bewildering and anxiety-provoking moment. "A lot of the stuff you're used to doing on a more able-bodied wrestler, you can't do," Matthew Snyder, Robles's first-round victim at the 2011 championships, told me. "You're looking for the leg and it's just not there." When this happened repeatedly, as it did for anyone who hadn't trained with a one-legged wrestler before facing Robles, frustration, confusion, and ultimately demoralization set in. This was a fatal combination. No wrestler can win with despondency in his heart, at least not against a foe as formidable as Robles.

What was an opponent to do? Robles's anatomy suggested at least two possibilities. One was to attack his leg relentlessly. Every time Robles scooted across the mat or attempted a takedown, he drove off the same leg. Every time a competitor yanked his ankle outward, the same knee got wrenched against the joint. As a result, the muscles, tendons, and ligaments of Robles's leg endured terrific strain, and thus were more prone to fatigue and injury than those of a wrestler who can distribute the same stresses over two legs. By his senior year of high school, his knee was so stiff after practices that he could barely move it. If an opponent could have somehow consistently circumvented Robles's hulking upper body, he might have eventually been able to take out his relatively vulnerable leg.

A second, and perhaps underutilized, strategy for scoring against Robles can be found 5,000 miles east of Arizona, in the Tuileries gardens of Paris. Among dozens of giant statues dotting the Tuileries is one of the Greek mythical hero Theseus, in close combat with the Minotaur, the bovine-headed, human-bodied offspring of Queen Pasiphaë and a white bull. In this depiction, Theseus forces the Minotaur's massive horned head down with his left hand as he prepares to bludgeon the beast with the club in his right. He triumphs not by evading the Minotaur's deadly horns, but by confronting them directly.

In the 2008 NCAA championships, Stanford's Tanner Gardner took an analogous approach against Robles. For much of the first period, Gardner plowed forward, ramming his head into Robles's and collaring his neck. In the second period he converted a head hold into a takedown, and, beginning the third period in the top position, he took the unorthodox course of releasing Robles's body and applying a headlock from behind. His tactics sent the match into overtime, where he again took Robles down with a head hold, earning himself the win. Theseus would have approved.

All of this—every detail of Robles's technique and virtually every square inch of his body—has been hotly debated in the fertile anonymity of cyberspace. Loyalists tend to concede his superior strength, but emphasize the many other variables that inform the outcome of a wrestling match. Robles both benefits and suffers from his anatomy, they argue, and to focus on a single metric is to miss the point. Many believe justice requires a long view, a weighing of equities and inequities over time. "It might have been unfair for us to have to wrestle him," Snyder said, "but it was more unfair what he had to go through to get there."

The detracting camp sometimes cites the numerous amputees in the sport as evidence of Robles's advantage. In 2001, for example, double-leg amputee Nick Ackerman (whose grandfathers, bizarrely, lost their legs in separate accidents) won the Division III tournament. Other critics linger over Robles's disproportionate upper-body strength. If they are aware of the irony of calling the man once considered too small to succeed at the Division I level too big, they don't let on.

This is not a position held only by a few angry bloggers on the periphery of the wrestling community. While many doyens of the sport have loudly hailed Robles as a deserving winner and a first-class human being, several of them have lowered their voices and confided to me—always "off the record"—that he wouldn't stand a chance against a wrestler with the same-sized torso. A 157-pounder, say.

But what most critics don't know is that Robles *did* wrestle a 157-pounder. Every day in practice at Arizona State, he worked out with Brian Stith, a former national runner-up in that weight class. Just as he did in high school with Freije, Robles trained with Stith so that, when it came time to compete in his own weight class, the job would be comparatively easy. And was he able to hold his own against one of the top 157-pound wrestlers in the country? "For sure," Stith told me. "Anthony would be a champion at any weight he wrestled."

*

In the last match of his career, the Division I championship, Robles found himself facing Iowa Hawkeye Matt McDonough, the defending national champion. The two had never wrestled before, but Robles had known all year that to win the title, he'd likely have to get through McDonough, the favorite going into the season. He'd kept a picture of McDonough in his locker, where he could look at it before and after practices.

Robles didn't sleep well on the eve of the match. He was up against not only one of the sport's biggest stars, but the coaches who had snubbed him, the critics who had dismissed him, and the hourglass he had turned over when he announced, three days earlier, his plan to retire from wrestling and become a motivational speaker. Robles tossed in his bed, with the knowledge that strange and unexpected things happen this deep in a tournament eating at his confidence. After four matches in two days, injuries flare. Legs and lungs give out. The body mutinies, and attention yields to momentary, decisive distraction.

But the instant the ref blew his whistle, the anxiety was gone. Robles dropped to his knee, and McDonough responded in kind, lowering his own stance to meet him. They vied for control of one another's hands and wrists. Twenty-five seconds in, Robles caught both of McDonough's wrists and spun behind him for a takedown. He then pried McDonough's supports from under him and drove him forward into the mat. With McDonough on his belly, Robles searched for an opening, shading to the right, then to the left.

At 88 seconds, he found it. As McDonough pushed his way up to all fours, Robles cinched his opponent's left wrist across his body and rolled hard across his own shoulders for a cross-wrist tilt. The torque was extraordinary, and the defending champion flipped like a pancake.

It was the most remarkable move of Robles's career. McDonough, inverted, pedaled vainly in the air as the crowd roared to its feet. Few of the 17,000 fans there had ever seen the Hawkeye on his back. McDonough kicked loose, but Robles kept him flat on his stomach. A minute later, Robles turned him with another tilt.

McDonough wriggled free again, but he was badly shaken. Robles had taken him down, kept him down, and was now turning him virtually at will. Tom Brands, Iowa's usually irascible head coach, stood mutely by. At the end of the first period, Robles was far ahead on points, with an even more commanding psychological lead.

Everyone loves an underdog. The problem here was figuring out who he was. Some saw in Robles's two tilts his latest crime against sport and man, others a great comeuppance to a world that had disbelieved. But the fans who watched the match had one thing in common: a year before they could not have imagined a one-legged man winning an NCAA Division I wrestling championship any more than they could have imagined him flapping his arms and taking flight. All of them—every last person who stood staring from the stands—must have felt the tethers loosen between what they beheld and what they thought they knew, the latter drifting away, into the rainy Philadelphia night.

Robles coasted the rest of the way. McDonough raced around him for the last two periods, seeking an opportunity, but there was none. Time expired. The referee raised Robles's hand.

McDonough hurried to the locker room, accepting no handshakes and no applause. There is no second place for Iowa wrestlers.

An interviewer stopped the new champion as he made his way off the mat. He told Robles he was an inspiration. "It's an honor," Robles said, breaking into a boyish grin. He took up his crutches and strode—there is no better word for it—over to the stands, where his mother and girlfriend jumped and cried and hugged each other. The crowd gave him a sustained standing ovation.

Later that day, the coaches in attendance voted Robles the outstanding wrestler of the tournament, making him, by consensus, the best college wrestler in any weight class, anywhere in the country.

Last year I chased down John Smith, a two-time Olympic gold medalist and Oklahoma State's head coach since 1992, to ask him why, for heaven's sake, he hadn't recruited Robles to Stillwater. I reminded him that Robles had won a high school national championship after wrestling for just three and a half years. "We ended up not going that route," Smith drawled, looking sheepish. "It was a mistake. I shoulda went that route."

I put the same question to Tom Brands, knowing that Iowa had been Robles's dream program. He fumbled through a couple of thin excuses, then suddenly erupted: *"Are you looking for a fight?"* Thanking Brands for his time, I turned to walk away. "Hey!" he barked after me. "Hey! *That's off the record!"*

A few weeks before the 2012 Olympic Trials, I told Robles about my encounters with college wrestling's two most revered coaches. He looked entertained, but not as gratified as I had anticipated.

I tried something more provocative. I told him how some former and would-be Olympians had reacted to his decision not to try out for the U.S. Olympic team. Kenny Monday, a 1988 gold medalist, and Raymond Jordan, who had helped coach Robles at ASU, both told me they consider the top position to be Robles's strongest, and that freestyle wrestling—a variant of the sport practiced at the Olympics—is better suited for wrestlers who excel in the neutral position. Jarod Trice, who wrestled at the Olympic Trials and calls Robles a close friend—"I just texted him this morning! He's my boy!"—reluctantly agreed: "I don't know how the leverage would work for him [in freestyle wrestling], because of the leg."

Where collegiate wrestling awards two points for any takedown, freestyle scoring is more variable. The simple leg tackles preferred by Robles earn just one point, while dramatic lifting-and-throwing takedowns—nearly impossible to execute while balancing on one leg—are worth three or five. Even more problematic, time on the mat, where Robles does most of his damage, is limited in freestyle wrestling.

Still, Robles might be a better freestyler than he at first appears. He may not throw many opponents, but his ultralow center of gravity makes him equally difficult to throw. And unlike college wrestling, where using the same tilt twice in a row without changing holds doesn't earn points, in freestyle wrestling Robles could repeatedly roll his opponent with a single tilt, scoring with every revolution.

I shared his colleagues' comments with Robles because I was frustrated by his choice to forgo the Olympic Trials. I was looking for an explanation, and somewhere in the recesses of my mind, I harbored a hope of spurring him to action, to prove the naysayers wrong. But before I let him speak, I goaded him one more time. Was it possible that he was too—ahem—*inhibited* to try out for London? Did he prefer walking away a college champion to risking a loss at the next level?

"A little bit," Robles confessed. He admitted to wanting to end his career on a high note, and to the seductive appeal of giving up to mitigate the pressure that accompanies sustained success.

"But my dream was never to win a gold medal," he said. "When I was in college, when I was wrestling in high school, my dream was to be a national champion." He said he missed wrestling, profoundly, but that he was happy with the direction his life had taken in the last year: connection with fans, lucrative motivational speaking engagements, Nike sponsorship, a book release, a movie deal in the works.

And then he hinted at the 2016 Olympic Games, in Brazil: "I'm still young. I'm only 23 . . . Four years from now, I'll still be prime age." (At the time the International Olympic Committee had dropped wrestling from the 2020 Games, and it appeared Brazil would be Robles's last chance at Olympic competition; the sport was reinstated in February 2013.)

I didn't find it an altogether satisfying answer, and suddenly I realized why. I'd been wanting Robles to see things my way. I'd seen his crossing over to freestyle wrestling, where his anatomical advantages are reduced, and *still* winning—as I imagined he would—as the ultimate rebuttal to his critics. I'd wanted him to erase the invisible asterisks that accompany every record he ever posted. I'd wanted Robles to demonstrate, once and for all, that ingenuity and discipline, not brawn, were the bedrock of his success, because these are attributes I value.

But I was just another guy reaching for phantom parts of Robles. His journey has been about many things, but it is not, fundamentally, about proving anybody wrong. Or being controversial. Or even about learning to wrestle with one leg. These are all epiphenomena of something larger.

Robles has been trying to solve the problems that life has been heaping on him since the moment he was born: a body that didn't look right and the bullies who wouldn't let him forget it, one father absent and another full of hate. Wrestling just happened to be an exquisitely efficient response to his dilemmas. It gave him, all at once, a sanctioned way of blowing off steam, an assessment of his abilities independent of other people's appraisals, and a vehicle for working collaboratively, for a change, with other men.

His decision to retire from wrestling had less to do with inhibition than with the challenge of how to be the 23-year-old he wanted to be. By *not* wrestling, Robles gets to support his family and through his words lift up the thousands of people who look to him for inspiration. And with a quiet pride that a less mature man might consider vanity, he allows himself to revel in the enormity of his achievements.

Before his final tournament, Robles told an interviewer that the thing he likes most about wrestling is the way it allows you to focus on your advantages—what you have rather than what you lack. Some people are tall and can use their length for leverage, he said. Some capitalize on physical strength.

Robles was suggesting, in essence, that as long as he didn't dwell on the nuisance of missing a leg, he could go about the business of becoming a champion wrestler. It was a preposterous remark, except that it turned out to be true. An absence isn't a weakness if you make it someone else's problem.

CHRIS JONES

When 772 Pitches Isn't Enough

FROM ESPN: THE MAGAZINE

HE IS OUT THERE SOMEWHERE on this all-dirt field; he is one of these few dozen possible boys. But on this overcast Saturday morning in June, before the start of the first of two exhibition games in Akashi City, the greatest teenage pitcher in Japan—the best since Yu Darvish—and one of the top 16-year-old prospects in the world—as can't miss as Stephen Strasburg—continues hiding in plain sight. Saibi High School isn't wearing numbers on its white uniforms today. These boys never wear names. And from a distance, as they practice their drills with alarming precision, looking less like ballplayers and more like a marching band, like toy soldiers, any single one of them disappears into the lockstep crowd. An arm like Anraku's, this inhuman appendage, must look different. It must have scales, or talons, or somehow drag across the earth, leaving fissures in its wake. But for now his arm is just another arm, and Anraku is just another player, his otherworldliness lost in this army of Japanese ordinary.

Masanori Joko, Saibi's 66-year-old manager, stands like a general on a hill overlooking the field. "Is Anraku the one with the shaved head?" someone asks him, and he smiles. "They all have shaved heads," he says through an interpreter, before he offers his only description: "He is the tallest one."

There he is. That must be him. He is the tallest one by several inches, more than six feet tall, with a cap perched high on his head and a red glove on his left hand. His back is so broad, his shirt—the only one its size on this entire team—rides up his long arms. He has thick legs and a surprisingly American ass, and when his feet dig into the dirt, he ripples like a sprinter. He runs with another, much smaller boy into right field, the pair lost in the same cloud of dust, where they wait for a coach to hit a ball their way. When a pop fly settles into Anraku's glove, his arm is put on display for the first time: he throws a one-hopper to the plate. A murmur rolls through the crowd. This is a good sign.

There has been talk in America that Anraku's arm had been destroyed weeks earlier, in April, stripped of its powers at Koshien—a high school tournament that happens twice a year in Japan, in spring and in summer. Robert Whiting, author of *You Gotta Have Wa* and one of the West's principal translators of Japanese culture, has a hard time capturing the meaning of Koshien, first held in 1915. "It's like the Super Bowl and the World Series rolled into one," he says. "It's the closest thing Japan has to a national festival." In the spring, 32 teams from across the country arrive at Koshien, the name of a beautiful stadium near Kobe but also the de facto title of the tournament that's played there. (In the summer, 49 teams participate, one from each of Japan's 47 diverse prefectures, plus an additional team from Tokyo and Hokkaido.) They meet in a frantic series of single-elimination games until a champion emerges. At any one time, 60 percent of Japan's TV sets will be tuned in to the drama. More than 45,000 fans will be packed into the stadium, and if the games are especially good, many of those fans will be weeping.

"It's not just baseball," says Masato Yoshii, who pitched in two Koshiens long before he joined the New York Mets. "It's something else. It's something more."

This spring, Anraku single-handedly carried Saibi, from his hometown of Matsuyama, representing Ehime prefecture, to the final. He stood on the mound and felt he was exactly where he should be. His parents met at Koshien as young concession workers. His father was a promising pitcher who blew out his arm even before high school; he started his son pitching when he was three years old. In some ways, it seems as though Anraku never had much choice about any of this, and he would agree. The Japanese don't use the word "destiny" very much. They call it fate.

He threw virtually every pitch for Saibi at Koshien, including a 13-inning complete game in which he threw 232 pitches. But in the awful final, he fell apart, terrifyingly and completely, eventually losing 17–1, pulled only after he'd thrown his 772nd pitch

over five games in nine days. His fastball was not nearly so fast; his
curveball no longer broke; his slider stayed flat. Every one of his
instruments abandoned him, and yet he had continued to throw
until his precious right arm hung limp at his side. Don Nomura,
the agent who represents Darvish, told Yahoo's Jeff Passan that
Anraku's treatment was nothing less than child abuse, a sentiment
shared by several American scouts. Those strong words traveled
over the ocean and upset many in Japan, where if anyone saw Tomohiro Anraku as a victim, he was blessed to be one. In fact, he's
been given the most coveted and celebrated title of all. He is a
kaibutsu.

Anraku is a monster. Anraku is a beast.

Yet even in Japan there has been a rising unease regarding Anraku's fate. Kazuhisa Nakamura, a 65-year-old journalist and former scout for the legendary Yomiuri Giants, sat in a Tokyo restaurant recently, stirring his coffee, shaking his head. "I felt sorry for
him," he said, remembering that final game. "It was so obvious.
Everybody could see something was wrong." The problem wasn't
that Anraku had thrown so many pitches. By Koshien's measures,
his performance was something like normal. Daisuke "Dice-K"
Matsuzaka had thrown 767 pitches in six games in 1998; even
Darvish, who allegedly had been protected from the excesses of
Japanese baseball culture by his Iranian father, threw 505 pitches
in five games in 2003. What separated Anraku was how plainly he
had faltered. It was like watching a prize colt find a hole in the
track, only no tarps were put up to protect us from his agony. The
torturous spectacle of this broken boy and the unkind Western
attention that followed were enough for some Japanese to wonder whether Anraku represented everything that's wrong with
Koshien rather than everything that's right. "Before, he was the
number-one prospect in Japan, easily," Nakamura said. "Now," he
said, and he stopped and shrugged. "Now we have to wait and
see."

Two months after that fateful Koshien, the waiting is almost
over. At last it's time to see. Except when Joko climbs down from
his hill and the game between Saibi and Kyoto–Gaidai West begins, Anraku stays in right field. One of Japan's potentially great
pitchers stands more than 200 feet from the mound, an exile from
the center of his former universe. He wades around in the sand,
chasing down fly balls that he misplays. He looks lost in every

sense. The only glimmer of his former light comes in the universal language of two admiring teenage girls, their hair and makeup immaculate, trying to get his attention through the fence. They know what he used to be and might still become, but the grim-faced object of their affection never looks their way. Entering the ninth inning, Saibi is losing 5–3. The Kyoto–Gaidai West players are shouting joyously in their dugout, and Anraku looks far from the tallest boy on the field.

Then his manager, Joko, makes some vague, almost invisible gesture, and Anraku releases his customary acceptance of com-mand—a chest-thumping shout that starts deep in his gut—bow-ing to his manager before he sprints to the mound.

And while this might sound like mythmaking, like some hin-terland baseball legend that's told by scouts to their children to explain why they are never home, this is a true account of what happens next:

The entire field goes silent. Not quiet. "Quiet" is not a strong enough word to describe this instant temple. It goes dead silent. What had been a consistent, heavy chatter just stops. Anraku's teammates, the opposing players in their dugout, the umpires, the mothers and fathers and tea-brewing booster club up on the hill—nobody says a word. Nobody claps or chants or boos. An opposing player noiselessly pulls out a radar gun, but nobody else moves. Even the two girls, gripped tight against the right-field fence, stop their lovesick parade.

Suddenly, there is a monster in their midst. He nods at his catcher, a tiny, brave boy built like a whippet. Anraku's huge hands lift slowly over his head, and he starts his big, leggy delivery, classi-cally Japanese, a full-body unwinding that culminates in a fastball thrown right down the throats of every last person here.

The radar gun is in metric: 148 kilometers an hour.

Ninety-two.

Anraku throws another pitch, and then another, and then an-other. He throws nine pitches in total, fastballs, sliders, and curves. He hits 94. There is one foul ball. Otherwise there are only un-touched strikes, called and swinging.

Nine pitches. Nine strikes. Three up, three down.

And then there is so much noise, a symphony rising up around Tomohiro Anraku once again.

*

In Japan there are things that should never be forgotten, and a baseball manager's job, at its essence, is to make such things hard to forget. In a country that can seem so modern in so many ways, with its bullet trains and capsule hotels, with its bento boxes that heat up with the pull of a string—seriously, it's like magic—there are also 2,000 years of history and nearly as many traditions. One of those traditions is called *nagekomi*. In America, nagekomi, like throwing 772 pitches in a single tournament, would be considered child abuse. Scientists would debunk it, and surgeons would decry it. But in Japan, nagekomi is important. It's maybe even essential. It is many things all at once, but mostly it is an exercise in remembering, and it is beautiful.

It was born, like so much else that matters in Japan, of Buddhism, of martial arts, of *bushido*—of the samurai spirit. At its purest, nagekomi is the repetition of a simple physical task beyond the point of exhaustion. It is the ceaseless completion of an exercise until you collapse. Baseball stuck so well here partly because in its routines, in its timelessness and pseudo-meditation, it might have been Japanese: a game of self-control, of precision, of craft. It also, conveniently, lent itself well to nagekomi. Baseball, as witnessed from a certain vantage point, could seem designed expressly to break you.

Take the infamous 1,000 Fungo Drill. For one day at Japanese spring training, professional players take a deep breath and begin fielding grounders. At first, fielding grounders is largely a mental exercise. You think about the process, about the careful placement of your feet, hands, and head. Left. Right. Left. Right. After a few hundred grounders, however, your brain will pack up and leave town for the beach. Your body will start acting automatically, without central systemic guidance, and in turn a mental exercise will become a more purely physical one. Left, right, left, right. But after another few hundred grounders, your body too will stop working the way it normally might. It is no longer yours, and you are no longer you. Now you will have reached that very particular departure lounge where what was once a physical exercise becomes spiritual. Now it's your soul at work. Leftrightleftright. And there is no axon or muscle fiber that remembers anything the way your soul remembers everything. That is the purpose of nagekomi: to open your soul as wide as a prairie, allowing it to swallow those secrets you have learned about yourself and lock them away inside the deepest parts of you, where they will survive long after your body dies. Nagekomi is that moment of clarity that comes in the last hundred yards of a marathon; it is that instant your throat closes and tears begin to run down your face. It is not a pursuit of a temporary, earthly glory. It is not gravity-bound. Nagekomi is weightless, and it is forever.

As far as Robert Whiting has been able to ascertain, the modern record for the 1,000 Fungo Drill is, in fact, around 900, attributed to Koichi Tabuchi in 1984. Like so much passed-down greatness here, the Legend of Tabuchi might or might not be true. But if he really did field 900 grounders one transcendent afternoon, he knows things that we will never know. He has visited places on no map. He has ridden Secretariat all those lengths clear at the Belmont; he has run the bases with Kirk Gibson, pumping his fist after that impossible home run.

Tomohiro Anraku didn't quite reach his spiritual end during that last game at Koshien. His soul opened; he just didn't have the strength to lock it back up before disaster struck. But he made it close enough to believe that this sacred moment really does exist and that one day he will know it.

"I left the mound feeling so bad," he says. "It was also an incredible experience for me. It's given me great confidence. I found my level. Now I know what I need to do to get to the next level."

What he needs to do—the answer to virtually every question that might be asked of him, the solution to virtually every problem that he represents—is to throw more pitches. These are the lessons of Koshien, and these are the lessons of nagekomi. In America, we build through rest and recovery. Young arms cspccially need time to heal, and there is little debate about it. (Dr. James Andrews, one of the country's leading sports surgeons, recommends that a 16-year-old pitcher be limited to 95 pitches an outing, with at least three days' rest between starts.) This is anathema in Japan. Only more throwing will allow Anraku to perfect his mechanics, and only perfect mechanics will prevent injury.

Tsuyoshi Yoda, a former pitcher and Japan's pitching coach at the World Baseball Classic, explains the Japanese obsession with mechanics. For him, the pitcher—Japanese pitchers in particular, he says, because they are smaller than Americans and can't rely solely on the strength of their arms—must begin his delivery either with his feet or his hands. Yoda compares good mechanics to a row of dominoes. If everything is lined up properly, the last domino will be released. But if any single domino is out of alignment, the entire construction falls apart.

Yoda believes so strongly in mechanics because pitching destroyed his wrist, elbow, shoulder, and knee. He can no longer touch his face with his right hand; he can't comb his hair or bring a drink to his mouth. He is 48 years old. According to Yoda, he was disabled like a factory worker not because he threw too much. "Bad mechanics," he says. "Too much thinking."

But more important than improving mechanics, only throwing will heal the scar tissue that Koshien left on Anraku's soul. He is already a kaibutsu. That gift is his. Now, if he works hard enough, if he continues to push through the ceilings that human biology might otherwise impose on him, he can become that most wicked of Japanese fantasies: the monster who can defeat even other monsters.

He is on his way. After he strikes out Kyoto–Gaidai West in that dramatic ninth-inning appearance, he starts the next game only minutes later, this one against the host high school, Takigawa II. Anraku throws 87 more pitches in seven innings of work—no runs, no walks, three hits, 12 strikeouts—leaving the mound only when a light rain begins to fall. (By Joko's odd calculus, throwing 772 pitches in sunshine is less risky than throwing one in the rain, and he pulls Anraku, fearing he might slip and get hurt.) Anraku is sent to the shelter of the bullpen. There, he throws yet more pitches, this time to cool down, which looks a lot like warming up.

Saibi has two more away games tomorrow, at a different field, near Osaka, against different high schools. Joko tells Anraku he will start the first game. He barks and bows to his manager, and he boards the bus with his teammates just when the rain really starts to fall. But those same two girls still stand at the end of the road, waiting for Anraku along with the rest of the world. Their hair is slick to their foreheads; their makeup has started to run. They might be crying, but the rain makes it hard to tell.

Anraku does not acknowledge them. He might not even see them. He says he'd like to come to America and pitch in the majors one day, but his professional aspirations remain vague. They have been assigned no dollar value. His ambitions are near-term, and they are specific and concrete. "I am a high school student," he says. "My only job is to win Koshien."

Because he is so big, and because he is so mature, people sometimes forget that he is only 16 years old. Most kaibutsu are seniors; their great Koshien is their last Koshien. Anraku was only a junior, pitching in the spring. Which means that if Saibi can qualify, Anraku and his all-too-human arm have three Koshiens left.

It's hard to think about Anraku pitching at another Koshien perhaps as soon as this August and not feel some combination of love and fear, as though we'll be watching not a monster but a human Mount Fuji, a beautiful bomb. Brian Cashman, the GM of the Yankees, has said he will be extraordinarily careful in his future pursuit of Japanese pitchers—a lesson taught him by Kei Igawa, a $46 million cautionary tale, a high price for an arm that wasn't what it was supposed to be. But Igawa is far from the only flawed import, and Cashman is far from the only burned buyer; since the rapture of Hideo Nomo's world-tilting migration in 1995, less happy patterns have emerged. Masato Yoshii's five-year American career ended with shoulder surgery. Cubs reliever Kyuji Fujikawa recently underwent Tommy John surgery after just 12 big league appearances. Even Dice-K, the kaibutsu of kaibutsu, is pitching for Cleveland's Triple-A affiliate after his elbow exploded, and after the Red Sox invested $103 million in him. Yu Darvish seems determined to be the exception, but it would be premature for the Rangers to boast. Dice-K looked like a relative steal for his first two seasons, especially 2008, when he went 18-3 with a 2.90 ERA. He hasn't posted an ERA below 4.69 in the four years since.

A growing number of Japanese observers, like Nakamura, the old Yomiuri Giants scout, have begun to feel a kind of creeping dread—the way our watching football now comes with its own brand of guilt. There are increasing reminders across Japan of the costs rather than the rewards of nagekomi. There are so many wounded soldiers like Yoda, the coach who can no longer bring his hand to his face.

One of the country's most famous former pitchers is a 74-year-old man named Hiroshi Gondo; he is thin and wiry with glasses to match. Strangers have always whispered about him when they see him on the streets, but lately he wonders what they're saying.

In 1961, during his rookie professional season for the Chunichi Dragons, Gondo appeared in 69 games, 44 as a starter. He pitched 429 innings, including 32 complete games, amassing a record of

35-19. "There were no excuses," he says today. His manager was a World War II veteran who carried an unusual standard of what was and what was not acceptable treatment. "You're not going to die out there," he told Gondo. His shoulder was never the same after that first season, and he pitched only three more years, with fewer appearances each season: 61, 45, 26. After three years away from the mound, he came back in 1968 but managed to muscle through only a few innings. "I was done," he says. There was no doubt, and neither did he doubt why.

Gondo stayed in the game as a manager and coach, a member of the Dragons staff as recently as last season. Because of his own experience, he was one of the few Japanese managers who believed in protecting his pitchers, in keeping careful track of their workloads during games and in practice. For this, he was often accused of being soft.

Change can come slowly in Japan, at least in baseball. Gondo remembers seeing a photograph of Sandy Koufax with ice on his arm and being amazed. He had always been prescribed heat. Today, Anraku ices his shoulder after his appearances, but his manager remains deeply suspicious of this strange, imported practice.

Ice isn't the only American given that's still met with Japanese uncertainty. After 2002, Koshien officials began spreading the quarterfinals over two days rather than whipping through them in one; such an imperceptible nod to arm preservation felt like a revolution. This summer, the quarterfinals will once again take place during a single marathon day—but for the first time in Koshien's history, there will be an off-day between the quarterfinals and semifinals. That day of rest will feel almost cataclysmic, a 24-hour chasm between the old and the new.

Even Gondo, the enlightened reformer, sometimes finds himself torn—between the past and the future, between the player and the game, between America and Japan. He says some brave manager needs to sit his star pitcher at Koshien when it counts, to break hearts in order to save arms, and yet Gondo doesn't fault Joko for sending Anraku out to the mound. For Gondo, for Japan, Koshien represents the greatest dilemma: how do you fix a tournament that is at its best when it is at its most brutal?

Gondo casts back to the Summer Koshien final of 2006, when his country was captivated by a display of teenage endurance that was equal parts moving and cruel. The game—two games, actually—was between Waseda Jitsugyo and Komadai Tomakomai high schools, but in truth it was a contest between two young pitchers: Yuki Saito, whose name you probably don't know, and Masahiro Tanaka, whose name you soon will.

In their first meeting, Saito started; Tanaka came on in early relief, in the third inning. They were studies in contrast. Saito had a loose, jangly delivery that sometimes made him look as though he were falling through space. Tanaka looked more American-made. He was bigger, and he threw much harder. Somehow they each pitched the rest of that game, all 15 innings of it, with the score tied 1–1. By Koshien's strange reckoning, that meant the game both would be remembered forever and did not happen. Games tied after 15 innings are ruled draws and erased from the ledger, and the teams play again tomorrow, new game.

The next day, Saito somehow returned to the mound; Tanaka again entered in relief, this time during the first inning. Nine innings later, an exhausted Saito nursed a 4–3 lead. In one of those cosmic baseball turns, Tanaka came to the plate, representing the tying run and the last out. After nearly 24 innings over two days, it came down to this—arguably the greatest at bat that most Americans have never seen.

Saito nodded to his catcher. He was about to throw his 942nd pitch of the tournament, on his way to a modern record. Tanaka had thrown 742 pitches. If the moment weren't so touching, so inspiring, if it didn't leave the boys watching it from their dugouts in tears, it would have been inhumane. Maybe it still was.

942. Fouled back for a strike.

913. Swinging strike.

944. Chopped foul.

945. High and outside. Ball one.

946. Fouled back again.

947. Fouled down the third-base line.

And then, at last: 948. Tanaka struck out, swing and a miss.

Saito lifted what was left of his arms into the air. Because he was small, and because he looked as though he'd been broken, he wasn't deemed a kaibutsu. There is more to the title than endurance, than simple suffering. A true kaibutsu inspires fear as well as awe. A true kaibutsu doesn't get damaged. He does the damage.

After graduating from high school, Yuki Saito played college baseball. Today he is in the Japanese minor leagues, presently out with a shoulder injury. It is unclear when he will pitch again. For now, his only physical reward for having sacrificed his arm to baseball is a plaque at Koshien, written entirely in Japanese, except for the three digits that shine like lights: 948.

Tanaka has gone on to become one of the top pitchers in Japanese professional baseball. At the end of this season, he will likely be posting, like Dice-K, like Darvish, auctioned off to the highest American bidder. A major league team will probably pay tens of millions of dollars for his rights and sign him for tens of millions more. Despite Cashman's misgivings, rumor has it that team might even be the Yankees. If not them, someone, somewhere, will overlook everything we now know about Japanese pitchers and the childhoods they survive, hoping against hope that Tanaka won't be the next Dice-K or Igawa or Yoshii or Fujikawa.

Or the next Yuki Saito. After telling the story of that fabled Koshien, Gondo rises out of his chair and reaches for his phone. He has been doing some math, some private equation, but he's not sure he's found the right answer. He calls Saito, whose voice crackles into the room.

Gondo asks Saito if he has any regrets.

No, Saito says. No regrets. He won Koshien, remember?

Gondo hangs up, and he brings his hand to his mouth. He remembers. He remembers two unstoppable boys throwing themselves into each other, inning after inning, pitch after pitch. He remembers how it was one of the most perfect, terrible, lung-heaving things he's ever seen. He remembers how that baseball game felt like love in his chest, how it still feels that way. His eyes glisten behind his glasses.

"I thought I had my mind made up," he says. "Now I'm not so sure."

On Monday afternoon, the boys of Saibi, now back home in Matsuyama, are informed that today's practice will be eight hours long. The first order of business is to tend to their field, on which heavy weekend rains have left a small lake where third base should be. Joko supervises the digging of a network of trenches that would impress a corps of engineers. Then most of the team sets upon the lake with wooden rakes and buckets and sponges. It takes them close to an hour of quiet, tireless work, but slowly the lake recedes. At last the bag is put into place.

All the while, Anraku has been nearby, working on his mound with his own rake, shaping its gentle curves. It is necessary, Joko says, that the boys maintain their own field. They need to learn a place in order to learn their places in it. Joko is not teaching them to be baseball players, he says, because most of them will not be baseball players. But one day all of them will be men. After they finish tending their field, they bow to it, because there is honor even in dust.

Next, they assemble in tight rows on the dirt, the starters sitting in the first row, the backups and the hopefuls sitting in two neat rows behind them. Joko gives them a talk, gentle, reassuring. "I have taught you the only way I know," he says. Then his voice grows stern. Between their weekend games, the boys had tucked into lunches behind one of the dugouts, and one of them had left his empty bento box on the ground. "We were their guests," Joko says. "We must leave these places cleaner than we found them." He turns to Anraku. "This is your responsibility," he says. "This is up to you."

At the end of his speech, Joko asks the boys to stand and turn to face toward home—not home plate but the place they were born. They turn in every possible direction, north and south, east and west, toward the cities and the mountains and the sea. They take off their caps and hold them to their chests. "I want you to think of where you come from," Joko says. "I want you to think of your mothers and fathers, of the people whose love brought you here. I want you to think of what you mean to them, how precious your gifts are. I want you to think of them and decide what it is you want to do today. Will you do your best? Will you make them proud?" And then he has the boys stand in quiet contemplation for a minute, for two minutes. Their faces crease; paths form in the dust under their eyes.

It's hard to imagine an American coach making the same speech. It's hard to imagine American boys taking off their caps and turning to face Philadelphia and Yonkers, San Antonio and St. Louis, and making up their minds about what it is they want to do today, and how well, and to honor whom. It's hard to imagine our physical pursuits also being spiritual ones. It's hard to imagine an America in which something as rare and special as a fastball is seen as less a possession than a sacrifice, more a communal property than a personal one.

It is just as hard to imagine an American manager asking his 16-year-old star to throw 772 pitches in a single tournament. The boys begin their practice. It too doesn't look like something we would ask our children to do. It is two hours before any of them touch a baseball. At one point, heavy logs are lifted and swung. Anraku, wearing a leather jacket to prepare his body for summer's heat, watches the sweat drip off the end of his nose. Soon he will leave for a six-mile run on a hilly golf course. He runs every day. He must get stronger. He must reach the next level.

"Let me ask you," Joko says to an astonished guest. "Why do Japanese arms break in America?"

He has heard many theories. He has heard that the Americans don't let the Japanese throw enough and they get weak. He has heard they get too muscle-bound, or too fat on American food, and it alters their formerly perfect mechanics. He has heard that the ball itself is different—the American ball is bigger—and so their grip must change, which changes everything else.

He has never heard that it's because Japanese children field too much, or hit too much, or throw too much. Nobody, he says, has blamed Koshien or nagekomi, or if someone has, he's been deaf to such complaints. American pitchers get hurt too, don't they? If anything, Joko says, the Japanese aren't working hard enough anymore. It's not that they risk losing something important to us, to our softer way of thinking. "We've already lost it," he says.

He is not alone in his fears. "If Koshien changes," the former Met Masato Yoshii says, "I think we would lose what is beautiful about baseball."

"What a game that was," Gondo says, remembering Saito's 948 pitches once again.

Joko concludes his chat about American misdeeds by walking onto the field with buckets of balls. The boys surround him in a tight circle. Joko picks one. The boy stands maybe 30 feet in front of him, and Joko starts rifling balls, left and right, left and right. The boy dives, gets up, dives again, again and again and again, the balls mostly just out of reach. A dozen, then two dozen, then three dozen, now four, until at last the spectacle is over. The boy retreats out of the circle, and he is dirt-caked and heaving. Sweat and snot and tears cover his face. Several minutes later, his hands are still on his knees, and he still struggles to catch his breath.

Meanwhile, another boy has been chosen. It's the catcher, the whippet. Now he too begins diving, left and right, left and right, left and right. The boys are screaming encouragement, and he continues, stretched out and back to his feet, again and again. He is covered in earth from head to toe, but Joko continues to throw, and the whippet continues to dive, until suddenly, out of the dust: he smiles. Somehow he is smiling, and Joko is smiling back at him, until finally the whippet catches one last ball, exhausted, facedown in the dirt. The boys roar in unison. They have just witnessed the difference between victory and defeat.

"That's how we communicate," Joko says, the smile still on his face. "We speak without talking."

The afternoon passes into evening, with so much speaking and so little talking, until the sun starts to set beyond right field and the brown earth goes golden. Anraku has returned from his run at the golf course. He is still wearing his leather jacket; his giant teenage body continues to cook. Joko has told him to be ready, that if they make Koshien again, he will throw every pitch. "I want to prove this is the right way," Anraku says. "I want to prove the Japanese way is the right way."

He knows that if he gets hurt, then the Japanese way might be finished along with him, his arm the final straw. It is his greatest fear. Unlike Hideo Nomo, he won't be the start of something. Anraku will be the end, the monster that leaves his city in ruins. "It will be my fault," he says. His manager was talking about a discarded bento box, but he wasn't really talking about a bento box: this is up to him.

If he were an American kid, if he really were Stephen Strasburg, he would be that almost mythical brand of prospect whose gifts are appraised by baseball jewelers looking at him through loupes and locked away in a vault. Instead, Anraku was born Japanese, which means he is a different commodity, measured by different values. Anraku is not from this place; he is of this place. He is this place. He is his high school and prefecture and Japan. He is his mother and father. He is his manager. Most of all he is the rest of these beautiful boys, everything they are and everything they hope they will be remembered for having been. He knows that his fate will also be theirs. He knows by heart which way is home. And so off Anraku goes unafraid into the night, swinging his arm at his shoulder, as though he's only just begun to warm up.

20 Minutes at Rucker Park

FROM SBNATION.COM

THOMAS "TJ" WEBSTER JR. waits impatiently for the ball to be tossed in the air. The only white player on the court, he can sense the eyes of the few dozen spectators lounging around the steel and plastic bleachers.

At half-court, the sole referee delicately balances the ball on his fingertips while simultaneously judging the slight breeze coming off the Harlem River.

Across the street, rising out of the ground where the once-famed Polo Grounds stood and Willie Mays tracked down fly balls, four 30-story housing projects known as the Polo Grounds Towers loom ominously over Holcombe Rucker Park.

TJ anxiously tugs at his long black shorts once, then again. The tattoos that start at his wrist and crawl toward his slender biceps glisten under the sun. At five-eleven, with a lithe upper body that more resembles that of a tennis player, he doesn't seem built for this game, or, perhaps, this place.

As the players wait for the scorer's table to set up, TJ bends his knees, then jumps straight into the air, landing with controlled force. It's as if he's testing the durability of the newly installed NBA-grade wood floor placed over the blacktop.

Despite his small size and light frame, he carries, like a weapon stashed under a vest, a 38-inch vertical jump. Along with his self-proclaimed "great" outside jump shot, he knows that during this 20-minute open tryout he'll have to do enough to impress one of the handful of coaches glaring at him from the stands. They represent teams in the upcoming Entertainer's Basketball Classic, an eight-week-long tournament and the jewel of New York's basketball summer circuit.

Just two days ago, TJ stepped off a cross-country bus with every penny to his name wedged into the bottom of his bag for a chance to change his life. It's a long shot; he understands that, and so do the other nine players on the court. There are only two ways to make an EBC team, either by reputation or by being selected after your performance in the open run.

Each year, one, maybe two players, at most, will be good enough to be granted a jersey and, in essence, a pass inside the halls of the cathedral of street basketball; a chance to feel the nearly religious power of Rucker Park—the same court that has hosted some of the greatest players to ever play the game.

In 1947, Holcombe Rucker, a Harlem teacher, started the predecessor to the EBC tournament on 128th Street, a mile south of its current location on West 155th Street, in the park now named in his honor. He viewed the tourney as a way to keep local youth busy during the summer months.

Over the next few decades, the tournament expanded and became vital to the community. Every local player with any game had to go through the crucible of Rucker's tournaments to prove he could play. Not only to himself and to other players, but also to the fans on the street who would sometimes wait for hours to squeeze inside the small park and watch basketball in its rawest form.

Although the tournament games are generally governed by the same rules as the indoor game, streetball has its own unique subculture. At its core, the attraction to the playground is the spontaneity and the depth of human expression. Without many, if any, set plays, extreme displays of individual skill and athleticism can flare at any moment. Early on, NBA players seeking a break from the stodgy confines of their winter league, and to solidify their street credentials, began flocking to the tournaments uptown. A young Lew Alcindor perfected his footwork there. Dr. J was a regular, and locals like Earl "The Goat" Manigault, Herman "The Helicopter" Knowings, and "Pee-Wee" Kirkland became legends almost equal in stature to their NBA counterparts.

On the court, other players with ability, but who lacked a name, had the opportunity to go toe-to-toe with the game's best. Overnight heroes and streetball legends appeared from seemingly nothing and nowhere in a way that could never happen in the inaccessible castle of the NBA. Reputations could be made, but dreams could be destroyed, at Rucker Park.

The success stories have become a part of the folklore of the game and are passed down from one era to the next. Joe "The Destroyer" Hammond was offered a contract by the Lakers after he scored 50 on Dr. J in the park. Harlem's Adrian "A Butta" Walton once dropped 33 on Vince Carter. Larry "The Bone Collector" Williams was an unknown Pasadena kid who earned himself an AND1 tour contract off the strength of his Rucker Park performances. The tales are endless. So too is the allure.

TJ knows all these stories by heart. He knows every last page of the history and anecdotes of New York street basketball and often spends his free time researching well-known streetball players, memorizing their achievements, but imagining their stories are about him and his life. This is his sustenance. It allows him to believe that a 24-year-old white kid, born and raised in stark poverty—who never played an organized indoor game in his life, never graduated high school—somehow not just belongs here in the open run standing on this court, but that one day his own story will also become part of the mythology of Rucker Park. A chance to not just earn himself a nickname, a reputation, and respect, but maybe if all the stars align the way he thinks they will, the way he believes they will, perhaps he'll get noticed by the right people and earn himself a basketball contract, maybe somewhere overseas, the AND1 Mixtape Tour, or the Ball Up Streetball Tour— *anywhere,* just to do what he loves, just to change things.

Really, he's given himself no other choice. He quit his job as janitor at the Greyhound bus station in his hometown of Sacramento, gave up his room in his grandfather's house, and cashed in every last penny he saved to take a three-day bus trip across the country to try out for these 20 minutes.

Twenty minutes. Running clock. That's all he has to make a team and continue his journey toward the gates of basketball heaven, or crumble and perish into the basketball hellfire below.

The referee bends his legs slightly as the longtime EBC announcer, Duke Tango, picks up the microphone.

"Welcome to Rucker Park, the start of the greatest outdoor tournament in the world." His husky voice shreds through the summer air, jolting the listless crowd.

The ball is tossed up—a knuckleball—and climbs toward its

apex before a pair of large hands meet it on the way down. It's tipped backwards in a slow, soft arc. TJ grabs it out of the air, then pauses and looks over at the scoreboard, at the clock that has already begun its slow descent toward judgment.

19:59 . . . 19:58 . . . 19:57 . . .

In the early afternoon, our bus pulls into Salt Lake City. The station is crowded, but it somehow seems vacant. A room full of exhausted, hungry people gives the long, cold hallways a feeling of vast emptiness. I've only been on the bus with TJ a relatively short 14 hours, but it's already begun to feel claustrophobic and restrictive, like a truck full of cattle.

I find a couple open spaces on the floor at the far end of the station; I put my bag underneath me and sit down. Soon the stench of hours of unchecked sweat spills out across the room. TJ seems unfazed. He pulls out his basketball, nearly worn to the rubber, signed by each of his family members and closest friends like an arm cast, wishing him luck on his journey. He begins casually spinning it around his finger in a tight circle, then around his thumb, then finally transferring the spinning ball to the edge of his cell phone. It's a party trick he's perfected to the point of boredom. A smallish man, with thick, worn lines across his forehead, comes closer to admire the skill. TJ smiles proudly.

This is the third time TJ has made this pilgrimage across country. The first time, in 2011, he had no expectations or even a place to stay. He was allotted a free ticket by virtue of working at Greyhound and simply wanted to take the three-day journey, place his feet on the Rucker Park playground, then get back on the bus and head home. However, a few days before he left, as if by divine intervention, he met a fellow streetballer at his favorite court on P Street and 10th in downtown Sacramento. He invited TJ to stay at his family's place in Queens for a few days, only a subway ride from Harlem.

"The first time I went there I took the subway to 145th Street," he explains to me through an awkward accent—a slow Northern California drawl (he'll say "hella" more than a few times) with touches of a Southern twang from his high school years spent in Oxford, Mississippi.

"As I'm walking I see the Polo Grounds Towers and my heart starts racing. I was shaking and nervous because I'm so excited. I sit down during a game and at halftime they ask if anyone wants to dunk. I was nervous, but I know for a fact if I raise my hand they'll pick me. Why? Because I'm white. Hannibal (an EBC announcer) picked me out of everyone. I went on the court, threw myself an alley-oop, cocked it back, and dunked it. It was 10 at night, street-lights on, music is going. The place went *crazy*. I dreamed about that my whole life."

A year later, he returned to Rucker, not just to dunk, but also to enter the open run and try to make a team. However, an ankle injury a few days before derailed his attempt. He stayed in New York a week longer, returning to Rucker Park nearly every day to watch the games, before eventually taking the bus home.

Over the last 12 months, he's been consumed with thoughts of playing in the EBC and excelling, seeking out that euphoric rush from the crowd on a weekly basis. He wakes up every day at 5:00 A.M., runs suicides, shoots an obscene number of jumpers, then plays in any game he can find.

But he's also taken to Facebook to boast he's one of the best in Sactown. He has announced that he is coming to Rucker Park this summer to score 40 to 50 points a game against the world's best.

People began to take notice. The director of the EBC heard about him, and so did others associated with the tournament. A film production team in Los Angeles got wind of the white kid with the unreasonable confidence and soaring leaping ability, and they got curious.

A producer friend of mine suggested I go up to Sacramento from LA and find out more about him, then document his journey across country. I played 10 years of pro ball overseas, and although I knew very little about street basketball in New York, my friend thought, if nothing else, I'd be a good judge of talent.

The day before we took off across country, I met TJ at his grand-father's house in the northern Sacramento neighborhood of Del Paso Heights (DPH, or "Deepest Part of Hell," as TJ calls it). It's a community of mostly small, decaying California bungalow houses built for migrant farmworkers from Oklahoma and Mexico during the Great Depression and workers at the McClellan Air Force Base during World War II. His place, near the end of the block, sits across from an alley of abandoned furniture and behind a pair of RV dealerships. A couple of the houses on the block are boarded up; the rest seem to be, if not neglected, barely functional, nothing more.

I walk past his uncle's old Camaro parked across the front lawn. TJ greets me and shakes my hand with an unconvincing flip of the wrist. His cutoff T-shirt shows off sleeves of colorful, cartoonish tattoos that start at his wrist and work their way up.

'80'S BABY, his left arm shouts; a Roc-A-Fella Records logo with the lines from a verse in Jay-Z's "Lost One": "Time don't go back, it goes forward / Can't run from the pain, go towards it"; a boom box animation with HIP-HOP tagged above it; a Wu-Tang Clan symbol near his right wrist; a large inscription of the '80s rap group Audio Two ("Milk is chillin'"); an array of colorful dollar signs and tiger-striped stars; and his self-anointed moniker, UPTOWN FINEST.

I wasn't quite sure what to make of his tattoos, and stared at them a few moments longer before I noticed his grandfather, hunched over on the blue cloth couch across the room, waving at me. He began to say something before picking up a glass marijuana pipe. He lit it up and took one long toke before turning back toward me and groaning some barely audible greeting.

After a lifetime of chronic back pain, he's usually stuck in a wheelchair and has spent most of the last few years under a haze of smoke and reruns of *Judge Judy*. At night, he simply curls up on the couch while TJ's older cousin sleeps on the love seat.

The house itself is crumbling. The bathroom is decaying and full of mold, and the kitchen floor seems to be rotting completely on one side. The only well-cared-for items in the entire place are two large cannabis plants on a circular plastic kitchen table, surrounded by bleach bottles, glowing under fierce HID lighting.

TJ has lived here almost six years, after homesickness brought him back from Mississippi. Born in Sacramento, starting in eighth grade when his father moved him to Reno, he had a nomadic childhood. He was there for a year before his dad abandoned him and his sister for another family—he hasn't spoken to him since. His mother remarried and took TJ to Oxford, Mississippi, during his high school years. He tried to adapt, but struggled in school, cutting classes to shoot hoops or just roam the streets with his new friends. He dropped out before graduation to help his family pay the bills. Eventually, one day when he'd had enough of the South, he walked to the bus station and headed back to Sacramento.

When he came home, after searching for months, he found the only job he could get in Sacramento's harsh, collapsed economy—cleaning bathrooms, part-time, at the local Greyhound station. In three years, he's never had a promotion or a pay raise.

Standing in TJ's kitchen, the inescapable smell of weed and beer drifts in from the yard. I walk through the back door and see 20 to 30 smaller marijuana plants lined up in neat rows, empty beer cans strewn across the concrete patio. The family pit bull lies in the sun, tongue out, and takes in the sweet smell of freshly grown weed.

TJ, who seems to be weary, ushers me back inside. We pass his uncle's bedroom. He's counting piles of green Ziploc bags, and shoving them into a box.

I walk behind TJ into his room, then freeze and look around. His bed is immaculately made, his sneakers lined up perfectly. A clothes iron is placed on the floor. There is the tidiness of a well-groomed man, but also innocence, the naïveté of a 14-year-old boy who still views the world in terms of heroes and candy money.

As he talks to me, he fiddles with his white headphones and moves them off his ears. I can hear the faint sounds of Mobb Deep's "The Infamous" eke into the air.

On his desk sits a large plastic jar filled to the brim with nickels, dimes, quarters, and pennies. Mostly pennies. It's money he's saving for food in New York. Next to the jar are spray cans and black markers for tags he's working on—"Brooklyn" and "Uptown Finest."

In the confines of his room, it's as if he's trying to live out his own fantasy of what he imagines an early-'90s childhood to be during the golden age of hip-hop on the streets of New York. A time that must seem romantic and authentic, in a way that his life now seems difficult and mundane.

On his desk, stacked neatly in two piles, seem to be every DVD or VHS tape ever produced about street basketball. *Above the Rim, Heaven Is a Playground,* a documentary about streetballer Earl "The Goat" Manigault.

These are the tapes he grew up with. "I was like, in the second grade watching a show with my dad and this commercial come on about streetball," he says. "I can't remember what it was, but the footage was fuckin' crazy. I was hypnotized, I couldn't get enough. Ever since that, that's all I want to do."

The rest of his room is a homage to his idols: quotes and pictures of Jay-Z over his window, an awkward life-size cutout of Michael Jordan leaned against the wall, a framed photograph he took with streetball legend Joe Hammond the first time he went to Rucker. "Joe didn't have to go to class, he was a legend," he says. "The entire Lakers flew to Rucker to see him play." He holds the picture in his hands, then puts it down and stares at it in admiration.

And above his bed, glaring down on him each night, is a mini-shrine to the fiery Boston Celtics playmaker Rajon Rondo. It's almost an unhealthy love. His entire bedroom is sprinkled with odes to Rondo—a jersey, his pictures, a warm-up shirt, and all types of assorted Boston Celtics paraphernalia.

When I ask him to name five players to comprise an all-time team, he mentions Jordan, then almost gushes with admiration just to say Rondo's name. He identifies with the antiauthoritarian point guard, who views the game through the lens of love, loyalty, and heart, and who shuns standardized versions of fundamentals and statistical analysis. A streetballer's baller.

"Rondo plays because he loves basketball," TJ says. "Basketball players in the NBA right now, like LeBron James, they're all about money. Like, Rondo dislocated his elbow and he *still* played."

Finally, he picks up his basketball off the carpeted floor, and tosses it to me. "You wanna play one-on-one?" he asks.

Seventy-four hours, 12 states, and eight bus changes. The distance from Sacramento to New York can be measured in many ways—hours wearing the same underwear, times stepping over a poor, passed-out soul in a bus station bathroom, centimeters of your swollen ankles, vending machine Snickers bars for lunch or dinner—but as the hours pass and sleep deprivation takes hold of you, your actual destination seems less and less important. It's almost as if you begin to just float alongside the bus in a sort of zombie-fied state, watching yourself through glossy eyes.

Still days away from New York, falling forward through the night across I-80, somewhere east of Utah, I looked over in TJ's direction and wondered what he was thinking. The lights inside the bus were off completely except for the thin strip across the roof that acted as a night-light.

Maybe he could sense me looking at him and he turned to-

ward me. "You know how the EBC started?" he offered, as if he's
been waiting for this moment to tell me. I say nothing. "You don't
know?" He leans in as if we're around a campfire. I can make out
the outline of his face across the aisle.

"It was 1982," he begins, and then proceeds to tell me about the
moment when modern streetball, as we know it—the marriage of
hip-hop and outdoor basketball—really started. It's his creation
myth, and happened seven years before he was born, but as far as
he's concerned, it's the beginning of time.

During a 2:00 A.M. broadcast of the legendary Mr. Magic and
Marley Marl radio show on WHBI in New York City (which Notorious B.I.G. later immortalized in the song "Juicy"), the local rap
group the Crash Crew issued a live on-air challenge to another up-
and-coming rap group, the Disco Four, to play a basketball game.

At the time, the show was the only strictly hip-hop broadcast
in the nation, and a must listen for many of the youth in Harlem.
Word spread fast and the next day hundreds of people turned up
to watch as the Disco Four destroyed the Crash Crew by 59 points
in the impromptu game.

Over the next few weeks, other pioneers of the genre, like the
Sugar Hill Gang and Grandmaster Flash, wanted to join in, so
Greg Marius of the Disco Four organized a round-robin tourna-
ment of rappers.

To up the stakes, some of the best ballplayers in New York City
were brought in as ringers to compete alongside the musicians
and rappers. Soon, as the quality of play went up, the rappers
were forced to the sideline (Nas and Rick Ross coached teams this
year). By 1987, crowds were so large that the EBC found a permanent home at Rucker Park.

TJ smiles proudly when he finishes the story. I could see his
white teeth through the dimness.

I feel my stomach grumbling and I reach into my bag for a granola bar. Despite being on a bus with 45 other people crammed
together for endless hours across the American landscape, there's
a distinct sense of isolation hovering over each of us. As the miles
pass and you're pushed further away from home, your thoughts
become more powerful; your dreams get bigger, and your fears
start to scream at you.

Minutes lapse in silence, maybe even hours. My red eyes flick-ered shut, then back open. TJ, who never seemed to sleep more than a few minutes, leans over and taps me on the shoulder. "You know what my goal is?" he says through the darkness. "Kevin Durant scored 66 points one game at Rucker. That would be cool if I beat that." His voice trails off. "There's a chance I could do that shit. There's a chance."

I finish my granola bar, and stash the wrapper back in my bag. Maybe, I wonder, it's better if he gets off the bus in Denver and turns back home, never attempts to play at Rucker, and just lives inside his own innocence, his own version of reality.

I felt as if I was escorting him to his own wake.

A couple of days before, he took me from his place to Roosevelt Park on 10th and P Street, a quiet, well-manicured playground just south of downtown. Right away, he asked again if I wanted to play one-on-one. I had on jeans and low-top sneakers and hadn't planned on playing, but he needed to prove to me he had game, so I agreed. He showed off his turnaround jumper, quick hops, and sharp lateral quickness. The hours of hard work had paid off and we split two games to 11. But when more players showed up for the noontime run, the crater-sized holes in his game became obvious.

He had never been coached, and had no understanding of the subtleties of basketball. When he didn't have the ball, he would shuffle toward the dribbler with his hands out, unaware of spacing, or search for steals on nearly every play. You could almost see the gears turning over in his head as he planned out each move. Nothing was natural.

He tried hard, and hustled, but overall he wasn't remarkable. Maybe if he had been relentlessly drilled from the age of 10 onward, things would be different, but he hadn't. Nobody had ever taken his hand and walked him into a gym. Instead, he was just a 24-year-old, stuck in a time that had already passed.

"Don't you think . . ."—I try to find the right way to say it— "Do you think maybe you should put your energy into something else? Maybe have some other options in case you don't make it at Rucker Park? Do you have a backup plan?" I ask. "Have you thought about going back to school?"

"No," he says. His headphones, which he rarely takes off, jiggle audibly as he shakes his head from side to side. "This basketball

thing is all I got," he says, almost pleading. "I'm 110 percent focused on this. People ask me if I have a Plan B. To be honest, I
don't. I think, like, nine out of 10 people with backup plans don't
succeed at their first plan because that backup plan is constantly in
the back of their head, and they lose focus on Plan A."

"But . . ." I began to say, shaking my head. I wanted to scold
him, tell him that he's wasting his time, and teach him, as I'd been
taught, to plan your life. The words, however, never came. I turned
away, back toward the desolate road, and breathed out.

For me, this trip was nothing more than an adventure, a story I
could tell my friends, a chance to laugh about the time I spent half
a week on a bus.

But for TJ, this trip wasn't his Kerouac novel, and didn't emerge
from Steinbeck's "virus of restlessness." It wasn't a modern-day vag-
abond's romantic jaunt around the country seeking to understand
the ills of America. This trip came from a deeper place. It was his
calling: he *had* to travel 3,000 miles from home on his own. He
had to believe in himself and that this lifelong fantasy to be a basketball star was, in fact, his reality. No one else would. To him, this
was all there was.

Perhaps he wasn't wrong to stake everything on this. He'd chosen a different path—a journey deep into the unknown to confront his self-doubts and fears head-on. He had to walk fearlessly
inside the gates of Rucker Park and believe it was all worth it . . .
then play the game of his life.

His choice to put everything on the line was rare, but it's not
unique. Nearly every culture and tradition has a similar story, real
or imagined. When a young man starts his journey, he must be
brave enough to take a metaphysical leap of faith. He must be willing to step foot on the bus and travel straight into the labyrinth of
his fears, toward whatever awaits him on the other end, even if it
may rip him to shreds.

It's the ultimate gamble. If the young man is successful, he
comes home a hero, and becomes important. His life has meaning
and purpose. But in order to succeed, he must first completely
open up his soul to the consequences of failure, knowing there
may be no way back out. This, above all else, is the hardest thing
to do.

TJ's quest reminded me of that of the Athenian warrior Theseus, who journeyed down into the impenetrable labyrinth, leaving only the slimmest thread to mark his path, and then, armed with only a shield and a small dagger, defeated the terrifying Minotaur. He was then able to follow the thread back out of the labyrinth to become king of Athens. He risked all, and gained all.

Or, maybe we all simply live within the confines of our own fears and TJ was just running away from his, afraid of slowly rotting inside a weed den in the Deepest Part of Hell. At least he was on the bus. And at 5:00 A.M., three days after we left, as we passed through Weehawken, New Jersey, and the Manhattan horizon came into view, I leaned over as a ripple of excitement rushed through the entire bus.

"So, are you ready?" I asked TJ.

He smiled from ear to ear. "Hell yeah," he said. "This summer at Rucker, I think no one's gonna be fuckin' with me. Think about it. I've been on a bus three days. No sleep. Just think when I go to Queens and get some rest. I'm gonna feel even better. No one's touching me."

As the bus hurtled toward New York, there was no turning back. He was going to Rucker Park almost bare, exposed, armed only with his hopes and his overconfidence. His abrasive arrogance— and his 38-inch vertical leap—were his only weapons. It was all he had, and, really, all he had left.

TJ got off the D train two hours early and sat down in the adjacent playground, and waited. There was no selection process or online registration for the open run; if you wanted to play, you just walked onto the court at 3:00 P.M. with a pair of sneakers.

A few minutes before his game was due to start, TJ's airtight ego was deflating. "I hope it works out," he said meekly. I peered inside the gate as a few players began warming up. I'd imagined a collection of ripped six-eight high jumpers and burly New York City point guards with lightning-quick handles. Instead, many of the players trying out struggled with basic dribbling skills, or would jump to dunk but fall short and tap the glass backboard furiously with their palm. Few, if any, looked as if they had ever played college ball. TJ saw what I saw and his eyes lit up, the hopefulness returned.

But as soon as he corralled the opening tip, the nerves began to show. He started to press. He'd pick up his dribble after only a few bounces, or guard too tightly on defense.

The third or fourth time down the floor, he got the ball at the top of the key. Before making a move, before even thinking about a move, he rose up and launched it at the hoop, missing everything. The ball bounced up and over the small fence into the empty steel bleachers behind the basket. He ran his hand through his hair in frustration, then jogged back on defense.

TJ had, over the years, made a shield for himself. Carefully constructed out of every hope or fantasy he'd ever had of being a basketball star, it helped him endure and survive DPH and everything else. As long as he never really tried to play at Rucker and see whether he was good enough to share a court with Kevin Durant, or "A Butta" and "The Bone Collector," the shield protected him.

But as he looked up at the scoreboard, maybe he was beginning to realize that once the fantasy starts to unravel, it can never come back. He missed another shot badly, and audible groans came from the stands.

As the minutes continued to pass and the players sprinted up and down the court, a set of clouds rolled by overhead, blanketing the sun. That seemingly innocent shift, however, changed TJ. As if the natural spotlight shining down on him had been turned off.

TJ still had a few skills he could showcase. He stole the ball near half-court and sped the other way, he stutter-stepped and readied himself for a dunk—his moment. Then, at the last second, he backed down and simply laid it in. Still, it was a start. It wasn't a dunk, but he had scored at Rucker Park.

On the next offensive possession, his confidence was soaring. He called for the ball. The small crowd seemed to sense something was about to happen and fell nearly silent in anticipation. TJ made a quick move right to left, skipped past his defender, then turned to make a no-look bounce pass through the key in between three defenders—the kind of out-of-nowhere, once-in-a-lifetime pass Rondo would have been proud of. The kind of pass that would earn you, by word of mouth, recognition in the streets, or, even better, a nickname.

In New York street basketball, your nickname is your identity. Once you're granted a nickname (and you can never give yourself one), it sticks with you for life. It's a sign you belong on the court. The nickname often comes from one of the announcers and it can be descriptive of your physical appearance ("Cabbie," "Eddie Kane," "Bodega"), your style of play ("Helicopter," "Dribbling Machine," "Cookie Monster"), something comical ("Clumsy Janitor"—"He does nothing but drop buckets!"), or simply your initials. But a streetball player hasn't arrived until he has a nickname.

TJ's pass didn't go as planned. Perhaps nothing ever does. It was half a second too late, knocked down inside the key, batted around, then picked up by the other team and tossed ahead for an easy layup.

Duke Tango, a childish grin on his face, squeezed his microphone tight. "That man's name isn't 'Uptown Finest.' His name from now on is 'Plastic Cup.' Because he *can't hold nothing*. That's 'Plastic Cup' right there," he said pointing at TJ. The entire crowd chuckled.

Every time TJ touched the ball, a chorus of "Plastic Cup" echoed from the bleachers to the project buildings across the street.

TJ heard the snickers and seemed to shrink, his shoulders hung low and his frail body slumped downward.

The shield that had protected him for so long was gone, disintegrated in his hand. He was completely naked, staring at the Minotaur, his deepest fears, flush in the eyes.

If I was his coach, I would have subbed him right there, spared him the humiliation, let him watch from the bench and just soak up the same Uptown air the legends once experienced.

Instead, I watched from four rows back, my hands at my side, and wished, like he wished, that life had been kinder; that he wasn't born a touch under six feet; that poverty isn't what it is; that he didn't have to clean up shit for a living; and that he didn't wrap so much of himself into a bouncing ball that was both his source of happiness and slowly strangling any hope of a future.

Still, as the minutes passed, there was a chance the basketball gods would smile down on him and the ball would bounce his way and this time he would dunk and the crowd could go crazy, and for a moment, or two, it would be different.

He shot another air ball, then another. The chuckles became laughs. "Plastic Cup! Plastic Cup!"

As the last few seconds ticked off the clock, TJ stood in the cor-

ner, away from the ball. The buzzer sounded, mercifully, and he
shuffled back toward the bleachers. He sat down, alone, leaned
forward, and dropped his head between his hands.

A couple weeks later TJ asked me to meet him at Port Authority
Bus Terminal in Manhattan's Hell's Kitchen, but he didn't tell me
where exactly, so I wandered around the web of concrete, past the
dull orange walls and narrow sloping walkways. The terminal is
designed in such a cold, impersonal way that it's impossible to tell
if you're standing two stories aboveground or two stories below it.

I finally found him standing by himself under a flight of stairs.
He had lost some weight, and his eyes looked worn and tired.

"I checked my card today," he said, to explain why he's leaving.
"I got $8 on my card. And cash, I got like $7 and some change."
He gnawed his teeth together and looked down.

After Rucker, TJ had floated around New York for as long as he
could, trying desperately to put off the inevitable. He'd wake up in
the morning, pick up his basketball, and head to one of the thousands of courts across the city. Goat Park, Tillary Park, West Fourth
Street, Wilkins Park—but usually by the end of the afternoon he'd
always travel toward Marcy Playgrounds in Brooklyn, underneath
the building where Jay-Z grew up.

He'd come back day after day, often shooting around by himself. Those walking past would pause by the fence surrounding the
courts and curiously peer in. It was as if he was hoping he would
somehow stumble across the ghost of a younger Jay-Z or someone
who knew him, that he would finally be seen. And that they would
then take him by the hand and offer him something, some mor-
sel of guidance or wisdom, something he so desperately sought; a
thread back out of his own personal labyrinth.

One afternoon while shooting around, he told me, someone
spotted his Roc-A-Fella Records tattoo with the Jay-Z quote on his
arm. They told him there was someone he needed to meet and
asked him to follow. He was nervous, but went anyway. And there,
waiting in front of a corner store, was Damon "Dame" Dash, veri-
fied hip-hop royalty, former best friend and Roc-A-Fella business
partner of Jay-Z.

They sat down, Dash and TJ, just the two of them, inside a small
café nearby and talked. TJ told him his story. Then he asked about

Jay-Z. He asked about how it all started—he wanted to know everything. Dash humored him and talked and listened. They exchanged numbers. After more than an hour, Dash got up, reached into his pocket, and took out a wad of hundreds.

TJ looked at the outstretched hand, the edges of the bills poking out. But TJ shook his head and turned down the offer. Dash put the money back in his pocket; they embraced and went their separate ways.

"So why didn't you take it?" I asked.

"I don't take nothin' from nobody," he said, hoping for it to come across as a statement of pride. "But you know, I think he respected that, I do." He shook his head, still in disbelief he had met Dame Dash.

He couldn't buy food with respect, he knew that, but that didn't scare him. He knew the taste of poverty. Respect, on the other hand, was something he was willing to starve for. Maybe this wasn't why he came to New York, but then again, maybe it was.

Rucker was over, his fantasies were dead. He had no job to go back to, he had almost nothing, nothing at all but the possible respect of Dame Dash. But this, this was a lot.

"Now boarding bus 4083 to Pittsburgh and all points further west," the bus driver announced. Everyone nearby got up and staggered into line.

"Maybe I should have taken it," he said reaching for his stomach. "I could use it, I could really use it." He zipped up his backpack and looked around as the passengers in front of him slowly shuffled forward.

As he neared the front of the line, the realization that maybe he would never be a Rucker Park legend was starting to sink in. "Three days on a fuckin' bus, to go back to . . ." His voice started to crack. "You know where I live. What if you were in my shoes?" He glanced down at his worn Nike sandals. "In these fuckin' flip-flops?"

He looked up at me. I reached in my pocket and handed him a granola bar.

TJ gave the driver his ticket outside of the gate, then turned and hugged me quickly, looking away.

I stood and watched him walk up the stairs of the bus and disappear back into the darkness.

I wanted to tell him that this would make him stronger. That he did something most people would never dream of, that he scored, that he earned Dame Dash's respect, that the trip to Rucker Park was just a start.

I wanted more than anything to tell him that in the end it would all work out.

But the truth was, I didn't know. I didn't know.

AMANDA RIPLEY

The Case Against High School Sports

FROM THE ATLANTIC

EVERY YEAR, THOUSANDS of teenagers move to the United States from all over the world, for all kinds of reasons. They observe everything in their new country with fresh eyes, including basic features of American life that most of us never stop to consider.

One element of our education system consistently surprises them: "Sports are a big deal here," says Jenny, who moved to America from South Korea with her family in 2011. Shawnee High, her public school in southern New Jersey, fields teams in 18 sports over the course of the school year, including golf and bowling. Its campus has lush grass fields, six tennis courts, and an athletic Hall of Fame. "They have days when teams dress up in Hawaiian clothes or pajamas just because — 'We're the soccer team!'" Jenny says. (To protect the privacy of Jenny and other students in this story, only their first names are used.)

By contrast, in South Korea, whose 15-year-olds rank fourth in the world (behind Shanghai, Singapore, and Hong Kong) on a test of critical thinking in math, Jenny's classmates played pickup soccer on a dirt field at lunchtime. They brought badminton rackets from home and pretended there was a net. If they made it into the newspaper, it was usually for their academic accomplishments.

Sports are embedded in American schools in a way they are not almost anywhere else. Yet this difference hardly ever comes up in domestic debates about America's international mediocrity in education. (The U.S. ranks 31st on the same international math test.)

The challenges we do talk about are real ones, from undertrained teachers to entrenched poverty. But what to make of this other glaring reality, and the signal it sends to children, parents, and teachers about the very purpose of school?

When I surveyed about 200 former exchange students last year, in cooperation with an international exchange organization called AFS, nine out of ten foreign students who had lived in the U.S. said that kids here cared more about sports than their peers back home did. A majority of Americans who'd studied abroad agreed.

Even in eighth grade, American kids spend more than twice the time Korean kids spend playing sports, according to a 2010 study published in the *Journal of Advanced Academics*. In countries with more holistic, less hard-driving education systems than Korea's, like Finland and Germany, many kids play club sports in their local towns—outside of school. Most schools do not staff, manage, transport, insure, or glorify sports teams, because, well, why would they?

When I was growing up in New Jersey, not far from where Jenny now lives, I played soccer from age seven to seventeen. I was relieved to find a place where girls were not expected to sit quietly or look pretty, and I still love the game. Like most other Americans, I can rattle off the many benefits of high school sports: exercise, lessons in sportsmanship and perseverance, school spirit, and just plain fun. All of those things matter, and Jenny finds it refreshing to attend a school that is about so much more than academics. But as I've traveled around the world visiting places that do things differently—and get better results—I've started to wonder about the trade-offs we make.

Nearly all of Jenny's classmates at Shawnee are white, and 95 percent come from middle- or upper-income homes. But in 2012, only 17 percent of the school's juniors and seniors took at least one Advanced Placement test—compared with the 50 percent of students who played school sports.

As states and districts continue to slash education budgets, as more kids play on traveling teams outside of school, and as the globalized economy demands that children learn higher-order skills so they can compete down the line, it's worth reevaluating the American sporting tradition. If sports were not central to the mission of American high schools, then what would be?

*

On October 12, 1900, the Wall School of Honey Grove played St. Matthew's Grammar School of Dallas in football, winning 5–0. The event was a milestone in Texas history: the first recorded football game between two high school teams. Until then, most American boys had played sports in the haphazard way of boys the world over: ambling onto fields and into alleys for pickup games or challenging other loosely affiliated groups of students to a match. Cheating was rampant, and games looked more like brawls than organized contests.

Schools got involved to contain the madness. The trend started in elite private schools and then spread to the masses. New York City inaugurated its Public Schools Athletic League in 1903, holding a track-and-field spectacular for 1,000 boys at Madison Square Garden the day after Christmas.

At the time, the United States was starting to educate its children for more years than most other countries, even while admitting a surge of immigrants. The ruling elite feared that all this schooling would make Anglo-Saxon boys soft and weak, in contrast to their brawny, newly immigrated peers. Oliver Wendell Holmes Sr. warned that cities were being overrun with "stiff-jointed, soft-muscled, paste-complexioned youth."

Sports, the thinking went, would both protect boys' masculinity and distract them from vices like gambling and prostitution. "Muscular Christianity," fashionable during the Victorian era, prescribed sports as a sort of moral vaccine against the tumult of rapid economic growth. "In life, as in a football game," Theodore Roosevelt wrote in an essay on "The American Boy" in 1900, "the principle to follow is: Hit the line hard; don't foul and don't shirk, but hit the line hard!"

Athletics succeeded in distracting not just students but entire communities. As athletic fields became the cultural centers of towns across America, educators became coaches and parents became boosters.

From the beginning, though, some detractors questioned whether tax money should be spent on activities that could damage the brain, and occasionally leave students dead on the field. In 1909, New York City superintendents decided to abolish football, and the *New York Times* predicted that soccer would become the sport of choice. But officials reversed course the next year, re-allowing football, with revised rules.

The National Collegiate Athletic Association had emerged by this time, as a means of reforming the increasingly brutal sport of college football. But the enforcers were unable to keep pace with the industry. Once television exponentially expanded the fan base in the mid-20th century, collegiate sports gained a spiritual and economic choke hold on America. College scholarships rewarded high school athletes, and the search for the next star player trickled down even to grade school. As more and more Americans attended college, growing ranks of alumni demanded winning teams—and university presidents found their reputations shaped by the success of their football and basketball programs.

In 1961, the sociologist James Coleman observed that a visitor entering an American high school

> would likely be confronted, first of all, with a trophy case. His examination of the trophies would reveal a curious fact: The gold and silver cups, with rare exception, symbolize victory in athletic contests, not scholastic ones . . . Altogether, the trophy case would suggest to the innocent visitor that he was entering an athletic club, not an educational institution.

Last year in Texas, whose small towns are the spiritual home of high school football and the inspiration for *Friday Night Lights,* the superintendent brought in to rescue one tiny rural school district did something insanely rational. In the spring of 2012, after the state threatened to shut down Premont Independent School District for financial mismanagement and academic failure, Ernest Singleton suspended all sports—including football.

To cut costs, the district had already laid off eight employees and closed the middle school campus, moving its classes to the high school building; the elementary school hadn't employed an art or a music teacher in years; and the high school had sealed off the science labs, which were infested with mold. Yet the high school still turned out football, basketball, volleyball, track, tennis, cheerleading, and baseball teams each year.

Football at Premont cost about $1,300 a player. Math, by contrast, cost just $618 a student. For the price of one football season, the district could have hired a full-time elementary school music teacher for an entire year. But, despite the fact that Premont's football team had won just one game the previous season and hadn't been to the playoffs in roughly a decade, this option never occurred to anyone.

"I've been in hundreds of classrooms," says Singleton, who has spent 15 years as a principal and helped turn around other struggling schools. "This was the worst I've seen in my career. The kids were in control. The language was filthy. The teachers were not prepared." By suspending sports, Singleton realized, he could save $150,000 in one year. A third of this amount was being paid to teachers as coaching stipends, on top of the smaller costs: $27,000 for athletic supplies, $15,000 for insurance, $13,000 for referees, $12,000 for bus drivers. "There are so many things people don't think about when they think of sports," Singleton told me. Still, he steeled himself for the town's reaction. "I knew the minute I announced it, it was going to be like the world had caved in on us."

First he explained his decision to Enrique Ruiz Jr., the principal of Premont's only high school: eliminating sports would save money and refocus everyone's attention on academics. Ruiz agreed. The school was making other changes too, such as giving teachers more time for training and planning, making students wear uniforms, and aligning the curriculum with more rigorous state standards. Suspending sports might get the attention of anyone not taking those changes seriously.

Then Singleton told the school's football coach, a history teacher named Richard Russell, who'd been coaching for two decades. Russell had played basketball and football in high school, and he loved sports. But he preferred giving up the team to shutting down the whole district. He told Singleton to do whatever he needed to do, then walked over to the gym and told the basketball players, who were waiting for practice to begin. At first, the students didn't seem to understand. "What? Why?" asked Nathan, then a junior and a quarterback on the football team. "Would you rather have sports or school?" Russell replied.

Out by the tennis courts, Daniel, a junior who was in line to become a captain of the football team, was waiting for tennis practice to start when a teacher came out and delivered the news. Daniel went home and texted his friends in disbelief, hoping there had been some kind of mistake.

"We were freaking out," says Mariela, a former cheerleader and tennis and volleyball player. American kids expect to participate in school sports as a kind of rite of passage. "We don't get these years back," she told me. "I'm never going to get the experience of cheering as captain under the lights."

As the news trickled out, reporters from all over America came to witness the unthinkable. A photographer followed Nathan around, taking pictures of him not playing football, which the *Corpus Christi Caller-Times* ran in a photo essay titled "Friday Without Football in Premont."

Many observers predicted that Singleton's experiment would end in disaster. Premont was a speck on the map, an hour and a half southwest of Corpus Christi. The town's population had dwindled since the oil fields had dried up, and a majority of the 282 high school students who remained were from low-income Hispanic families. How many football players would drop out? How many cheerleaders would transfer to the next town's school? How would kids learn about grit, teamwork, and fair play?

Last fall at Premont, the first without football, was quiet—eerily so. There were no Friday night games to look forward to, no players and their parents cheered onto the field on opening night, no cheerleaders making signs in the hallway, no football practice 10 or more hours a week. Only the basketball team was allowed to play, though its tournament schedule was diminished.

More than a dozen students transferred, including four volleyball players and a football player. Most went to a school 10 miles away, where they could play sports. Two teachers who had been coaches left as well. To boost morale, Principal Ruiz started holding sports-free pep rallies every Friday. Classes competed against each other in drum-offs and team-building exercises in the school gym.

But there was an upside to the quiet. "The first 12 weeks of school were the most peaceful beginning weeks I've ever witnessed at a high school," Singleton says. "It was calm. There was a level of energy devoted to planning and lessons, to after-school tutoring. I saw such a difference."

Nathan missed the adrenaline rush of running out onto the field and the sense of purpose he got from the sport. But he began playing flag football for a club team on the weekends, and he admitted to one advantage during the week: "It did make you focus. There was just all this extra time. You never got behind on your work."

That first semester, 80 percent of the students passed their classes, compared with 50 percent the previous fall. About 160 people attended parent-teacher night, compared with six the year before. Principal Ruiz was so excited that he went out and took pictures of the parking lot, jammed with cars. Through some combination of new leadership, the threat of closure, and a renewed emphasis on academics, Premont's culture changed. "There's been a definite decline in misbehavior," says Desiree Valdez, who teaches speech, theater, and creative writing at Premont. "I'm struggling to recall a fight. Before, it was one every couple of weeks."

Suspending sports was only part of the equation, but Singleton believes it was crucial. He used the savings to give teachers raises. Meanwhile, communities throughout Texas, alarmed by the cancellation of football, raised $400,000 for Premont via fund-raisers and donations—money that Singleton put toward renovating the science labs.

No one knew whether the state would make good on its threat to shut the district down. But for the first time in many years, Premont had a healthy operating balance and no debt. This past spring, the school brought back baseball, track, and tennis, with the caveat that the teams could participate in just one travel tournament a season. "Learning is going on in 99 percent of the classrooms now," Coach Russell told me, "compared to 2 percent before."

In many schools, sports are so entrenched that no one—not even the people in charge—realizes their actual cost. When Marguerite Roza, the author of *Educational Economics*, analyzed the finances of one public high school in the Pacific Northwest, she and her colleagues found that the school was spending $328 a student for math instruction and more than four times that much for cheerleading—$1,348 a cheerleader. "And it is not even a school in a district that prioritizes cheerleading," Roza wrote. "In fact, this district's 'strategic plan' has for the past three years claimed that *math* was the primary focus."

Many sports and other electives tend to have lower student-to-teacher ratios than math and reading classes, which drives up the

cost. And contrary to what most people think, ticket and concession sales do not begin to cover the cost of sports in the vast majority of high schools (or colleges).

Football is, far and away, the most expensive high school sport.
Many football teams have half a dozen or more coaches, all of
whom typically receive a stipend. Some schools hire professional
coaches at full salaries, or designate a teacher as the full-time athletic director. New bleachers can cost half a million dollars, about
the same as artificial turf. Even maintaining a grass field can cost
more than $20,000 a year. Reconditioning helmets, a ritual that
many teams pay for every year, can cost more than $1,500 for a
large team. Some communities collect private donations or levy a
special tax to fund new school sports facilities.

Many of the costs are insidious, Roza has found, "buried in
unidentifiable places." For example, when teacher-coaches travel
for game days, schools need to hire substitute teachers. They also
need to pay for buses for the team, the band, and the cheerleaders,
not to mention meals and hotels on the road. For home games,
schools generally cover the cost of hiring officials, providing security, painting the lines on the field, and cleaning up afterward.
"Logistics are a big challenge," says Jared Bigham, until recently
the supervising principal of two schools in Copperhill, Tennessee, and a former teacher, coach, and player. "Even though the
coaches are in charge of the budgets, I still have to oversee them
and approve each expenditure. You're looking at 10 different budgets you have to manage."

That kind of constant, low-level distraction may be the greatest
cost of all. During football season in particular, the focus of American principals, teachers, and students shifts inexorably away from
academics. Sure, high school football players spend long, exhaust-
ing hours practicing (and according to one study, about 15 percent experience a brain injury each season), but the commitment
extends to the rest of the community, from late-night band practices to elaborate pep rallies to meetings with parents. Athletics
even dictate the time that school starts each day: despite research
showing that later start times improve student performance, many
high schools begin before 8:00 A.M., partly to reserve afternoon
daylight hours for sports practice.

American principals, unlike the vast majority of principals
around the world, make many hiring decisions with their sports

teams in mind—a calculus that does not always end well for students. "Every school in the entire country has done this," Marcia Gregorio, a veteran teacher in rural Pennsylvania, told me. "You hire a teacher, and you sometimes lower the standards because you need a coach."

But here's the thing: most American principals I spoke with expressed no outrage over the primacy of sports in school. In fact, they fiercely defended it. "If I could wave a magic wand, I'd have more athletic opportunities for students, not less," Bigham, the former Tennessee principal, told me. His argument is a familiar one: sports can be bait for students who otherwise might not care about school. "I've seen truancy issues completely turned around once students begin playing sports," he says. "When students have a sense of belonging, when they feel tied to the school, they feel more part of the process."

Premont is not alone. Over the past few years, budget cuts have forced more school districts, from Florida to Illinois, to scale back on sports programs. But in most of these places, even modest cuts to athletics are viewed as temporary—and tragic—sacrifices, not as necessary adaptations to a new reality. Many schools have shifted more of the cost of athletics to parents rather than downsize programs. Others have cut basic academic costs to keep their sports programs intact. Officials in Pasco County, Florida, have considered squeezing athletic budgets for each of the past six years. They've so far agreed to cut about 700 education jobs, and they extended winter break in 2011, but sports have been left mostly untouched.

In these communities, the dominant argument is usually that sports lure students into school and keep them out of trouble—the same argument American educators have made for more than a century. And it remains relevant, without a doubt, for some small portion of students.

But at this moment in history, now that more than 20 countries are pulling off better high school graduation rates than we are, with mostly nominal athletic offerings, using sports to tempt kids into getting an education feels dangerously old-fashioned. America has not found a way to dramatically improve its children's academic performance over the past 50 years, but other countries have—and they are starting to reap the economic benefits.

Andreas Schleicher, a German education scientist at the Organization for Economic Cooperation and Development, has visited schools all over the world and is an authority on different regional approaches to education. (I profiled Schleicher for this magazine in 2011.) He is wary of the theory that sports can encourage sustained classroom engagement. "Our analysis suggests that the most engaging environment you can offer students is one of cognitive challenge combined with individualised pedagogical support," he told me in an email. "If you offer boring and poor math instruction and try to compensate that with interesting sport activities, you may get students interested in sports but I doubt it will do much good to their engagement with school."

Though the research on student athletes is mixed, it generally suggests that sports do more good than harm for the players themselves. One 2010 study by Betsey Stevenson, then at the University of Pennsylvania, found that, in a given state, increases in the number of girls playing high school sports have historically generated higher college attendance and employment rates among women. Another study, conducted by Columbia's Margo Gardner, found that teenagers who participated in extracurriculars had higher college graduation and voting rates, even after controlling for ethnicity, parental education, and other factors.

But only 40 percent of seniors participate in high school athletics, and what's harder to measure is how the overriding emphasis on sports affects everyone who doesn't play. One study of 30,000 students at the University of Oregon found that the grades of men who did not play sports went down as the football team's performance improved. Both men and women reported that the better their football team did, the less they studied and the more they partied.

Exercise, without a doubt, is good for learning and living. But these benefits accrue to the athletes, who are in the minority. What about everyone else?

At Spelman College, a historically black, all-women's college in Atlanta, about half of last year's incoming class of some 530 students were obese or had high blood pressure, type 2 diabetes, or some other chronic health condition that could be improved with exercise. Each year, Spelman was spending nearly $1 million on athletics—not for those students, but for the 4 percent of the student body that played sports.

Spelman's president, Beverly Daniel Tatum, found the imbalance difficult to justify. She told me that early last year, while watching a Spelman basketball game, "it occurred to me that none of these women were going to play basketball after they graduated. By that I don't mean play professionally—I mean even recreationally. I thought of all the black women I knew, and they did not tend to spend their recreational time playing basketball. So a little voice in my head said, *Well, let's flip it.*"

That April, after getting approval from her board and faculty, she gathered Spelman's athletes and coaches in an auditorium and announced that she was going to cancel intercollegiate sports after the spring of 2013, and begin spending that $1 million on a campuswide health and fitness program.

Many of Spelman's 80 athletes were devastated, needless to say, and it is too early to tell whether the new swim, aerobics, and Zumba classes, among other offerings, will lead to healthier students on campus. But Tatum's signal was clear: lifelong health habits matter more than expensive, elite sporting competitions with rival schools. One priority has real and lasting benefits; the other is a fantasy.

Imagine, for a moment, if Americans transferred our obsessive intensity about high school sports—the rankings, the trophies, the ceremonies, the pride—to high school academics. We would look not so different from South Korea, or Japan, or any of a handful of Asian countries whose hypercompetitive, pressure-cooker approach to academics in many ways mirrors the American approach to sports. Both approaches can be dysfunctional; both set kids up for stress and disappointment. The difference is that 93 percent of South Korean students graduate from high school, compared with just 77 percent of American students—only about 2 percent of whom receive athletic scholarships to college.

As it becomes easier and more urgent to compare what kids around the world know and can do, more schools may follow Premont's lead. Basis public charter schools, located in Arizona, Texas, and Washington, DC, are modeled on rigorous international standards. They do not offer tackle football; the founders deemed it too expensive and all-consuming. Still, Basis schools offer other, cheaper sports, including basketball and soccer. Anyone who wants to play can play; no one has to try out. Arizona's mainstream league is costly to join, so Basis Tucson North belongs to an alternative league that costs less and requires no long-distance travel, meaning students rarely miss class for games. Athletes who want to play at an elite level do so on their own, through club teams—not through school.

Basis teachers channel the enthusiasm usually found on football fields into academic conquests. On the day of Advanced Placement exams, students at Basis Tucson North file into the classroom to "Eye of the Tiger," the *Rocky III* theme song. In 2012, 15-year-olds at two Arizona Basis schools took a new test designed to compare individual schools' performance with that of schools from around the world. The average Basis student not only outperformed the typical American student by nearly three years in reading and science and by four years in math, but outscored the average student in Finland, Korea, and Poland as well. The Basis kid did better even than the average student from Shanghai, China, the region that ranks number one in the world.

"I actually believe that sports are extremely important," Olga Block, a Basis cofounder, told me. "The problem is that once sports become important to the school, they start colliding with academics."

In a column published in 1927, Roy Henderson, the athletic director of the University Interscholastic League, a public-school sports organization in Texas, articulated the challenge of keeping sports and academics in balance: "Football cannot be defended in the high school unless it is subordinated, controlled, and made to contribute something definite in the cause of education."

The State of Texas announced in May that the Premont Independent School District could stay open. The district has a lot of work to do before its students can feel the kind of pride in their academics that they once felt in their sports teams. But Ernest Singleton, Enrique Ruiz, the teachers, and the students have proved their ability to adapt. Nathan, the onetime quarterback, started college this fall, as did Mariela, the cheerleader—and, as it turns out, the valedictorian. This fall, Premont brought back a volleyball team and a cross-country team, in addition to basketball, baseball, track, and tennis. But for now, still no football.

PATRICK HRUBY

The Choice

FROM SPORTSONEARTH.COM

MARIETTA, GEORGIA — His name is Parker. Everyone called him Tank. In his first season of youth football, he made two boys cry. Knocked three boys out. He was four years old, going on five, big and strong for his age. A bobble-headed bulldozer. His mother didn't mind. She was too busy cheering. *Boy, get out there and hit somebody!*

Besides, Monet Bartell was the one who signed her son up.

"My husband wanted him to play chess," she says.

Her husband, Melvin Bartell, concurs. The three of us are having dinner. It's August. Another season is about to begin, and I'm here to answer a question: should your child play football? The answer, of course, is complicated, because the question is complicated. It's hard to know where to begin. What to believe. Who to trust. How to weigh the risks against the rewards. I'm hoping Monet can help. Only now she's asking *me* for help.

"Do I want my son to play football?" she says.

A long pause. Melvin is silent. Monet lets the question hang. Her father, Mel Farr Sr., played in the NFL for seven seasons. Her uncle also played in the league, as did both of her brothers and a number of cousins. Before Parker was even born, Monet had his life mapped out: play football at UCLA, and then play in the NFL. Just like her dad. Just like her brothers, Mel Jr. and Mike. Such was the plan. It did not include chess. And then one day in 2011 — around the same time Parker first put on a helmet and shoulder pads — a relative wanted to talk. About the problems in his life. The problems in his head. Dark, desperate thoughts. He was done with football—had been for years—but scared that football wasn't done with him.

"Have you heard of CTE?" he said. "I believe that is what I am suffering from."

Monet had heard a little. Not a lot. She knew it was a disease, a bad one, and that it happened to other people. She started going online, searching for answers, for help. She read about concussions. Suicides. Lawsuits. Brain bleeds. Blows to the head. Former football players suffering from depression and memory lapses, cognitive and emotional dysfunction, weird neurological diseases with hard-to-pronounce names, like *chronic traumatic encephalopathy* and *amyotrophic lateral sclerosis*. She learned that helmets protect the skull, not the brain, and that even boys as young as Parker could suffer lasting damage. She found herself sitting in the stands at the youth league championship game, chatting with another team mother. Both had a choice to make, and the choice was harder than ever before.

Would their sons continue to play football?

Earlier that season, Parker had leveled another boy. He earned a personal foul. Monet remembered the moment, how proud she felt as her son skipped back to the sideline.

Mommy! Mommy! I made a kid eat dirt!

"I sat back and said, 'Wow,'" she says. "What if I'm the parent of that other kid?"

Football is fun. And football means eating dirt. That's the trade-off. Always has been. The game is inherently dangerous, rooted in violence and physical domination, hitting and tackling, knocking your opponent on their ass before they do the same to you. Football breaks bones, shreds ligaments, ruptures internal organs. Occasionally, it kills.

And yet for just about forever, the harm has seemed manageable. Perfectly acceptable. A reasonable price to pay for both Friday Night Lights and weekend tailgating. Because bones heal, and ligaments can be fixed. Deaths are horrific, but freaky and rare. Week after week, season after season, the sport teaches life lessons, rallies communities, provides excitement and entertainment for millions, inspires military flyovers and breast cancer awareness drives. It helps define American masculinity and pays NFL commissioner Roger Goodell's $29.5 million salary. At the youth level, most players walk away from the game with fond memories and without serious, lasting harm; for parents and society alike, football's rewards largely have outweighed its risks, so much so that even in an era of helicopter parenting and school safety zones, more than four million American children play high school and youth football.

Because of brain damage, that calculus is changing.

Scott Hallenbeck is sweating. Profusely. Like a human lawn sprinkler. I can't blame him. It's an early November morning in Washington, DC, and the Aspen Institute's "Sport and Society" program is hosting a roundtable discussion on youth football safety and the sport's future. The NFL's top lobbyist is here. So is the head of the players' union. There are journalists and academics, lawyers and school officials, coaches and scientists.

Almost everyone is a parent.

Sports concussion expert Robert Cantu proposes that children under age 14 not play tackle football, largely because both their brains and bodies are still developing and therefore more vulnerable to serious injury. This puts Hallenbeck in a tight spot. He's the executive director of USA Football, the NFL's national youth arm. His day job involves telling America why its children *should* play tackle football, the same way his 16-year-old son does.

"I think we all recognize there are challenges," Hallenbeck says. "We're all looking for ways to try to create a better and safer environment for parents and players. I also hope that we're in this to provide accurate and whenever possible evidence-based data for parents. I think we have to be careful certainly not to scare parents."

Too late. A recent Marist College poll found that roughly one in three Americans say that knowing about the damage concussions cause would make them less likely to allow their sons to play football. Earlier this year, a *Washington Post* survey of more than 500 NFL retirees found that less than half would recommend that children play. According to the National Sports Goods Association, tackle football participation has dropped 11 percent between 2011 and now. The National Federation of State High School Associations reports decreasing football participation numbers since 2008–2009. And according to ESPN's *Outside the Lines,* Pop Warner—the nation's largest youth football program—saw participation drop 9.5 percent between 2010 and 2012. Even President Obama has expressed doubts about letting his hypothetical son play the sport.

Still, fear is not the problem. Physics and biology are the problem.

Reliable youth sports brain injury statistics are hard to come by. A USA Football study of almost 2,000 youth football players reported a concussion rate of 4 percent; however, non-industry-funded research suggests that concussions are chronically under-diagnosed and -reported. Meanwhile, the American Association of Neurological Surgeons estimates that between 4 percent and 20 percent of college and high school football players will sustain a brain injury during the course of one season. The Institute of Medicine reports that football consistently has the highest concussion rate of any high school sport (11.2 percent), and that the concussion rate in prep football is nearly double that in the college game (6.2 percent). The Centers for Disease Control and Prevention, which has labeled sports concussions "an epidemic," reported in 2011 that roughly 122,000 children between the ages of 10 and 19 went to emergency rooms annually for nonfatal brain injuries—and for boys, the top cause was playing football.

This is no coincidence.

Football isn't NASCAR. It's demolition derby. The collisions aren't accidents. Head trauma is baked into the game. Boston University researchers estimate that the average high school football player absorbs 1,000 blows to the head per season. In a pair of studies, Virginia Tech and Wake Forest researchers recently found that seven- and eight-year-old boys received an average of 80 head hits per season, while boys ages nine through twelve received 240 hits. Some of the impacts were 80 g's of force or greater, equivalent to a serious car crash.

Now consider the human brain. It's essentially a blob of Jell-O, floating inside the skull like an egg yolk. Getting hit in the head—or just experiencing a sudden change in momentum, like the kind that comes from a blindside tackle—can cause the brain to stretch, warp, and collide with the bony inner surface of the skull. This produces damage. The damage can be structural, akin to a cracked microchip in a laptop computer. It can be metabolic, like the same computer suddenly losing its electrical supply. Some damage is obvious, visible from the sidelines. Other damage is subtle, almost impossible to detect, even for trained experts in a clinical setting.

With adequate rest and recovery, most concussions resolve themselves in a relatively short period of time. But other damage—such as neurodegenerative diseases and severe cases of postconcussion syndrome—never does. Current research indicates that damage can be cumulative; that getting hit in the head repeatedly is worse than getting hit once or twice; that both concussive and subconcussive blows are dangerous; and that getting hit while recovering from a previous blow or concussion is particularly risky. There currently is no definitive causal link between youth football and long-term neurodegenerative disease. Yet depending on duration and severity, brain damage can mean missed games. Missed classes. Learning disabilities. Changes in mood, memory, personality. It can permanently alter who you are, and who you have a chance of becoming.

Three years ago, Purdue University researchers compared brain scans of concussed and nonconcussed high school football players. They found changes in brain function—evidence of damage—in both groups. The results were stunning, so much so that the researchers initially thought their scanners were broken. The changes appeared to subside in the off-season. However, the researchers still don't know what that means, or if those same players' brains suffered lasting harm. In a subsequent study, they found that high school players exhibit brain function changes long before they have recognizable signs of a concussion—and that the more hits a player endured on the field, the more their brain function changed.

"No brain trauma is good brain trauma," Cantu says. "We're not paranoid about it, but when you can reduce it—or every chance you get to eliminate it short of stopping something completely—it's a good thing."

Should your child play football? Start with a simple fact: no helmet can prevent any of the above.

As a child, Monet didn't worry about what football helmets can't prevent. She enjoyed what the sport could provide. The game took her father, Mel Sr., from a home without indoor plumbing in segregated Beaumont, Texas, to his first drink of cold water from a refrigerated fountain on the UCLA campus. He parlayed his standout career with the Lions—two Pro Bowl selections and the 1967 Rookie of the Year Award—into an off-season job with Ford, later building a network of car dealerships that eventually became one of the largest black-owned businesses in the U.S.

"When I went to college, I shrunk my first comforter," Monet says. "Because I didn't know how to do laundry. I had never bothered to learn. That's when I realized I grew up rich."

Monet grew up with money, and she grew up with football. Lions running back Billy Sims was a frequent guest at her family's suburban Detroit home. Hall of Famer Barry Sanders showed up to watch one of her high school plays. Dad had a box at the Pontiac Silverdome. Monet was there with him for every Lions home game. When her brothers played at UCLA, Monet would get out of school on Friday afternoons, hop on her father's plane, and fly to wherever the Bruins were playing. When her brother Mel Jr. played for the Los Angeles Rams, she went to the American Bowl in Germany, right after the fall of the Berlin Wall. "I had pieces of it," she says. "I can't find them. That's how carefree we were. It's all a blur. We were always at a game. Every single weekend."

In high school, Monet played tennis. It was a choice made out of chromosomal necessity. Her uncle, Miller, played 10 seasons in the NFL and the American Football League. Cousins Jerry Ball and D'Marco Farr also played in the NFL. When Mel Sr. met Monet's mother, Mae, he told her that he wanted 11 sons. An entire football team. Some of Monet's earliest memories are of her father coaching her brothers in Pee Wee football. Dad was a drill sergeant. Every morning, he ran the boys through backyard agility exercises. He would sit in a sled and have his sons drag it up a large hill. On the sidelines, he wore a leather visor and pork chop sideburns. He smoked Kool Milds. The Birmingham-Bloomfield Vikings went undefeated. Didn't give up a single point. Monet was a cheerleader—and again, it wasn't her first choice.

"I would have played [football] if I could have, absolutely," she says. "Even today, I've never sat and watched my nephew play. My brother Mike coaches him, and I'm on the sideline, yelling at him."

"I stand on the sideline too," says Monet's mother, Mae.

"The other moms drink wine from coffee cups," Monet says. "I don't dress up cute. I'm there for the game."

When Parker turned four, Monet searched for a local youth football league that would take children that young. She wanted him to play. Get his first taste of the family business. No question in her mind. When she found one, she was pumped. *God bless the South.* "Our coach's son was three years old when he first came out," she says. The boys went through spring training—no, really—doing bear crawls and running through tires. They had full-contact practices, complete with Oklahoma drills, coaches screaming *Knock his lights out!* The actual games were full-fledged events, with packed stands and tailgating adults.

For Monet, all of it felt familiar. Like an old childhood blanket. Was she worried about brain trauma?

"No," she says. "I was getting mad at [Parker] if he didn't tackle, like, 'What are you *doing* out there?'"

University of North Carolina researcher Kevin Guskiewicz studies football collisions for a living. Big hits and little ones. Full-speed human missile strikes. Mundane helmet-to-helmet blows delivered across the line of scrimmage after every snap of the ball. Much of his analysis involves using sensor-equipped helmets to measure impact forces and locations. Guskiewicz has been doing this since the 1990s, and his campus office is home to one of the world's most extensive databases of football brain-rattling.

He also has three sons. One of them, a high school junior, plays football. The other two have given up the sport in favor of baseball and basketball.

"I never pushed or pulled them to play," he says. "As long as I knew there was a coach out there who cared about health and safety, it was fine."

Guskiewicz published some of the earliest research linking football to long-term cognitive harm. At one point in time, he was an outspoken critic of the NFL's decades-long campaign to deny and minimize that connection. While working as an athletic trainer for the Pittsburgh Steelers, he saw the sport's brutality up close.

That said, he coached his sons in youth football, and says he would do so again.

"For some reason everybody thinks there is a concussion epidemic," he says. "That frustrates me. I sustained two concussions playing football in high school myself. There's not an epidemic.

We just know a lot more about them and care more about them than we ever have. We need to be smart about how we're doing this."

Should your child play football? In most cases, Guskiewicz isn't against it. But he can't really answer for anyone else. Not his place. There are too many variables to consider. Besides, his work focuses on a different question: what, if anything, can be done to make football safer?

The NFL, some college conferences, and a number of high school and youth leagues have mandated limits on full-contact practice, the better to reduce the total number of head hits that players absorb. Guskiewicz believes that's a good first step. So do many others. He also advocates for state laws requiring that players who show signs of being concussed be removed from games or practices and not be allowed to return until they're cleared by a health care professional—largely because research indicates that unresolved concussions leave the brain more vulnerable to additional damage and concussions, which in turn increase the risk of long-term harm. The worst-case scenario? A condition called second-impact syndrome, in which an athlete suffers a second concussion while still recovering from a previous one. Though the precise physiological cause is uncertain, the outcome is not: the brain swells rapidly and catastrophically, causing severe disability or death.

Of course, there's a problem with said laws, a problem that dogs football at every level. How do you spot concussions in the first place? Self-reporting is unreliable. Players are conditioned to hide injuries. The sport's entire ethos revolves around playing through pain. Moreover, brain damage affects the seat of awareness, so even a player who *wants* to report a concussion may not realize that he has one. As for coaches? They're distracted. Mostly unqualified. Asking them to consistently diagnose a mysterious, invisible injury is foolhardy. Would you ask a neurologist to draw up a goal line defensive play?

Speaking of neurologists: the NFL recently required teams to have an independent one on the sideline at every game. During Philadelphia Eagles home games, said neurologist is joined by an orthopedic surgeon, an internal medicine specialist, a spine specialist, a chiropractor, a dentist, a podiatrist, an ophthalmologist, and an anesthesiologist.

By contrast, a recent survey of Chicago public high school football teams found that only 10.5 percent had a physician present during games. Only 8.5 percent had an athletic trainer. During practices, no school had a physician, and only one school had a trainer. This is hardly unique. According to the National Athletic Trainers' Association, only 42 percent of high schools nationwide in 2010 had access to a certified athletic trainer educated in concussion care—and while the numbers for junior varsity, middle school, and youth squads are unknown, they unquestionably are far lower.

"If I said that one in ten middle schools has an athletic trainer, I'd probably be overestimating," Guskiewicz says. "Having a trainer isn't going to prevent every injury or solve every problem. But it's important. Some people say this is extreme, but I think that at the high school level, if you can't afford to hire a certified athletic trainer, then you shouldn't field contact sports at your school."

No trainer? No contact sports for kids. A simple formula. But doesn't it imply that the vast majority of youth football programs—short of trainers but stocked with vulnerable young brains—ought to be shut down?

Guskiewicz winces.

"It's a problem," he says.

Cantu has written an entire book arguing that children under 14 shouldn't play contact sports. NFL Hall of Famer Ron Mix thinks the prohibition on youth football should extend to age 15. Hockey Canada recently outlawed bodychecking for 11- and 12-year-old players, citing a study that showed that youth players in checking leagues were four times more likely to suffer concussions than players in leagues without contact. Numerous NFL players—including New England Patriots quarterback Tom Brady—didn't start playing tackle football until high school, and New Orleans Saints quarterback Drew Brees says he won't *consider* allowing his three sons to play tackle until they're teenagers. Should children be playing flag football exclusively?

Guskiewicz says no.

"I'm adamantly opposed to the suggestion of banning contact sports for kids under some age," he says. "One, we don't even know what that age should be. Two, if the first time a kid is going to strap on a helmet or shoulder pads and play football or hockey is at age 15 or 16 when the weight differential between players [colliding] could potentially be 80 to 90 pounds—like a 210-pound senior linebacker tackling a 130-pound freshman—that is when you're going to have problems, if it's the first time you're trying to protect yourself. I'm a proponent of teaching kids how to tackle and block properly at younger ages."

Guskiewicz brings up a football video on his desktop computer. A North Carolina player lowers his head while making a block. *Thwack!* The collision delivers 104 g's of force to the side of his helmet. He sustains a concussion. Up comes a second video, this from a game that took place a month later. The same player makes another block—only this time, he strikes his opponent with his left shoulder, remaining mostly upright and turning his body to shield his head.

"See that?" Guskiewicz says. "It's an entirely different approach. We taught him to do that. We can change behavior. And that's in a college player. It's a hell of a lot easier to do with a high school team."

This, according to Guskiewicz, is the future. Behavior modification. Teaching players to tackle *without* hitting their heads, assuming that's possible. Guskiewicz is a member of the NFL's Head, Neck and Spine Committee. In conjunction with USA Football, the league is aggressively pushing the safe tackling concept on youth coaches and nervous parents through a program called "Heads Up." Goodell himself insists that it works, that it makes the sport "safer than it has ever been" and moves closer to "taking the head out of the game" entirely.

I have doubts.

In USA Football's glossy tutorial videos, boys practice their new-and-improved tackles against empty air, foam pads, and stationary opponents who seem to be imitating scarecrows. Tackling is broken down into five distinct stages. There's plenty of time and space to take just the right angle, launch into a tackle, maintain perfect form, keep one's head from getting bashed by tucking it under an opponent's armpit. Football becomes an exercise in aggressive, studied chest-bumping. It really does look safer.

Thing is, the actual sport is completely different. Uncontrolled chaos. Players of varying sizes and strength run at full speed. They trip and shove and hit and fall, pinballing around at ever-changing heights and angles. When I showed a "Heads Up" tackling video to a pair of college football players, both shook their heads. When

I asked former NFL player Nate Jackson about it, he laughed. Knocking someone else to the ground, he explained, means getting leverage on them. Which means getting low. Which means dropping your shoulders. Drop your shoulders, and your head will follow.

I also asked longtime *Chicago Sun-Times* sports columnist and former All–Big Ten defensive back Rick Telander about "Heads Up." His reply was dryly incredulous: "Does the ball carrier cooperate with you?"

"Have I seen behavior modification not work?" Guskiewicz says. "Absolutely. It doesn't work 100 percent of the time. But I've seen it work."

In fairness to Guskiewicz, his program is far more involved than the NFL's youth tackling clinics. This season, players at nearby Chapel Hill High School have been outfitted with special helmets that measure the location and intensity of hits to the head. When a player suffers a series of what Guskiewicz calls "bad hits"—that is, head hits that are too hard, too frequent, or too often on the crown of the helmet, based on deviations from previously established positional averages—trainers and coaches will study video with the player and attempt to make changes to their collision technique.

"During the first half of the season, we identify who has a bad hit profile," he says. "We put them into a coaching intervention that links video footage and data from accelerometers in their helmets. Then we study them for the second half of the season to see if we can reduce those bad hit numbers and put them into safer play."

One problem: the force threshold for "bad hits" is largely a matter of guesswork—while some studies suggest that hits over 60 to 80 g's significantly increase the likelihood of concussion, there is no hard-and-fast rule. One player can absorb a 100 g blow and appear perfectly fine; another can take a 30 g hit and be knocked out cold. No hits are *good* hits. Moreover, basing the "bad hits" frequency threshold on positional averages seems odd. A defensive back who absorbs 250 hits to the head during the first half of a season might be in line for an intervention; a defensive lineman who absorbs the same total might not. Are their brains all that different?

More doubts. I express them to Guskiewicz. I tell him that both the "Heads Up" push and new rules across football penalizing certain types of helmet hits seem like a replay of the 1970s, when football responded to criticism from the American Medical Association by banning "butt-blocking" (blows delivered with the face mask or front and top of the helmet to an opponent in close line play) and "face-tackling" (driving the face mask or front and top of the helmet into a runner), all while calling on coaches to teach "correct, head-up blocking and tackling."

Has anything really changed?

"We have a kid at the high school who I already know—based on watching video from last year on kickoffs—has a bad hits profile," Guskiewicz says. "We're already starting to work with him for this season. I can show you video footage of a guy who changed his behavior in three weeks. We've been working on this for eight years. We didn't come up with it overnight."

Suppose Guskiewicz is right. Suppose he's on to something. Sensor-equipped helmets are expensive. Video intervention takes time. Guskiewicz's lab is partially funded by the NFL, and staffed by paid research assistants. What about the typical Pop Warner squad? Or high schools that already are facing budget shortfalls? I'm reminded of something journalist Stefan Fatsis said at the Aspen Institute roundtable:

> You're talking about putting accelerometers in equipment. Equipment specialists to outfit our children. Having independent observers of coaches on the sidelines at practices and games to monitor what's going on. At what point are we kidding ourselves about youth football, that this is not a sensible proposition when you need this superstructure for every game in the country?

I'm also reminded of something else Guskiewicz told me, the first thing out of his mouth when I asked him if children should play the sport.

"It's not for everyone," he said.

Monet shakes her head. She knows it sounds ridiculous. Looking back, she really should have known better. After all, she once watched her brother Mike get knocked unconscious during a Lions game. Her mom ran down to the team's bench. Monet stayed put and bawled. Sitting in the very same Pontiac Silverdome skybox, she also saw Detroit lineman Mike Utley taken off the field on a stretcher after suffering a 1991 spinal injury that left him paralyzed from the waist down.

Monet felt a chill, a queasy sensation in her stomach. But never mind that.

"I honestly didn't realize that football was *violent*," she says. "It was just football. Even now, with my [family member] suffering, when I watch a game and they're trying to make calls about players hitting too hard, fining them, I don't know if they should do that. It's like, 'That's football!'"

On the same afternoon that Utley lost the use of his limbs, Mike Farr caught his first and only NFL touchdown pass. That's football. Three years later, as paramedics treated Monet following a car accident, Mike saw his bloodied sister on a stretcher and cried. He immediately thought of Utley. That's football.

Two summers ago, Monet was watching the Pro Football Hall of Fame induction ceremony with a relative. The one who suspects he has CTE. He recalled constant headaches, keeping Advil in his football pants, popping pills on the field; he remembered washing down caffeine pills with cola in the locker room after games, the better to not fall into a woozy sleep. He hardly knew what concussions were, let alone what they could do. He didn't care. He just wanted to play the game.

That's football too.

"I always say it's like a drug or alcohol addiction," Monet says. "Leaving the sport is like trying to quit cold turkey. It's very difficult to lose it."

Monet saw her relative's life crumble. Weight loss. Erratic behavior. Bad decisions. Family problems. A short stint in a mental health facility. In public, he was charismatic and charming; in private, brooding and lethargic. He all but lived in a basement. No one in the family knew what was wrong. No one knew what to do about it. "At first it was just like, 'What happened to you?'" Monet says. "'Snap out of it. It's not that big of a deal!' But now we see that he can't snap out of it."

The family closed ranks. Wouldn't let Monet's relative be alone. They started reading. Talking. Reaching out. Monet contacted former NFL running back Dorsey Levens, who was producing a documentary film on football and brain damage. Mel Sr. found himself attending more and more funerals for men he played football with. Strong, proud men, like Hall of Famer John Mackey. Mackey

was the first head of the players' union. Monet's father looked up
to him. Calls him "a god." He died at 69, after struggling with
dementia. Mel Sr. started emailing articles to his daughter, stories
about former players suffering from mental problems. *Wow. Did
you read about this guy?*

Monet came across a story about the first concussion lawsuits
filed against the NFL. She learned that former league commissioner Paul Tagliabue created a committee in the mid-1990s to
study football-induced brain damage. That the committee put out
a series of since-discredited scientific papers asserting that concussions posed neither short- nor long-term health risks, defying both
independent research and common sense. That league doctors
used those papers to justify and continue the longtime practice of
clearing concussed players to return to action in the same games
they were injured in, increasing the odds of lasting damage. That
league scientists suggested in print that the same practice might
be fine for college and high school players. She learned that the
NFL had waged a scientific and public relations war to downplay
and dismiss the link between football and brain damage, and that
Goodell had presided over a pattern of ongoing denial—one that
extended all the way down to youth football, and by extension, her
son Parker.

This was football? Monet was furious.

"I had no idea about the first NFL committee," she says. "I had
chill bumps when I read that. My eyes turned red. Nobody wants
to admit the fact that their organization is costing lives and people
having decent lives. Who wants to go to bed saying, 'That was my
fault'? It's so much easier to say it's not."

Last year, former NFL linebacker Junior Seau committed suicide by shooting himself in the chest. At the league's direction,
scientists from the National Institutes of Health subsequently examined his brain. They diagnosed him with CTE. Publicly, NIH
doctors declined to speculate on the cause of Seau's disease; privately, they reportedly told Seau's family that football was responsible.

Monet's brother Mel Jr. played football with Seau. Monet attended the grand opening of Seau's San Diego restaurant. Both
were watching television news coverage on the day of Seau's death,
along with Mike and their mother. During a live press conference

outside Seau's home, his mother, Luisa, stood at a podium. She broke down in grief.

Take me! she sobbed. *Take me!*

"My whole family was in tears, watching her crying," Monet says. "As a parent, as a mom, that was the hardest thing to watch."

Imagine this: A pharmaceutical company invents a new drug. A drug with many benefits. It increases cardiovascular fitness, facilitates friendship, creates feelings of excitement, euphoria, and community pride. As a side effect, however, the drug also produces varying degrees of acute and chronic brain damage in an indeterminate number of users, for reasons that are only crudely understood.

The drug, of course, is football. Which is why Lewis Margolis can't help but ask: should *anyone's* child play the sport?

"I'm not saying that everyone should be placed into bubbles," he says. "But we have enough evidence now to know that there are harmful consequences from these traumatic brain injuries. We know that. And kids are exposed to this. To continue to allow children to participate [in football] in an unencumbered way, to me, is no different than exposing them to an untested medicine or medical device. Only it's being done without the tools, procedures, and protections essential to medical research."

A public health professor at the University of North Carolina, Margolis specializes in maternal and child health. His campus office is a 10-minute walk from Guskiewicz's. His views on youth football might as well be from another planet. In an opinion article published on the website Inside Higher Ed, Margolis argued that allowing children to play tackle football is not only the equivalent of an uncontrolled, nationwide research project in concussion medicine and science, but also an unethical project that parallels the infamous Tuskegee Study—in which the U.S. Public Health Service monitored but did not treat a group of rural African Americans suffering from syphilis over a period of decades.

"That article raised the eyebrows of people around here," Guskiewicz says. "The analogy is absurd and embarrassing."

Guskiewicz has a point: likening football to venereal disease is pretty out there, even as a thought exercise. Margolis admits as much. He also notes that parents, coaches, school administrators, and concussion researchers all have the best interests of children at heart—unlike the Tuskegee scientists, who didn't even tell their research subjects what was happening.

Still, Margolis maintains that the football-to-research comparison is apt. And he's not alone. According to the book *League of Denial: The NFL, Concussions, and the Battle for the Truth*, the NFL once contracted with a bioengineering firm to help run a first-of-its-kind epidemiological study of concussions in professional football. A memo from the firm read as follows:

> A major obstacle to head injury research is the unavailability of willing test subjects. The NFL has graciously sponsored a research program offering its players as those living subjects.

"Just because you're doing something with goodwill doesn't make it ethical," Margolis says. "If Kevin [Guskiewicz's] research or my research generates a risk, then we have to ask, 'Is that risk acceptable?' Is an 80 percent increased risk of brain damage acceptable? Fifty percent? Ten percent? If football generates a risk, then we have to ask the same question. This is a discussion for public health. Not just coaches."

Public health focuses on preventing predictable problems. On stopping harm before it happens. Last year, the Consumer Product Safety Commission banned the sale of Buckyballs, small magnetic toys that can pinch intestines and require surgery when swallowed by children. Federal regulators enacted the ban following 22 swallowing cases over a three-year span. By contrast, youth football has produced far more than 22 concussions among children over the last three years. Seven high school football players have died this year, five from brain injuries and two from spine and neck injuries.

Yet society's response—from the NFL to Pop Warner—has been akin to running a yellow traffic light. Look into the problem, be more aware, spend some money on research, change a few rules. But keep driving. Margolis thinks it should be more like stopping on red: figure out the risks of football in a controlled setting under established clinical standards, and *then* decide if children should participate.

This goes double for schools.

Schools, Margolis says, have two primary duties. Nurture young minds. And protect the children in their care. Hence, homework.

Study halls. Anti-bullying campaigns. Not allowing drugs or guns on campus. Schools receive public funds—and are tax-exempt institutions—to help carry out these duties. No high school would start and sponsor an official mixed martial arts team. Not without provoking parent outrage.

What makes football—a known vector of student brain damage—so different?

"I'm not saying sports don't belong on campuses," he says. "But take UNC. How do they tolerate that they are knowingly sending kids out there [to play football] with some risk—and we can disagree on the level—when it's not consistent with the mission of the institution?"

In medical research, children cannot legally agree to participate in studies. Their parents or guardians have to give permission—and even then, the consent has to be informed. Participants have to know what they're getting into. How much do most families know about brain damage and football? How much *can* they know, given both scientific uncertainty about the sport's risks and the football industry's concerted, ongoing effort to downplay those risks, particularly to children?

Last year, Goodell gave a speech on football safety at Harvard University's School of Public Health. He cited a recent study by the National Institute for Occupational Safety and Health (NIOSH), debunking the notion that NFL players had shorter life spans than the general population. He did not mention a second NIOSH study suggesting that pro football players were four times more likely to develop Alzheimer's or Lou Gehrig's disease. During an appearance on *Face the Nation* last February, he was asked to acknowledge the link between football and brain damage—and promptly ducked the question, stating that "we're going to let the medical individuals make those points."

About those medical individuals: sports concussion expert Cantu is an adviser to the league's health and safety committee. He recommends no tackle football for children under age 14. He was not present at a recent NFL-sponsored "Football Safety for Moms" clinic in Chicago. Instead, the league rolled out Chicago Bears neuropsychological consultant Elizabeth Pieroth, who, according to the Associated Press, "presented checklists for recognizing concussion symptoms and recommendations for treatment, but suggested on balance that 'boys like to hit things' and without proper channels for their aggression, they might do other things like drive too fast or drink too much."

None of this should be surprising. In the mid-1990s, then NFL commissioner Tagliabue worried that football was losing cultural cachet. That the game wasn't cool. The league hired top executives from MTV, who reportedly drew up a marketing plan entitled "Game Plan 1997." The document addressed Tagliabue's concerns:

> Nothing can be more important than how we manage young people (particularly ages 6–11 . . .) into our fan continuum and begin to migrate them toward becoming avid/committed fans . . . Critical action: Generate early interest and enthusiasm. Transform/convert their casual interest into commitment. Amplify to avidity.

As one of the former MTV executives explained to *New Yorker* writer John Seabrook, "It's all about getting a football, this unusual-looking object, into a kid's hands as soon as you can. Six years old, if possible. You want to get a football in their hands before someone puts a basketball in their hands, or a hockey stick or a tennis racquet or a golf club."

Between 1998 and 2007, the NFL reportedly spent more than $100 million promoting youth football. Former league director of youth development Scott Lancaster said the league's strategy was to "take out all the negatives and emphasize the positives" of the sport. At a 2005 youth marketing conference titled "Making Your Brand Cool and Mom Acceptable," Lancaster also said that children were important to the NFL, because they would someday become adult football fans with discretionary income.

Four years later, Goodell was invited to a congressional hearing on brain trauma. He was scheduled to appear with the father of a Texas high school quarterback who had died after suffering a concussion. According to *League of Denial,* NFL lobbyist Jeff Miller was apoplectic. He demanded that Goodell be placed on a different panel. Congressional staffers acquiesced.

Today, Miller is the league's director of health and safety. Meanwhile, Goodell is pushing to increase the NFL's annual revenue from $10 billion to $25 billion over the next 15 years.

"It's in the interest of the National Football League to cultivate doubt around this," Margolis says. "To say, 'We're interested in the well-being of kids, college players, and our players—but we need to be certain. Let's be certain about this brain trauma stuff. Don't want to jump to conclusions.' It's all about creating a sense of doubt and not being willing to address the problem."

Should your child play football? The choice, Margolis says, isn't just for parents. It's for all of us. Society needs to seriously weigh the risks and rewards, the games won and the damage done, the same as it has with lead paint and cigarettes.

He shows me an article. It's from the *Wall Street Journal*. The title? "In Defense of Football." Written by a military historian, it acknowledges that brain damage is a problem, but lauds the sport as a civic religion and argues that society should not "overreact to a handful of tragic injuries and legislate or litigate away a game that means so much to so many Americans." The author concludes by citing Teddy Roosevelt, who warned that abolishing the game would be "simple nonsense, a mere confession of weakness," and result in society producing "mollycoddles instead of vigorous men."

"It's the old thing about the Battle of Waterloo being won on the playing fields of Eton," Margolis says. "I don't disagree with that. My son played sports. My daughter played sports. Sports can produce laudable outcomes."

But?

"But whether you need to have people scrambling their brains in the process is doubtful," he says.

Monet's mother is showing me pictures. Photo albums. Framed shots. A family's football life. Mel Jr. in his UCLA uniform, featured in an advertisement on the side of a Los Angeles city bus. Mae and Mel Sr. with singer Smokey Robinson. Mike and Mel Jr. with their beaming father, all three wearing Lions uniforms. A collage of Mel Jr. and Mike's undefeated youth squad. Mike's 12-year-old son, Mikey, in his youth league uniform. Mae on a football field, holding a camera.

"I didn't want my boys to play football at first," Mae says. "But look at me. I would run up the sidelines when they would score a touchdown."

"It's almost like a bipolar love of the sport," Monet says.

"It gets your adrenaline going," Mae says.

"Then you go home and think about it," Monet says. "My gosh, it's a rough sport. I think about my family. When it hits home it's completely different."

"I used to sit in the [team] medical room with my mother-in-law when Mel [Sr.] would play," Mae says. "I never understood why she was so concerned. Not until my boys started to play did I understand what that was like for her."

"But even though I have that feeling, I'm still right down there on the field," Monet says. "If it's fourth-and-goal at my nephew's games, I can't watch."

"My mother watches football and she is 95," Mae says. "I'm missing Mikey's scrimmage right now. Football gave our lives such dimension."

Remember that Marist College survey? The one in which a third of Americans said concussion concerns would make them less likely to allow their children to play football? Seventy percent of the respondents thought the benefits of the sport outweighed the risks. The choice is hard. Football is a new car and a full tank of gas. Brain damage is climate change.

It's a Saturday morning. Monet is making breakfast. Mike couldn't join us. He's coaching his son's scrimmage. I ask Monet's 14-year-old daughter, Paige, if football is a big deal at her high school. She nods. Her eyes go wide.

"When they have games, you can't find a place to park," Monet says.

"People who live across the street from school charge to park," Paige says.

Young Parker Bartell isn't playing football this year, though even if his parents let him, he doesn't really want to. "There are thousands of people there," Monet says. "Everything at the school is scheduled around football season. My daughter is in a play. The dates of the play coincide with the playoffs. If the team makes the playoffs, they've already planned on moving the play."

Parker wants to show us something. His football trophy. It's nearly as tall as he is. He received it at the end of his first season, and it was pretty much his favorite thing about the sport. Well, that and the team banquet. Turns out Tank didn't really *like* football — he would knock opposing boys down, sure, but only so he could more quickly get back to the sideline and continue playing his Nintendo DS.

"Whenever I talk to him about football, he is not interested,"

Melvin says. "Like, period. He won't even watch it with me for more than three minutes."

Parker is now seven. He's playing chess. Taking karate lessons. Asking about soccer and basketball. He's a whip-smart student but also a handful, the kind of boy who finishes an assignment and then celebrates by doing cartwheels in the middle of the classroom. He says he wants to be an engineer when he grows up—that is, after he learns how to cook at Le Cordon Bleu.

"He's into being a Ninja Turtle," Monet says.

Parker isn't playing football. Not this season. But if he asks to play again in the future, Monet and Melvin have made their choice. They'll definitely say no. Unless they say yes.

"Deep down, there's a side of me that would love him to go to the NFL and keep up the tradition," Monet says. "Do I *want* him on a football field? Absolutely. Do I know the repercussions? Absolutely. Do I think he *should* play? As a mom, absolutely not."

The phone rings. It's Mel Sr. We talk about football. About the choice. He thinks children should be allowed to participate. Thinks the sport builds character. Provides opportunity. He tells me a story: Back in Beaumont, his mother didn't want him and his brother, Miller, to play. But Mom also worked. So the boys joined their school team in secret. Didn't tell their parents. They got away with it for about two weeks, until Miller came home with a busted lip.

"When I retired from football, I told my mom, 'My knees have given up,'" Mel Sr. says. "And she said to me, 'What do you think about my knees? I don't have to go on the floor anymore to pray.'"

Football is like the lottery. Thrilling to play. You probably won't win. But if you do, it can change your life. Forever. Only the prize isn't money.

Monet hugs her son.

"What do you want to be when you grow up?" she says.

"An engineer," Parker says.

"Where do you want to go to school?"

"Georgia Tech."

Tank grins. He's missing two of his baby teeth. Monet smiles too. She looks relieved. For now, at least, the choice has been made for her.

TIMOTHY BURKE AND JACK DICKEY

Manti Te'o's Dead Girlfriend, the Most Heartbreaking and Inspirational Story of the College Football Season, Is a Hoax

FROM DEADSPIN.COM

NOTRE DAME'S MANTI TE'O, the stories said, played this season under a terrible burden. A Mormon linebacker who led his Catholic school's football program back to glory, Te'o was whipsawed between personal tragedies along the way. In the span of six hours in September, as *Sports Illustrated* told it, Te'o learned first of the death of his grandmother, Annette Santiago, and then of the death of his girlfriend, Lennay Kekua.

Kekua, 22 years old, had been in a serious car accident in California, and then had been diagnosed with leukemia. *SI*'s Pete Thamel described how Te'o would phone her in her hospital room and stay on the line with her as he slept through the night. "Her relatives told him that at her lowest points, as she fought to emerge from a coma, her breathing rate would increase at the sound of his voice," Thamel wrote.

Upon receiving the news of the two deaths, Te'o went out and led the Fighting Irish to a 20–3 upset of Michigan State, racking up 12 tackles. It was heartbreaking and inspirational. Te'o would appear on ESPN's *College GameDay* to talk about the letters Kekua had written him during her illness. He would send a heartfelt letter to the parents of a sick child, discussing his experience with disease and grief. The *South Bend Tribune* wrote an article describing the young couple's fairy-tale meeting—she, a Stanford student; he, a Notre Dame star—after a football game outside Palo Alto.

Did you enjoy the uplifiting story, the tale of a man who responded to adversity by becoming one of the top players of the game? If so, stop reading.

Manti Te'o did lose his grandmother this past fall. Annette Santiago died on September 11, 2012, at the age of 72, according to Social Security Administration records in Nexis. But there is no SSA record there of the death of Lennay Marie Kekua, that day or any other. Her passing, recounted so many times in the national media, produces no obituary or funeral announcement in Nexis, and no mention in the Stanford student newspaper.

Nor is there any report of a severe auto accident involving a Lennay Kekua. Background checks turn up nothing. The Stanford registrar's office has no record that a Lennay Kekua ever enrolled. There is no record of her birth in the news. Outside of a few Twitter and Instagram accounts, there's no online evidence that Lennay Kekua ever existed.

The photographs identified as Kekua—in online tributes and on TV news reports—are pictures from the social-media accounts of a 22-year-old California woman who is not named Lennay Kekua. She is not a Stanford graduate; she has not been in a severe car accident; and she does not have leukemia. And she has never met Manti Te'o.

Here is what we know about Manti Te'o: He is an exceptional football player. He's a projected first-round NFL pick. He finished second in the Heisman voting, and he won a haul of other trophies: the Walter Camp, the Chuck Bednarik, the Butkus, the Bronko Nagurski. In each of his three seasons as a full-time starter, he racked up at least 100 tackles.

We also know that Te'o is a devout Mormon. When asked why he picked Notre Dame over Southern California, the school he had supported while growing up in Hawaii, he said he prayed on it. "Faith," he told ESPN, "is believing in something that you most likely can't see, but you believe to be true. You feel in your heart, and in your soul, that it's true, but you still take that leap."

We know, further, that Te'o adores his family. Te'o's father said that Manti had revered his grandfather, who died in January 2012, since the day he was born. He ran his sister's postgraduation luau. And he loved his late maternal grandmother, Annette Santiago.

But that's where the definite ends. From here, the rest of Te'o's public story begins to grade into fantasy, in the tradition of so much of Notre Dame's mythmaking and with the help of a compliant press.

Assembling a timeline of the Kekua-Te'o relationship is difficult. As Te'o's celebrity swelled, so did the pile of inspirational stories about his triumph over loss. Each ensuing story seemed to add yet another wrinkle to the narrative, and details ran athwart one another. Here is the general shape of things, based on occasionally contradictory media accounts:

November 28, 2009: Te'o and Kekua meet after Stanford's 45–38 victory over Notre Dame in Palo Alto, according to the *South Bend Tribune:* "Their stares got pleasantly tangled, then Manti Te'o extended his hand to the stranger with a warm smile and soulful eyes." Kekua, a Stanford student, swaps phone numbers with Te'o.

2010–2011: Te'o and Kekua are friends. "She was gifted in music, multi-lingual, had dreams grounded in reality and the talent to catch up to them" (*South Bend Tribune*). "They started out as just friends," Te'o's father, Brian, told the *Tribune* in October 2012. "Every once in a while, she would travel to Hawaii, and that happened to be the time Manti was home, so he would meet with her there."

Early 2012: Te'o and Kekua become a couple. They talk on the phone nightly, according to ESPN.

Sometime in 2012: Kekua has a car accident somewhere in California that leaves her "on the brink of death" (*Sports Illustrated*). But when? Eight months before she died of cancer, in September, reports ESPN. "About the time Kekua and Manti became a couple," reports the *South Bend Tribune.* April 28, reports *SI.*

June 2012: As Kekua recovers from her injuries, doctors discover she has leukemia. She has a bone marrow transplant. ("That was just in June," Brian Te'o told the *South Bend Tribune* in October of 2012. "I remember Manti telling me later she was going to have a bone marrow transplant and, sure enough, that's exactly what happened. From all I knew, she was doing really, really well.")

Summer 2012: Her condition improves. Kekua "eventually" graduates from Stanford, according to the *South Bend Tribune.* (A *New York Times* story, published October 13, identifies her as a "Stanford alumnus.") She soon takes a turn for the worse. At some point, she enters treatment, apparently at St. Jude Medical Center in Fullerton, California. (In a letter obtained by Fox Sports published October 25, Te'o writes to the parents of a girl dying of cancer: "My girlfriend, when she was at St. Jude's in LA, she had a little friend.")

Te'o talks to Lennay nightly, "going to sleep while on the phone with her," according to *Sports Illustrated.* "When he woke up in the morning his phone would show an eight-hour call, and he would hear Lennay breathing on the other end of the line."

September 10, 2012: Kekua is released from the hospital; Manti's father, Brian, congratulates her "via telephone" (*South Bend Tribune*).

September 11–12, 2012: Te'o's grandmother dies in Hawaii. Later, Kekua dies in California. Or is it the other way around? "Te'o's girlfriend, Lennay Kekua, died Sept. 11 of complications from leukemia. His grandma, Annette Santiago, died after a long illness less than 24 hours later," according to the September 22 *South Bend Tribune.* No, Annette dies first, according to the October 12 *South Bend Tribune.* In fact, Lennay lives long enough to express condolences over the death of Annette:

> Less than 48 hours later [after Lennay's release from the hospital], at 4 A.M. Hawaii time, Kekua sent a text to Brian and Ottilia, expressing her condolences over the passing of Ottilia's mom, Annette Santiago, just hours before.
> Brian awakened three hours later, saw the text, and sent one back. There was no response. A couple of hours later, Manti called his parents, his heart in pieces.
> Lennay Kekua had died.

Or does Kekua die three days later (*New York Post*)? Four days (ESPN, CBS)?

In any case, according to Te'o's interview with Gene Wojciechowski in a segment aired during the October 6 episode of *College GameDay*, Lennay's last words to Te'o were "I love you."

September 12, 2012 (morning): Te'o is informed of his grandmother's passing (*Sports Illustrated*).

September 12, 2012 (afternoon): Te'o is informed of Kekua's passing by her older brother, Koa (*Sports Illustrated*).

September 15, 2012: Te'o records 12 tackles in leading the Irish to an upset win over Michigan State.

September 22, 2012: Kekua's funeral takes place in Carson, California. (The Associated Press puts it in "Carson City, Calif.," which does not exist.) Te'o skips the funeral, saying Kekua had insisted that he not miss a game (*Los Angeles Times*). Her casket is closed at 9:00 A.M. Pacific time, according to Te'o. That night, Notre Dame beats Michigan, 13–6, to go to 4-0, the school's best start in a decade. Te'o intercepts two passes. After the game, he says of Lennay: "All she wanted was some white roses. So I sent her roses and sent her two picks along with that." Notre Dame head coach Brian Kelly awards the game ball to Lennay Kekua, handing it to Te'o to "take back to Hawaii."

It was around this time that Te'o's Heisman campaign began in earnest, aided in part by the *South Bend Tribune*. He appeared on the cover of *Sports Illustrated*'s October 1 issue, above the headline "The Full Manti."

And it was around this time that Manti and his father began filling in details about the linebacker's relationship with Lennay. Brian Te'o told multiple reporters that the family had never met Kekua; the Te'os were supposed to spend time with her when they visited South Bend, Indiana, for Notre Dame's Senior Day on November 17. The elder Te'o told the *South Bend Tribune* in October, "We came to the realization that she could be our daughter-in-law. Sadly, it won't happen now."

Lennay Kekua's death resonated across the college football landscape—especially at Notre Dame, where the community immediately embraced her as a fallen sister. Charity funds were started, and donations poured into foundations dedicated to leukemia research. More than $3,000 has been pledged in one Indie-Gogo campaign raising money for the Leukemia & Lymphoma Society.

Te'o's story moved beyond the world of sports. On the day of the BCS championship game between Notre Dame and Alabama, *CBS This Morning* ran a three-minute story that featured a direct quote from Lennay Kekua:

> Babe, if anything happens to me, you promise that you'll stay there and you'll play and you'll honor me through the way you play.

CBS also displayed a photo of Kekua several times throughout the piece.

This week, we got in touch with a woman living in Torrance, California. We'll call her Reba, to protect her identity. She was initially confused, then horrified to find that she had become the face of a dead woman. "That picture," she told us over the phone, "is a picture of me from my Facebook account."

Manti Te'o and Lennay Kekua did not meet at Stanford in 2009. The real beginning of their relationship apparently occurred on Twitter, as an encounter between @MTeo_5 and @lovalovaloveYOU, on October 10, 2011. Here's the moment they first made contact.

> @lovalovaloveyou nice to meet u too ma'am
> —Manti Te'o (@MTeo_5) October 10, 2011

Lennay Kekua's Twitter name was @lovalovaloveYOU from 2011 until April 2012, @LennayKay from April until September 2012, and has been @LoveMSMK ever since. Their interactions, by and large, consisted of mild flirting. By January 2012, they were a "couple," and Te'o sprinkled #LMK (for Lennay Marie Kekua) throughout his Twitter timeline in 2012.

As for what Kekua was tweeting, we have only bits and pieces. Her Twitter was private during most of this time, though various Google caches reveal her ever-changing series of avatars and a handful of Twitpics.

All of those photographs—with one important exception— came from the private Facebook and Instagram accounts of Reba, whom we found after an exhaustive related-images search of each of Lennay's images (most of which had been modified in some way to prevent reverse image searching). We sent her a number of photographs that had appeared on Lennay's Twitter account, which is now private but apparently still active. One picture in particular brought Reba to a start. It had been used briefly as @LoveMSMK's Twitter avatar and later in the background of the page.

That photo hadn't appeared on the Internet—at least, not to Reba's knowledge. She had taken it in December 2012 and sent it directly to an old high school acquaintance. The two hadn't talked since graduation, but the classmate, whom Reba remembered fondly, contacted her on Facebook with a somewhat convoluted request: His cousin had been in a serious car accident, and he had seen her photos before and thought she was pretty. Would she be so kind as to take a picture of herself holding up a sign reading MSMK, to put in a slide show to support the cousin's recovery? (He didn't explain what MSMK meant, and Reba still doesn't know.) Baffled but trusting, Reba made the sign and sent along the photo.

And now here it was on a dead girl's Twitter profile. After Googling Lennay Kekua's name, Reba began to piece things together. She called up the classmate. He expressed alarm, Reba told us later, and "immediately began acting weird." "Don't worry about it," he told her. Moments after the phone call, Reba's picture was removed from the @LoveMSMK Twitter profile. Then, in a series of lengthy phone calls, Reba told us everything she knew about the classmate, a star high school quarterback turned religious musician named Ronaiah Tuiasosopo.

Ronaiah Tuiasosopo comes from a big football family. His father, Titus, played for USC in the late '80s and early '90s. One uncle, Navy, played for the LA Rams; another uncle, Mike, coaches the defensive line at Colorado. A cousin from an older generation, Manu, went to Seattle in the first round in 1979; another cousin, Marques, went to Oakland in the second round in 2001. A cousin from a different side of the family, Fred Matua, earned All-America honors at guard for USC and played on several NFL teams, before dying this past August of a heart-related issue. (He was 28.)

Tuiasosopo, now 22, had once been something of a football prospect himself. In 2005, the *Los Angeles Daily News* wrote that the young Tuiasosopo, then the sophomore starting quarterback for Antelope Valley High School in Lancaster, California, "looked like a star" in practice, despite some in-game growing pains. His coach said he was a "great kid" who did a fine job leading the older seniors. He was an honorable mention for the all-league team. But then he transferred out of town, to Franklin High in Stockton, where he spent his junior year living with an aunt and handing the ball off. His team featured two 1,000-yard rushers, and he completed only five passes all season. He transferred again: his senior year, he turned up at Paraclete High in Lancaster. Titus, his father, had become an assistant coach there. That's where he encountered Reba. His team lost in the semifinals. A season recap article suggested that he might sign with Hawaii, but that evidently went nowhere.

Once high school ended, in 2008, Tuiasosopo threw himself into his father's church. Titus is the pastor at the Oasis Christian Church of the Antelope Valley, and Ronaiah leads the church's band. He also has his own little YouTube music career. He sings secular songs, with a cousin (Conan Amituanai, a former Arizona lineman whom the Vikings once signed), and religious songs, both solo and as part of an ensemble. "Ignite," the lead single on the group's ReverbNation page, is a likable enough song. It borrows its chorus from Katy Perry's catchy "Firework." But the song only has 10 Facebook likes, a fairly low figure that seems especially low once one considers who plugged Tuiasosopo's single on Twitter in December 2011: Manti Te'o.

Te'o and Tuiasosopo definitely know each other. In May 2012, Te'o was retweeting Tuiasosopo, who had mentioned going to Hawaii. Wrote Te'o, "sole"—"bro," in Samoan—"u gotta come down." In June, Te'o wished Tuiasosopo a happy birthday. How they know each other isn't clear. We spoke to a woman we'll call Frieda, who had suggested on Twitter back in December that there was something fishy about Lennay Kekua. She was Facebook friends with Titus Tuiasosopo, so we asked her if she knew anything about Ronaiah.

"Manti and Ronaiah are family," she said, "or at least family friends." She told us that the Tuiasosopos had been on-field guests (of Te'o or someone else, she didn't know) for the November 24 Notre Dame–USC game in Los Angeles. USC was unable to confirm this, but a tweet from Tuiasosopo's since-deleted account suggests he and Te'o did see each other on that West Coast trip. "Great night with my bro @MTeo_5! #Heisman #574L," Ronaiah tweeted on November 23, the night before the game.

And there was something else: Tuiasosopo had been in a car accident a month before Lennay's supposed accident.

Was this Lennay Kekua? We spoke with friends and relatives of Ronaiah Tuiasosopo who asserted that Ronaiah was the man behind Lennay. He created Lennay in 2008, one source said, and Te'o wasn't the first person to have an online "relationship" with her. One mark—who had been "introduced" to Lennay by Tuiasosopo—lasted about a month before family members grew suspicious that Lennay could never be found on the telephone, and that wherever one expected Lennay to be, Ronaiah was there instead. Two sources discounted Ronaiah's stunt as a prank that only metastasized because of Te'o's rise to national celebrity this past season.

The hoax began crumbling around the edges late last year. On November 4, 2012, an "U'ilani Rae Kekua," supposedly Lennay's sister, popped up on Twitter under the name @uilanirae. Manti Te'o immediately tweeted out the following:

> Shout out to Ms.@uilanirae she's new to twitter and really needs some followers! One of the realist people I know.

Te'o also wished U'ilani a happy Thanksgiving on November 22.

Numerous Notre Dame fans sent U'ilani messages of condolence, and she responded with thanks. On November 10, U'ilani tweeted the following:

> I miss you @LennayKay our dinner for Daddy today was beautiful & it hit me hard that you weren't at the table. Rest easy lala, love you sis.

A few weeks later, the @uilanirae account was deleted. The deletion came immediately after tweets from two now-suspended Twitter accounts had alleged that U'ilani was a fraud, that the same person behind Lennay was operating the U'ilani account, and that the images of "U'ilani" were really of a woman named Donna Tei.

Tei's Twitter account is @FreDonna51zhun; Fred Matua wore number 51, and Tei's profile is full of pictures of herself with the late football star (and cousin of Tuiasosopo's). We showed U'ilani's Twitter avatar to one of Tei's friends, and he confirmed it was her.

In yet another now-deleted tweet, Tei herself reached out to Nev Schulman, star of the 2010 film *Catfish* and executive producer of the MTV program of the same title. Schulman's movie and show are about romantic deception through fake online personas.

Manti Te'o, meanwhile, has deleted his tweets mentioning U'ilani.

There was no Lennay Kekua. Lennay Kekua did not meet Manti Te'o after the Stanford game in 2009. Lennay Kekua did not attend Stanford. Lennay Kekua never visited Manti Te'o in Hawaii. Lennay Kekua was not in a car accident. Lennay Kekua did not talk to Manti Te'o every night on the telephone. She was not diagnosed with cancer, did not spend time in the hospital, did not engage in a lengthy battle with leukemia. She never had a bone marrow transplant. She was not released from the hospital on September 10, nor did Brian Te'o congratulate her for this over the telephone. She did not insist that Manti Te'o play in the Michigan State or Michigan games, and did not request he send white flowers to her funeral. Her favorite color was not white. Her brother, Koa, did not inform Manti Te'o that she was dead. Koa did not exist. Her funeral did not take place in Carson, California, and her casket was not closed at 9:00 A.M. exactly. She was not laid to rest.

Lennay Kekua's last words to Manti Te'o were not "I love you."

A friend of Ronaiah Tuiasosopo told us he was "80 percent sure" that Manti Te'o was "in on it," and that the two perpetrated Lennay Kekua's death with publicity in mind. According to the friend, there were numerous photos of Ronaiah Tuiasosopo and Te'o together on Tuiasosopo's now-deleted Instagram account.

The sheer quantity of falsehoods about Manti's relationship with Lennay makes that friend, and another relative of Ronaiah's, believe Te'o had to know the truth. Mostly, though, the friend simply couldn't believe that Te'o would be stupid enough — or Ronaiah Tuiasosopo clever enough — to sustain the relationship for nearly a year.

Since Notre Dame was blown out in the BCS national championship game, Te'o has kept a low profile. He has tweeted sparingly, and he declined an invitation to the Senior Bowl. His father made news recently when he announced on the "Manti Te'o 'Official' Fan Club" Facebook page that he had "black listed" the *Honolulu Star-Advertiser*, which had carried a photo on its front page of Manti getting bowled over by Alabama's Eddie Lacy in the title game.

Te'o hasn't tweeted at Lennay since November 6, when he wrote:

@lennaykay I miss you!
—Manti Te'o (@MTeo_5) November 7, 2012

As of this writing, Te'o's Twitter profile carries a quotation from Alexandre Dumas's *The Count of Monte Cristo*, the great adventure novel about a man in disguise.

Life is a storm. You will bask in the sunlight one moment, be shattered on the rocks the next. What makes you a man is what you do when that storm comes.

We called a cell phone for Manti Te'o, but the number we had is not accepting calls. Brian Te'o, Manti's father, was in a meeting when we called, according to a text message he sent in response. Ronaiah Tuiasosopo did not answer his phone or respond to multiple text messages. We left a message with Notre Dame earlier this afternoon. We'll update with comments when and if we get any.

Update (5:17 P.M.): Notre Dame responds:

On Dec. 26, Notre Dame coaches were informed by Manti Te'o and his parents that Manti had been the victim of what appears to be a hoax in which someone using the fictitious name Lennay Kekua apparently ingratiated herself with Manti and then conspired with others to lead him to believe she had tragically died of leukemia. The University immediately initiated an investigation to assist Manti and his family in discovering the motive for and nature of this hoax. While the proper authorities will continue to investigate this troubling matter, this appears to be, at a minimum, a sad and very cruel deception to entertain its perpetrators.
Dennis Brown
University Spokesman/Assistant Vice President

Update (6:10 P.M.): Manti Te'o's statement:

This is incredibly embarrassing to talk about, but over an extended period of time, I developed an emotional relationship with a woman I met online. We maintained what I thought to be an authentic relationship by communicating frequently online and on the phone, and I grew to care deeply about her. To realize that I was the victim of what was apparently someone's sick joke and constant lies was, and is, painful and humiliating. It further pains me that the grief I felt and the sympathies expressed to me at the time of my grandmother's death in September were in any way deepened by what I believed to be another significant loss in my life. I am enormously grateful for the support of my family, friends and Notre Dame fans throughout this year. To think that I shared with them my happiness about my relationship and details that I thought to be true about her just makes me sick. I hope that people can understand how trying and confusing this whole experience has been. In retrospect, I obviously should have been much more cautious. If anything good comes of this, I hope it is that others will be far more guarded when they engage with people online than I was. Fortunately, I have many wonderful things in my life, and I'm looking forward to putting this painful experience behind me as I focus on preparing for the NFL Draft.

DON VAN NATTA JR.

The Match Maker

FROM ESPN.COM

"HELLO AGAIN, EVERYONE, I'm Howard Cosell. We're delighted to be able to bring you this very, very quaint, unique event."

On Thursday night, September 20, 1973, 50 million Americans, fatigued by Vietnam and Watergate, tuned in to see whether a woman could defeat a man on a tennis court. Dubbed "The Battle of the Sexes," the match pitted Billie Jean King, the 29-year-old champion of that summer's Wimbledon and a crusader for the women's liberation movement, against Bobby Riggs, the 55-year-old gambler, hustler, and long-ago tennis champ who had willingly become America's bespectacled caricature of male chauvinism.

Before 30,472 at the Houston Astrodome, still the largest crowd to watch tennis in the United States, the spectacle felt like a cross between a heavyweight championship bout and an old-time tent revival. Flanked by young women, Riggs, in a canary-yellow Sugar Daddy warm-up jacket, was imperiously carted into the Astrodome aboard a gilded rickshaw. Not to be outdone, King, wearing a blue-and-white sequined tennis dress, sat like Cleopatra in a chariot delivered courtside by bare-chested, muscle-ripped young men. Moments before the first serve, King presented Riggs with a squealing, squirming piglet. "Look at that male chauvinist pig," Cosell told viewers. "That symbolizes what Bobby Riggs is holding up . . ."

All of the vaudevillian hoopla made it easy to forget the enormous stakes and the far-reaching social consequences. King was playing not just for public acceptance of the women's game but also an opportunity to prove her gender's equality at a time when women could still not obtain a credit card without a man's signature. If she were to defeat Bobby Riggs, the triumph would be shared by every woman who knew she deserved equal pay, opportunities, and respect. Equally sweet, King would cram shut the mouth of a male chauvinist clown who had chortled that a woman belonged in the bedroom and the kitchen but certainly not in the same arena competing against a man. For Riggs, the $100,000 winner-take-all match offered big money and a perfect launching pad to a late-in-life career playing exhibition matches against women.

It seemed a certain payday for him. Four months earlier, Riggs had crushed Margaret Court, the world's number-one women's tennis player, 6–2, 6–1, in an exhibition labeled by the media as the "Mother's Day Massacre." Court's defeat had persuaded King to play Riggs. Nearly everyone in tennis expected a similarly lopsided result. On the ABC broadcast, Pancho Gonzales, John Newcombe, and even 18-year-old Chrissie Evert predicted Riggs would defeat King, then the number-two-ranked woman. In Las Vegas, the smart money was on Bobby Riggs. Jimmy the Greek declared, "King money is scarce. It's hard to find a bet on the girl."

But by aggressively attacking the net and smashing precision shots, King ran a winded, out-of-shape Riggs all over the court. Riggs made a slew of unforced errors, hitting soft returns directly at King or into the net and double-faulting at key moments, including on set point in the first set. "I don't understand," Cosell said after a King winner off a Riggs backhand. "He's been feeding her that backhand all night." Midway through the third set, Riggs looked drained and complained of hand cramps. After King took match point, winning in straight sets, 6–4, 6–3, 6–3, Riggs mustered the energy to hop the net. "I underestimated you," he whispered in King's ear.

Several hours later, Bobby Riggs lay in an ice bath in the Tarzan Room of Houston's AstroWorld Hotel. Despondent and alone, Riggs contemplated lowering his head into the icy water and drowning himself.

"This was the worst thing in the world I've ever done," Bobby Riggs later told his son, Larry, about his defeat before the whole world. "The worst thing I've ever done."

*

When Hal Shaw heard the voices at the Palma Ceia Golf and Country Club in Tampa, Florida, on a winter night some 40 years ago, he turned off the bench light over his worktable and locked the bag room door. He feared burglars. Who else would be approaching the pro shop long after midnight? Then Shaw, who was there late rushing to repair members' golf clubs for the next day's tournament, heard the pro shop's front door unlock and swing open.

Peering through a diamond-shaped window, Shaw, then a 39-year-old assistant golf pro, watched four sharply dressed men stroll into the pro shop. He says he instantly recognized three of them: Frank Ragano, a Palma Ceia member and mob attorney whose wife took golf lessons from Shaw, and two others he knew from newspaper photographs—Santo Trafficante Jr., the Florida mob boss whom Ragano represented, and Carlos Marcello, the head of the New Orleans mob. Trafficante and Marcello, now deceased, were among the most infamous Mafia leaders in America; Marcello would later confide to an FBI informant that he had ordered the assassination of John F. Kennedy. A fourth man, whom Shaw says he didn't recognize, joined them.

Shaw's workroom was about 20 feet from the men, who sat at a circular table. Through the window to the darkened bag room door, he could see them, but they couldn't see him. Shaw says he was "petrified" as he tried to remain completely still, worrying that the men would find him lurking there. Then Shaw heard something he'd keep secret for the next 40 years: Bobby Riggs owed the gangsters more than $100,000 from lost sports bets, and he had a plan to pay it back.

Shaw, now 79, told the story of what he saw and heard that Tampa night to a friend late last year for the first time. This spring, he told it to *Outside the Lines.*

The men, Shaw says, used an array of nicknames for Riggs— "Riggsy," "BB," "Bobby Bolita." Ragano told the men that "Riggsy" was prepared to "set up two matches . . . against the two best women players in the world," Shaw says. "He mentioned Margaret Court—and it's easy for me to remember that because one of my aunt's names was Margaret so that, you know, wasn't hard to remember—and the second lady was Billie Jean King."

Ragano explained that Riggs "had the first match already in the works . . . and the second match he knew would follow because of Billie Jean King's popularity and everything that it would be kind of a slam-dunk to get her to play him bragging about beating Margaret Court," Shaw says Ragano told the men. Shaw also says he heard Ragano mention an unidentified mob man in Chicago who would help engineer the proposed fix.

"Mr. Ragano was emphatic," Shaw recalls. "Riggs had assured him that the fix would be in—he would beat Margaret Court and then he would go in the tank" against King, but Riggs pledged he'd "make it appear that it was on the up and up."

At first, Trafficante and Marcello expressed skepticism, Shaw says. They wondered whether Riggs was in playing shape to defeat Court or King, but Ragano, now deceased, assured them Riggs was training. The men also wondered whether there would be enough interest in exhibition tennis matches to generate substantial betting action. In the early 1970s, as it does today, tennis attracted a tiny fraction of sports betting dollars. Ragano assured them that there was ample time for Riggs to get the media to promote the matches so enough people would be interested to place bets with the mobsters' network of illegal bookmakers.

Finally, Shaw says, the men asked about Riggs's price for the fix. "Ragano says, 'Well, he's going to [get] peanuts compared to what we're going to make out of this, so he has asked for his debt to be erased.'" Riggs "has also asked for a certain amount of money to be discussed later to be put in a bank account for him in England," Ragano told the men, according to Shaw.

After nearly an hour, the four men stood up, shook hands, and agreed they'd move forward with Riggs's proposal, Shaw says.

Lamar Waldron, an author of several books about the Mafia, says Shaw's account of the meeting rings true. "In the early 1970s, proposed deals were usually brought to Trafficante and Marcello by other cities' mob leaders, businessmen and lawyers for the mob," says Waldron, whose book *Legacy of Secrecy* is being developed into a film by Leonardo DiCaprio, with Robert De Niro slated to play Marcello. "They'd accept some, pass on others. I know Marcello and Trafficante also met during that period in the Tampa area."

After the men left the pro shop, Shaw says he stayed hidden in the darkened room for a half-hour until he was certain they were gone.

"Mobsters have been here for centuries," Shaw says of Tampa, where he has lived his entire life. "There were gangland murders on top of one another. I was brought up with the fear factor. You don't mess around with these people. You stay clear of them, and you don't do anything that would make them angry."

But as he approaches his 80th birthday this December, Shaw says he is motivated to tell his story. "There are certain things in my life that I have to talk about, have to get off·my chest," he says of the meeting, which he says occurred during the last week of 1972 or the first week in 1973. "It's been 40 years, okay, and I've carried this with me for 40 years . . . The fear is gone . . . And I wanted to make sure, if possible, I could set the record straight— let the world know that this was not what it seemed to be."

Robert Larimore Riggs, the youngest of six children, was born in Los Angeles in 1918. His father was a minister, but young Bobby ignored his father's warnings about the evils of gambling. He won nickels racing boys in a Los Angeles park, played marbles and penny-ante poker, and mastered his own invented games of chance. After winning his first racket on a bet at the age of 11, Riggs played the game nonstop, using smarts and guile to compensate for his five-foot-seven-inch frame, and became a dominant amateur tennis player.

Before Wimbledon in 1939, Riggs visited the London betting shops and was stunned to see he was listed at 25–1 odds to win the men's singles championship. So he placed a remarkably presumptuous parlay bet on himself that would only pay off if he'd win the singles title, the doubles championship, and the mixed-doubles title. At Wimbledon, then an amateur tournament, no one had ever won all three in the same year. But at age 21, Riggs pulled off the remarkable feat and won, from the bookmakers, a total of $108,000, more than $1.7 million in today's dollars. "I blew it all back on gambling like any young kid will do," he told *Tennis Week* in 1995. "I liked to go to the casinos and bet on the horse races and play gin. I got overmatched a few times."

But Riggs was rarely overmatched on the tennis court. Twice, he won the U.S. singles championships at Forest Hills, in 1939 and 1941. After serving in the Navy during World War II, Riggs won U.S. Pro singles titles in 1946, 1947, and 1949.

And always, Riggs had a bet on the outcome of his match. "I've got to have a bet going in order to play my best," Riggs wrote in his 1973 memoir, *Court Hustler.* At least once, he had a bet going and played his worst. Tennis historian Bud Collins recalls a 1940s doubles match in which Riggs and his partner cruised to a two-set lead. But they then lost by dumping the next three sets, Collins says. The fix was obvious. "Well, there's always money with Bobby," Collins says. "The jingle of tennis was always there."

After Riggs's tennis career ended, he continued to play against seniors and amateurs at clubs in Chicago, New York, and, later, in California. He was in such supreme control of a match that players say he had the ability to drop a first set or even two sets, bet on himself at fatter odds, and then come storming back to win. "Staying in the barn" is what Riggs's best friend, Lornie Kuhle, calls this hustle. "[It] means you're not giving it your full effort, yet your opponent thinks you are," Kuhle says. "He led you to believe you really had a chance to beat him. As soon as the bet was increased, he came out of the barn, and he beat you. Then everybody would scream bloody murder and foul. Bobby would stay in the barn a lot—on the golf course, on the tennis court."

Before long, Riggs was playing more golf than tennis. That was because golf's handicap system made it easier for Riggs to disguise his true talent; every golf gambler knows most wagers are won during the first-tee negotiations. "The second worst thing in the world is betting on a golf game and losing," Riggs often said. "The worst is not betting at all."

In the 1950s, Riggs was the resident tennis pro at the Roney Plaza Hotel, a Miami Beach artdeco magnet for celebrities and mobsters who enjoyed wagering. "Bobby was hanging around the unsavory people," says Gardnar Mulloy, 99, a close friend of Riggs's and a former U.S. number-one player. "I'd seen him with people that normally you would think you wouldn't want to be with. And he was always betting big money—it was always, it seemed to me, a fix." In those days, Riggs played golf for money with South Florida mobster Martin Stanovich, nicknamed "The Fat Man."

Riggs also gambled on the links with Jackie "The Lackey" Cerone, a hit man for the Chicago Mafia and protégé of mob boss Sam Giancana, according to Riggs's son and Kuhle. As he caddied for his father as a teenager in a money match against Cerone, Larry Riggs says he noticed that Cerone and his pals kept brazenly riding their carts over his father's ball. They kicked the ball too, when they thought no one was looking.

Bobby Riggs just smiled. "These are rough guys," he told his son. "These guys—you don't mess with these guys. Just don't ask any questions. Just keep your mouth shut."

Larry Riggs was a child of Bobby Riggs's first marriage, which ended in divorce. Riggs's second marriage was to a woman whose family owned the American Photographic Cos. in New York, a $20 million a year corporation where Riggs worked during the 1960s. He wore a suit and necktie and took the commuter train from Long Island to Penn Station. He tried to satisfy himself by playing cards and golf on the weekends, but it wasn't enough action. His second wife divorced him in 1972, handing Riggs a $1 million-plus divorce settlement.

With that stake, Riggs moved into his older brother's duplex apartment in Newport Beach, California. Riggs wagered every day on things he could control, like tennis and golf. "Bobby had the guts of a burglar on a tennis court or on a golf course," says tennis legend Tony Trabert, 82, a close friend. "He could goad people or needle people or set people up by purposefully losing a set or two and get the bet up to higher stakes and then win with ease. He just had amazing control."

But Riggs was also betting on contests he couldn't control: like horseracing and pro and college football. With California bookmakers, he'd place bets on every televised football game and often on games that weren't on TV. On a New Year's Day in the early 1970s, he lost every bowl game, dropping nearly $30,000 to the bookmakers, his friends said. At Caesars Palace, Kuhle recalls that Riggs, sloppy from too much bourbon, lost $17,000 playing baccarat in a few hours.

Riggs enjoyed far more betting success on the seniors' tennis circuit, dominating his opponents. In the early '70s, he beseeched the top women players to play him in a series of exhibition matches, but no one agreed. After having vanished from the public eye for nearly two decades, Riggs saw the proposed matches as a chance to climb back into the spotlight and make some easy money.

Six weeks after Hal Shaw heard the mob leaders weigh the appeal of a fixed tennis match, Bobby Riggs held a news conference at the Westview Hotel in downtown San Diego. It was February 1973. Before a roomful of reporters, Riggs held up a $5,000 cashier's check—the money was staked by a local developer—that he was offering to Margaret Court or Billie Jean King. All either one had to do was agree to play him.

Court, then 30, agreed to a match with the 55-year-old Riggs, telling friends it would be an easy payday. Almost overnight, there was worldwide interest; Riggs made sure of it with quotable chauvinistic rants against women that sounded as if they were intended to get under the skin of King, a crusader for the women's liberation movement and a cofounder that year of the Women's Tennis Association.

"He took the most basic conflict in the world, which is man versus woman, and he took that conflict and used tennis as the metaphor and created the match," says Kuhle. "And therefore the whole world became interested."

Riggs had no doubt he would defeat Margaret Court. "I'm just going to destroy her," he told his son, Larry.

And over the next three months, Riggs trained 10 to 12 hours a day, playing hours of tennis against outstanding young male players and running miles alongside a San Diego golf course. This was Riggs's usual routine: train, rigorously, for a big match. "Never underestimate opponents," Riggs advised in his list of rules for competition titled "You Too Are Champions" published in the late '60s.

By the time she faced Riggs, Court was 30 years old and had won 18 of her previous 25 tournaments, including three majors—the U.S. Open, Australian, and French. She was one of the most dominant players of all time, having won a total of 62 Grand Slam singles and doubles events in her career—a feat never matched by a man or a woman. Still, the oddsmakers, all men, installed Riggs as the betting favorite in the Las Vegas sports books. The match attracted a fair amount of action; nearly everyone bet on Bobby Riggs.

On May 13, 1973, an overflow crowd of fans and celebrities assembled at San Diego Country Estates in Ramona, California, and more than 30 million people watched on CBS. Before the first serve, Riggs handed Court a bouquet of red roses. She curtsied.

Riggs made few errors and relied on his masterful service game and trademark lob while Court looked flummoxed and hit shot after shot into the net. Riggs coasted, winning 6–2, 6–1. "Sometimes

I look back and think, *Why did I need to do it?*" Court now says. "I was number one in the world in tennis . . . Look, we all make mistakes in life, and probably that was one of my mistakes."

"As soon as Margaret lost, I said, 'I have to play,'" King, 69, told *Outside the Lines* in an interview last week. "I knew I was going to say yes and I knew that it was on, the match was on." And she knew she had to win. A boxing promoter and television producer named Jerry Perenchio, who promoted the Ali-Frazier bout in 1971 as "The Fight," organized "The Battle of the Sexes" between King and Riggs. He put up a $100,000 winner-take-all prize for the best-of-five-sets match and arranged for it to be played in the Houston Astrodome in prime time on national television.

A week after Wimbledon, which King had won for the fifth time, Riggs and King hammed it up at a raucous news conference at the Town Tennis Club in Manhattan. "Personally," Riggs said, "I would wish that the women would stay in the home and do the kitchen work and take care of the baby and compete in areas where they can compete in because it's a big mistake for them to get mixed up in these mixed sex matches." (Kuhle and Riggs's son, who was in his midtwenties at the time, say this was pure shtick, that Riggs was not a chauvinist, but viewed women as equals; his first tennis coach back in LA was a woman.)

Riggs flew home to California. His son, Larry, says he was friendly with an investor named Steve Powers, who had a Beverly Hills estate renowned for its wild, all-night parties. "Bobby and I had a deal—he got to stay at my house as long as he entertained my guests, and he did that," Powers says. "He didn't ask much of me—just get him laid with the wild women in LA. And I did that."

In July, Riggs moved into Powers's guesthouse, where he lived—and partied—during the eight weeks prior to the King match.

"Steve had his maid, and she wore the French maid outfit with no underwear on the top or the bottom," Larry Riggs says. "That set the tone for the parties at nighttime . . . It was just a wild time to be had by everybody, including my dad."

With a glass of bourbon in his left hand and a glass of Coca-Cola in his right, Bobby Riggs would take big swigs from both glasses and mix the liquids in his mouth before swallowing. And he was always puffing on a fat cigar. "I had never seen him really drink as much as he was then," Larry Riggs says. "And it concerned me."

Kuhle's job was to train Riggs, but for the first time anyone could remember, Riggs refused to practice with solid players or even exercise, his son says. Not once did he use Powers's lighted tennis court to do anything but goof around for the cameras or hustle matches. Instead, he'd play stragglers off the street for a few quick bucks. "It's very hard to turn down $500 if a guy wants to come out and play for $500. He can put that in his pocket," Kuhle says. "There was so much commotion going on, and he just felt he could beat her on roller skates."

Riggs tirelessly promoted the match, filming several TV commercials (American Express, Sunbeam Curling Iron) and seemingly never refusing an interview request or a party invite. Early one morning, Riggs realized $1,500 had been stolen from his wallet by a young woman he had been drinking with the night before. He grumbled that the woman hadn't even slept with him.

Riggs relished playing the impish, gambling-mad, chauvinistic court jester for enthralled members of the national media. On its cover, *Time* magazine called Riggs "The Happy Hustler." *Sports Illustrated* warned, "Don't Bet Against This Man." A recording artist named Lyle "Slats" McPheeters recorded "The Ballad of Bobby Riggs," for Artco Records. On *60 Minutes,* Riggs tossed playing cards at a wastebasket for money, played tennis with eight chairs on his side of the court, and ran around Las Vegas looking for action on anything, from tennis and golf to backgammon and card tosses, with everyone he met.

"All of the running, all of the chasing, all of the betting, all of the playing—what's it all about?" Mike Wallace asked Riggs. "Do you do it for money, Bobby?"

"No," said Riggs with a smirk. "I do it for fun, the sport, it's the thing to do. When I can't play for big money, I play for little money. And if I can't play for little money, I stay in bed that day."

This wasn't a midlife crisis. This was a midlife Mardi Gras.

During those weeks, Larry Riggs noticed some "unsavory characters" kept showing up at Powers's house to meet privately with his father. "They weren't golfers," Larry Riggs says. "I called them shady characters with the kind of flashy suits on and the ties and whatever. They just didn't fit in."

After one of the visits, Larry Riggs confronted his father. "Who are those guys?"

"Friends of mine from Chicago."

That's when Larry Riggs says he recognized the men as associates of Jackie Cerone, the Chicago mob hit man with whom his father had played golf and cards back at the Tam O'Shanter Country Club outside of Chicago. "Very not upright citizens of our country," Larry Riggs now says of the men visiting his father.

"What the hell are those guys doing?" Larry Riggs asked his father.

"They're here to see me. We have a little business that we're doing. Don't worry about it. Everything's okay."

But Larry Riggs says he worried obsessively. And he says his father never identified the men or explained why they flew from Chicago to Los Angeles to meet with him several times before the King match.

As Riggs lived the high life on the West Coast, King trained in South Carolina with the focus of a boxer preparing for a prizefight. Larry Riggs was so sure his father was going to lose to King that he refused to accompany him to Houston for the match. "You're going to embarrass yourself," he told his father before he left. Larry Riggs says he bet $500 on King. King says she told her brother "to bet the house" on her.

On the eve of the match in Houston, Mulloy, the tennis legend who was Riggs's close friend, visited him in his leopard-patterned Tarzan Room at the AstroWorld Hotel. A party was raging. Riggs looked heavier to Mulloy; he had gained 15 pounds in the four months since the Court match. "Bobby was in his pajamas," Mulloy recalls, "and I looked around at a half a dozen cuties there, and they're all having their drinks and laughing."

Mulloy asked, "Bobby, what the hell are you doing? You got to play tomorrow."

"Oh, there's no way that broad can beat me," Riggs replied.

The next morning, Mulloy was scheduled to warm up Riggs on the Astrodome court for one hour, but Riggs quit after 10 minutes. Mulloy was stunned. He was even more astonished to find Riggs that afternoon in a nearby practice facility, standing on a court with a brown dog tied on a leash to his left ankle and an umbrella in one hand. People off the street with tennis rackets were lined up to play Riggs. If they won a game, they played for free; if Riggs beat them, they owed him $100. Riggs's brother, John, was collecting fistfuls of cash.

Mulloy says Riggs urged a millionaire friend named Jack Dreyfus not to bet on him against King. "Prior to the match, Jack Dreyfus had called him and said he wants to make a bet, how do you feel, where should I get odds," Mulloy recalls. "Bobby says, 'Don't bet on me.' That made me believe he was going to tank it."

Moments before the match at the Astrodome, some spectators say Riggs appeared sullen, almost angry—the opposite of the happy hustler. "He wasn't having any fun," says Cliff Drysdale, a 72-year-old tennis broadcaster and former top-ranked pro who attended the match. With the first serve, Billie Jean King attacked aggressively in a bid to send a message to Riggs that this would not be another Margaret Court cakewalk. When one of King's early forehands rocketed past him, Riggs told King, "Atta girl." Still wearing his Sugar Daddy warm-up jacket, Riggs moved as if he were underwater. "I was surprised," King says. "He was extremely nervous. So was I."

"He was in slow motion," says Donald Dell, a 75-year-old lawyer, former Davis Cup captain, and one of the first professional sports agents. "It was as if he had taken a sleeping pill."

"Well, as I watched the match, I was surprised that he wasn't attacking more," says Stan Smith, a 66-year-old two-time major winner and a former number-one men's player in the world.

King was ahead 2–1 in the first set. During a break, Riggs finally peeled off his Sugar Daddy jacket. His blue shirt was soaked with sweat.

At the LA Tennis Club where Riggs had won tens of thousands of dollars hustling its members on the tennis court, the golf course, and at the card table, the members watched the match on a large television. Riggs looked nothing like the spry, dominant player who had crushed Margaret Court four months earlier. During the first set, says tennis broadcaster Doug Adler, a friend of Riggs's since they met at the club, someone shouted, "Looks like Bobby bet on Billie Jean!"

Riggs lost a game late in the first set on a double fault, something he rarely did. After losing the first set, Riggs told Kuhle to offer a friend of King's, named Dick Butera, a $5,000 bet that he'd come back to win, at 2–1 odds. Prior to the match, Riggs had bet $10,000 with Butera that he'd beat King. But Butera, who was sitting courtside, refused this midmatch bet, apparently assuming Riggs was once again keeping his game "in the barn."

From across the net, King says, Riggs looked "a little bit in shock" by his first-set loss. And she says she is certain he wasn't tanking: "Bobby Riggs wanted to win that match. I saw it in his eyes. I saw it when we changed ends, and there is no question. I have played matches where players have tanked, and I know what it feels like and I know what it looks like, and he did not. He just was feeling the pressure."

Riggs played even worse in the second set, moving around even more listlessly.

In the broadcast booth, Howard Cosell and tennis analysts Rosie Casals and Gene Scott repeatedly sounded puzzled by Riggs's soft, erratic play. "He doesn't look right to me," Casals said. After Riggs hit a weak return right at King, Casals said, "That's pretty unusual for Bobby." And later, she asked, "Where is Bobby Riggs? Where did he go?"

Scott said Riggs was "just nonchalant with the forehand."

Riggs was well known for a nearly flawless service game, but he missed on nearly half of his first serves. Four times, he double-faulted, all on critical points. The level of play hardly lived up to all the hype and the anticipation. King was grinding down the old man, who was the same age as her father. "Funny, with this match I guess we all expected some high humor involved in it," Cosell said. "Instead, it's become a very serious, serious thing because the comedy has gone out of Bobby Riggs."

When it was finally over, fans stormed the court and engulfed King, and Riggs hugged her. "You could just see he wanted it so badly and couldn't get it going," she says. "I think he got so nervous—it exhausted him." He just "choked," she says. "We've all done it. I've choked. Everybody chokes."

At the postmatch news conference, a subdued Riggs saluted King's performance. "Billie Jean was too good, too quick," he said. "I know I said a lot of things she made me eat tonight. I guess I'm the biggest bum of all time now. But I have to take it." Prior to the match, King says she told Riggs, win or lose, she would never play him again. But before the assembled reporters, Riggs quickly called for a rematch. "I would've given Billie Jean a rematch if I had won, so I want a rematch."

"Why should there be a rematch?" she said. Billie Jean King had nothing left to prove.

*

Nearly 40 years later, "The Battle of the Sexes" is one of the most iconic sporting events in American history. The match's value is especially cherished by tennis people because it proved the game, like King, was a trailblazer for society. King planted a flag for women's equality. Gradually, America followed.

"I think it wasn't just for women," says King. "It was really about both genders. Men come up to me constantly, many times with tears in their eyes, and tell me their story, like 'Oh, I was 12 years old when I saw that match, and now I have a daughter and I have a son, and I really want both of them to have equal opportunity.'

"So I think for men, it changed them to think differently about things. For women, also, they thought differently about themselves—they were much more empowered to ask for what they want and need to have more self-confidence."

This past July, King and several hundred members of tennis's elite gathered at the International Tennis Hall of Fame, in Newport, Rhode Island, for the annual induction ceremonies. On a Sunday evening, they watched a new documentary film that will air September 10 on PBS that salutes King's victory. Afterward, Martina Hingis, a Hall of Fame inductee who wasn't alive in 1973, appeared awestruck by what she had just seen on the big screen. "This was bigger than anything probably anyone can go through . . . so, congratulations," Hingis told King. "I mean—amazing."

In attendance were the aging male members of tennis's old guard, who applauded for King. None of these men knew about Hal Shaw's allegations, and only a few knew about Bobby Riggs's mob friends. Still, the men remarked among themselves that there wasn't a single word in the film about the belief by some that Bobby Riggs had thrown the match for a big payday.

Across nearly 40 years, some of the men who knew Riggs best have wondered: was "The Battle of the Sexes" nothing more than a cultural con job?

"A lot of my tennis friends immediately suspected something was up, and many of us still believe something was up," says John Barrett, the longtime BBC tennis broadcaster. "It wasn't so much that Bobby lost. It was that he looked as if he had almost capitulated. He just made it too easy for Billie Jean King. We all wondered if the old fox had done it again."

"Everything was different," says Adler. "If you were a tennis person that knew Bobby Riggs, the first thing that comes to your mind is he threw the match."

Steve Powers, who owned the guesthouse where Riggs stayed prior to the match, says, "If Bobby had an opportunity to fix the match, he would have jumped at it. Ethics wouldn't have stopped him."

Tennis great Gene Mako, who died in June, had insisted for years that Riggs had thrown the match. "You have to know Bobby," Mako told author Tom LeCompte in the 2003 Riggs biography, *The Last Sure Thing*. Mako believed Riggs was so vain that his play was just awful enough to demonstrate to smart tennis people that he had tanked the match.

Almost right after the match, King says she began hearing the rumors that Riggs had thrown it. The rumors were started by "people who were unhappy—guys who lost money," she says. "And a lot of people, men, particularly, don't like it if a woman wins. They don't like it. They make up stories. They start just thinking about it more and more. It's hard on them. It's very hard on their egos."

King also says because of all the stories about Riggs's betting and hustling, especially in Los Angeles, it was just natural that some people would assume the fix was in.

Asked recently whether she could believe Riggs had thrown the match, former world number-one player Chrissie Evert said she wouldn't think so but you could never be sure. "Ninety-nine percent of me would say [King] beat him fair and square," Evert says. "But if you know Bobby Riggs, you can't put anything past him."

The assumption by some was that Riggs would not have been able to resist the odds on Billie Jean King, who was listed as high as 5–2 in the Las Vegas sports books. Tennis legend Don Budge, who died in 2000, had told one of his sons he had no doubt Riggs threw the match for money. "In no uncertain terms, he definitely heard from people that Riggs had thrown it," says Budge's son, Jeffrey. "And it was huge money—more than $100,000, perhaps $200,000 to $500,000. Dad said, '[Riggs] could have run her off the court any day of the week as he did against Margaret Court.'"

But Kuhle denies Riggs threw the match, arguing it would have been impossible for Riggs to have quietly placed large bets on King in Vegas. In the 1970s, as they do now, sports books had strict wagering limits and large bets would have moved the odds in an obvious way. "It just makes no sense," Kuhle says.

If Riggs had thrown the match for the Mafia, how would that kind of fix have benefited Carlos Marcello and Santo Trafficante Jr.? Both men controlled networks of illegal bookmaking operations. From New Orleans, Carlos Marcello ran "the wire" that took bets on horse races and sports wagering across the country, Mafia experts say. Gambling experts said that "a perfect fix" is a result known to illegal bookmakers. That knowledge allows them to offer fatter odds on a betting favorite knowing it would attract far more action.

London betting shops listed odds on "The Battle of the Sexes," which had been scheduled to be shown on closed-circuit TV at a half-dozen London movie houses. But the bookmakers viewed the match with "huge suspicion," recalls Graham Sharpe, a 62-year-old media relations director at William Hill, the UK's largest bookmaker. "This thing was regarded as a freak show, a sideshow. And we were concerned because one of the guys is a noted hustler and a compulsive gambler, who is not as pure as the driven snow. If anyone tried to bet more than a few pounds, we'd reject the bet and figure he knew something that we didn't."

The Mafia expert and author Lamar Waldron was told about Riggs's Mafia acquaintances and what Hal Shaw had heard. "Given all the connections that Riggs had and the way these Mafia leaders operated, it would be unusual if they didn't look to him to throw the match," Waldron says. "Certainly it appears the motive and opportunity was there."

When Shaw watched Riggs lose to King, he says he knew the scheming he had overheard in Palma Ceia's pro shop had been executed. "There's nothing impossible when money's involved and power's involved," he says. Shaw says he is glad he decided to come forward and tell his story and has nothing left to fear. "You can ask me a thousand questions, I would still tell you what happened that night, you know, 40 years ago," he says. "I got no ax to grind. I don't get anything for this. I know deep in my heart—Riggsy had taken a fall, but made it look good. He was a showman, and he pulled it off."

But Lornie Kuhle angrily denied Shaw's allegations during an interview at his home in Decatur, Illinois. "I've never heard any-

thing so far-fetched," he says. "It's just complete bulls——." As for
Shaw, he said, "I mean, that's ridiculous—unless he's got Alzheimer's, and people do get that when they're 79 years old." He
added, "I never heard anything so far-fetched as this guy in Tampa.
I'd like to meet that guy sometime."

Kuhle also vehemently disputed the suggestion that Riggs owed
mob-linked bookmakers any money, at any time. "You can say the
mob killed John Kennedy," he says. "We could rationalize that one,
but Bobby never owed anybody a dime—football bets, basketball
bets, or anything like that . . . There are no mob people involved
with this match. The mob doesn't even play tennis . . . I think
that's a funny story."

Kuhle, who is the founder and owner of the Bobby Riggs Tennis Center and Museum in Encinitas, California, also denied that
Riggs received a Mafia payment deposited in a bank account in
England, as Shaw had heard. "Listen, I'm with Bobby night and
day for 20 years," Kuhle says. "I'm the executor of his estate. I
know every nickel he had in the bank. I know every check he's
written, every bet he made. There was never any bet with anybody
in the mob or anything like that."

However, Larry Riggs did not dismiss Shaw's story outright because, after all, his father knew and gambled with a lot of mob guys
all over the country. Bobby Riggs was also a longtime member of
the La Costa Country Club in Carlsbad, California, a reputed mob-
built country club where mob leader and Riggs's acquaintance
Moe Dalitz was a member. And Larry Riggs had never understood
why those Chicago pals of hit man Jackie Cerone had visited his
father several times prior to the King match.

"Did he know Mafia guys? Absolutely," Larry Riggs says. "Is it
possible these guys were talking some s——? Yes, it is possible. They
talked to him about doing it? Possible." However, Riggs says, it was
more likely his father purposefully lost with an eye toward setting
up a bigger payday rematch—and a continuation of the national
publicity that he so craved—than throw the match for mob money.
Larry Riggs also says he remains baffled by the fact his father did
not prepare for the King match—the only match in Bobby Riggs's
life for which he had failed to train. "Never understood it," Larry
Riggs says.

King says Riggs underestimated her. He was devastated that
he lost, though King acknowledges he might have been capable

of throwing a match. "Oh, I'm capable of tanking; everyone can tank," King says. "It depends on the situation. But that was not really in Bobby's best interest in any way to lose that match."

When Mulloy was told about Shaw's story, he says, he believed it. "I think that the mobsters of some sort were in on the match with Billie Jean King," he says. "He didn't put himself in a position to win, and I think he did it on purpose to make a buck." Besides, Mulloy adds, Riggs knew his defeat would create intense interest— and money—for a rematch with King.

In the contract signed by Riggs and King, there was an ironclad clause for a rematch, Kuhle and others say. Riggs considered suing King to force a rematch, but friends urged him not to do it. He was "crushed" by King's decision to deny him a rematch. King says she knows nothing about a rematch clause, wouldn't have agreed to one, and had never heard that Riggs contemplated suing her. Perenchio, the match promoter who is now 82 years old, did not respond to questions from *Outside the Lines* along with a request to review the contract.

For Riggs, who was often quoted as saying, "I want to be remembered as a winner," the aftermath of a loss on such a big stage to a woman he had ridiculed could not have been easy to endure. "He thought for sure she would play him in the rematch," Larry Riggs says. "He thought for sure he would have redemption."

Bobby Riggs's friends say he was depressed for at least six months after his "Battle of the Sexes" loss. Even so, he had become a legitimate national celebrity. (On an airplane, *Laugh-In* star Arte Johnson told Riggs, "People tell me I look like you," to which Riggs replied, "Funny—no one tells me I look like you.") He would do humorous star turns on *The Odd Couple* and other TV shows. By early 1974—only a few months after the loss to King—Riggs moved to Las Vegas and worked at the Tropicana Hotel and Casino as the resident tennis pro and casino greeter. Paid an annual salary of $100,000, he moved into a house on the hotel's golf course.

The Tropicana was the casino where mobsters had skimmed packets of $100 bills from the counting room—the crime immortalized in the film *Casino*. One of the men who benefited from the Tropicana skim was Riggs's Chicago golfing buddy Jackie Cerone. In 1986, Cerone and four other men, from the Chicago, Detroit, and Kansas City mobs, were convicted of skimming a total of $2 million from the Tropicana during the mid-'70s. Larry Riggs says he is unsure who had arranged the job at the Tropicana for Bobby Riggs.

Through the late '70s and early '80s, whispers about an alleged Bobby Riggs fix only grew louder. In 1983, Riggs appeared on a syndicated television show called *Lie Detector*, hosted by the famous criminal defense lawyer F. Lee Bailey. On the show, Bailey asked Riggs if he had thrown the match, and he said no. Bailey declared for viewers that Riggs had passed the lie detector test. Kuhle says Riggs did the show for $5,000, not because he had felt a need to deny the allegation.

Few people who watched knew that Bailey had helped Santo Trafficante Jr. in the late 1970s avoid a congressional subpoena to testify in the House's JFK assassination inquiry. Trafficante had faced jail time, but he thwarted the subpoena with Bailey's help. Now 79 and living in Maine, Bailey says he helped Trafficante as a favor to his lawyer, Henry Gonzalez, whom Bailey called a close friend. "I knew Santo and Henry, but I didn't represent either one of them," Bailey says. Waldron, the Mafia expert, says Frank Sturges, one of the Watergate burglars, also appeared on the show and passed his lie detector test. Waldron says Sturges was a bagman for Trafficante.

For years, Riggs's gambling buddies often asked him about a fix. "Of course it wasn't on the level," says Jim Agate of Las Vegas, a golf gambling pal of Riggs's. He said when he asked Riggs what had happened against Billie Jean King, "he'd laugh and giggle, and roll his eyes and say, 'Oh, well, you know, it wasn't my day.'"

Over the years, King has repeatedly denied there was a fix, saying the suggestion was preposterous because, if Riggs had beaten her, he could have parlayed the victory into additional big money exhibitions against other top women players. He had plenty of incentive to win, she says. When told about Hal Shaw's story, King laughs. "I would bet my life that Bobby never had that discussion with them," she says of Marcello, Trafficante, and Ragano. "Maybe they had that discussion with themselves because they're mobsters, but that's not Bobby. Bobby doesn't get involved with mobsters . . . If I really thought there was even a glimmer of possibility of that, I would think about it, but I know it's not."

In 1995, during the last year of his life, Riggs was 77 years old and suffering from prostate cancer. And reporters were still asking him about a fix. "I know there was a rumor about that match," he told tennis writer Steve Flink. "People said I was tanking, but Billie Jean beat me fair and square. I tried as hard as I could, but I made the classic mistake of overestimating myself and underestimating Billie Jean King. I didn't really think she had a chance . . . Even though we had put up a million dollars in escrow for her to play the rematch, she just wouldn't do it."

The day before Riggs died in October 1995, King called him at home. Over the years, the two adversaries had become good friends.

"I love you," King told him.

"I love you," Riggs said.

Then Billie Jean King told the happy hustler how important their match's result will always be to all women.

"Well, we did it," Bobby Riggs finally told her. "We really made a difference, didn't we?"

MARY PILON

Tomato Can Blues

FROM THE NEW YORK TIMES

GLADWIN, MICHIGAN — Scott DiPonio raced to make sure everything was in order—the fighters were ready, the ring girls were on time, and the Bud Light was cold.

DiPonio was a local promoter who organized amateur cage fights that looked more like barroom brawls than glitzy Las Vegas bouts. With a mix of grit, sweat, and blood, the fights had caught on in rural Michigan, and DiPonio's February 2 event, called Caged Aggression, drew hundreds of fans, even with cage-side seats going for $35.

Charlie Rowan, an undistinguished heavyweight, was scheduled to fight that night at Streeters, a dank nightclub that hosted cage fights in Traverse City.

Rowan's cage name was Freight Train, but he was more like a caboose—plodding and slow, a bruiser whose job was to fill out the ring and get knocked down.

He was what the boxing world used to call a tomato can. The term's origins are unclear, but perhaps it's as simple as this: knock a tomato can over, and red stuff spills out.

Rowan certainly wasn't in it for the money. He was an amateur who loved fighting so much he did it for free.

An hour before the Caged Aggression fights began, DiPonio's cell phone rang. It was Rowan's girlfriend, so frantic she could hardly get the words out, DiPonio said. He asked her to take a deep breath, and, on the verge of tears, she told him that Rowan had crashed his car. He was being airlifted to a hospital. It didn't look good.

Two days later, DiPonio said, she called back. Rowan, only 25 years old, was dead.

DiPonio drove for two hours from Traverse City to Gladwin for a makeshift memorial at the home of Rowan's girlfriend. Rowan's mother sat in the living room, quietly weeping.

DiPonio and other promoters planned a string of benefits for the Rowan family, including one called the Fight for Charlie. The fighters were enemies in the cage, but they pulled together to help one of their own. A heavyweight who had once knocked out Rowan in less than 90 seconds agreed to work as a judge at the largest benefit.

The Fight for Charlie took place March 9. Ring girls sold raffle tickets to a crowd of about 1,000. A young fighter declared from the cage that he was dedicating his bout to Rowan's memory.

"Thank you for helping us raise money for Charlie Rowan's family," a promoter wrote on Facebook after one of the benefits. "Thank you for letting it all out in the cage for us." He added that Rowan was "there with us in spirit and would have been very proud of all of you!"

Less than two weeks later, a Gladwin gun store was robbed.

When Scott DiPonio, the fight promoter, saw the suspect's mug shot on the next day's news, his stomach dropped. It was the late Charlie Rowan, back from the dead.

A Blood-Soaked Allure

Mixed martial arts was born as a seedy sport on the fringes of society. The matches were short, loud, and brutal, fights for those who found boxing too tame. Over the years, it's grown into a mainstream spectacle that now draws millions of viewers on television.

The sport blends techniques from jujitsu, kickboxing, karate, tae kwon do, judo, and wrestling. Certain moves, like eye gouging and shots to the crotch, are generally not allowed. Across America, kids squabbling in their backyards now dream of making it to the Ultimate Fighting Championship, just as playground basketball players picture themselves in the NBA.

But far from the bright lights of professional matches, shadow fighting circuits have sprung up around the country, in small towns like Kingston, Washington, and big cities like New York. It's like the early days of boxing, but with more kicks to the face.

"It's amazing that guys will get beat up for free," Christos Piliafas, a top fighter in Michigan, said. "They just love to fight."

In Michigan, the bouts take place in nightclubs, community centers, and casinos. Most are unregulated, with few safety requirements to speak of. In April, a 35-year-old died after losing a fight in Port Huron.

The crude violence and underground feel of cage fighting draw lusty cheers across the state. These are not carefully negotiated bouts between millionaires trailing personal nutritionists and publicists. Inside the cage at Streeters, unknown Michigan men—factory workers, fathers, soldiers, and convicts—become the Wolverine, the Bloodbath, the Spider Monkey, and the Nightmare.

"You build a brotherhood," said Justin Martinson, a fighter and former Marine. "It's the closest thing to combat."

Finding a Family

When Rowan entered the cage for the first time, he felt electric. Part of it was the cocaine—he was high, as he was for most of his fights. But he also loved the atmosphere: the chain-link walls, the heavy metal music, the screaming fans.

Rowan could take a punch, but he was out of shape and showed little promise. "He was a horrible fighter," said Piliafas, who competes professionally. "He just showed up and would fight. He was a great first fight for someone."

Rowan kept his brown hair cut close and wore a thin mustache. He had a tattoo of a Viking on his left shoulder, the Grim Reaper on his right; Jesus's face on his right leg; and MOM on his left wrist. His newest tattoo was a gothic D inside a diamond, the logo for DiPonio's mixed martial arts team. To Rowan, the Diamond D fighters were family, even if they didn't know what to make of him.

Rowan had struggled to find meaningful work since dropping out of school before 10th grade. He spent time in telemarketing and pipeline installation. He even worked on the carnival circuit assembling rides. He fathered three children with three women, but he drifted from all of them.

Rowan's real family admired his passion for the cage. "I thought maybe it would be good for him," his mother, Lynn Gardner, said. "He seemed to like it, and I thought finally he found something and can take out his aggression. Maybe it could help him turn his life around."

Troubled Beginnings

Rowan was from Gladwin, a city of 3,000 that's barely a blip amid Central Michigan's endless wheat, corn, and soybean farms. His story was pieced together from more than 50 interviews with relatives, local fighters, and Michigan law enforcement officials, as well as police reports, court records, and family letters.

Gladwin families hunt on weekends, and the town's quiet roads include Deer, Elk, and Antler Streets. It takes five minutes to drive across town, from McDonald's to the west to Shopko to the east. Jobs are hard to come by. Slouching houses with plywood-covered windows are as common as stop signs.

In some ways, Rowan had been preparing for the cage his whole life. His father, also named Charles, had beaten him and his brother ever since they were little.

"His dad would put him on the floor and stomp him in the head," his mother said. "When he couldn't take it out on Chuckie, he would take it out on me."

Home was cigarettes, beer, and the blare of a television over his parents' constant arguments. The family moved around Michigan as Rowan's father picked up and lost factory jobs. For a while, the family gathered soda bottles for spare change.

"I thought about leaving a lot," his mother said. "But I was never confident enough in myself and my abilities."

Rowan's father died of cancer in 2001. "He told Chuck that he would rather it was him"—his son—"that was dying," she said.

Even as a kid, Rowan was always in trouble. He stole from neighbors and relatives—"guns, dumb things, work tools, money," Scott Gardner, his stepfather, said.

In the years after his father's death, Rowan was arrested on charges of marijuana distribution and failure to pay child support. He was charged with criminal sexual misconduct as a teenager and failure to register as a sex offender in 2007. Those records are sealed under state law. Rowan spent most of 2012 in jail on check fraud charges.

During those years, he used cocaine and did some work for drug dealers, but he kept that a secret from his family.

Through mutual acquaintances, he met Michael A. Gomez, a convict with drug and weapons charges dating back at least 20 years. The sheriff's office knew Gomez had ties to the Latin Kings and the Mexican Mafia Gang.

While Rowan was ferrying drugs in Three Rivers in 2010, before he began cage fighting, he claimed to have lost Gomez's shipment, maybe worth as much as $80,000. As Rowan told it, a group of thieves jumped him, cracked his ribs, and stole the drugs.

Now, Rowan owed money to impatient people. He tried to lie low, but in January, a group of men beat him up behind Shopko, leaving him with two black eyes, broken ribs, and blood on his baseball cap, he told friends at the time.

Rowan was desperate. Then, while he was watching TV at his girlfriend's house, a show caught his attention. It was on the Investigation Discovery channel, something about a guy who staged his own death so he could start his life anew.

A Way Out

Rowan had felt as if he were drowning for a while now. He owed money to drug dealers. He couldn't keep a job. His hobby was getting beaten up in public. Now this fake-death scheme landed like a life preserver.

If people thought he was dead, he and his girlfriend, Rosa Martinez, could move far from Michigan. Maybe New Mexico. They could begin again.

"I wanted a fresh start," he said in one of a series of interviews conducted both in person and over the phone. "To pick up and start someplace new where no one knew us."

The phone calls were the first step—Rowan said he was there when Martinez called DiPonio, the fight promoter, to announce the car crash. She later called his mother. Rowan said it broke his heart to think of his mother picturing him dead, but he saw no other way. He could hear Martinez as she made the calls, and he said that first step of the hoax "almost killed me."

When Martinez called back two days later to say Rowan was dead, he said, he choked up and had to leave the room.

In Memory of Charlie

The mourners gathered at Martinez's home to remember Charles H. Rowan, father, son, friend, and cage fighter. The guests walked up a wooden ramp leading to the front door, past a sprinkling of cigarette butts that dotted the yard's patchy snow.

Inside the small living room, lined with brown carpet and wood-paneled walls, sat two young children, along with Rowan's mother, who was sobbing.

Martinez looked grief-stricken. She brushed off questions about funeral arrangements and other practical matters, making clear she was not yet ready.

As the group sat quietly in the living room, she stepped away to collect a bag that she said had been retrieved from the accident.

She pulled out a white baseball cap that was stained with blood. A young boy began to cry.

They mourned Rowan as a lost soul gone too soon. But he had not gone anywhere. Rowan was upstairs throughout the memorial, he said, hiding in a child's bedroom until the guests left. While his mother cried and his girlfriend accepted condolences, Rowan worked hard not to make a sound.

He said he thought about walking downstairs to interrupt the grieving, ending the ruse right there. But he decided not to.

From upstairs, he said, he could hear the sobs coming from the living room, sounds that took him by surprise. "For people to care about me," he said, "it meant something."

But now, he needed to play dead, which meant he needed to block all that out. He looked out the bedroom's small window, past the lawn and out toward the Rite Aid. He tried not to break his gaze.

Trapped

If this was the afterlife, Rowan didn't much care for it.

He spent most of the next six weeks hiding out in his girlfriend's home, watching TV and working out in a small makeshift gym. He said he closed his bank account and disabled his Facebook page. He made late-night trips to Rite Aid and even kept Martinez company for a meeting at her children's school. The couple said they were possibly moving to New Mexico, a school official later told the police.

"I went stir-crazy," Rowan said. "I couldn't call any of my friends; I couldn't go anywhere. I love Rosa more than life itself, but it's just too much to be around the same person all of the time."

Despite his efforts, the hoax began to fray. Skeptics took to Facebook, where they peppered the fight promoters with questions about death certificates and obituaries.

The promoters took offense. "I said: 'How dare you question this? The dude is dead! Have some respect,'" the promoter Joe Shaw said.

Rowan's family wanted to know what happened to his body. Scott Gardner, his stepfather, called local hospitals but didn't find anyone who could help. "We felt like we didn't have any facts," Gardner said. Sympathy cards began to arrive, some of them with checks included, but the family set them aside.

Rumors about Rowan were bound to reach the people he owed money, and by mid-March, they apparently had. While his loved ones still thought he was dead, he sneaked away to meet with Michael Gomez in Gladwin—the circumstances remain murky. Gomez and his lawyer did not respond to multiple requests for comment.

At the meeting, Gomez threatened to hurt Martinez and her kids, Rowan said.

The walls were closing in. But Charlie Rowan, still presumed dead, had one last idea.

An Opportunity to Strike

On a cold March afternoon, Roxie Robinette served lunch to her husband, Richard. The bell rang next door in their store, Guns and Stuff: a new customer.

Richard got up, leaving Roxie behind to fold laundry in front of the TV.

Guns and Stuff was a mom-and-pop shop that sold revolvers,

pistols, and shotguns, along with hunting jackets and Skittles. Mounted buck heads eyed customers from the wall. A sign read, NO PISSY ATTITUDES.

The gun store played the role a diner might in another town—the place where neighbors gossip about the weather and one another. All of Gladwin knew Richard Robinette, a retired plumber and banjo player who'd been in poor health. Even Rowan knew Robinette: he had recently sold Robinette a rifle he stole from a relative, Rowan said.

On the afternoon of March 18, the sheriff said, Michael Bowman drove Rowan and his girlfriend to the store in a maroon Chevrolet Blazer. Bowman was among Rowan's closest friends, a lanky, baby-faced man in his early twenties with a criminal history of his own. A lawyer for Martinez did not respond to multiple requests for interviews. Bowman's lawyer declined to comment.

Rowan sat in the backseat, wearing a trench coat and sneakers. He smeared black dollar-store makeup around his eyes and tied a red bandanna around his mouth. The finishing touch was a Batman mask he said he took from his girlfriend's son.

Rowan was going to rob Guns and Stuff—"hit a lick" was his term. His girlfriend would be the decoy.

The police said she walked into the store first, carrying an iPhone in her pocket that was on an open call to Rowan, waiting down the road. That way, he could listen in and find the right moment to strike.

After a few minutes, Rowan got out of the car and headed toward the neon OPEN sign. But on the way, he realized he had made a mistake: he forgot the weapon, a pink canister of pepper spray. He had left it in the car.

He was carrying a hammer from his toolbox—he was going to use it to break into the cases holding the guns. But now, the hammer would take on a starring role.

He pushed open the door and swung the hammer at Robinette's head, knocking him from his stool. Rowan later said he had been aiming for Robinette's shoulder and missed.

The blow opened up the side of Robinette's head, spilling a pool of blood. The sheriff's report called the wound a "jagged hole approximately the size of a quarter, which appeared to go through his skull." The bloodstain soaking the carpet was, a county detective wrote, the "size of a dinner plate."

Even Rowan was shaken. "There was a lot of blood," he said. "Enough to scare me. I'm a man used to seeing a lot of blood, but that was a lot of blood."

Rowan kicked his girlfriend in the arm, hoping to make her seem like a second victim. He shoved eight handguns into his red-and-black duffel bag and then, on his way out, noticed Robinette's wallet sticking out of his pocket. He grabbed that too, and tore off through the woods, toward a church parking lot where Bowman was waiting.

In the car, the two hardly spoke.

"I was in shock with what had just happened," Rowan said. "I thought I had just killed somebody."

Martinez kept to her part of the plan and called 911 from Guns and Stuff. Within minutes, Detective Sergeant James Cuddie and Officer Eric Killian were en route. They stopped 100 yards from the store, on the shoulder of the road, to put on bulletproof vests.

They approached on foot, and inside found Rowan's girlfriend cowered in the back. Robinette sat on a stool, holding the left side of his head. Cuddie asked him what happened, and he replied slowly, "I don't know, Jim."

Cuddie then turned to interview Martinez. She hadn't herself been in trouble before, but her social circle sometimes overlapped with Cuddie's investigations. Martinez told him she had been there to sell some of her family's guns when a masked robber burst through the door.

Meanwhile, Bowman later told the police, he and Rowan drove toward a vacant home where the mother of Rowan's girlfriend had recently lived.

Rowan stashed the robbery evidence around the house—two pistols in the dining room vent, the duffel bag behind the refriger-ator, the sneakers in the garage attic. He stuffed the Batman mask above the kitchen sink, still filled with dirty dishes and an empty bottle of Diet Pepsi Wild Cherry.

Rowan paced the house, waiting for news, waiting for his girl-friend. He smoked an entire pack of Newports.

Finally, Rowan called the phone his girlfriend had carried dur-ing the robbery. Cuddie answered and identified himself as Jim. He asked who was calling. Rowan, flustered, gave his cousin's name.

He could tell that Cuddie was suspicious. The life preserver had begun to feel like a noose.

Connecting the Pieces

With a thick mustache, his hair cut short, and a no-nonsense demeanor, James Cuddie would have a hard time passing as anything other than a cop. Not that he would try—everyone in Gladwin County knew him as Jim, the county detective, including many of the people he arrested. Sometimes, as Cuddie eased suspects into the back of his police car, they apologized to him by name.

It didn't take long for Cuddie and his colleagues to connect Rowan with the Guns and Stuff robbery. When officers dropped off Martinez, they saw his ID in her home.

Then Bowman visited the sheriff's office and said that Rowan might have been involved in the robbery. That was also a roundabout way of saying that Rowan might not be quite as dead as people had thought.

For weeks, Cuddie had heard rumors about Rowan's death, but he didn't think much about them one way or the other. "I didn't know it to be true or untrue," he said. "At that point it wasn't an issue. I'm working on other cases."

But now, with Richard Robinette in intensive care, Cuddie's interest was piqued.

It should have been the most straightforward of questions: is Charlie Rowan dead or alive? But it had become bizarrely muddled.

The day after the robbery, Cuddie called the Saginaw County medical examiner's office, which housed records for the county's deceased. Officials there confirmed that there was no death certificate for Charles Howard Rowan. The medical examiner declared it "unlikely" that Rowan had died.

That was enough for Cuddie to surmise that Rowan was out there on the run. "Rowan and Martinez were people of interest that needed to be located," he wrote in his report.

On March 19, the sheriff's office released Rowan's mug shot to the local news media.

"I Know That Guy!"

Big John Yeubanks, a fight promoter, was smoking a cigarette in his home office, half-listening to the TV news. The story of the day was a robbery of Guns and Stuff.

The suspect's mug shot flashed across the screen, and Yeubanks snapped to attention.

There was no mistaking it, yet it could not be.

"I know that guy!" he shouted. "He's not supposed to be alive!"

Yeubanks called the sheriff to say there must have been a mistake—they were looking for a dead man.

Word quickly spread through the cage fighting world. DiPonio's girlfriend pulled up the mug shot on her phone. Goatee, square jaw, pursed lips—it was Charlie Rowan.

"She showed it to me," DiPonio said, "and I nearly threw up right there."

At the Gladwin County Sheriff's Office, the phone had been ringing steadily since the mug shots were released. The officers kept hearing the same strange thing: the suspect, Charlie Rowan, was already dead.

Weeks later, sitting in his cluttered basement office, Cuddie laughed at the deluge of calls. He described the one he received from DiPonio, so sure that Rowan was dead.

"I told him that I had reason to believe," Cuddie said, "that Mr. Rowan was very much alive."

Voice from the Beyond

Rowan's vision of starting a new life, in New Mexico or anywhere else, was turning to dust.

He and his girlfriend were hiding out from the local police, from federal agents working the case, from the people Rowan owed money, and from the fight promoters he tricked.

The Guns and Stuff robbery and the manhunt had put the town on edge. Rowan's mother, still grieving for her son, was at the Chappel Dam Grocery when she heard about the attack. "I thought, *At least I know my son didn't do it,*" she said.

Her relief wouldn't last long. Soon, her phone rang. It was her son, Charlie, no longer dead.

For six weeks, she thought she'd lost him, at age 25. She never said good-bye. Now, here he was, on the phone. He had one question for her: could she give him a ride?

His mother drove in a fog, past the familiar barns, churches, and homes that lined the road. Finally, on the right, she saw her son, waving his arms to flag her down.

Still confused, she asked where he'd been for so long. This was all a lie? They both started crying. Rowan mumbled something about being "out of state." He got out of the car at his girlfriend's home, the same place his mother had cried during his memorial the month before.

His mother went to the sheriff's office in tears the next day to tell Cuddie that her son was indeed alive. She said she was afraid he'd robbed Guns and Stuff and hit old man Robinette.

That night, Rowan said, he went to Saginaw, where he gave Gomez six of the stolen guns to pay down his debt, worth $1,000 per handgun. Gomez later told the authorities that he bought only one pistol from Rowan, according to a police report. Gomez was arrested soon after on charges of possessing weapons as a felon.

Rowan and his girlfriend were still hiding out. They booked a room at the Knights Inn in Saginaw, where a bed cost $50. "I was on edge all night, me and Rosa," Rowan said. "I knew I was fighting a losing battle."

Betrayal and Regret

They stayed on the run for about 48 hours, moving from one spot to another. The scrambling didn't throw off Cuddie and his colleagues.

On March 20, two days after the robbery, they tracked Rowan and his girlfriend to a friend's apartment in Unionville. The couple were arrested about 7:15 A.M.

It was all over—and Cuddie had a definitive answer. Charlie Rowan was not dead. But he would be going away for a long, long time.

He told Cuddie that he didn't mean for it to happen this way.

He walked the officers through the robbery and told them where they could find the guns, the Batman mask, the stolen wallet.

The news was out. A front-page headline in the *Traverse City Record-Eagle* read, "Fighter Accused of Faking Death."

The cage fighters felt betrayed, furious that Rowan had sullied their sport's name.

"He's lucky the cops got him before the fighters did," Big John Yeubanks, the promoter, said. Organizers of the Fight for Charlie recently filed a police report in Traverse City accusing Rowan of fraud.

After the hoax was exposed, the cage fighting promoters decided to hold another benefit, this time to raise money for the Robinettes, the owners of Guns and Stuff. They have collected more than $15,000.

"We got sick of hearing about Charles Rowan and we thought, *What about the Robinettes?*" Yeubanks said. "Everybody was looking at this guy like he was an MMA fighter from Michigan, but in fact he was a small-time tough guy who got in a cage a couple of times."

Today, Richard Robinette is back home after a recovery that's surprised even his family and his doctors. He started playing his banjo again. He recently fixed the bathroom sink.

He doesn't remember much of the robbery, but he showed off a horseshoe of stitches on the left side of his head.

"You can't sit and cry about it," he said. "They thought I was going to die."

A few miles away, Rowan sits inside another cage, in the Gladwin County Jail. He pleaded guilty last month to armed robbery. He'll be sentenced in October.

In jail, Rowan wrote letters to his mother, trying to atone. "I did not mean to hurt that man and his family," one letter read. "I hope to see you at my visit."

Rowan's mother usually goes to see him once a week. On a recent afternoon, the two put their hands against the clear divider that separated them.

"I'm sorry you did this too," his mother said. Rowan, wearing an orange jumpsuit, told her he figured he'd be locked up for the rest of her life.

He reads mysteries in jail. During his first few weeks behind bars, he tried to catch glimpses of his girlfriend, who was being held nearby. She recently pleaded guilty to armed robbery charges.

He goes over the whole strange story, step by step. He finds himself returning to the fake memorial, and the sounds of people sobbing for him.

"I didn't realize how I impacted other people's lives," he said. "I don't hold myself in high regard. I'm not a good person, I'm not a good dad, and most of the time I'm not a good son."

He thinks about his girlfriend, Rosa, and wonders whether they'll ever be together again.

"It's like . . ." He struggled to get the words out. "It's like we just died."

JAY CASPIAN KANG

The End and Don King

FROM GRANTLAND.COM

IN THE BACK ROOM of Manhattan's Carnegie Deli, Don King picked at a pastrami sandwich with his fingers. He had just been asked a question about his electric hair and, for the first time in a day filled with radio and television interviews, King paused before he spoke. A cautious look crept over his graying eyes. As he silently deliberated between several well-worn origin myths about the height of that hair, King tweezed a scrap of pastrami between two well-manicured fingernails and dragged the meat through a puddle of deli mustard. "My hair is God's aura," King explained while chewing. "Everything went up when I got home from the penitentiary. One night I went to lie down next to my wife and my hair started popping and uncurling all on its own—ping, ping, ping, ping! I knew that it was God telling me to stay on the righteous path so he could one day pull me up to be there with him."

King smiled, but not the smile you remember. That smile—the screwed-on mask of boundless optimism—had been on full display throughout this week of promotions, but at the Carnegie, King had finally succumbed to exhaustion. "When I'm doing good, the hair goes straight up," King said, a bit wearily. "Now that things are difficult, the hair has gotten a little flatter."

I had been trailing Don King for two weeks between Boca Raton, Florida, and now New York City. This was the closest he had come to admitting that things just weren't what they used to be. In three days' time, Tavoris "Thunder" Cloud, King's last fighter of any consequence, would step into the ring against Bernard

Hopkins at the Barclays Center in Brooklyn. The story of the fight should have been about the 48-year-old Hopkins and his quest to become the oldest champion in boxing history. But because Don King was involved, the focus during fight week had been on Don King and his uncertain future. If Cloud lost to Hopkins—especially in a boring way—his short career as an opponent in televised events would be put in serious jeopardy and King would have very little left to promote. In a prefight interview, Hopkins, who, like so many other fighters, had worked with King before an inevitable falling-out, had this to say about his old promoter: "What a way to put the last nail in the coffin. Who thought it would be me that would shut him down?"

At the Carnegie, nobody was talking much about Tavoris Cloud or Bernard Hopkins or the impending end of Don King Promotions. King had come to one of his favorite New York landmarks to enjoy a quiet lunch with three longtime employees. They talked, mostly, about music and old times in Manhattan, the city where King lived and worked during the majority of his reign at the top of boxing. The conversation eventually turned to James Brown. Don King, still digging his fingers into his sandwich, muttered, "James Brown died owing me $50,000. But I loved James Brown."

Don King no longer sits on boxing's throne, but he has nostalgia by the balls. Fights are best enjoyed through old film, which means that if you want to watch Muhammad Ali or Larry Holmes or Mike Tyson or Julio Cesar Chavez or Evander Holyfield raise his arms in triumph at the end of a fight, you're also going to see the big man with the bigger hair climbing in through the ropes. You see him in the Philippines in 1975, hovering over a near-death Muhammad Ali after the Thrilla in Manila. You see him in Japan, 15 years later, looking more or less like the same man, crowding in on a battered and finally defeated Mike Tyson. He has negotiated deals with Mobutu Sese Seko and counted Hugo Chavez as a personal friend. Nobody alive, save some presidents, has taken more photos with world leaders and celebrities. As a boxing fan growing up in the '80s and early '90s, I cannot remember a single fight that didn't end with Don King in the ring, cigar clamped between his teeth. He is one of those big American men who distort our collective memory—I'm sure King's rival Bob Arum promoted some of the fights I watched as a kid, but when I think of the final bell, I still see the menacing hulk of Don King smiling for the cameras.

So it's a little sad to sit across from Don King at the Carnegie Deli and see the tourists line up at our table to take a photo with him, and to overhear them talk about the man in the past tense as if he were already dead. Not because Don King deserves our sympathy, but because it's always jarring to see a once-robust American institution fall into disrepair and decay. The cuffs on King's "Only in America" denim jacket—the same coat he wore to the Thrilla in Manila—are badly frayed. He sometimes stumbles over his words. There's a distinct sag in his once-static face. Don King never thought he would live past 50. He is 81 years old now and has been in the public's eye since the early '70s.

Don King was born in Cleveland in 1931 and grew up in the city's numbers racket, a lottery-style game that King describes as "hope for people who don't have hope." As a kid he wanted to be Clarence Darrow, and set himself up to study law at Kent State University. The summer before he was to matriculate, King's older brother Connie recruited him to "take numbers," whereby the younger King would walk around Cleveland's black neighborhoods and record $1 lottery-style bets. Players would submit a three-digit number to King, who was somehow able to keep track of everything in his head. At the end of the business day, if a player's number matched up with the middle three digits in a predetermined market quote, he or she would win somewhere around $600. King's phenomenal memory and his talent for talking made him a natural at the numbers game, and before too long he started his own production.

Despite his involvement in the mob-controlled rackets, King managed to mostly avoid legal problems during his youth. But on December 2, 1954, King shot and killed Hillary Brown after Brown and two associates tried to rob one of King's gambling houses in Cleveland. The judge in the case decided that King had acted in self-defense and declared the act a justifiable homicide. King was released and continued running numbers.

Over the next 12 years, King continued to grow his empire and took over ownership of several businesses in Cleveland, including the Corner Tavern, a music joint that has since been enshrined into the Rock and Roll Hall of Fame and Museum. The law eventually caught up to him again. On April 20, 1966, King stomped a former employee named Sam Garrett to death over a $600 debt. In a trial overrun with witness tampering and bizarre judicial motions, King was eventually convicted on a reduced first-degree manslaughter charge. "When they sentenced me," King told me, "they said it was a probationary shock. Like I would go in and come out quickly and they hoped that the experience of the penitentiary would *shock* me into going straight. Turns out they kept me in there for four years."

King says he divides his life into two categories—Before the Penitentiary and After the Penitentiary. There is no doubt that his time in prison expanded King's ambitions. He read voraciously, and by the time he got out he had built up the lexicon of quotations and malapropisms that would turn him into one of the great talkers of his time.

Within a year of his release, Don King was putting together his first fight. With the help of Lloyd "Mr. Personality" Price, a close musician friend of King's from the Corner Tavern, King convinced Muhammad Ali to come to Cleveland to put on a boxing exhibition to help save a black hospital from going under. As part of the night's festivities, King put on a concert featuring Marvin Gaye, Lou Rawls, and Wilson Pickett. The Don King template for big-time promotions was set—a superstar boxer, some vague social mission, and a whole lot of great music. He also found his cash cow in Ali, and although Ali's camp never fully trusted Don King, the champ was impressed by the new promoter's grand visions. In 1973, King attended the George Foreman–Joe Frazier title bout in Kingston, Jamaica. King, as his own legend goes, rode to the fight in Frazier's limousine, and after Frazier got knocked out in the second round, King jumped into the ring, hugged Foreman, and left Jamaica with the new champ. By 1974, King's ambition and hustle produced the Rumble in the Jungle, arguably the greatest sporting event of the 20th century. Everything else—the notoriety, the Thrilla in Manila, the hundreds of millions of dollars, the multiple investigations by Interpol and the FBI and CIA, the dozens of lawsuits, Larry Holmes, Mike Tyson, Julio Cesar Chavez, Tito Trinidad—came as a direct result of King pulling off the impossible in Zaire. An ex-con numbers runner, three years removed from the penitentiary, somehow brokered deals with Mobutu Sese Seko, Muhammad Ali, George Foreman, James Brown, the country of Liberia, Barclays Bank of London,

and several other operations that could have killed a fight that
was perpetually in danger of being canceled or moved back to the
United States.

But none of that—the killings, the jail time, the extraordinary
hustle—matters much when it comes to Don King's legacy. In the
eyes of the public, Don King is a monster because he stole from
his fighters. After Muhammad Ali's brutal loss to Larry Holmes
on October 2, 1980, King shortchanged Ali about $1.2 million of
an $8 million guaranteed payout. While Ali was laid up in Los An-
geles, his career finally dead and buried, King coerced Jeremiah
Shabazz, one of Ali's trusted associates, to bring the champ a suitcase filled with $50,000 and a contract that not only released the
right to pursue any further punitive damages, but also gave King
the option to promote any of Ali's future fights. Ali, wearied and
confused, signed the contract and took the briefcase. King repeated this process with nearly every fighter he worked with in the
'70s and throughout the '80s. In doing so, he violated Mike Tyson,
Larry Holmes, Evander Holyfield, and a long list of other fighters
who came up, like King, from impoverished backgrounds to claim
glory found "Only in America!"

King speaks of himself as a transformative figure, someone who
through sheer intellect, hard work, and determination overcame
racism, both overt and institutional, and brought millions of dollars and international adulation to the young black men he promoted. All of this is undeniably true. But Don King's PR problem
is that we don't see him as a civil rights pioneer. We see him as a
gangster—and as a gangster, he must adhere to the strict ethics of
a gangster movie. He stole, without a hint of mercy or contrition,
from his own people.

There is no forgiveness for the hypocritical gangster.

> It is not the critic who counts: not the man who points out how the
> strong man stumbles or where the doer of deeds could have done
> better. The credit belongs to the man who is actually in the arena,
> whose face is marred by dust and sweat and blood, who strives
> valiantly, who errs and comes up short again and again, because
> there is no effort without error or shortcoming, but who knows
> the great enthusiasms, the great devotions, who spends himself for
> a worthy cause; who, at the best, knows, in the end, the triumph
> of high achievement, and who, at the worst, if he fails at least he

fails while daring greatly, so that his place shall never be with
those cold and timid souls who knew neither victory nor defeat.
—Theodore Roosevelt

As King recited the quote above, he slapped excitedly at my wrist.
Certain words deserved a certain emphasis, and Don King delivered them by slapping me a little harder. "Valiantly" was one of
those words. So were "worthy," "greatly," and, of course, "victory."
We were standing in the museumlike hallways of Don King Productions in Florida. The Roosevelt quote, printed out in neat, uniform
calligraphy, hung directly underneath a letter from Jimmy Carter
and the 1980 Democratic National Convention that thanked Don
King for his work as "the cornerstone of the Mideast Treaty between
Egypt and Israel." After King finished his recitation, he looked
down at me, his face lifting up into one hellish grin, and said, "You
and I are colored people and therefore we operate at a psychic
handicap. White people, institutionally, have made us believe that
we cannot achieve what we, in our hearts, know we can achieve."

I shrugged and tried to suppress a smile. King caught me slip-
ping and squawked with laughter.

"But real life, boy, is stranger than fiction," he yelled. "Who
could ever dream up a life like mine? I still can't believe it! I wake
up every morning and I'm shocked that I'm alive."

Don King Productions moved from the Upper East Side of Manhattan down to South Florida in the late '80s. Today, King works
out of a two-story office building in Deerfield Beach. Out the back,
you'll find a low-slung stretch of I-95 and a slow line of Buicks
heading up to Boca Raton. Out the front, it's pure Florida office
park—smelly tropical trees, overgrown lawns, all of which cast an
eerie, green glow on Don King's two-tone blue-and-stainless-steel
Rolls-Royce Phantom. Like all tropical places, Don King Productions is in a state of decay—the carpets have picked up the mold
that can only be kept out with the greatest vigilance in South Florida. The plants droop. Throughout the late '90s and early aughts,
when King promoted Felix Trinidad, Bernard Hopkins, Roy Jones
Jr., Hasim Rahman, and a host of other big-name fighters, somewhere around 50 employees worked at DKP. Today, no more than
10 of King's longtime advisers and employees remain.

We moved on down a hallway filled with framed photographs.

"That's the former president of Pepsi," King reported, pointing at a black-and-white photo of himself with four people in businesswear. "We did the biggest endorsement deal in the history of America together." The next photo was of the Jackson Five. "That's from the *Victory* tour," King explained, referring to the 1984 worldwide showcase that brought in a reported $75 million. "We set the record for the most money ever made on a tour." King then pointed at the image at the end of the hallway and smirked. "And that's Mobutu Sese Seko."

Don King's office takes up two large rooms on the second floor. Memorabilia has been crowded onto every available surface—in one corner, you'll find a LeRoy Neiman painting collection. In another, you'll find a truly unusual number of swords from every culture around the world. At a desk littered with bags of candy and gum-ball dispensers, Don King took phone calls and signed contracts for an upcoming fight he wanted to put on in Germany. During pauses in his work, he talked to me about what should have been a variety of different subjects. But when you're talking to Don King, all discussions quickly funnel back down to what he calls "the color barrier." Our talks almost always returned to the history of racism, and it struck me as strange that a man whose work ethic and unfailing optimism placed him so squarely in the present seemed to only be concerned with the past.

He rambled on about Frederick Douglass and Adolf Hitler and Martin Luther King Jr. and Simon Wiesenthal and Porfirio Diaz and Shimon Peres. All these anecdotes and references seemed strangely rehearsed—propelled by a meandering yet insistent boredom. Like many men in their eighties, King seemed to be talking mostly because he could not believe the young man sitting across the desk was so dumb. By way of example, during our first interview, King lectured for 10 straight minutes about Joseph Goebbels and Nazi propaganda. By the time it was over, I had already forgotten the question that launched this particular history lesson. Upon review, I had asked him something about Beyoncé, Jay-Z, and the new Barclays Center.

Over the course of the next two weeks, I heard King talk about Goebbels and Willie Lynch and the Declaration of Independence and Thomas Jefferson and W.E.B. Du Bois and Frederick Douglass and dozens of other historical people, events, and phrases. When I read books and articles about King, some written as far back as 20 years ago, I'd find those same phrases, almost verbatim. In the past, several boxing writers would make fun of King for mispronouncing the names of prominent philosophers or misquoting famous passages in their work. Having spent enough time with him to watch the repetition of these mistakes (my favorite example: "Beware the Ids of March, young man! Beware the Ids of March!"), it's ludicrous to believe that Don King's famous malapropisms are unintentional.

For Don King, everything is strategy and payback. And if someone thinks King is a buffoon because he mispronounces "Nietzsche," the real buffoon will pay at the negotiating table. King might mispronounce "Sun Tzu" and misquote him, but he sure as hell understands *The Art of War* better than anyone who might point out his mistakes.

"There's nothing I love more in life than turning around a bigot," King told me repeatedly. I took him at his word on this statement, not because I thought Don King relished the opportunity to teach people about the history of Willie Lynch or Joseph Goebbels, but because I believed that he takes outsize pleasure in outsmarting someone who has underestimated him because of who he used to be—a black numbers runner from the streets of Cleveland. King told me that when he arrived in New York in the mid-'70s, he made sure everyone in town knew that he was an excon. "They'll always underestimate you for who you are," he said, "and then they'll try to use all that against you. So you've got to use that to your benefit, because they're never going to change."

This strategic intelligence extends to every part of King's life. He does not answer questions as much as he circles and hypnotizes them to the point of exhaustion, but in our later interactions, he could quote back, verbatim, questions I had asked him several days before. He could recall the specific numbers that people in his old neighborhood in Cleveland would play back in the 1950s. He could recite almost any line of any contract that he had ever signed. When Norman Mailer wrote about meeting King in Zaire, he portrayed King as a self-proclaimed genius who sprayed every negotiable issue with a cloud of fast-talking bullshit. In his account of the Rumble in the Jungle, Mailer wrote, "It would be hard to argue that King was not a genius." This is undeniably true. Don King, even at 81, possesses the sort of bullying intellect that lets you know, almost immediately, that you will never, *ever* outsmart him.

*

Four days before Cloud vs. Hopkins, King arrived at the Barclays
Center for the last press conference. He had been in Panama the
night before, setting up the details of a fight he wanted to hold
in Russia in the upcoming months. His flight into New York had
arrived at four in the morning. When he saw me in the open-air
concourse in front of Barclays, King yelled, "Jay, baby! I want you
to listen up because I was so saddened to hear about the death
of my dear friend, *mi hermano* Hugo Chavez last night. I first met
Chavez when he was a lieutenant in the Venezuelan army in 1971.
He was my security when we opened the Poliedro de Caracas!"*

Once inside, King held court with the 20 or so reporters who
had shown up. He talked to anyone who would listen about Chavez
and all the medical care he gave to the poor mountain people
of Venezuela. A vaguely European reporter shoved a camera in
King's face and asked, "Is your story possible in any other country?" King took the bait and bellowed, "Only in America!"

It had been a while since anyone had seen Don King at one of
these things, especially in a city like New York. Before Cloud, King's
last notable fighter was Devon Alexander, whose last two fights with
Don King Productions had been held at the Silverdome in Pontiac,
Michigan, and at the Family Arena in St. Charles, Missouri. Onstage
in front of an audience of about 50, King sang the praises of New
York City—"The city so great, they named it twice!"—and talked
about the importance of promoting the spirit of the people, but he
did not talk very much about Tavoris Cloud. Earlier in the week, I
talked to Cloud at Gleason's Gym in Brooklyn. When he realized
that all my questions were going to be about Don King, Cloud
threw his head back and chuckled sarcastically. He then gave one
minute of boilerplate about Don King's greatest hits. When asked
if he felt any pressure for being Don King's last hope, Cloud said,
"Nobody's going to ever stop Don King from promoting, man."

At the press conference at Barclays, Cloud spoke softly but
firmly about his confidence heading into the fight. Like so many
other fighters, Cloud carries himself with an almost genteel modesty. He does not crave any spotlight. It's not even clear whether
he enjoys boxing, or simply sees it as a way to support his growing family. As Cloud spoke unsteadily into the microphone, King

---

* The Poliedro de Caracas was actually opened in 1974 with a fight between
George Foreman and Ken Norton.

punctuated the end of each sentence with a "Yes!" or a "That's right!" or a "Thunder and Lightning Cloud!" Earlier, King had rambled on about Tito Trinidad's post-9/11 fight against Bernard Hopkins and how Tito had not really been in the proper state of mind when he entered the ring. He then talked about a possible rematch between Trinidad, who is 40, and Oscar De La Hoya. It was unclear if King was talking about the past or if he was proposing Trinidad–De La Hoya II for the immediate future, but if you want to know how far Don King has fallen, consider that in his first meaningful press conference in years, he talked, mostly, about the "Fight of the [Last] Millennium."

The assembled press mostly chuckled at King's outbursts and asked him questions about the past. But there was a hard edge to their laughter. In the past, these same journalists would have either cowered or steeled their nerves for a confrontation over a question that Don King didn't want to answer. The menace and the power have left Don King—to most people these days, he's little more than a rap sheet and a haircut. Old American icons should never play their younger selves in public. When the aura fades, the seams start to show. And Don King, with his bombast, his circuitous way of talking, and his faded set of affectations, is nothing but seams.

> Most people will look at the black and believe that he is what they say he is—lazy, lethargic, can't rise to the occasion, all lies, cheat and steal, shiftless, worthless, no good, no account, he's a heathen and a savage.
> Martin Luther King Jr. said, "No lie can live forever."
> I'm a promoter of the people, by the people, and for the people, and my magic lies in my people ties.
> Yesterday's nobody becomes today's somebody.
> You must be able to deal with what is real.
> How long? Not long!
> They blamed me for the Lindbergh kidnapping, World War II, the invasion of Poland, they made me the villain and tried to tarnish my reputation.
> I'm a promoter of peace, unanimity and zeal, constricting negativism to its narrowest form and working for the betterment of mankind.

When asked a direct question, especially one about money, Don King hems dozens of these phrases together into a dazzling yet utterly meaningless tapestry of pretty much everything that has ever happened in the history of the world. By the time he's done quoting Saint Thomas Aquinas and Frederick Douglass and William Cullen Bryant, you're so confused and exhausted that you're willing to accept any statement that's not tied to a historic event or quotation. It's a performance worthy of a Borges story—Don King is one of those rare orators who understands the inverse value of words, whereby the most momentous phrases, especially those that have been stamped by history, can stand in for straight bullshit. There was always a bullying element to King's plundering of history. In the past, as long as King talked about matters of political importance at a loud volume—especially those that make white people uncomfortable—nobody would cut him off and redirect him to the matter at hand. At the height of his considerable powers in the '80s and '90s, King used these types of historic words to help convince young black fighters to sign with the only black promoter in the game. Now, they're mostly used as a diversionary tactic, a way to duck questions about Ali, the briefcase, and Mike Tyson's expense accounts.

It's almost as if the man dislikes the act of giving a straight answer so much that he's figured out a way to play a puzzle game that would make Baudrillard swoon. There's a library of puffed-up phrases stored inside Don King's head and if you take Quotation 1.4 and match it with Historic Event B7 and then transition over to Quotation 2.17, you'll get something like Don King's explanation for why he wants to put an upcoming second-tier fight in Russia.

> I have a special affinity for the Russian people for their resilience. In World War II they stood up and fought and endured the inclement weather, and that was a big part of their victory against the Nazis in Stalingrad and Moscow, and that's something I love about our people, how they resist the oppression and no matter what they say or do they fight and stand up for what they believe in—liberty and freedom and justice and equality—and even if the goal is not fulfilled, you'll find me there with the downtrodden and the underprivileged. Every country I go to I do the same thing. I'm a promoter of the people, for the people, and by the people. My magic lies in my people ties.

This is maddening, I know. But if you listen to King long enough, you'll start to trace out patterns that hint at an underlying system of beliefs. Now, it's possible that the symmetries are illusions and nobody will ever know, possibly not even Don King himself, just how much he believes in his own stated politics. But it goes something like this: Over the course of Don King's 81 years, the problem of what W.E.B. Du Bois called "the color line" has gone underground. What used to be a simple proposition—an oppressed people fighting against their oppressors—has gone institutional. Black people, according to King, still live their lives at a distinct handicap, and whenever they try to accomplish anything the white men will discredit them and try to destroy them. King, of course, uses his own life as the great example of this and argues that before his time, boxing was controlled by mobsters like Frankie Carbo and Blinky Palermo, who fixed bouts and stole much more from fighters than Don King ever did. He points out that his longtime rival Bob Arum has been sued by fighters and managers and pretty much everyone else who came in contact with him.

Today, Don King stands in for every shady backroom deal, every shortchanged interaction, and every time a greedy promoter pushes a shot fighter into the ring to get pummeled to death. In the business of boxing, everyone is a hypocrite and a liar, but in the eyes of the public, Don King is the only hypocrite and the only liar.

Notorious men make for bad relics. Don King was vilified throughout his three decades on top, but like all self-made men, his power stood in as its own rebuttal. You didn't need to wonder if a black man could rise to the top of boxing, because Don King was there. But now that the avenues of influence built up over a career have been shut down, Don King has started thinking about what it all might have meant. In his office, he began talking about the "evening of his career" and how he wanted to help poor white people understand that the black man was not the enemy. After he finished his usual 10-minute response, I asked him a follow-up question: "Don, now that you're in your last act—"

"Last act?" he bellowed. "I said evening, not last act!" He turned to one of his advisers, who had come into the room carrying an armload of paperwork. "This motherfucker's trying to bury me," King said, incredulously, "and I ain't even close to be done yet!"

If King wants to reflect on the past during this, the evening of his career, he only has to look around his offices at Don King Productions, where he has surrounded himself not only with memorabilia, but also with the same people who helped him rise to the top. Dana Jamison, King's vice president of operations, has worked with King for 27 years. His personal photographer has been around for two decades. Of all the people I met associated with Don King, only Tavoris Cloud was under the age of 40. King's productions feel even older and more out-of-date. While waiting for him to show up back at the headquarters of Don King Productions, I squeezed into a long-since-abandoned cubicle, careful not to disturb an ancient Brother typewriter and a stack of press releases and legal documents from the late '90s. In the lobby, there was an old movie theater popcorn machine stamped with Don King's emblem. One of his employees told me that in the '90s, that machine had pumped the smell of fresh popcorn into the vents of the building. He couldn't remember the last time it had been turned on. Out back in a warehouse behind the offices, more than 20,000 square feet of King's possessions—mostly ornate furniture and towering bronze statues of lions—gathered dust along with seven of King's cars. Earlier this month, Jessica Lussenhop of the *Riverfront Times* published an excellent article about King's ongoing legal battle with St. Louis boxer Ryan Coyne, a conflict that started in November 2012. If you go to donking.com today, you will find a story titled "Undefeated National Champion Boxer Ryan Coyne Meets Cardinals Three-Time MVP Albert Pujols."

But nothing about Don King feels older than those interchangeable phrases, quotations, and exclamations that make up his public persona. His is a civil rights gospel straight out of 1974—everything King talks about when it comes to race in this country has since been co-opted and turned inert. (I wouldn't be surprised if it turned out that the phrase "playing the race card" was coined by someone who wanted to figure out a way to shut up Don King.) It's a commonly held belief among boxing people that King ran boxing with the same exact ruthless street ethic that carried him to the top of Cleveland's numbers game, and that he is categorically incapable of change. This might very well be true. But that's not why every conversation with Don King inevitably circles back to Martin Luther King Jr., Frederick Douglass, and W.E.B. Du Bois. King talks about those great men because he believes himself to be in their company as a pioneer for his people.

In an otherwise scathing book about King's career in boxing titled *The Life and Crimes of Don King,* investigative reporter Jack Newfield wrote,

The great tragedy is that if Don King had gone straight after [the Rumble in the Jungle], he could have become one of the great black role models in contemporary history. He could have been the black Horatio Alger hero. King could have become a universal inspiration, a black man given a second chance, who rose from prison to the pinnacle of entrepreneurship by hard work, desperado bravado, grand ambition, evangelical salesmanship and by the mean standards of boxing — merit.

I asked King on several occasions if he saw himself as a civil rights hero. It took five tries, but he finally gave me something of a straight answer. We were riding in a limo down Second Avenue in Manhattan. King had just accompanied Tavoris Cloud for an appearance on *Good Day New York*. In the green room of the Fox studios in the Upper East Side, King ran into the actor Terrence Howard. "They should create an Oscar category for black actors who play Uncle Toms," King said to Howard. "And the award should be given to Samuel L. Jackson for his role in *Django Unchained*." Once Cloud and King got on the air, the show's host asked King about his relationship with Mike Tyson. King gave his standard answer to all questions about Tyson and claimed that Tyson loved King and said those horrible things only because he had been conditioned to believe that the only way a black man could get attention in America was to denigrate another black man. King then started yelling about Roger Ailes, the head of Fox News, and ended the interview by waving a miniature Venezuelan flag and yelling some more about Hugo Chavez. The segment did little to promote Cloud or the fight, but the rare spotlight had put King in a good mood. He talked to me about his life in Florida, a place he calls "God's waiting room," and reiterated that he would retire only when he was dead. I wondered aloud whether King saw himself as a transformative figure, if he believed that his accomplishments could serve as inspiration for the breaking down of his despised color barrier. "They'll never give me the credit for what I accomplished!" King shouted. "Who else came out of poverty and desperation and got to where I got? Who else brought millions of dollars to young kids who didn't have nothing? Who has lived a life like mine? And still, they demonize me!

"Sheeeeeeeit," King spat. "They'll *never* acknowledge me!" He reminded me of something he had told me in his offices back in Florida about the prospects for minorities, including myself, to really get their due respect in America: "If you poor, you a poor n——, if you rich, you a rich n——, if you dancing, sliding, and gliding n——, you a dancing, sliding, and gliding n——. If you have intellect, you're an intelligent n——. But you're going to be a n—— till you die."

Then, with all the brass in his body, King bellowed, "They'll shut you out, man, they'll shut you out. I can't get eye water to cry with."

In the locker room before the fight at Barclays, a subdued Don King sat next to Thomas Hauser, a former lawyer and longtime boxing writer. In 1992, Hauser and Joseph Maffia, the former chief financial officer of Don King Productions, put together a series of affidavits that ultimately led to King's indictment on nine counts of wire fraud. Early on in the investigation, a lawyer from a Senate subcommittee investigating corruption in boxing came to interview Maffia and asked him if Don King was tied to organized crime. Hauser, who was in the room as Maffia's legal adviser, told the lawyer, "You don't understand. Don King *is* organized crime."

But all that seemed in the past. King sat in a chair near the locker-room door, an iPod Touch cradled in his massive hand. He took Hauser through four decades of photographs and gave long, rambling captions for each one. He told stories about Christie Brinkley, Henry Kissinger, Ali, Martin Scorsese, Michael Jackson, and Jacques Chirac. As the two old men, awash in nostalgia, stared down at those tiny, digital images, Cloud went through his prefight preparation. Once Cloud's hands were taped up and gloved, he sat down in a corner and tried to have a quiet moment to himself. King was talking to Hauser about Shimon Peres and Israel and Cloud yelled out, "Don, you giving *interviews* now?" King grinned and waved him off. King then talked about his plans to take a victorious Cloud to fight in North Korea. "It'll be my show this time," King said while waving the flags of North and South Korea. "A real event for the people!"

On a TV in the locker room, the last round of the last undercard fight came to an end. Cloud hopped up and down and slapped his gloves together. His trainer and his childhood boxing coach both shouted their encouragement. The excitement in the room finally drew King out of his melancholy mood. He pointed at Cloud and yelled, "We gonna keep going where we gonna go and that man there is gonna strike a blow to free us all!"

*

Cloud lost. In the ring after the fight, Bernard Hopkins screamed something at Don King that nobody in his camp would repeat. In his postfight press conference, Hopkins said, "Who would ever think in anybody's wildest dream? I wouldn't even bet on it! That Bernard Hopkins would be the one that put Don King out of business. I did Richard [Schaefer] a favor, I did HBO a favor, I even did Bob Arum a favor. I did everybody a favor. Don King, whether you like him or not, is no more."

King did not attend the press conference. He was back in the locker room with Cloud and the remaining employees of Don King Productions. There was still the matter of paying out everyone who had worked on the fight, including the fighter himself. King sat slouched in a folding chair. Dana Jamison, his longtime assistant, knelt on the floor in front of a calculator and a giant three-ring binder. This was Don King's checkbook. Someone in the room told me that King had been shaken by Hopkins's outburst in the ring. When he saw me enter the locker room, King raised his head and gave a weak smile. Cloud, who was undefeated going into the fight, didn't seem to be too upset. After about five minutes of quiet payouts, King ordered everyone out into the hallway. It was time for him and Cloud to negotiate a payment.

After about an hour, King and Cloud emerged from the locker room. I asked King what he had planned next. King said, "This is a setback. You get back up, you dust yourself off, and you get back in the game. We had a great singer named Ray Charles who wrote a song called 'Drowning in My Tears.' You can't afford to drown in your tears. You gotta go back, rededicate yourself, redouble your efforts, and persevere."

In our prior conversations, King had talked frequently about setbacks. Every time he said the word "setback," he would immediately follow it with this phrase: "I have completely eradicated the word 'failure' from my vocabulary." This time, he did not.

IAN FRAZIER

The Last Days of Stealhead Joe

FROM OUTSIDE

THE POLICE REPORT listed the name of the deceased as Joseph
Adam Randolph and his age as 48. It did not mention the name
he had given himself, Stealhead Joe. The address on his driver's license led police to his former residence in Sisters, Oregon, where
the landlord said that Randolph had moved out over a year ago
and had worked as a fishing guide. In fact, Randolph was one of
the most skilled guides on the nearby Deschutes River, and certainly the most colorful—even unforgettable—in the minds of
anglers who had fished with him. He had specialized in catching
sea-run fish called steelhead and was so devoted to the sport that
he had a large steelhead fly with two drops of blood at the hook
point tattooed on the inside of his right forearm. The misspelling
of his self-bestowed moniker was intentional. If he didn't actually
steal fish, he came close, and he wanted people to hear echoes of
the trickster and the outlaw in his name.

I spent six days fishing with Stealhead Joe in early September of
2012, two months before he died. I planned to write a profile of
him for this magazine and had been trying for a year to set up
a trip. Most guides' reputations stay within their local area, but
Joe's had extended even to where I live, in New Jersey. Somehow,
though, I could never get him on the phone. Once, finding myself
in Portland with a couple of days free, I drove down to Sisters in
the hope of booking a last-minute trip, but when I asked for him at
the Fly Fisher's Place, the shop where he worked, I was told, in essence, "Take a number!" Staffers laughed and showed me his com-

pletely filled-out guiding schedule on a calendar on an office door, Joe himself being unreachable "on the river" for the next x days.

The timing sorted itself out eventually. Joe and I spoke, we made arrangements to fish together, and I met him in Maupin, a small town on the Deschutes about 90 miles from Sisters. Joe had moved to Maupin for personal and professional reasons by then. On the day we met, a Sunday, I called Joe at nine in the morning to say I was in town. He said he was in the middle of folding his laundry but would stop by my motel when he was done. I sat on a divider in the motel parking lot and waited. His vehicle could be identified from far off. It was a red 1995 Chevy Tahoe with a type of fly rod called a spey rod extending from a holder on the hood to another holder on the roof like a long, swept-back antenna.

I have seen a few beat-up fishing vehicles and even owned one or two of them myself. This SUV was a beaut, and I chuckled in appreciation as Joe got out, introduced himself, and showed me its details. The Tahoe's color was a dusty western red, like a red shirt that gets brighter as you slap dust off of it. (To maintain that look, he deliberately did not wash his vehicle, a girlfriend of Joe's would later tell me.) The grille had been broken multiple times by deer Joe had hit while speeding down country roads in predawn darkness in order to be on the water before everybody else, or returning in the night after other anglers had gone home. He had glued it back together with epoxy, and there was still deer hair in the mends.

Hanging from the inside rearview mirror was a large red-and-white plastic fishing bobber on a loop of monofilament line, and on the dash and in the cup holders were coiled-up tungsten-core leaders, steelhead flies, needle-nose pliers—"numerous items consistent with camping and fishing," as the police report would later put it. While Joe and I were admiring his truck, I didn't guess I was looking at the means he would use to take his life. He died in the driver's seat, which he pushed back into its full reclining position for the occasion. The report gave the cause of death as asphyxiation from carbon monoxide poisoning.

Something momentous always seems about to happen in canyon towns like Maupin, where the ready supply of gravity suggests velocity and disaster. Above the town, to the east and west, the high desert of central Oregon spreads its dusty brown wheat fields toward several horizons. Below the town, in a canyon that is wide in some places and narrow in others, 4,500 cubic feet per second of jade-colored river go rushing by. Four-hundred-some people live in Maupin in the winter; several thousand might occupy it on any weekend from June through Labor Day. People come to white-water raft, mainly, and to fish. Guys plank on bars in the wee hours, tequila shots are drunk from women's navels, etc. Sometimes dare-devils pencil-dive from Maupin's one highway bridge; the distance between the Gothic-style concrete railing and the river is 98 feet. They spread their arms and legs in the instant after impact so as not to hit the bottom too hard.

Maupin, an ordinary, small western town to most appearances, actually deals in the extraordinary. What it offers is transcendence; people can experience huge, rare thrills around here. Fishing for steelhead is one of them.

Steelhead are rainbow trout that begin life in freshwater rivers, swim down them to the ocean, stay there for years, and come back up their native rivers to spawn, sometimes more than once. They grow much bigger than rainbows that never leave fresh water, and they fight harder, and they shine a brighter silver—hence their name. To get to the Deschutes from the ocean, the steelhead must first swim up the Columbia River and through the fish ladders at the Bonneville Dam and The Dalles Dam, massive power-generat-ing stations that (I believe) add a zap of voltage to whatever the fish do thereafter. Some are hatchery fish, some aren't, but all have the size, ferocity, and wildness associated with the ocean. "Fishing for steelhead is hunting big game," says John Hazel, the senior of all the Deschutes River guides and co-owner of the Deschutes An-gler, a fly shop in Maupin.

Steelhead are elusive, selective, sometimes not numerous, and largely seasonal. They seem to prefer the hardest-to-reach parts of this fast, rock-cluttered, slippery, rapid-filled, generally unhelpful river. On the banks, you must watch for rattlesnakes. Fishing from a boat is not allowed. You wade deeper than you want, and then you cast, over and over. You catch mostly nothing. Casting for steel-head is like calling God on the telephone, and it rings and rings and rings, hundreds of rings, a thousand rings, and you listen to each ring as if an answer might come at any moment, but no an-swer comes, and no answer comes, and then on the 1,001st ring, or the 1,047th ring, God loses his patience and picks up the phone and yells, "WHAT THE HELL ARE YOU CALLING ME FOR?" in a voice the size of the canyon. You would fall to your knees if you weren't chest-deep in water and afraid that the rocketing, leaping creature you have somehow tied into will get away.

Joe's other nicknames (neither of which he gave himself) were Melanoma Joe and Nymphing Joe. The second referred to his skill at fishing for steelhead with imitations of aquatic insects called nymphs. This method uses a bobber or other floating strike indicator and a nymph at a fixed distance below it in the water. Purists don't approve of fishing this way; they say it's too easy and not much different from dangling a worm in front of the fish's nose. For himself, Joe believed in the old-time method of casting downstream and letting the fly swing across the current in classical, purist style. But he also taught himself to nymph, and taught others, and a lot of Joe's clients caught a lot of fish by this method. In one of Joe's obituaries, Mark Few—Joe's prized and most illustrious client, the coach of the highly ranked men's basketball team at Gonzaga University, whom Joe called, simply, "Coach," who liked to catch a lot of fish, and who therefore fished with nymphs—praised Joe's "open-mindedness" as a guide.

The nickname Melanoma Joe came from Joe's habit of fishing in board shorts and wading boots and nothing else. Most guides long-sleeve themselves, and lotion and hat and maybe glove themselves, and some even wrap a scarf around their heads and necks and faces like mujahedeen. Joe let the desert sun burn him reddish brown. Board shorts, T-shirt, sunglasses, baseball cap, flip-flops—that was his attire when we met. He grew up mostly in California and still looked Californian.

He smoked three packs of Marlboros a day.

For a guy as lost as Joe must have been, he gave off a powerful fatherly vibe. Even I was affected by it, though he was 13 years my junior. An hour after we met, we waded out into the middle of the Deschutes in a long, straight stretch above town. The wading freaked me out, and I was frankly holding on to Joe. He was six-five, broad-shouldered, with a slim, long-waisted swimmer's body. I wore chest waders, and Joe had put on his waders too, in deference to the colder water. I held tightly to his wader belt. Close up,

I smelled the Marlboro smell. When I was a boy, many adults, and almost all adult places and pastimes, smelled of cigarettes. Joe had the same tobacco-smoke aroma I remembered from dads of 50 years ago. I relaxed slightly; I might have been 10 years old. Joe held my hand.

That day we were in the river not primarily to catch fish but to teach me how to cast the spey rod. I had been dreading the instruction. Lessons on how to do any athletic activity fail totally with me. Golf coach reprimands like "You're not opening up your hips on the follow-through" fall on my ears as purest gibberish, talking in tongues, like the lost language of a tribe of Israel that has been found again at Pebble Beach—

—Where Joe was once a golf pro, by the way, as he told me in passing. The only athletic enterprises he had never tried, he said, were boxing and wrestling. Now he demonstrated to me the proper spey-casting method. Flourishing the rod through positions one, two, three, and four, he sent the line flying like a perfect tee shot down fairway one. From where we were standing, above our waists in water, it went 90 feet, dead straight. You could catch any fish in the river with that cast.

Regular fly-casting uses the weight of the line and the resistance of the air to bend the rod—or "load" it—so that a flick of the wrist and arm can release the tension and shoot the line forward. Spey casting, an antique Scottish technique from the heyday of water power, uses a longer rod, two hands, and the line's resistance on the surface of the river to provide the energy. You lay the line on the water beside you, bring the rod up, sweep it back over the line against the surface tension, and punch it forward with an in-out motion of your top and bottom hands. The spey cast is actually a kind of water-powered spring. It throws line farther and better than regular fly-casting does, and because it involves no backcast it is advantageous in closed-in places like the canyons of the Deschutes.

If Joe showed any signs of depression in the first days we fished together I did not notice them. Walking along the railroad tracks beside the river on our way to a good place to fish, he seemed happy, even blithe. As we passed the carcass of a run-over deer with the white of buzzard droppings splattered all around, he said,

"I've been fly-fishing since I was eight years old. Bird hunting too. My grandfather sent me a fly rod and a 12-gauge shotgun for my eighth birthday, because he fished and hunted and wanted me to be like him. He was a Cajun from south Louisiana. His last name was Cherami. That was my mom's family, and my dad's family was also from the South, but they were more, like, aristocrats. My last name, Randolph, is an old Virginia name, and I'm actually a direct descendant of Thomas Jefferson. My dad's father is buried at Monticello."

We went down the riprap beside the tracks and held back the pricker bushes for each other. They were heavy with black raspberries; the smell in the cooler air by the water was like someone making jam. He stopped to look at the Deschutes before wading in. "This is the greatest river in America," he said. "It's the only one I know of that's both a great steelhead river and a blue-ribbon trout stream. The way I came to it was, I was married to Florence Belmondo. Do you know who Jean-Paul Belmondo is? Famous French movie actor? You do? Cool! A lot of people never heard of him. Anyway, Florence is his daughter. She's an amazing person, very sort of withdrawn in a group, but warm and up for anything— like, she has no fear—and knockout beautiful on top of that. We met on a blind date in Carmel, California, and were together from then on. Flo and I got married in 2003, and we did stuff like stay at Belmondo's house in Paris and his compound in Antigua."

I looked at Joe, both to make sure he was being serious and to reexamine his face. I observed that he looked a bit like Belmondo himself—the same close-set, soulful eyes, big ears, and wry, down-turned mouth.

Florence skis, Joe was a snowboarder. They began to visit central Oregon for the snow at Mount Bachelor, Joe discovered the Deschutes, Florence got him a guided trip on the river as a present, he fell in love with the river, they moved to Sisters, and she bought them a big house in town in 2005. "After I learned the river and started my own guiding, I think that was what created problems between Florence and me," Joe said. "Being a kept man sounds great, but it's really not. To be honest, there were other problems too. So finally we divorced. That was in '08. We tried to get back together once or twice, but it didn't work out. Well, anyway—man, it was awesome being married to her. I'll always be grateful to her,

because she's the reason I came here and found this river. And I
have no desire to fish anywhere else but on the Deschutes for the
rest of my life."

The railroad tracks we were walking on belong to the Burlington
Northern and Santa Fe Railway. During the day, the trains sound
their horns and rattle Maupin's stop signs and bounce echoes
around the canyon. At night they are quieter; if trains can be
said to tiptoe, these do. The rhythmic sound of their wheels rises,
fills your ears, and fades; the silence after it's gone refills with the
sound of the river. We were out in the night in Maupin a lot because first light and last light are good times to catch steelhead. It
seems to me now that I spent as much time with Joe in the dark as
I did in the light.

On my second night, he and I went to a fish hatchery downstream from town. We parked, zigzagged down a slope, passed
dark buildings, crossed a lawn, and wrong-footed our way along
the tracks, on whose curving rails the moon had laid a dull shine.
After about a mile, we plunged through some alders and into the
river and stood in the water for a long time waiting for dawn to
start. This all felt a bit spooky and furtive to me.

My instinct, I later learned, was right. I had a fishing license,
and Joe had licenses both to fish and to guide. He did not, however, possess a valid permit to be a fishing guide on the Deschutes.
Two months earlier, he had left the Fly Fisher's Place in Sisters (actually, he had been fired), and thus he had lost the guiding permit
that the shop provided him. His attempt to jury-rig a permit from
a rafting guide's permit loaned to him by an outfitter in Maupin
was not enough, because it allowed him to guide rafters but not
anglers. Joe was breaking the law, in other words, and the consequences could be a fine of up to $2,500, a possible prison term,
and the forfeit of his guiding license—no small risk to run.

On some evenings, after fishing, Joe and I went to Maupin's
bars. They were packed with a young crowd that included many
rafting guides, and everybody seemed to know Joe. He sat drinking
beers and watching two or more baseball games on the bar TVs
while young guys came up to him, often asking for advice—"She's
kissed me twice, Joe, and I mean, *she* kissed *me*. But I haven't even
brought up anything about sex." Joe: "Hell, tee her up, man, and

ask questions later!" At the end of the night a barmaid announced last call, and Joe told her, "I'll have another beer, and a cot."

When Tiger Woods fished the Deschutes some years ago (with John Hazel, not with Joe), he did not pick up the spey cast right away, so I guess it's no surprise that I didn't either. I simply couldn't get the message, and I told Joe I wanted to go back to the fly rod. Not possible, he said. He had no fly rod; and, at his insistence, I had not brought mine. He was a patient and remorseless coach, smoking and commenting on each attempt as I tried over and over. "You fucked up, Bud. Your rod tip was almost in the water on that last one. Keep the tip high." A failed spey cast is a shambles, like the collapse of a circus tent, with pole and line in chaos, and disgrace everywhere.

But he wouldn't give up. I worried that it might be painful for him to watch something he did so beautifully being done so wrong, but now I think his depression gave him a sort of immunity. The tedium of watching me may have been nothing compared with what he was feeling inside. And when occasionally I did get it, his enthusiasm was gigantic: "That's it! *Money!*" he would holler as the line sailed out.

So I'm in my motel cabin the night before our three-day float trip, and I can't sleep. I keep practicing the motions of the cast— one, two, three, four—like the present-arms drill in a commercial for the Marine Corps on TV. I practice the cast when I'm pacing around the motel-cabin floor and when I'm lying on my back in the bed. Joe has told me that the first pool we will fish is the best pool on the entire lower river. If I don't catch a fish there, I figure, my chances for success will go way down. He has shown me how to cast from the right side of the river and from the left; you turn the motion around, like batting from opposite sides of the plate. He has said we will fish this first pool from the right side, so I practice that cast only. I keep remembering that I have never caught a steelhead. I do not sleep a wink.

He has told me to come to his house at 3:45 A.M. The early start is essential, he has assured me, because another guide is likely to be in the pool before us if we're late. At 3:15 I put on my gear and drive to his house. All his windows are dark. The moon is up, and

I wait in the shadow of Joe's trailered drift boat. No sign of activity in the house. At the tick of 3:45, I step noisily onto the front porch in my studded wading shoes and rap on the door. Through the window I can see only darkness, and the corner of a white laundry basket in a patch of moonlight. I call Joe's name. A pause. Then, from somewhere inside: "Th'damn alarm didn't go off!"

He comes out, rumpled and sleepy, and puts on his waders, which were hanging on the porch rail. We get in the Tahoe and take off, stopping on the way to pick up some coffee and pastry from the free breakfast spread at a motel considerably more expensive than my own. Joe assures me this is okay; no one is around to disagree. We rattle for half an hour down a county road beside the river, leaving dust behind, and then pull into a location he asks me not to disclose. He backs the drift boat down to the river and launches it and we get in. At the second or third scrape of the oars against the boat's aluminum sides, headlamps light up at a place not far from the boat launch. Guys are camped there so as to get to this pool at first light, and we have beaten them to it, Joe says with satisfaction. We go a short distance downstream and stop under the branches of trees on the right-hand bank.

The moon is not high enough to reach into the canyon, so the water is completely dark. We wait, not talking. I unwrap and eat the Heartland Bakery cinnamon Danish from the more expensive motel's breakfast spread and crumple the wrapper and put it in the top of my waders and rinse my fingers in the river. The sky lightens and the water becomes a pewter color. Faintly, its ripples and current patterns can now be seen. Joe puts out his cigarette and applies ChapStick to his lips. We slide from the boat into the river.

My fear of wading has receded, thanks partly to my new wading staff. We go halfway across the pool. Joe tells me where to put the fly—a pattern called the Green Butt Skunk—and I begin to cast. Suddenly, I'm casting well and throwing line far across the river. Joe exclaims in astonishment and yells, "Money! Goddamn! You're throwing line as good as Abe Streep!" (He is referring to an editor of this magazine, a fine athlete who fished with Joe the year before.) I am elated and try not to think about how I am managing to cast this well. I fish the fly across and downstream as the line swings in the current. I strip in the line, take a step downstream, and cast again.

Cast, step, cast again; I work my way down the pool, Joe next to me. We pause as a train goes by, hauling a collection of graffiti on the sides of its white boxcars. I notice a purple, bulbous scrawl that reminds me of something. Joe tells me to cast toward a pile of white driftwood on the bank. I send 50 or 60 feet of line straight at it, lay the fly beside it, swing the fly across. The light is now high enough that the ripples and the lanes of current are distinct. At the end of the swing, a swift, curved disturbance appears in the pewter surface of the river, and the line pulls powerfully tight.

Joe's father, William Randolph, was a Navy pilot who flew many missions in Vietnam and could be gone for months at a time. Brenda, Joe's mother, stayed home with Joe (called Joey), his older sister, Kay, and his younger sister, Fran. The family spent much of the kids' childhood at Naval Air Station Lemoore, south of Fresno, California, where Joe often rode his bicycle down to the Kings River to fish. Sometimes he hunted for ducks with family friends. Later he even had a scabbard on his bicycle in which he could carry his shotgun. His friends had shotguns too, and sometimes they would stand about a hundred yards apart in a field and shoot at each other with the lighter sizes of birdshot. The pellets did not penetrate but "stung like crazy" when they hit. Once, when Joe was speeding along on his bicycle without a helmet, he came out from behind a Dumpster and a passing garbage truck ran into him and knocked him unconscious. There was not much male supervision on the base with the dads away at war.

Joe's mother had problems with depression, which the kids did not understand until they were in their twenties. Once or twice they went to stay with relatives while she was hospitalized. When Joe was in grade school, she and his father divorced. Joe's main emotional problem, as Kay remembers, was getting angry, often at himself for personal frustrations. As a boy, he played tennis and traveled to tournaments and earned a national junior-level ranking. Being tall, he had a big serve, but his inability to avoid blowups on the court ruled out tennis for him. Other sports he excelled in were basketball, baseball, track, and volleyball. He went to high school in Fresno but did not graduate, although he did get his GED. To acquire a useful trade, in the late 1980s, he attended a school in the Midwest where he learned to be a baker; then he decided that was not for him and returned to California. He was kicked off the basketball team at Monterey Peninsula College for skipping practice to fish. Various injuries—elbow, knee, a severe fracture of the left ankle—interfered with his promising college baseball career. He once watched a doctor chip a bone spur off his knee with a chisel and did not pass out.

In his thirties, in Monterey, he tried to qualify for the semipro beach-volleyball circuit and took steroids to improve his game. The drugs caused him to feel invincible and aggressive and righteously angry, and added a foot to his vertical leap, but he did not make the roster. While playing volleyball he met a woman named Tricia, and they married. The couple had two children—Hank, born in 1995, and Maddi, born in 1997. He and Tricia separated in about 2000 and later divorced.

Now the sun had risen over the canyon, and Joe was navigating us through rapids whose splashes wet my notebook as I recorded the details of my first steelhead—a six-pound hatchery fish from far upstream, according to the identification made by Joe on the basis of the fish's clipped maxillary fin (a tiny fin by the mouth).

"The tug is the drug," steelheaders say, describing that first strike and the fight that follows. This was true, as I could now affirm. The afterglow was great too. I looked up at the canyon walls rising like hallelujah arms, their brown grasses crossed by eagle shadows, and at the green patches where small springs came up, and the herd of bighorn sheep starting mini-rockslides behind their back hooves, and the hatch of tiny crane flies like dust motes in the sunlight.

Happiness! The pressure was off, I had caught the fish, defeated the possible jinx, the article would now work out. In this mood, I could have fallen out of the boat and drowned and not minded, or not minded much. The morning had become hot, and Joe asked if I wanted some water. He opened the cooler. Inside I saw a few bottles of spring water and a 30-pack of Keystone beer in cans. Joe's assistant for the trip, a young man named J.T. Barnes, went by in a yellow raft loaded with gear, and Joe waved. He said J.T. would set up our evening camp downstream.

Every fishing trip reconstructs a cosmogony, a world of angling defeats and victories, heroes and fools. Joe told me about a guy he fished with once who hooked a bat, and the guy laughed as the bat flew here and there at the end of his line, and then it flew directly at the guy's head and wrapped the line around the guy's neck and was in his face flapping and hissing and the guy fell on the ground screaming for Joe to get the bat off him and Joe couldn't do a thing, he was laughing so hard.

"Do your clients ever hook you?" I asked.

"Oh, hell yes, all the time. Once I was standing on the bank and this guy was in the river fly-casting, and he wrapped his backcast around my neck, and I yelled at him, and what does the guy do but yank harder! Almost strangled me. I'll never forget that fucking guy. We laughed about it later in camp."

The next pool we fished happened to be on the left side. I had not practiced the left-side cast during my insomniac night. Now when I tried it I could not do it at all. The pool after that was on the right, but my flailing on the left had caused me to forget how to cast from the right. Again the circus-tent collapse, again chaos and disgrace. My euphoria wore off, to be replaced by symptoms of withdrawal.

I liked that Joe always called me "Bud." It must have been his standard form of address for guys he was guiding. The word carried overtones of affection, familiarity, respect. He got a chance to use it a lot while trying to help me regain my cast, because I soon fell into a dire slump, flop sweat bursting on my forehead, all physical coordination gone. "Bud, you want to turn your entire upper body toward the opposite bank as you sweep that line . . . You're trying to do it all with your arms, Bud . . . Watch that line, Bud, you're coming forward with it just a half-second too late." I was ready to flip out, lose my temper, hurl the rod into the trees. Joe was all calmness, gesturing with the cigarette between two fingers of his right hand. "Try it again, Bud, you almost had it that time."

By midafternoon Joe started in on the 30-pack of Keystone, but he took his time with it and showed no effects. Our camp that night was at a wide, flat place that had been an airfield. J.T. served shrimp appetizers and steak. Joe and I sat in camp chairs while he drank Keystone and told more stories—about his Cajun grandfather who used to drink and pass out on fishing excursions, and Joe had to rouse him so he wouldn't trail his leg in the gator-infested waters; about a stripper he had a wild affair with, and how they happened to break up: about playing basketball at night on inner-city courts in Fresno where you put quarters in a meter to keep the playground lights on. At full dark, I went into my tent and looked through the mesh at the satellites going by. Joe stayed up and drank Keystone and watched sports on his iPhone.

I was back in the river and mangling my cast again the next morning while Joe and J.T. loaded the raft. Out of my hearing (as I learned afterward from J.T.), their conversation turned to J.T.'s father, who died when J.T. was 15. Joe asked J.T. a lot of questions about how the death had affected him.

J.T. misunderstood Joe's instructions and set up our next camp at the wrong place, a narrow ledge at the foot of a sagebrush-covered slope. Joe was angry but didn't yell at him. During dinner that evening, J.T. told us the story of his recent skateboarding injury, when he dislocated his right elbow and snapped all the tendons so the bones of his forearm and hand were hanging only by the skin. Joe watched a football game and talked about Robert Griffin III, who was destined to be one of the greatest quarterbacks of all time, in Joe's opinion. As I went to bed I could still hear his iPhone's signifying noises.

At a very late hour, I awoke to total quiet and the sound of the river. The moon was pressing black shadows against the side of my tent. I got out of my sleeping bag and unzipped the tent flap and walked a distance away, for the usual middle-of-the-night purpose. When I turned to go back, I saw a figure standing in the moonlight by the camp. It was just standing there in the sagebrush and looking at me. At first I could not distinguish the face, but as I got closer I saw that it was Joe. At least it ought to be, because he was the most likely possibility; but the figure just stood in silence, half-shadowed by sagebrush bushes up to the waist. I blinked to get the sleep out of my eyes. As I got closer, I saw it had to be Joe, unquestionably. Still no sound, no sign of recognition. I came closer still. Then Joe smiled and said, "You too, Bud?" in a companionable tone. I felt a certain relief, even gratitude, at his ability to be wry about this odd moonlight encounter between two older guys getting up in the night. Now, looking back, I believe that more was going on. I believe that what I saw was a ghost—an actual person who also happened to be a ghost, or who was contemplating being one.

The poor guy. Here I was locked in petty torment over my cast, struggling inwardly with every coach I'd ever disappointed, and

Joe was . . . who knows where? No place good. In fact, I knew very little about him. I didn't know that he had started guiding for the Fly Fisher's Place in 2009, that he'd done splendidly that year (the best in modern history for steelhead in the Deschutes), that he had suffered a depression in the fall after the season ended, that he'd been broke, that friends had found him work and loaned him money. I didn't know that after his next guiding season, in 2010, he had gone into an even worse depression; that on December 26, 2010, he had written a suicide note and swallowed pills and taped a plastic bag over his head in the back offices of the Fly Fisher's Place; that he'd been interrupted in this attempt and rushed to a hospital in Bend; that afterward he had spent time in the psychiatric ward of the hospital; that his friends in Sisters and his boss, Jeff Perin, owner of the fly shop, had met with him regularly in the months following to help him recover.

I didn't know that after the next season, in late 2011, he had disappeared; that Perin, fearing a repetition, had called the state police; and that they had searched for him along the Deschutes Valley with a small plane and a boat and eventually found him unharmed and returning home. Joe later told Perin he had indeed thought about killing himself during this episode but had decided not to.

I didn't know that Perin had refrained from firing Joe on several occasions—for example, when Joe was guiding an older angler who happened to be a psychiatrist with the apt name of Dr. George Mecouch, along with one of Dr. Mecouch's friends, and a repo man showed up with police officers and a flatbed, and they repossessed Joe's truck (a previous one), leaving Joe and his elderly clients stranded by the side of the road in the middle of nowhere at 11 o'clock at night. Dr. Mecouch, evidently an equable and humorous fellow, had laughed about the experience, thereby perhaps saving Joe's job. I did not know that Perin had permanently ended his professional relationship with Joe when Joe refused to guide on a busy Saturday in July of 2012 because he had received no tip from his clients of the day before.

The spot where Joe killed himself is out in the woods about six miles from Sisters. You drive on a rutted Forest Service road for the last mile or two until you get to a clearing with a large gravel pit and a smaller one beside it. Local people come here for target practice. Splintery, shot-up pieces of plywood lie on the ground, and at the nearer end the spent shotgun-shell casings resemble strewn confetti. Their colors are light blue, dark blue, pink, yellow, forest green, red, black, and purple. Small pools of muddy water occupy the centers of the gravel pits, and the gray, rutted earth holds a litter of broken clay-pigeon targets, some in high-visibility orange. At the clearing's border, dark pine trees rise all around.

Probably to forestall the chance that he would be interrupted this time, Joe had told some friends that he was going to Spokane to look for work, others that he would be visiting his children in California. On November 4, 2012, he spent the afternoon at Bronco Billy's, a restaurant-bar in Sisters, watching a football game and drinking Maker's Mark with beer chasers. At about six in the evening he left, walking out on a bar tab of about $18. The bartender thought he had gone outside to take a phone call. At some time after that, he drove to the gravel pit, parked at its northwest edge, and ran a garden hose from the exhaust pipe to the right rear passenger-side window, sealing the gaps around the pipe and in the window with towels and clothes. A man who went to the gravel pit to shoot discovered the body on November 14. In two weeks, Joe would have been 49 years old.

He left no suicide note, but he did provide a couple of visual commentaries at the scene for those who could decode them. The garden hose he used came from the Fly Fisher's Place. Joe stole it for this purpose, one can surmise, as a cry for help or gesture of anger directed at his former boss, Jeff Perin. Over the summer, Joe's weeks of illegal guiding had caught up with him when the state police presented him with a ticket for the violation. He would be required to go to court, and in all likelihood his local guiding career would be through, at least for a good while. Joe thought Perin had turned him in to the authorities; and, in fact, Perin and other guides had done exactly that. Joe was often aggressive and contentious on the river, he competed for clients, and his illegal status made people even more irate. But, in the end, to say that Joe's legal difficulties were what undid him would be a stretch, given his history.

Joe's friend Diane Daviscourt, when she visited the scene, found an empty Marlboro pack stuck in a brittlebrush bush next to where Joe had parked. The pack rested upright among the branches, where it could only have been put deliberately. She took it as a sign of his having given up on everything, and as his way of saying, "Don't forget me."

John Hazel, the Deschutes River's senior guide, said Joe was a charismatic fellow who took fishing too seriously. "I used to tell him, 'It's only fishing, Joe.' He got really down on himself when he didn't catch fish. Most guides are arrogant—Joe possessed the opposite of that. Whoever he was guiding, he looked at the person and tried to figure out what that person wanted." Daviscourt, who had briefly been Joe's girlfriend, said he was her best friend, and made a much better friend than a boyfriend. "He fooled us all," she said. "I haven't picked up a fly-fishing rod since he died." She made a wooden cross for him and put it up next to where she found the Marlboro pack. The cross says JOE R. on it in black marker, and attached to it with pushpins is a laminated photo of Joe, completely happy, standing in the river with a steelhead in his hands and a spey rod by his feet. On the pine needles beside the cross is a bottle of Trumer Pils, the brand Joe drank when she was buying.

Just before Joe died, J.T. Barnes was calling him a lot, partly to say hi, and partly because Joe had never paid him for helping on the trip with me. (He did split the tip, however.) For someone now out $600, J.T. had only kind words for Joe. "He was like the ideal older brother. And he could be so up, so crazy enthusiastic, about ordinary stuff. One day we were packing his drift boat before a trip, drinking beer, and I told him that I play the banjo. Joe got this astonished, happy look on his face, and he said, 'You play the banjo? No way! That is so great—I sing!' That made me laugh, but he was totally being serious. I play the banjo, Joe sings!"

Joe had six dollars in his wallet when he died. Kay, his sister, who lives in Napa, thought Joe's chronic lack of money was why he lost touch with his family. "Joe was always making bad decisions financially. Maybe, because he had a lot of pride, that made him never want to see us. But he was doing what he loved, supporting himself as a famous fishing guide. He had no idea how proud his family was of him."

Alex Gonsiewski, a highly regarded young guide on the river, who works for John Hazel, said that Joe taught him most of what he knows. When Gonsiewski took his first try at running rapids that have drowned people, Joe was in the bow of the drift boat helping him through. "It's tough to be the kind of person who lives for extreme things, like Joe was," Gonsiewski said. "His eyes always looked sad. He loved this river more than anywhere. And better than anybody, he could dial you in on how to fish it. He showed me the river, and now every place on the river makes me think of him. He was an ordinary, everyday guy who was also amazing. I miss him every day."

The paths along the river that have been made by anglers' feet are well worn and wide. Many who come to fish the Deschutes are driven by a deep, almost desperate need. So much of the world is bullshit. This river is not. Among the many natural glories of the Northwest that have been lost, this valley—still mostly undeveloped, except for the train tracks—and its beautiful, tough fish have survived.

Joe was the nakedest angler I've ever known. He came to the river from a world of bullshit, interior and otherwise, and found here a place and a sport to which his own particular sensors were perfectly attuned. Everything was okay when he was on the river . . . except that then everything had to stay that way continuously, or else horrible feelings of withdrawal would creep in. For me the starkest sadness about Joe's death was that the river and the steelhead weren't enough.

At the end of my float trip with Joe, just before we reached the river's mouth, he stopped at a nondescript, wide, shallow stretch with a turquoise-flowing groove. He said he called this spot Mariano, after Mariano Rivera, the Yankees' great relief pitcher, because of all the trips it had saved. I stood and cast to the groove just as told to, and a sudden river quake bent the spey rod double. The 10-pound steelhead I landed after a long fight writhed like a constrictor when I tried to hold it for a photograph.

The next evening, not long before I left for the airport, Joe and I floated the river above Maupin a last time. Now he wasn't my guide; he had me go first and fish a hundred yards or so ahead of him. Dusk deepened, and suddenly I was casting well again. I looked back at Joe, and he raised his fist in the air approvingly. At the end of his silhouetted arm, the glow of a cigarette could be seen. I rolled out one cast after the next. It's hard to teach a long-time angler anything, but Joe had taught me. He knocked the rust off my fishing life and gave me a skill that brought back the delight of learning, like the day I first learned to ride a bicycle. I remembered that morning when we were floating downstream among the crane flies in the sunlight. Just to know it's possible to be that happy is worth something, even if the feeling doesn't last. Hanging out with Joe uncovered long-overgrown paths back to childhood. Peace to his soul.

JEREMY MARKOVICH

Elegy of a Race Car Driver

FROM SBNATION.COM

SOMETIME AFTER 10:30 on a Thursday morning in May, after he'd had his cup of coffee, Dick Trickle snuck out of the house. His wife didn't see him go. He eased his 20-year-old Ford pickup out on the road and headed toward Boger City, North Carolina, 10 minutes away. He drove down Highway 150, a two-lane road that cuts through farm fields and stands of trees and humble country homes that dot the Piedmont west of Charlotte, just outside the reach of its suburban sprawl. Trickle pulled into a graveyard across the street from a Citgo station. He drove around to the back. It was sunny. The wind blew gently from the west. Just after noon, he dialed 911. The dispatcher asked for his address.

"Uh, the Forest Lawn, uh, Cemetery on 150," he said, his voice calm. The dispatcher asked for his name. He didn't give it.

"On the back side of it, on the back by a '93 pickup, there's gonna be a dead body," he said.

"Okay," the woman said, deadpan.

"Suicide," he said. "Suicide."

"Are you there?"

"I'm the one."

"Okay, listen to me, sir, listen to me."

"Yes, it'll be 150, Forest Lawn Cemetery, in the back by a Ford pickup."

"Okay, sir, sir, let me get some help to you."

Click.

The funeral was four days later. It was small. There weren't many people. Maybe 50, mostly family. A few were old crew members from Wisconsin and Kansas City. Kenny Wallace, a driver who made Dick Trickle his mentor, was there. So was Kenny's older brother Rusty, the former Winston Cup champ who used to call Dick every Monday. Mike Miller and Mark Martin, both drivers, came. Nobody else from NASCAR did. Dick wanted it that way.

There was no eulogy. The pastor only said a few words. But he didn't go on long. Soon, everybody had left the church and headed down the road to Dick and Darlene's place in Iron Station. Kenny hugged Dick's son Chad.

"I'm so sorry," Kenny said.

"Aw, come on, man," Chad told him. "Seventy-one years. That's pretty good." Kenny thought Chad sounded a lot like his father.

The suicide. That didn't seem like Dick at all. People who knew Dick had heard something was wrong. A lot of them weren't sure what it was. Kenny asked Darlene if she'd seen this coming. No. She had no idea anything was wrong until a Lincoln County sheriff's deputy pulled into her driveway on Thursday afternoon.

After Dick shot himself, Chad called Kenny. Darlene wants you at the funeral, he said. "You know," he said next, "we're all big Kenny Wallace fans." That sounded like a Dick Trickle call. There weren't many short phone conversations between Kenny and Dick. If the phone would ring and Dick's name was on the caller ID, Kenny would think twice about answering if he didn't have an hour to talk. But they still talked all the time. Dick was still giving him advice. Back in 2011, Kenny called to talk about his new Nationwide Series race team. He told Dick he'd lost some weight. He was ready. You've got a new car now, Dick told him. Do not change your driving. Let the car do the work for you. Kenny had 11 top 10s and finished seventh in points, his best showing in years.

The calls started to slow down. Kenny wasn't sure why. Dick really didn't talk about it. In 2011, Kenny's father, Russ, an old-school racer who won a lot around St. Louis, died at age 77. Your dad lived a great life, Dick said. He was in pain, but he's fine now. Dick could justify anything, but Kenny thought it was odd how quickly he'd made sense of his father's death.

After Dick's funeral, Kenny had an idea. "Darlene, maybe we should make some T-shirts," Kenny said. New ones. With Dick

Trickle's name on the front. Just something so his fans could remember.

"Nope," she said. "We're done."

Darlene hadn't talked publicly about what happened to Dick. She still hasn't. And so Dick Trickle's closest friends were left with memories from a lifetime of friendship and a couple of clues and hindsight to make sense of his death. Darlene knew that the people who loved her husband needed to know what happened. So before Kenny and the rest of Dick's friends left the house after his funeral, she gathered up some manila envelopes and handed them out, one by one.

Here, she said. The answers to your questions are inside.

Most of the stories people tell about Dick Trickle aren't quite right. They aren't wrong, but they just aren't what they appear to be. He was bowlegged, and walked with a slight limp. That must be from a lifetime of crashes, right? Wrong. There was that commercial from 1997 where Dick Trickle talked about a contest for guessing the winner of the Napa 500. "A little tip," he smirked, "it's gonna be me." Instantly, text flashed on the screen: *Dick is 0 for 243 in Cup races.* "And remember, November 16 could be a real big day." *That's 0 for 243,* the screen said. If you saw that, and didn't know much about racing, you'd get the impression that Dick Trickle never won anything.

Same thing if you watched *SportsCenter* in the early '90s. You'd hear Dick Trickle's name alongside a litany of middle- to back-of-the-pack finishes. Dan Patrick and Keith Olbermann thought the name sounded like a joke, so they said it as often as they could after NASCAR highlights. "I thought, *Well, this guy's not any good,*" Patrick told *Spin* magazine in 1996, which pointed out Trickle's last-place finish in the Daytona 500 that year. "But he's a good old boy and he really represents what NASCAR used to be. He just loves to drive." Patrick and Olbermann weren't the only people who kept referring to Dick Trickle by his full name. Announcers did it. Fans did it. At the track, only his wife called him Richard. To everyone else, Dick Trickle had that three-syllable cadence that made you want to say the whole thing, like Kasey Kahne or Ricky Rudd. At first, it's funny, then familiar, and finally it just feels easy, not formal. When you say Dick Trickle, you know a story is coming.

When Dick Trickle finally got to NASCAR, to the biggest stage he'd ever been on, he was fading. By that time, people had attached a lot of labels to him, some true, some half true, and some not true at all. Hard drinking. Hard partying. Hard living. Veteran. Journeyman. Chain-smoker. Respected by racers and loving fans who could appreciate who he was and what he'd done, he had become a caricature to many, misunderstood by a new group of people who only saw him as a coffee-drinking, cigarette-smoking, old-school racer. If you were one of them, you might think that Dick Trickle wasn't good enough to hack it in NASCAR. That he never got the chance to run in the Cup series as a young man. And that too, like so many of the labels, is not quite right either.

"He was definitely one of the most talented race drivers that we've ever had in America," says Humpy Wheeler, the former promoter and president of Charlotte Motor Speedway. "He's up there with A. J. Foyt, [Richard] Petty, [Mario] Andretti, Cale Yarborough, Dale Earnhardt, Jeff Gordon." Wheeler once stuck his face in a tiger's mouth. He knows hyperbole. But he's being serious.

"Today, had he been 25 years old, his looks would have gotten him into a race car," Wheeler says. But today, he would have had to deal with sponsors who squirm at habits like smoking cigarettes or personalities that aren't squeaky clean. Dick Trickle was the last NASCAR driver to keep a pack of smokes in his car. Imagine that now. These days sponsors create a whitewashed version of the drivers that fans fell in love with when racing was racin', and stock cars were actually stock cars. "Today, they would have tried to put him through the clothes wash, and he wouldn't have gotten in the clothes wash," says Wheeler. "If you start off and you don't have perfect size, perfect weight, perfect teeth, perfect hair, and perfect speech, you're probably not going to get in a Cup car."

Dick Trickle could have. But he didn't. To understand why, you need to look at his life in reverse. That way the quirks become more commonplace, the near misses become wins, and the legend becomes real. The pain he endured at the end of his life washes away. He was a family guy from Rudolph, Wisconsin—a working-man whose work just happened to be racing cars.

"He liked the simple life, he liked the simple people, he liked the working people," Wheeler says. "And that's where racing's always been, and despite all the people today that have entered this sport, particularly working for companies, that have led cloistered lives and don't understand working people, Dick Trickle sure did. And that's why they didn't understand Dick Trickle."

Up All Night

It was 6:30 A.M. on a summer morning in 1996, and Dick Trickle threw the door open and walked into the conference room at the Chose Family Inn in Stoughton, Wisconsin. He had a somber look on his face. He stood on a cooler and looked around.

"You all are a bunch of drunks," he said.

The men in the room laughed. They weren't up early. They were up late. They were Rich Bickle's race team, which had beaten Trickle the night before at Madison International Speedway and clinched the championship in a series of races called the Miller Nationals. Once the race was over, they drank in the pits. It was always a contest between Bickle and Trickle to see who would leave last.

Once the track kicked them out, Bickle's team found a bowling alley and drank there. Then they found some bars that were still open. They drank there. When the bars closed, they ended up back at the motel in Stoughton. And that's where Trickle found them. At 6:30 A.M.

"Give me a beer," he said.

Dick always seemed to have a brewing company's logo on his car, and a can of beer in his hand. He joked about a sponsorship deal that gave him $100,000 and 350 cases of beer. But there are 365 days in the year, he said. What am I supposed to drink on the other 15 days?

The fans and friends who drank with him tended to miss something—Dick didn't actually drink all that much. Once he got down to the end of his PBR, he'd just stand there, holding a nearly empty can for as long as he could. Everybody else kept drinking. Dick kept holding. If someone threw him a beer, he'd take it. But people don't tend to do that when you've already got one in your hand.

His close friends had never seen him drunk, even though his close friends got drunk with him. Kenny Wallace finally figured out his trick. "You know how many times I've gotten drunk because of you?" he asked.

Dick would much rather talk. He'd stay up late to talk racing. Cars. Anything. If you'd ask him how on earth his parents named him Dick Trickle, he'd matter-of-factly tell you that his parents named him Richard. If you asked him how often he smoked in the car, through a special hole he'd drilled in his helmet, he'd ask: How many yellow flags have I had in my career? If you'd seen him rolling up to the track in the morning and asked him how late he was up the night before, he'd probably say it would depend on the race. The rumor about him, spread by him, was that he needed one hour of sleep for every 100 miles he'd have to drive the next day. He once said he probably drank 40 cups of coffee a day. The man ran on caffeine and conversation.

You could tell when Trickle was going to say something important. "My boy," he'd start off, and then he'd tell you something simple that made a lot of sense. Don't say you finished sixth, he'd say. You *won* sixth place, because guys who finished seventh and eighth would love to have had the race you did. Don't race the other drivers. Just race the leader. Race the track. Don't crash. To finish first, he'd say, you must first finish. Guys like Mark Martin made that their mantra.

By that day in 1996, he'd been racing for nearly four decades. He had plenty of fans. But he was still more popular in the Midwest than he ever was outside of it. In 1995, he flew to Minnesota for an American Speed Association race at the State Fair, and his PR guy remarked that he seemed more popular than Richard Petty.

Dick Trickle had always been a big fish in a small pond. Before the 1990s that was about the best you could hope to be, a local hero. But during the 1990s, NASCAR shook off its reputation as a regional, Southern sport and turned into a national phenomenon. Petty retired and Jeff Gordon debuted in the same race in 1992, the Hooters 500. North Wilkesboro Motor Speedway shut down and Las Vegas Motor Speedway opened up in the same year. Neil Bonnett died on the track. Alan Kulwicki died in a plane crash; Davey Allison died in a helicopter crash. Before the '90s, a lot of races were still shown on tape delay. By 2000, a half-dozen channels had broadcast live racing. The money started rolling in, and drivers who used to spend their time riding from track to track on the interstate began to buy their own private buses and airplanes. The King Air 200 became the most popular jet in racing.

Dick would fly with people, but he didn't buy a plane. He didn't even buy a big RV. He built a big garage behind his house in 1991, but that was it. "My boy," he told Kenny, "I don't need none of that stuff." The Wisconsin in him kept him incredibly frugal. Although he didn't like to talk money, he had a lot of it. In 1989, arguably his most successful year in the Winston Cup, he made $343,000. He struggled in 1998, with only one top-10 finish. It was his final full season. He still won $1.2 million.

His biggest problem was his age. By the time he ran his last Cup race in 2002, he was 61. Too long in the tooth, as Humpy Wheeler would say. At that age, your eyes get to you. When you're down at Daytona or up in Charlotte, you're running at 300 feet a second. Sooner or later, your age is going to creep up on you. "Your eyes are what bring you down," Wheeler said.

Great race drivers don't hang around, Wheeler says, they fade away like old soldiers. When Trickle stopped racing in the Winston Cup, he didn't come out and announce his retirement. There was nothing official. He was just done. That was it. He didn't become a team owner like Junior Johnson. He'd get invited back up to Wisconsin every once in a while to grand-marshal a race, or he'd show up to sign autographs, but mostly he'd hang out in Iron Station with Darlene and his family. He went on a cruise for the first time in his life. He played with the grandkids, cut down trees on his property, picked up garbage along the road. He didn't need NASCAR. He never did. "Who knows," he told now-defunct bgnracing.com after his final Cup race, "maybe I'll be revived and get the support of the right sponsor and team and be out there every weekend. But if I don't, life isn't bad."

Trickle didn't need to win anymore. He didn't need the money. "I had a new challenge when I went to Cup," he told nascar.com in 2007. "I had a refreshing life, from 48 to 60. I was excited. I was pumped up. I enjoyed it. I got a second lease on life."

Back on that morning in 1996, at that little two-story motel in Stoughton, Wisconsin, the party was still going for Dick Trickle. Around 8:00 A.M., when it was time for either breakfast or bed, the long night started making memories foggy and Bickle's crew began to split up into two groups, those who fell asleep and those who passed out. One by one, they started heading off to bed.

Dick Trickle was one of the last to leave. He took a can of beer back to his room.

Rookie of the Year

It was 1989, and Dick Trickle was trying to buy a fake Rolex on the street in Manhattan. He was willing to pay $10. But he wanted a guarantee first. If it falls apart, the guy who was selling told him, you come and find me, and I'll give you another one.

This was a little bit of a stunt, done for the cameras. *Motor Week Illustrated* was putting together a story called "Trickle Takes Manhattan." A television crew followed Dick and Darlene around New York City. He bought a hot dog. He took the subway to Grand Central Terminal. "Man, look at all these trains!" he said. "You think you've got one that goes to Wisconsin Rapids?"

A few days later, on December 1, Trickle stood onstage in a tuxedo at the Waldorf Astoria, listening to people talk about how old he was. "Luckily, this year's rules do not include any age restriction," an executive from Sears said, to mild laughter. He presented Dick with a painting of himself and his car. Dick got a check for $20,000. He'd just won NASCAR's Rookie of the Year Award. At age 48.

"I'd like to thank Champion and Sears DieHard Batteries for giving us young racers a chance to come up through the ranks," he said. More laughs.

He thanked his kids for coming. He thanked Darlene for putting up with 31 years of racing. He thanked his sponsors. And he thanked Bill and Mickey Stavola, who owned the car. He had no contract. No guaranteed ride. He drove all year on a handshake.

"If you'd have told me last December that I would be on the stage at the Waldorf Astoria, I'd have said no way," Trickle said. "But one phone call last spring changed it all."

It started one year before, in 1988, actually, with the crash that ended Bobby Allison's career. Allison blew a tire at the Miller 500 at Pocono in June, and then Jocko Maggiacomo came along and T-boned him so hard that Bobby still doesn't remember the crash, nor winning the Daytona 500 the February before. Mike Alexander drove Allison's car for the rest of the season. Afterward, at the Snowball Derby in December, Alexander hit an embankment with the driver's side of his car. Something happened to him. But he didn't tell anyone for months.

A few days before the 1989 Daytona 500, Alexander did a media tour during the day but was too worn out to keep going through the evening. His PR guy, Tom Roberts, thought that was strange. On Sunday, after 188 laps, Alexander hit the wall in turn two and that was it.

The next race was the Goodwrench 500 at Rockingham in early March. Alexander and Roberts were having dinner and Alexander confessed he shouldn't be out on the track. He'd had blurry vision and severe headaches since the Snowball Derby. Roberts told him to fess up to his crew chief, Jimmy Fennig, and he did.

Now Stavola's car needed a new driver. A few years before, Fennig had been Mark Martin's crew chief when Martin was running American Speed Association races in Wisconsin. That's how Fennig knew Trickle. He convinced Stavola to bring him in for the race, and that Thursday night, Dick Trickle got The Call.

He started in the last row. During the race, he kept pitting on yellow flags, and one of his pit crew members kept leaning way in through the passenger window. The TV announcers thought there was a problem with the transmission. The transmission was fine. But the heat near the throttle was causing Trickle's right foot to swell, and the guy from the pit crew was trying to pull off his snakeskin cowboy boot. He kept trying until they finally swapped it out for a regular driving shoe.

Trickle finished 13th at Rockingham, ahead of Richard Petty. The next week, in Atlanta, Trickle finished third. He went on to nine top-10 finishes. Larry Pearson, son of NASCAR legend David Pearson, had been the favorite to win Rookie of the Year. That changed when Trickle came along.

Roberts knew Trickle could drive. But he also knew Trickle didn't have that much pressure on him. Opportunity just came to him. Trickle was just the fill-in guy and knew it.

Off the track, he hedged. For the first month, Trickle lived in a motel off of Interstate 85 in a rough area of Charlotte, just to be ready to go back home to Wisconsin Rapids with some cash in his pocket if NASCAR didn't pan out. But at the track, he was still the same guy he'd been up north, smoking and drinking coffee and talking to everybody. His family came to every race. He didn't want people to line up for his autograph—he wanted to buy fans beers and talk with them and work the crowd. Sometimes, after two-hour meet and greets, he'd ask if he could stay longer.

He didn't always qualify well, but he knew how to pass. He never tired out. He said he didn't need to work out. Got his workout in the race car, he said, and since he'd been driving so much in so many features on so many short tracks, he was in pretty good shape. At the gas pumps after the race, Roberts would see the other drivers worn out and sucking down oxygen. Trickle would just be standing there, cigarette in hand. I could go another hundred laps, he'd say.

He smoked outside of the car. He smoked in the car. When the yellow flag came out, so did the lighter. Trickle was a Marlboro man, but had the sense to put them into an empty pack of Winstons whenever he was at a Winston Cup race. He'd show up at races with a briefcase, just like the one Alan Kulwicki, another short track racer from Wisconsin who was named NASCAR Rookie of the Year, in 1986, made popular. Kulwicki would keep shock charts, setups, and notes from the last race in his. Trickle's carried a schedule, a ball cap or two, cheap Miller High Life sunglasses, and a carton of cigarettes.

By the time he was named Rookie of the Year, Trickle had already lined up a full-time ride for 1990, driving for Cale Yarborough's Phillips 66 team. Two months after his trip to New York, Dick and Darlene bought a modest, 11-year-old Cape Cod house in Iron Station, North Carolina, along with the eight acres of land that came with it, leaving Wisconsin behind. Their new home was less than an hour away from Charlotte, near where most all the other drivers kept their race shops.

One of the stories that is not quite right is this: Dick Trickle never won while he was racing in NASCAR's Winston Cup. That is wrong. In May 1990, he qualified for the Winston Open, a 201-mile precursor to the Winston, NASCAR's All-Star race. But neither one was a points race, so it doesn't show up in most recaps. Still, the Open was big. Winning it gave you the 20th and final spot in the Winston, and the winner of that race got $200,000.

Ernie Irvan led a third of the race before Trickle took the lead with a dozen laps to go. Then Rob Moroso, the 1989 Busch Series champion, all of 21 years old, crept up behind Trickle. When the white flag flew, Moroso and Trickle traded spots, one and two, with Trickle taking the high side. When they hit the final straightaway and crossed the finish line, Trickle beat him by eight inches.

He got out of the car, grabbed a cup of water, and thanked his sponsors. He thanked Cale Yarborough, who hadn't had a win as a car owner. The reporter asked him what he needed to do to be ready for the Winston, which started in 20 minutes. "I'll be ready," he said, sweaty, his hair mussed. "Just get the car ready." Then he hugged Darlene and answered another question about his car and Darlene buried her face in his shoulder. And then Dick Trickle went out and finished sixth in the Winston. Once again, he came from behind.

The Short Track

Dick Trickle had a crown on his head. He'd just won the 1983 World Crown 300 in Georgia and the $50,000 that came with it. Dick looked over at the guy who'd just presided over his coronation in the victory lane. "I'm not a king," he said. "I'm a race car driver."

This was, at the time, the largest prize Dick Trickle had ever raced for. He spent a month preparing the car. If anyone else did any work on it, he went back and did it over. "I never look at the purse," Trickle told Father Dale Grubba, a Catholic priest and chronicler of Wisconsin racing who'd known him since 1966. "My wife does. I come to race."

But for the World Crown 300, Trickle broke his rule. He did look at the purse. The race itself had been nearly rained out, and instead of thousands of fans at the Georgia International Speedway in late November, there were only a couple of hundred. It was a problem for Ron Neal, the engine maker who owned the speedway. He promised a huge purse for the short track race, one that now, because of the weather, he might not be able to pay for in cash. It's okay, Trickle said. I'll barter with you. So instead of getting the entire purse, Trickle also got new engines, and engine service, for his cars. He did things like that.

There are tons of stories about Dick Trickle from the short track days. He once told a *Milwaukee Journal-Sentinel* reporter about the time when he blew a water pump in a race, got on the PA, and asked if anyone in the crowd had a Ford. A guy drove his car down to the pits. Trickle pulled the water pump off, put it on his car, won the race, and gave it back. Another time he blew an engine, pulled one out of a tow truck, dropped it in his car, and won that race also.

Trickle won a lot on the short tracks. Maybe more than any other driver. The number of wins that Trickle is supposed to have is 1,200, legitimized by a *Sports Illustrated* article in 1989. But unlike NASCAR, which has precise records, Wisconsin's short track racing record book isn't a book at all, but a patchwork of newspaper clippings and memories and word of mouth. One man, who has tried to piece together records of every race Trickle entered, says he's found evidence of 644 wins up through 1979. He's not sure of the '80s. Trickle would have needed 556 more victories before heading off to the Winston Cup in 1989 to hit 1,200.

Might have happened.

He was good at the little things. He knew how to power through the corners. He always kept his car in control, even in traffic. Pit stops were critically important, because when a race was long enough to require one, one was all you got. At the 200-lap races at Wisconsin International Speedway in Kaukauna, he would pit on around lap 70 or 80 when everybody else thought about heading in around 120. After his stop, he'd drive conservatively, waiting for a yellow flag. When everybody else went in to change tires, Trickle would stay out, take the lead, and a lot of times take the checkered flag. He won at least 34 races at Kaukauna. At least.

In central Wisconsin, the same drivers went to the same circuit of tracks, which all ran races on different nights of the week. Drivers didn't bump and grind because they couldn't afford to, and you didn't have a week between races to fix your car. You only had a matter of hours. If Dick Trickle couldn't get around you cleanly to win, he'd settle for second. It wasn't worth the risk.

Almost all of the other drivers had day jobs. They had to go home after the races. Trickle could hang out at the track all night. He could hit the bar. He could hang out with fans. "Just because the races were over didn't mean pulling up the shades and going to bed," he told Father Grubba for his book *The Golden Age of Wisconsin Auto Racing.* "You are still pumped up. What are you going to do, stop at a corner church?" When Trickle left the track, people would follow him. They knew he'd stop somewhere for a drink.

The things that made Dick Trickle old-school later were quite ordinary then. He drank canned beer because that's what most bars served. He smoked because people smoked. He wore cowboy boots in his stock car because they were thick and durable, and that's what people wore to race.

He started to get a reputation. One time, at an ASA race, the fans booed him when he was introduced. Doesn't that bother you? another driver asked. "When you get introduced there may be 500 or a thousand people that cheer," Trickle told him. "But when I get introduced, 100 percent of the crowd reacts, one way or the other."

He was always racing, stock cars, snowmobiles—anything. In the beer garden after a race at the Milwaukee Mile in 1969, Trickle got to talking with another short track racer, Dave Watson, and they decided they needed to race again. The two drivers and three crew members grabbed mats and walked to the top of a nearby giant blue carnival slide. They sat, counted down, and pushed off. Dick Trickle won.

In 1972, he entered 107 races, and won 68. He got his 49th on August 4 in his 1970 Mustang, starting at the back of the field, taking the lead on lap 9, and taking the checkered flag on lap 30. By this time, he was starting to make the number 99 car legendary. He was called the White Knight, named for the mascot of Super America, his sponsor. He won seven ARTGO short track championships in 11 years, from 1977 to 1987. He was the ASA champion in 1984 and 1985.

There was a point, in 1979, when Humpy Wheeler tried to bring Trickle down to NASCAR full-time. Trickle had driven in 11 Winston Cup races up to that point, starting at Daytona in 1970. He ran four Cup races between 1973 and 1974 and won at least eighth place every time. The big question about a short track guy like Trickle was focus. The longer the race, the longer you're required to maintain that intense concentration. That was never a problem for Dick Trickle. Focus ran in his family. "They could focus so hard," said his brother Chuck, "and forget there was another world and get things done."

He made the calculations. There wasn't big money in NASCAR. Not yet. He could make more money in short track. So he told Wheeler, I can't afford to come down there. Promoters are paying me to show up at the tracks up here.

He had all the ingredients to be a great Cup driver. He just didn't need to be one. All he needed to do was win.

The Start

Rudolph, Wisconsin, where Dick Trickle was born in 1941, was race-crazy in the 1950s. At one time, Father Grubba says, there were 26 race cars in a town of just a few hundred people. Nearly every driveway had a race car in it.

When Dick Trickle was nine, a neighbor took him to a race at Crown Speedway in Wisconsin Rapids, and he thought that was the greatest thing he'd ever seen. For the next seven years, he focused on how to get behind the wheel of his race car. Problem was, the Trickles were on welfare. Dick's father, Lee, came down with an ear infection that led to medical problems and was hospitalized for years. There was no money for racing. Dick had to work for his money, on farms and in his father's blacksmith shop. He swept the floors, but he also learned how to use the arc welder.

In 1958, at age 16, when he'd welded together enough parts and came up with enough money to buy a 1950 Ford, he dropped the engine from a 1949 Ford in it and started racing. It was slow, and during his first race, in Stratford, Wisconsin, he finished way back in the end.

When the nearest racetrack, Griffith Park in Wisconsin Rapids, found out he was too young to race, he was kicked out for a year. After that, Dick never took racing for granted. Whenever he raced, he raced hard, and smart, as if he might not have another chance.

But he still had a day job, working 66 hours a week at a service station in Rudolph while racing four nights a week. With his free time, he worked on his cars at night, using what he'd learned about fixing cars during the day.

He married Darlene in 1961, paid $8 for a motel room the night of the wedding, and then ran two races the next day at Wausau and Griffith Park. Dick started working for a telephone company, and hated it, being up high on the poles. So he started doing the math: Gas was cheap. Parts were cheap if he scoured through the junkyard and did the work himself. If he owned his own car, he wouldn't have to split up his winnings. Dick could bring in the money, and Darlene could stretch it as far as it would go, but the racing season in Wisconsin ran from only May to September, so he didn't have all year to make money, and the payouts for winning races were maybe $100 one week, maybe $300 another. He would have to be on the road constantly, going from track to track, from LaCrosse to Wausau, from Madison to Wisconsin Dells. He couldn't afford to lose. Wherever there was a race, Dick Trickle would have to go there and win.

I think I can make it, Dick told Darlene. And he did.

The End

Chuck Trickle doesn't want to talk much more about the suicide. He's on the phone from a water park.

"It's not the right thing to do, and I'm upset the way he did it, but you know, I wasn't in his shoes," Chuck says.

"Now they're turning on the music," he says, changing the subject.

"That's my story anyway." The music gets louder.

"The park is closing in 15 minutes," he says.

"Anyway, that's about it. Is there anything else you want to know here?"

Tom Roberts says he struggles with Dick Trickle's suicide. So does Father Grubba. John Close, who partied with Dick Trickle in Stoughton, is saddened by it. Humpy is too. Kenny Wallace put a Dick Trickle sticker in the cockpit of his dirt car in memory of Trickle. But he had to take it off. It bothered him too much. He had a hard time driving.

Kenny Wallace tries to justify it like the others. He doesn't agree with suicide, but he's not going to question it. Dick had been through a lot over the last couple of years, he said.

Kenny has been talking about Dick Trickle for about two hours when he stops for a second. "You know, this has been like therapy for me," he says. His voice sounds tired. "I want to make sure you understand that he was a good man," he says. "I want to make sure you know the full story.

"Don't you fuck it up," he says.

So he tells me what was in the envelope.

There were medical records inside. Computerized forms. Test

results. Findings from doctors. Charts. They detailed a day-by-day, doctor-by-doctor struggle with pain.

Dick Trickle chain-smoked for his entire life. But he didn't have cancer. Aside from some stents, his heart was healthy.

To understand the end, maybe you have to go understand the beginning, way before racing, back to 1949, when Dick was eight years old. He was playing tag with a cousin up in the rafters of the house his uncle was building in Rudolph when he fell and broke his hip. He dragged himself home, and his mother took him to the hospital. He spent six months there, and missed a year of school. Doctors weren't sure if he'd ever walk again.

Once he got home, he wore a cast on his leg for months before he and his brothers got tired of the thing and cut it off. He'd walk again, but always with a slight limp.

In 2007, 58 years after the fall, that hip needed to be replaced. The limp was becoming too painful. He also had stents put in, doctors put him on blood thinners, and told him he ought to stay off the track. In 2009, he told the *Milwaukee Journal-Sentinel* he still felt good enough to race, but he admitted to feeling the wear and tear from years of bumping cars and hitting walls. "I'm paying for some of my good times," he said, "but at the same time, I'm getting better and better with old age."

But sometime after, only his family knows when, he began feeling a stabbing pain two inches under his left nipple. Dick Trickle didn't cuss all that often, but when the pain became too much he started to really let the words fly. His phone conversations got shorter because he just couldn't go on. He went to doctor after doctor, looking for help, for years. We can't help, they told him, because we can't find the pain.

The problem with pain is that most doctors need to know what's causing it before they can treat it. Prescribe the wrong drug, and you might mask the real problem. Prescribe the drug to the wrong person, and they might abuse it. One study found that chronic pain increases the risk of suicide by 32 percent. It can leave people desperate. It can change people.

After the pain started, Dick Trickle stopped smoking. But by that point, he was already dealing with another kind of pain too.

In 2001, Vicky's daughter Nicole, Trickle's granddaughter, was on the way home from volleyball practice. She stopped for gas at a minimart and was pulling back onto the road when a pickup truck smashed into her side of the car. She died instantly. Dick never talked about it with Kenny all that much. That wasn't surprising. "You are never going to get a feeling out of Dick Trickle," he said. Still, Kenny knew he was grieving. Other friends said he never got over her death.

They buried Nicole at Forest Lawn. Her death came just three years after his nephew, Chuck's son Chris, died after being shot in Las Vegas. Police there have never solved the crime. Chris was an up-and-coming race car driver. He called Dick for advice all the time.

"You never know what a man is thinking," Kenny said. Maybe it was grief. Maybe it was pain. Maybe it was a combination of both.

Race car drivers don't like to talk about pain. It shows vulnerability. And besides, it might keep them off the track. Dick Trickle endured a lifetime of crashes and hard hits. He wasn't a complainer. But he'd been through a lot of pain. His chest. His hip. His granddaughter. His nephew. Dick Trickle was always a guy who looked ahead. He didn't dwell on the past. He always raced so he could race again. But there were no more races. Ahead, all Dick saw was suffering.

A week before his death, Dick called Chuck. I don't know how much longer I can take it, he said.

On May 15, Dick Trickle went to the Duke Heart Center in Durham. This was his best chance to get better. Doctors ran more tests. But it was the same answer. We can't find anything wrong with you.

On May 16, he was dead.

Kenny thinks everything was done deliberately. Dick Trickle didn't kill himself at home. He didn't do it on a piece of property that somebody else could buy sometime. He ended his life at the same cemetery where his granddaughter was buried, where he would be buried. He made sure Darlene and the family had enough money.

The Trickle family is still private. Chad Trickle politely declined to talk about his father. Vicky didn't return an email. Their racing days are done. But they still know there are a lot of people out there who loved Dick Trickle. Two weeks after the funeral, Kenny got a package in the mail from Darlene. It was an old Dick Trickle T-shirt.

Most of the grave markers at the Forest Lawn Cemetery are

flush to the ground, so from a distance, one looks the same as the next. You almost have to know where you're going to find the spot where Dick Trickle is buried, on the gentle slope of a North Carolina hill. You can barely see a gas station across Highway 150. Beer, coffee, and cigarettes aren't too far away.

His grave is right in front of Nicole's. There are a few trinkets on it. A little number 99 checkered flag. A toy John Deere tractor. A Titleist golf ball with the words MISS YOU DAD. Some flowers. There's an oak tree nearby. It's sunny. The driveway through the cemetery is a small asphalt oval.

Fitting, really. Dick Trickle always liked a short track best.

STEPHEN RODRICK

Serena the Great

FROM ROLLING STONE

WHO IS THE MOST DOMINANT FIGURE in sports today? LeBron James? Michael Phelps? Please. Get that weak sauce out of here. It is Serena Williams. She runs women's tennis like Kim Jong-un runs North Korea: ruthlessly, with spare moments of comedy, indolence, and the occasional appearance of a split personality.

Here are the facts. Serena is the number-one tennis player in the world. Maria Sharapova is the number-two tennis player in the world. Sharapova is tall, white, and blond, and, because of that, makes more money in endorsements than Serena, who is black, beautiful, and built like one of those monster trucks that crushes Volkswagens at sports arenas. Sharapova has not beaten Serena in nine years. Think about that for a moment. Nine years ago Matchbox Twenty and John Edwards mattered. The chasm between Serena and the rest of women's tennis is as vast and broad as the space between Ryan Lochte's ears. Get back to me when LeBron beats Kevin Durant's Oklahoma City Thunder every time for nine years.

Serena's dominance has been fueled by not giving a shit what you or anyone else thinks about her methods. Serena has been giving tennis the two-finger salute for more than half her life. Not that she cops to it. "Lots of my friends have been telling me lately that I'm spoiled," Serena says with a baffled look on her face. "And I'm like, 'Really? I'm not spoiled.'"

I almost spit Coke through my nose. Serena does what she wants, when she wants. If she'd pulled a Jamesian I'm-taking-my-talentsto-South-Beach event, she would have put it on pay-per-view and hawked her Home Shopping Network all-under-a-hundred-bucks fashion line during the commercial breaks. And she would not have given a flying fuck what you thought. This is a woman who one minute is reading inspirational notes during changeovers and then, in the 2009 U.S. Open semifinals, threatening to personally make a line judge eat a tennis ball.

Tennis ninnies chided Serena for taking months off earlier in her career to flirt with fashion and make cameo TV appearances, you know, like a normal person might do after making tens of millions of dollars. Chris Evert, an icon of the game, questioned Serena's dedication just 18 months ago.

Evert couldn't have been more wrong. The players Serena entered the game with are long retired, burned out, and discarded. Meanwhile, Serena came back last year from foot problems and blood clots that could have killed her. Instead, she has gone 74-3 since losing at the 2012 French Open and won three Grand Slams and an Olympic gold medal. After each one, tennis gurus whispered, "That was Serena's last hurrah."

Not quite. This year she has won the past four tournaments she's entered and is on a 31-match winning streak, the longest of her career. If she doesn't pocket her sixth Wimbledon and her fifth U.S. Open titles this summer, check the ground because the world may have spun off its axis. She's never been more dominant than now, at the age of 31, which is about 179 in tennis years. (Evert now says Serena is the best of all time.) Hell, even dating Brett Ratner couldn't stop her. Neither could older sister Venus, merely the second-best tennis player of the past 20 years.

What's her secret? Serena only compromises with herself.

"I've thought it would be cool to have a baby young," says Serena. "You know, be my road dog—like my dogs, they travel the world—but there's always something you have to give up for success. Everything comes at a cost. Just what are you willing to pay for it?"

Good question.

Serena and Venus Williams share a house in a gated community in Palm Beach Gardens, Florida, where the rest of the residents have been enjoying the early-bird specials for years. They like it that

way; it keeps out the riffraff. On a misty March morning, Serena
answers the door in sweats and a T-shirt, her long hair flowing in
about seven directions.

"Come on in," she says, rubbing the sleep out of her eyes. "I've
got to practice, ugh." Then her face brightens. "But then we'll go
get my nails done. I'm getting them done in colors that change
with my mood. Now, *that* I'm looking forward to."

She turns around and sarcastically sings a few bars of "Oh What
a Beautiful Morning" in a not-bad voice. The sisters have lived here
for a decade, but the house still has a transient, hedge-funder's-
second-home feel. Amazon boxes and dozens of shoes sit stacked
in the foyer next to a giant painting of Venus. (She's not around.)
There's a sparkly chandelier and a massive antique mirror leaning
against the wall. But the action takes place in the kitchen, where a
cook hands Serena a green potion. She drinks it reluctantly.

"I had chicken and waffles the other day, so I've got to make up
for it," she says. "Ai-yi-yi."

An assistant brings in some new Green Day T-shirts—they're her
favorite band. Serena reanimates and does a bunny hop around
the dining room. "These are cool, so cool!"

Patrick Mouratoglou, her newish French coach and possibly
her boyfriend, emerges from a back room. He's handsome in that
dark-haired Frenchman kind of way. He says nothing but carries a
bagful of rackets.

Serena sighs.

"I guess it's time to do it."

We head over to some nearby courts in my rental car (there's a
white Rolls in the driveway).

"That's Casper," says Serena. "I like to name my cars. And, you
know, Casper seemed obvious for that one."

Like most everyone in modern America, Serena travels with
an entourage. There's Mouratoglou, the cook, the physical therapist, and Aleksandar "Big Sascha" Bajin, her much-put-upon hitting partner. The caravan heads to a court about a half-mile from
the house and begins loading out the gear. It's two days before
the start of the Sony Open in Miami, one of the circuit's premier
nonmajors and the first significant test for Serena since she was
upset in the quarterfinals at the Australian Open after spraining
an ankle that had ballooned to three times its normal size.

Serena was beaten by the beautiful and—for sportswriters—conveniently black Sloane Stephens, leading tennis commentators to call her the "New Serena." Stephens proceeded to lose seven of her next 10 matches and earned Serena's annoyance when the press suggested that Stephens regarded Serena as a mentor. Stephens objected, saying no way in hell was Serena her mentor, and questioned whether Serena had dissed her on Twitter, proving the tennis tour is much like *Mean Girls* with prize money. ("I don't know where all that mentor stuff came from," Serena says. "I am definitely not that girl's mentor.")

She's been recovering from the ankle injury for two months, but if anyone is feeling the pressure, nobody shows it. Jackie, Serena's beloved old white dog, curls up in her tennis bag and goes to sleep. Serena changes from the Green Day shirt—she doesn't want to get it sweaty—and slips on an Incredible Hulk T-shirt festooned with six-pack abs.

Bajin is ready to warm up, but Serena has other things on her mind. "I had a dream last night," she says to no one in particular. "My dad was in the Mafia, and he'd done something bad, and there were body parts everywhere, but I didn't want to see them." Bajin stops stretching and listens in. "Then the Mafia came over to our house, but it wasn't our real house, and they had grenades and rifles."

Everyone in the entourage looks at their collective feet, and Serena goes on. "My dreams always have a twist. Then I was swimming with Venus, and then she was holding a shark in her hands pushing at me. I mean, what does that mean?"

This seems like an easy one. The Williams sisters are known inside the tennis world equally for their on-court achievements and for being the offspring of one Richard Williams, who was raised by a single mom in Shreveport, Louisiana, and schooled the girls for hours on the glass-strewn courts in Compton, California, from the age of seven. Richard turned two children of the ghetto into legends in a gilded sport run by Veuve Clicquot–sipping country-club types. This has not always gone over well. Richard has steamrolled other players and tour staffers—hence the dead bodies—to get his girls their just due. Sometimes, he's been heroic—he gave the black-power salute at a tournament in Indian Wells, California, a decade ago—after the crowd shamefully booed Serena with racial overtones. And sometimes he has been insufferable—dancing on the broadcasting booth at Wimbledon, proclaiming his daughters the best ever.

Richard's antics so sucked the oxygen out of the girls' worlds that most fans forgot it was the Williams sisters' mother, Oracene Price, who shared in the coaching and steadied the girls whenever Richard went slightly cuckoo. (Serena's parents divorced years ago. Richard was suspected of assault in 1999 after his wife was hospitalized with several broken ribs. He denied assaulting her, and no charges were ever filed.)

Part of the myth of Richard was you didn't know when he was telling the truth—he once said a businessman offered him $78 million for the rights to Serena's and Venus's future winnings—or when he was trying to mind-fuck you on behalf of his daughters. But you can watch grainy footage of Richard, Venus, and Serena piling out of a VW bus with a seat taken out to hold more baskets of tennis balls. He was the magical-realism version of Earl Woods, Tiger's military dad. And there was a method to his demented psychology. While many of his fellow tennis dads were entering their kids into cutthroat junior tennis tournaments at the age of 10, Richard kept his girls largely sequestered, hitting with men and working on their fundamentals so that when they turned pro at 14 they were almost fully hatched with power strokes never seen in the women's game. Along the way, Richard has jettisoned coaches, trampled officials, and browbeaten reporters, all in the name of his girls.

The shark part with Venus? Well, Serena's a girl who, by her own admission, cheated her sister at line calls when they were young and once cut off another sister's braids. There's a bit of the bad seed in her, and Venus is a sweetheart. Venus would never toss a shark at her, but Serena might feel like she deserves it.

Just as Serena finishes dream therapy, Richard arrives on the court. Despite having recently fathered a son, Richard, 71, walks with a stoop and has the permanently bewildered smile of an elderly man. He spends the first 20 minutes of Serena's practice watching the lawn mowers outside the court cut their swaths. He wanders over and says hello with a question.

"Do you play tennis?"

"No."

Richard looks sorrowfully at me and pats me on the shoulder. He spends the next half-hour shagging balls for his daughter. Every once in a while, I track a ball down, and he shouts, "Thank you very much, sir! Kind of you!"

Today, Mouratoglou is trying to get Serena to plant her feet a centimeter closer together. Serena isn't buying it.

"It just doesn't feel right."

Mouratoglou gently pushes Serena while she's in her stance. She almost topples over.

"See?"

Serena gives him a secret smile.

"I'm not saying you're not right—I'm saying it doesn't feel right."

Eventually, Serena moves on to her serve. Power is the dominant part of the game, which is sort of like saying speeches are the dominant part of Obama's game. She simply hits the ball harder than any woman who has ever played the game.

Most women on the tour serve in the 95-mile-per-hour zone; Serena's serve breaks well into triple digits. Her power just obliterates opponents. In May, at Roland Garros, Serena played Caroline Garcia, a waifish French player, in the second round. Most of their points went like this: Serena crushing a 100-mile-per-hour serve, Garcia weakly returning, Serena slamming a ground stroke, Garcia popping it up, and Serena then driving the ball down her gullet. Once, Serena thundered toward the net—and Garcia, understandably, looked terrified. When Serena changed up and dinked a return barely over the net, it didn't seem quite fair. Garcia's thin shoulders sagged. If this were MMA, she would have just tapped out.

Serena's power is key because she isn't the most nimble player. "I'm a total klutz," she says. "I fall over for no reason. I have a scar on my face because I fell off a bike."

Her klutziness is a bit of an old cliché. Under Mouratoglou's tutelage, Serena's footwork has vastly improved, and she's getting to balls she could never have reached a decade ago. Still, she ends most points before her opponent can trip her up. Serena starts serving, and the balls sound like they are exploding as they whiz over the net and then bounce off the lines. She tugs at her ankle occasionally, checking on it like a mother making sure her baby hasn't kicked off her blankets. Richard watches and smiles. "Good, that's good."

Now it's time for Bajin, a funny Serb, to bang some serves at Serena. But she wants to make it interesting.

"If you can't get an ace in five tries, then you have to kiss Jackie, with tongue."

"No way," Bajin protests. "You know what that dog licks? Other dogs' butts."

Serena grins.

Bajin and Serena have a classic Serena relationship. Bajin joked two years ago that he was going to go work with a more easygoing contender, and Serena gave him the silent treatment. But when she washed out in the first round of last year's French Open, it was Bajin's shoulder she cried on. They are like an old married couple who no longer argue about who wears the shorts in the family.

Bajin chokes on the first four serves—they're not even close. Serena cackles.

"Get ready to make out!"

Bajin takes a breath and hits a borderline ace. Serena momentarily howls in protest but gives in.

"Okay, but I still want you to kiss Jackie."

Bajin shakes his head and gets the hell off the court.

Serena piles into my car for the half-mile drive to the gym. I ask her if she hates training, and she shoots me a "What do you think?" look.

"When I stop playing, it's not going to be because I'm sick of playing," she says. "It's going to be because I'm sick of practicing."

The phone rings. It's Venus.

If they weren't actually sisters, the two could make a perfect CBS sitcom, *Two Rich Girls*. Venus is slim and elegant—Serena wears a "Don't sass me" look. Venus plays with grace and little emotion—Serena is all grunts and glares. While Venus dated a golfer named Hank, Serena was with Ratner, a middle-aged Hollywood *enfant terrible*. Serena drives a Rolls-Royce, and Venus shyly replied to a question about her cars with, "Uh, I get rides."

But whatever their differences, they share a sisterly alliance of Venus and Serena versus the universe. It was Venus who made Serena go to the hospital in 2011 when her leg swelled up because of a pulmonary embolism. Now it is Serena who consoles Venus through Sjögren's syndrome, an autoimmune disease that threatens the elder Williams's career.

They talk at this time every day. After chattering about their dad, they move on to gossip. As usual, Serena does most of the talking.

"There are people who live, breathe, and dress tennis. I mean, seriously, give it a rest." Serena exits the car and the conversation moves on to a top-five player who is now in love. "She begins every interview with 'I'm so happy. I'm so lucky'—it's so boring," says Serena in a loud voice. "She's still not going to be invited to the cool parties. And, hey, if she wants to be with the guy with a black heart, go for it." (An educated guess is she's talking about Sharapova, who is now dating Grigor Dimitrov, one of Serena's rumored exes.)

This is sort of how Serena rolls. There's Serena and then the rest of the tennis world. She likes to say, "Good match, girl," and condescendingly pat her vanquished rival on the shoulder after a match. Virginie Razzano, who upset Serena at the French Open last year, said that she has encountered Serena twice since and got the Serena death glare both times.

"I'm there to do a job, not to make friends," says Serena, before hastily adding, "but I'm not there to make enemies."

Serena clicks off the phone and drags herself into the gym.

Did you ever want to have one thing in common with a world champion? Now you can! Nobody dreads the gym like Serena. She plugs in her iPod and lets a trainer manipulate her legs without making eye contact. She lifts light weights with her left hand while texting with her right. The most painful part comes when she has to run intervals on a treadmill. Her trainer tries to talk her through them, forcing her to remove her earbuds, an impossibly annoying imposition to Serena.

"Are we done?" asks Serena.

"Two more," says the trainer.

"One more."

"Okay."

Serena climbs off sweaty and relieved, a kid whose calculus class ends early for a fire drill. We head back to the house.

"Okay, shower and then nails!" Her whole demeanor changes;

the face lightens up. "Finally, something I've been looking forward to."

Serena Williams toggles between global sports icon, international financial concern, and misunderstood little girl in less time than most of her rallies with Sharapova. I drive her to the manicurist, and she asks me whom else I've written about. I mention a comedian or two. She sighs.

"Can you believe I've never been asked to host *Saturday Night Live?*" she says. "And I'm funny. Ask my friends."

We get off I-95, and I stupidly turn into oncoming traffic, nearly killing a tennis legend. Serena doesn't shout, "Watch out!" Instead, I hear, *"Attention, attention!"*

I apologize, and Serena lets out an embarrassed giggle. "I've been spending too much time in Paris. I can't believe I just said that."

In addition to the Florida home, Serena has a place in LA, but over the past 18 months she's spent much of her time in Paris. (She won't cop to a relationship with her coach, but the paparazzi have caught them arm in arm.) "I lost in the first round in the French Open last year, and I just decided to stay." I asked her if it was because of the defeat. She laughed a little sadly. "No, I had a bad breakup, and I just didn't want to be in the same country as the guy."

We turn onto a street lined with strip malls. Serena bangs her hand on the dashboard. "Look, that place has a happy hour! I've never been to one." Serena was raised a Jehovah's Witness, but I tell her that she's not really missing anything. She isn't convinced. "Maybe, but I'd like to go. Just one happy hour."

We pull into the parking lot with the nail salon, but Serena hasn't eaten lunch yet, so we pop into a Panera. Serena looks at the displays and then turns to me.

"Can I ask you a real question?"

She points to some pastries.

"See that cinnamon roll? Why do you think that calls to me?"

"Because cinnamon rolls are delicious?"

I tell her that to cut down on my french-fries intake from room service I throw them in my toilet. She jumps with glee. "Me too! Well, I just have them empty the minibar before I get there."

Sure, Serena has been accused of being, uh, slightly self-centered, but she's done heaps of good as a role model for the non-Sharapovas of the world.

"I had to get comfortable with knowing that one of my weaknesses was my weight," says Serena, eating a sandwich with no cinnamon-bun chaser. "Especially growing up with Venus, who's so tall and slim and model-like, and me, I'm thick and hips and everything." A teenager comes over for a picture with her, and Serena poses and then continues. "I used to feel like I wanted to be her. I wanted to be thin, but it wasn't me, so I had to learn that I'm going to have larger boobs. I'm going to be bigger, and just enjoy that. So I think it's good for a lot of other girls who are curvy or more bodacious to be confident in themselves."

We walk over to the salon and Serena slips off her sandals, displaying toes marked and torn from a quarter-century of tennis. She's assigned a Korean manicurist who recognizes Serena and then gets nervous. There's some miscommunication about what shade to use, and the manager comes over.

"Do you want to work with someone with better English?"

Serena shakes her head.

"Absolutely not. We're fine."

I wait until Serena is in a trancelike state before asking her about her anger issues. In the recent documentary *Venus and Serena,* Serena listed her different personas: Summer, the one who writes thank-you notes; Psycho Serena, the tennis player; and Taquanda, whom Serena describes simply as "not a Christian." It was Taquanda, according to Serena's mom, who threw the tantrum at the U.S. Open in 2009. "Taquanda got loose," Oracene says.

Serena happily cops to the multiple personalities. After she struggled in an early match at the Sony Open, a reporter asked her what she was saying to herself on the court. Serena just laughed.

"When I'm down, I talk to myself a lot. I look crazy because I'm constantly having an argument with myself. We're going back and forth and then I tell her she sucks and she tells me to shut up. Then we get along."

There's been an uneasy truce between the many faces of Serena for two years. Serena followed her 2009 U.S. Open outburst with another one in 2011, when she accused a chair judge of being "the one who screwed me last time." (She wasn't.) Serena knows she doesn't play best out-of-control angry and talks frankly about what it has cost her. When we met, she had won the French Open only once, and she blamed near misses on her psyche.

"I've choked a lot there," she says. "I should have won a few years ago. Just not playing well when the pressure is on. I just get too far ahead of myself, and I crumble."

But Serena's renaissance during the past two years correlates roughly with the taming of Taquanda, her blood-clot scare, and working with Mouratoglou.

"The funny thing, at first with him, I was struggling—all my matches going to three sets," says Serena, admiring a hot-pink shade of nail. "And he came to me and said, 'Bring that angry Serena out. I want you relaxed, but I want you to be good angry.' A little bit of me does need a little anger."

We watch the news for a while, and the infamous Steubenville rape case flashes on the TV—two high school football players raped a drunk 16-year-old, while other students watched and texted details of the crime. Serena just shakes her head. "Do you think it was fair, what they got? They did something stupid, but I don't know. I'm not blaming the girl, but if you're a 16-year-old and you're drunk like that, your parents should teach you: don't take drinks from other people. She's 16, why was she that drunk where she doesn't remember? It could have been much worse. She's lucky. Obviously, I don't know, maybe she wasn't a virgin, but she shouldn't have put herself in that position, unless they slipped her something, then that's different."

Serena's Hannity-like take on the case isn't her only rightward lean. She is baffled by the tax rate in France. "Seventy-five percent doesn't seem legal. Nobody does anything because the government pays you to be broke. So why work?"

Agree or disagree, Serena's no-safety-net political philosophy is rooted in her Compton childhood, one where there wasn't a lot of money and where gun violence claimed her older sister Yetunde in 2003. Today, Serena mother-hens every expenditure. "I'm an athlete and I'm black, and a lot of black athletes go broke. I do not want to become a statistic, so maybe I overcompensate. But I'm paranoid. Oprah told me a long time ago, 'You sign every check. Never let anyone sign any checks.'"

All the talk of finances and self-reliance is a bit of a stand-in for the ghost in the room: How long can Serena Williams keep playing at this level? And is there an exit strategy? She recently had an internal dialogue with herself, and it didn't go well. She props up her foot so the beautician can get a better handle on her cuticles.

"I had a panic attack," she says with a shiver. "I was like, 'I have no idea what I'm going to do next.'"

Then there's the whole kids thing. She's only 31, but she can hear the clock ticking.

"I've seriously thought of freezing my eggs—no joke. I've thought about it, but with all the drug testing, if you do that, then you can test positive or something. Maybe I'll check into it again."

That all seems far away, at least for a moment. She wants to play through the 2016 Olympics, so she's got at least three years to come up with a master plan or maybe even a new persona. Over the next two months, she sweeps through the Sony Open, from there cruising to victories on clay in Rome and Madrid. And then it was on to the French Open, her old nemesis. All Serena did, according to sometimes-doubter Chris Evert, was play some of the best tennis Evert had ever seen. She lost only one set all tournament. In the finals, she rolled past Sharapova in straight sets. Afterward, she spoke to the crowd in French. Serena smiled and shouted, *"Je suis incroyable"*—aka "I am incredible." Folks said she misspoke, meaning to say, "That's incredible," but it doesn't matter. As usual, Serena Williams told the truth.

But that's all in the future. Right now, Serena is simply happy with her nails.

"I can't wait until I get mad about something and they change colors." She frowns. "But now everyone will know what I'm feeling. I'm not sure if that's good or bad."

BROOK LARMER

Li Na, China's Tennis Rebel

FROM THE NEW YORK TIMES MAGAZINE

THE PATCH OF WIMBLEDON GRASS known as the Graveyard of Champions was supposedly exorcised four years ago, when the blue-blazered gentlemen of the All England Lawn Tennis Club demolished Court 2, built a new grandstand in its place, and, in 2011, renamed the haunted space Court 3. But the tennis fans watching the 2013 championships still knew. Li Na, China's tennis rebel, knew too. This was the same cursed court where top seeds like Pete Sampras and Serena Williams had suffered ignominious defeats, falling to unheralded players in the early rounds. Now Li, the former French Open champion and sixth-ranked player in the world, teetered one game away from a third-round loss to the Czech veteran Klara Zakopalova. "At that moment," she told me later, "I suddenly saw myself with my bags going to the airport. It made my heart ache."

For two hours, Li had struggled against her hard-hitting opponent. Trailing 5–6 in the third set, she walked to the baseline knowing that she had to break serve just to stay alive. Lose the next four points, and she might carry out her pretournament threat to quit the sport she had been forced to start playing nearly a quarter-century ago. Her spring season had been a bruising free fall from the heights of her second Australian Open final in January to her second-round flameout at the French Open in May. Now the graveyard was calling.

As Li crouched at the baseline, the cluster of Chinese fans waving little red flags went still. On the first serve, Li blasted a winner down the line. Five points later, she pounced on her first breakpoint opportunity, scorching a forehand winner—and letting out a scream—to even the set at 6-all. Two more games, another roar: Li had survived. It was just a third-round match, and she had played erratically. But after her recent run of defeats—marked by what appeared to be a lack of conviction at decisive moments—pulling out this victory felt redemptive. "I fought like mad," she said with a grin. "Winning this match felt as good as getting to a Grand Slam final."

One more obstacle awaited Li that afternoon. Walking into the press room in her sleek white sweatsuit, she looked warily at the assembled Chinese reporters. Her smile was pinched. China's state-run media, which happily extols her victories for bringing glory to the motherland, had recently intensified its attacks on her streak of individualism, which has grown only stronger since she left the Chinese sports system in 2008. The furor began after her collapse at the French Open a month earlier, when a reporter for the government's Xinhua News Agency asked her to explain her disappointing result to her nation's fans. "I lost a match and that's it," Li snapped. "Do I need to get on my knees and kowtow to them?" Her comment ignited a round of official criticism, rebuking her lack of patriotism and manners. Now, the very same reporter raised his hand to ask Li, once again, to address her fans. She glared at him for almost a full minute before mumbling, "I say, 'Thank you, fans.'"

Li Na might prefer that we forget about China and judge her by her character and accomplishments alone. Hers, after all, is the tale of a conflicted working-class girl—the daughter of an athlete whose own dreams were thwarted by political strife—who rose to become one of the finest, richest, and most influential players of her generation. All in a sport that most of her compatriots had never watched before.

A mercurial star who blends speed and power—and occasional meltdowns—Li became Asia's first and only Grand Slam singles champion when she won the French Open in 2011. She is also the first Chinese-born player to crack the world's top five—an elite group she rejoined last month after her run at Wimbledon. With nearly $40 million in sponsorship deals signed in the past three years, she is now the third-highest-compensated female athlete in *any* sport, trailing only Maria Sharapova and Serena Williams.

Still, it is impossible to separate Li from China. She is one of the country's biggest celebrities, with more than 21 million followers on the Twitter-like Weibo. (By comparison, LeBron James has 9.4 million Twitter followers.) A record 116 million Chinese viewers watched her triumph in the French Open, a bigger audience than the Super Bowl attracted that year. The tens of millions of dollars in endorsements that Li has collected depend on her connection to the Chinese market. Had she been born in Chile, Chad, or even Chicago, she would not be one of the top three earners. Nor would the Women's Tennis Association be unveiling a new pro tournament next year in her home city of Wuhan, in central China. Five years ago, the WTA staged two tournaments in the country; in 2014, there will be eight. The WTA's chief executive, Stacey Allaster, credits Li with helping spark a tennis explosion in Asia. "If the Williams sisters had the greatest impact on the first decade of this century," Allaster says, "then I would say, without a doubt, that Li Na will be the most important player of this decade."

But even now, Li's game is plagued by a maddening unpredictability—not unlike the WTA in general, where a decade of relative instability at the top has led to a few players reaching number one without winning a Grand Slam. (Caroline Wozniacki, of Denmark, was only the latest example.) This situation has prompted unfavorable, often unfair, comparisons with the men's tour, which has been defined over the past decade by scintillating battles among four of history's greatest players (Roger Federer, Rafael Nadal, Novak Djokovic, and now Andy Murray).

On the women's side, the only truly dominating player this decade has been Serena Williams. Her return to the sport full-time last year after being sidelined by injuries has reestablished a more natural order in women's tennis, with two Grand Slam winners, Maria Sharapova and Victoria Azarenka, serving as her worthy, if not yet equal, adversaries. But Wimbledon blew that order into disarray—none of the four semifinalists had ever won a Grand Slam—and showed how erratic the women's game can still be.

As the U.S. Open begins this week, Li senses an opportunity. At 31 years old, she still possesses great foot speed and thunderous ground strokes, including what many consider to be the most cleanly struck backhand in the game. In the past, Li has tended to fade in the later majors from a lack of fitness and focus. (At the

U.S. Open, she's gotten to the quarterfinals only once, in 2009.) But this summer, after watching her at Wimbledon, I followed Li back to Beijing to witness up close her demanding midseason training regimen with her coach, Carlos Rodriguez. Li is making a big push to make the world's top three and to win another Grand Slam. "Anybody could win the U.S. Open this year," Li said. "Why not me?"

Born in 1982, Li Na was, like many Chinese athletes, pushed into sports against her will. Her father—a former badminton player whose career had been cut short by the chaos of the Cultural Revolution—was the "sunshine of my childhood," she said. Even so, he gave his daughter no choice when he enrolled her at age five in a local state-run sports school. Though she was a strong athlete, her shoulders were deemed too broad and her wrists not supple enough to excel at badminton. A coach persuaded her parents that she would have a better chance in a sport that few Chinese at that time had ever seen. "They all agreed that I should play tennis," she said, "but nobody bothered to ask me."

From the beginning, Li chafed at the harsh strictures of the state-run sports machine. China's *juguo tizhi*—or "whole-nation sports system"—churns out champions by pushing young athletes to their limits every day for years on end. The first time Li defied her coach came at age 11, when, on the verge of collapse, she refused to continue training. Her punishment was to stand motionless in one spot during practices until she repented. Only after three days of standing did Li apologize. She continued training for her father's sake—"His love was my source of strength," she said—even though her coach never uttered a word of praise in their nine years together.

When she was 14, her father died of a rare cardiovascular disease. She was playing in a tournament in southern China at the time, and her coach didn't tell her for several days, waiting until the competition was over. "It is my deepest pain that I did not make it to say goodbye to him," Li wrote in her autobiography. Her mother sank into debt, and Li remembers being driven to win in tournaments so that she could earn small bonuses to fend off creditors.

Despite the turmoil, Li's tennis flourished. Her first national junior title came just months after her father's death. The following year, she was invited to a 10-month Nike-sponsored training program in Texas. After her return, she told an interviewer that she aimed to make the top 10 in the world, and by early 2002, her goal actually seemed attainable: the 20-year-old was ranked number one in China and had even climbed, at one point, into the world's top 135. And then she disappeared.

Without telling any of her coaches, Li slipped out of the national training center one morning later that year. To avoid suspicion, Li said, she carried only a small bag of necessities. On the desk in her dorm room was a letter she had written to tennis authorities requesting an early retirement. The note didn't elaborate on her reasons: the burnout from excessive training, the outrage at her coaches' attempts to squelch her romance with a male teammate named Jiang Shan, and the debilitating period that the team leader wanted her to play through by taking hormone medicine.

Within hours, Li was in Wuhan with Jiang, planning their new life as university students. "As soon as I got home, I turned off my mobile and refused to take any phone calls," Li later wrote. "Freedom was delicious."

Tennis is infamous for tumultuous relationships, usually between parent and child star, coach and protégé. Li is now married to Jiang, a former Davis Cup player. Jiang became her first and only boyfriend at age 16. Romances between teammates were technically forbidden, but Jiang was Li's refuge—first from the system, then from the vicissitudes of success and failure.

Over the years, Jiang has often served as Li's coach—only to be demoted to the roles of sparring partner, cheerleader, and punch line. In postmatch interviews, Li likes to joke about Jiang's snoring, his weight fluctuations, his control of the family credit card. The couple have been together so long—almost exactly half of Li's life—that Rodriguez said, "They are not two people, but one person, fused together." That doesn't stop them from bickering in public. During an early-round match at Wimbledon, when Jiang exhorted her after a missed shot, she retorted in Mandarin, "You're not my coach!"

Just hours before her fourth-round Wimbledon match with the 11th-seeded Roberta Vinci, Li seemed annoyed with her husband again. They were warming up on one of the practice courts. As Jiang hit an amped-up version of Vinci's skidding slice backhand, Li looked out of sorts, netting backhands, lifting forehands long. At one point, Jiang whipped a shot past her and Li responded by angrily crushing a winner. "Sometimes," she said later, arching an eyebrow, "I think my husband's purpose is simply to make me unhappy."

Once the match began, though, Li couldn't miss. She handled Vinci's slice with ease and breezed into the quarterfinals. "I felt so good I could've run for another three hours," she said. Li had matched her deepest Wimbledon run, and with Williams, Sharapova, and Azarenka gone, the highest seed left, at number four, was Li's next opponent, Agnieszka Radwanska, whom she had beaten handily at the Australian Open in January.

The vibe in Li's camp was so positive that nobody anticipated the attack on her that same day in *People's Daily,* the official mouthpiece of the Chinese Communist Party. "When star athletes' personalities have become insufferable by the standard of social customs and traditions," the editorial read, "who is to rein in their unchecked insolence?"

Despite China's desire to have Li embody the country's ambitions, she has made it clear that she plays for herself as much as, if not more than, for her homeland. "When people say that I represent the nation," she told me later, "that is too big a hat for me to wear." Li's independent streak is part of what makes her resonate deeply with China's younger generation, who have nicknamed her Big Sister Na. But for the country's leaders (be they national, athletic, or media), this is a fundamental challenge to the way the Chinese Communist Party has rallied its subjects for 64 years.

Li said she didn't see the *People's Daily* editorial. Rodriguez forbids her, as best he can, from reading media coverage during tournaments, and Jiang acts as sentry to shield her from articles that might affect her mood. Still, when the coverage stings, Jiang tries to soothe her. "We Chinese have a saying: 'For any hero, half will compliment, half will slander,'" he said. "I tell her to forget the attacks, the pressure, the expectations. But it's hard to forget. We're only human."

Li tried to be lighthearted when I asked her about the Chinese press: "In the past, I used to be really bothered by [bad stories].

Now I just think that perhaps [the Chinese media] think that I'm not famous enough, so they want to help me out." Her laugh sounded hollow.

Li has become a lightning rod in China, provoking a conversation about the role of freedom—and patriotism—in sports and society. When the editorial came out, her fans angrily defended her right to be herself in an online debate that consumed Chinese microblogs. "At the beginning, I would be affected by everybody's expectations, but I came to realize that people were just projecting their own dreams onto me," she said. "I'm not a saint. I too am an ordinary person. I have my ups and downs. So all I can do is focus on doing my job well." She added: "I really, truly think that I am just an athlete. I can represent nothing but myself."

More than a year into what Li calls her "first retirement," in 2003, the new head of China's state tennis program, a former volleyball star named Sun Jinfang, visited her in Wuhan. As Li remembered the meeting, Sun said: "I have heard from many people that there was a Li Na who played very well, but she suddenly quit. So I decided to come see for myself." At 22, Li was reveling in the joys of ordinary life for the first time: taking university classes in journalism, freely pursuing her relationship with Jiang, even playing a stint of intramural tennis with classmates who had no idea who she was.

"Why don't you play for yourself?" Sun asked her. The question surprised Li. No other official had ever spoken to her this way. But it wasn't clear what "playing for yourself" meant in a system that managed every aspect of players' lives—from dictating the coaching, training, and tournament schedule to taking 65 percent of players' earnings. Even so, in early 2004, Li put her academic plans on hold (she would eventually graduate five years later) and headed back to the court, unencumbered by a WTA ranking or outsize expectations.

That year, she became the first Chinese player to claim a WTA title by winning a tournament in Guangzhou as a qualifier. By 2006, she had climbed into the top 25 in the world, but to break into the top 10, Li believed she needed the freedom to manage her own career, something only a few Chinese athletes, such as the former NBA star Yao Ming, had ever been offered. That freedom wouldn't be granted before the 2008 Beijing Olympics, the pridefest in which the supremacy of the Chinese sports system—its 51 gold medals topped the Americans' 36—was meant to mirror the rise of the nation.

With a Chinese flag affixed to her red Nike outfit, Li made an unexpected run to the semifinals, seemingly untroubled by the knee surgery she had undergone just months before. The local fans cheered her so wildly—even in the middle of points—that at one stage she yelled, "Shut up!" Li regretted the outburst, but reflected later: "Chinese people needed a victory so badly to prove ourselves. I used to think tennis was simply a sport, but the craziness of that match made me realize that it was endowed with meanings that are far more significant."

Once the Games ended, Li said she issued Sun an ultimatum: "I told her, 'If I have no freedom, I'm going to quit.'" Another young player, Peng Shuai, had been making similar demands. Whether to avert the desertion of her top stars or to help them realize their potential (as it was later presented), Sun soon introduced a policy called *danfei,* or "fly solo." Under the new rules, Li, Peng, and two others would still have obligations to the national and provincial teams, but they would be allowed to hire their own coaches, set their own schedules, and keep a far greater percentage of their earnings. Instead of giving 65 percent of her income back to the federation and her provincial team, Li now pays between 8 and 12 percent, even as she bears the cost of travel, training, and coaching. For China—and for Li's career—this was a radical change.

Flying solo was scary at first. "Jiang Shan and I made plans for the worst-case scenario, where our savings would be reduced to zero," Li said. She'd never had to deal with the minutiae of finances or logistics before, since the state had done everything for her. But the benefits soon became indisputable. In 2010, with Jiang as her coach, Li reached the semifinals at the Australian Open and broke into the world's top 10 for the first time—just as she had vowed so improbably a decade before. A year later, she swept all the way to the Australian final, charming fans with her verbal volleys as well as her ground strokes. Asked to describe what motivated her back-from-the-dead semifinal victory over top-seeded Wozniacki, she said: "Prize money."

The date that changed everything for Li—and for the global landscape of tennis—was June 4, 2011. There were no memorials in China that day for the protesting students who were massacred

around Tiananmen Square exactly 22 years earlier. But 116 million Chinese fans—nearly double the population of France—gathered around their television sets to watch Li defeat the defending
champion, Francesca Schiavone, for the French Open title. LI NA,
WE LOVE YOU! read the banner on the screen of national broadcaster CCTV, while a presenter raved: "A miracle, a breakthrough,
a first in more than 100 years of tennis!" The Chinese website
Sohu Sports calculated that the victory would net Li 234 times the
annual earnings of an average Chinese worker. "But she absolutely
deserves it!"

Stunned by the size of the Chinese audience, the WTA ramped
up its plans for expanding its presence in Asia while top brands
rushed to sign endorsement deals with Li. With Rolex and Nike
already signed up, her agent, IMG's Max Eisenbud (who also represents Sharapova), struck multiyear deals with Mercedes-Benz,
Samsung, and Häagen-Dazs, among others, pushing Li's total annual earnings to more than $18 million.

But fame and fortune seemed to disorient Li. She lost early in
nearly every other event that year, and failed to make the quarterfinals in six consecutive majors. Last summer, at her request,
Eisenbud put together a list of coaches from which she could
choose. One of them was Carlos Rodriguez, an Argentine who had
guided Justine Henin her entire career, including 117 weeks as
world number one, and had recently opened a tennis academy
in Beijing. "I told Max immediately, 'Him, him!'" Li recalled. "I
thought if he could make Justine a champion . . ." She made the
Montreal finals the first week they worked together in August
2012, and then won the Masters in Cincinnati the following week,
her first tournament victory in 15 months.

On a muggy afternoon this past July, Li Na's quads were burning.
It wasn't the heat, exactly, though the temperature at her training
base in Beijing hovered around 94 degrees. Nor was it the torturous workout she'd endured so far: half an hour of running, jumping, and agility drills; an hour of rapid-fire core and upper-body
training in the gym; then two 90-minute sessions on court, honing
her fitness and footwork—and an attacking game she is sharpen-
ing for the U.S. Open.

The burning sensation came from the deep sand Li was churning underfoot—part of a beach-volleyball court that Rodriguez has turned into a terrain of pain at his sprawling tennis academy called Potter's Wheel. For 45 minutes, Rodriguez pushed her through a series of lunging exercises in the sandpit, giving her only 30 seconds of rest in between (not coincidentally, almost the same amount of time a tennis player is allowed between points). The day before, during a timed cycling session, Li had screamed, "I'm on the verge of dying!" Today, after a set of lunging volleys in the sandpit, she bent over her aching legs, her entire body soaked in sweat, and exclaimed, "Now I think I'm actually dying."

At five feet eight inches tall and 143 pounds, Li has an almost perfect body for tennis: agile feet, pistonlike legs, and a sculptured core and upper torso. "I'm as fast and strong as I've ever been," Li said earlier that day, as she hunched over a full plate of rice, eggplant, pork, and tofu at the academy's cafeteria. "It just takes me longer to recover than when I was younger." As Li finished off her food, Jiang dumped several spoonfuls of a high-energy protein powder into a bottle of water and shook it vigorously. "It tastes terrible, but I have to drink it every day," she said, grimacing as she forced it down.

The dozens of young tennis players eating at the tables around us were under strict orders not to bother Li. But a trio of boys, 12 or 13 years old, kept sauntering by, stealing glances at the small stud earrings that ringed Li's upper lobe and her tanned forearms, glaring white strips marking where her wristbands normally were. (The rose tattoo on Li's chest, which caused such a controversy in China when she got it at age 19 that she covered it up during televised matches, was hidden under her T-shirt today.) After she cleared her tray, separating plates and utensils just like all the other players, one of the boys sidled up to her. Li smiled and posed for a photo, but there was little small talk. She only wanted to get to her dorm room upstairs for a quick nap before another grueling afternoon with her coach.

Rodriguez is the ultimate guru, with an intellectual approach to the physical and psychological aspects of the game. Despite his gentle demeanor, his training regimen is so relentless that when Li began in earnest last winter, she told Jiang: "How did Justine continue with Carlos for 15 years? I was ready to die after just three days." Returning midseason to this kind of training, Rodriguez

believes, will help Li avoid a late-season slide. "Li Na has the resources for two more years at the top," Rodriguez said. "The only
question mark will be her motivation at the end of the season."

For now, at least, Li seems invigorated to be adding new dimensions to her game. At one point during practice, Rodriguez had Li
stand on one leg on a wobbly pedestal near the net, cracking volleys without losing her balance. Coming to the net behind forceful
approaches, Rodriguez says, will help her end points more quickly
(key for a veteran) and add an element of surprise. "I was reluc-
tant at first," Li said. "But if I don't try it now, perhaps I'd regret
it when I retire. As Carlos told me, 'Without trying, you'll never
know how good you can be.'"

A glimpse of that future may have come on Wimbledon's Center Court, during Li's quarterfinal match against Radwanska. Her
net-rushing tactics earned Li four set points in the opener. She
served an ace on one of them, but when it was called out, she
neglected to challenge, and the set went to the Polish player. Li
battled back to win the second set before finally succumbing in the
third. When a reporter asked Li if she wanted to know the correct
call on the serve that would have won her the set—and perhaps
the match—she stared in disbelief. "Was it in?" she asked.

Still, Li had a right to seem upbeat afterward. This was the first
time since 2010 that she had reached the quarterfinals at Wimbledon—fulfilling a goal that Rodriguez had set for her—and
the lifelong baseliner charged the net an astonishing 71 times in
the quarterfinal match, winning 48 of those points. "Many people
maybe thought I was mad, coming up to the net again and again,"
she said. "But I'm glad I was brave enough to try something new."

Sinking into her white Mercedes coupe after a day of training, Li
Na craved one thing above all: a massage. The manicure, the shopping, the spicy Sichuan meal: all those little luxuries would have to
wait while her aching body got pounded and kneaded back into
some semblance of normalcy. "When I was growing up, I never
got a massage, never needed one," Li said, as Jiang maneuvered
into Beijing's snarled late-afternoon traffic. "But now, anything less
than a 90-minute massage and I won't be able to walk tomorrow."

From the car, Li rang up the spa at their five-star hotel and was
told that the early-evening slots were all booked. It would have
been easy for Li to mention her name, but she enjoys a little an-

onymity, especially in China. Their suite was registered under a pseudonym, so she left the spa their room number. "Yesterday, the receptionist said, 'You know, you look a bit like that tennis player.' Later, when she found out, she said: 'No way! But you're so skinny in person!'" Li threw her head back and laughed.

The question of retirement looms over Li. Among the world's top 30, only Serena Williams is older—by five months. Relaxing on a rumpled single bed in her dorm room at Rodriguez's academy, Li laughed when the subject of age came up. "I didn't like tennis for the first 15 years I played," she said, as Jiang, carrying an armful of dirty clothes, asked if there was any more laundry for him to do. "But now, when I'm finally at a stage where I'm enjoying my tennis life, everybody keeps asking me when I'm going to leave."

Age may be a subject Li avoids, but she makes no secret about wanting children—and becoming "a housewife trailing after my husband." The couple recently began renovating their three-story villa in Wuhan, where her mother and his parents still live. While Li trained in Beijing, Jiang flew down to shop for curtains and light fixtures, emailing her photos for approval. (When Li objected to the $10,000 price tag on one designer fixture, Jiang replied that it was the cheapest one he'd been shown.) If motherhood comes, Li is adamant that her offspring would not pursue a tennis career. "It's too painful," she said.

In the state-run Chinese system, Li "never heard a single positive word in a decade or more," Rodriguez told me, noting that she can still turn that negativity, at low moments, into a corrosive form of self-loathing. Henin was once psychologically fragile too, he said. But he worked with her from age 13; Li, at 31, has a fully formed character shaped, in large part, by the Chinese sports system and her reaction to it. "When I ask how she's doing, she almost never mentions anything good. I have to force her to tell me also what she is doing right."

Rodriguez's probing into Li's feelings has provoked greater discomfort than his demanding workouts. In all her years in China, no coach ever asked Li about them. But Rodriguez pushes her to express herself so that her innermost thoughts—and the experiences that shaped them—can be dealt with. "All of her sad memories and experiences are imprinted on her," Rodriguez said. "They can never be erased, but she has to acknowledge that they have also helped forge her into the person and player she is." The process, Li told me, "felt like spreading salt over a wound at first. It has been hard and painful, but once I spill things out, Carlos can help me find ways to get over it. He's made me much stronger mentally."

Just days before Wimbledon began, Li vowed to quit in anger when she lost early—her tailspin continuing—at a warm-up tournament in Eastbourne. To her surprise, Rodriguez agreed. "Everybody always says, 'No, no, Li Na, don't quit,'" he recalled. "I told her: 'Fine, you can quit. Stop playing if that's what you feel. But if you're quitting because you didn't like what happened today, have some courage. This is just a game, but you can't continue to run away from your problems. They'll follow you until the end of your life.'" Shaken by his words, Li agreed to train hard for Wimbledon. "At Wimbledon, we started to see a different person emerge—more relaxed, more positive," Rodriguez said. "Now I think she's hungry for more."

By the time her three weeks of training ended in late July, Li seemed primed, physically and mentally, for the hard-court season leading up to this week's U.S. Open. Nothing is guaranteed, of course, and that unpredictability is part of what makes Li so intriguing. She still aims to win another Grand Slam, and she's doing everything she can in the time she has left on court to make that happen. But under Rodriguez's guidance, she now seems motivated less by pride and prize money than by the desire to leave the game on her own terms, with no regrets. "I know I can't win every match," she said. "But as long as I've gone through this difficulty, this process, all I need to do is try my best. Then I can be happy, whether I win or lose."

AMANDA HESS

You Can Only Hope to Contain Them

FROM ESPN: THE MAGAZINE

MINUTES AFTER RONDA ROUSEY bounded into the Octagon this past February for the first women's fight in UFC history, she found herself grappling with two formidable opponents. The first was former Marine Liz Carmouche, who was suddenly suctioned to Rousey's back, strangling her and twisting her head. The second was her low-cut black crop top, whose elastic spaghetti straps were no match for Carmouche's moves.

In a last-minute mishap, handlers had failed to order Rousey a formidable fight-night bra and instead handed her one of the light-as-air chest coverings she usually wears for weigh-in. Now that teensy swath of fabric was the only thing standing between Rousey's goods and 13,000 onlookers at the Honda Center in Anaheim, California—and it was inching closer and closer to the mat.

"When someone's on your back trying to rip your head off, things tend to slip around a bit," Rousey says. After one failed attempt at a wardrobe adjustment, she switched her focus to freeing herself from the choke hold "so she wouldn't snap my neck in half." As soon as she flipped Carmouche to the floor, Rousey went straight for her own neckline. Bad move: "I got kicked straight in the chest right as I was trying to adjust my bra."

Rousey eventually finished Carmouche with her signature arm bar. But the rumble over the bra had only just begun. Online commentators asked whether the UFC's new female fighters required a dress code to fight modestly. Others immortalized the near nip slip as an ever-refreshing animated GIF.

The episode was the latest skirmish in a long-standing war over the place of the mammary in the pectoral-dominated world of sports. Breasts are an impressive network of milk glands, ducts, and sacs, all suspended from the clavicle in twin masses held together by fibrous connective tissue. But a mounting body of evidence suggests that they pose a serious challenge in nearly all corners of competition. Gymnasts push themselves to the brink of starvation to avoid developing them. All sorts of pro athletes have ponied up thousands of dollars to surgically reduce them. For the modern athlete, the question isn't whether breasts get in the way—it's a question of how to compete around them.

"Gina Carano was an amazing fighter, and she had a fantastic rack," Rousey says of the MMA fighter-turned-actor. But then again: "You don't see big titties in the Olympics, and I think that's for a reason."

Breasts have taken a metaphorical beating from the sports world ever since women first entered the arena. Greek folktales spun the myth that a race of all-female Amazons lopped off the right breast in order to hurl spears and shoot arrows more efficiently. (In Greek, *a-mazos* means "without breast.") Centuries later, in 1995, CBS golf analyst Ben Wright controversially told a newspaper that "women are handicapped by having boobs. It's not easy for them to keep their left arm straight. Their boobs get in the way."

Wright's commentary wasn't exactly the result of careful scientific review. ("Let's face facts here," he opined in the same interview: "Lesbians in the sport hurt women's golf.") But what if he had a point? Research shows a typical A-cup boob weighs in at 0.43 of a pound. Every additional cup size adds another 0.44 of a pound. That means a hurdler with a double-D chest carries more than four pounds of additional weight with her on every leap. And when they get moving, the nipples on a C- or D-cup breast can accelerate up to 45 miles per hour in one second—faster than a Ferrari. In an hour of moderate jogging, a pair of breasts will bounce several thousand times.

None of this feels good. Large breasts are associated with back and neck pain, skin rashes, carpal tunnel syndrome, degenerative spine disorders, painful bra strap indentations, and even anxiety and low self-esteem. In one study of women racing in the 2012 London Marathon—cup sizes AA to HH—about a third reported breast pain from exercise. Eight percent of those described the pain as "distressing, horrible or excruciating." Reports of pain grew with every cup size.

It's no wonder that athletes rack up strategies—and bills—for battling the bulge. Well-endowed golfers flock to former player-turned-coach Kellie Stenzel, who teaches them to shift their posture forward so their swing clears the top of their breasts; the bigger the chest, the deeper the lean. "These women have a real feeling of relief, like, 'Nobody ever told me that before,'" Stenzel says, adding that despite Wright's claims, she's never seen a chest she couldn't coach into compliance.

American archer Kristin Braun says her chest causes clearance issues as she draws her bow; in order to get around it, she anchors the string farther away from her body, which can diminish power and consistency. Australian hurdler Jana Rawlinson received breast implants in 2008, then promptly removed them in hopes of speeding up her times. "Every time I raced, I panicked about whether I was letting my country down, all for my own vanity," she told reporters. And inside the Octagon, Rousey's boob issues go deeper than the cotton-Lycra blend. "The bigger my chest is, the more it gets in the way," says Rousey. When she's fighting at her most curvaceous weight, "it just creates space. It makes me much more efficient if I don't have so much in the way between me and my opponent."

But nowhere do breasts pose more of a liability than in the world of elite women's gymnastics, where any hint of a curve can mean early retirement. "Look at missiles that shoot into the air, batons that twirl—they're straight up and down," says Joan Ryan, author of the 1995 exposé of gymnastics and figure skating, *Little Girls in Pretty Boxes*. In order to stay stick straight, elite gymnasts undereat and overtrain, which delays menstruation. "You can't afford to have a woman's body and compete at the highest level," Ryan says.

To keep competitors from reaching puberty, coaches would push away bread baskets at the table and rifle through their belongings to sniff out hidden treats, says Dominique Moceanu, who was, at 14, the youngest, teensiest competitor on the 1996 gold medal USA Olympic team. "The sport pushes us to be breastless little girls as long as possible," she says. But though breasts were forbidden, privately "we longed for them."

Laying off the carbs may do the trick for preteens, but most adult athletes can't starve their boobs out of existence. So every year, some competitors head to the Marina del Rey, California, office of Dr. Grant Stevens in pursuit of a streamlined frame.

Stevens, a plastic surgeon with backswept blond hair and a boyish face he maintains through injections of Botox and Restylane, is known as the inventor of a scalpel-free procedure that leaves women multiple cup sizes (and up to $15,000) lighter with minimal recovery time. The doctor says he's treated volleyball players, golfers, ballet dancers, and assorted Olympians, though he won't name names. (He trains his lasers on men as well, because nothing calls their abilities into question like a pair of man boobs.) But many of his patients have already lost out on the years of weightless chests needed to reach the highest levels of competition. At the size they walk in with, Stevens says, "they would never get to be a pro athlete."

Not all athletes agree that large breasts constitute a competitive disadvantage. In 2009 then 18-year-old Romanian tennis player Simona Halep announced she was having her breasts surgically reduced from a 34DD to a 34C, saying they were slowing her reaction time and causing back pain. Upon hearing about Halep's plan, retired South African beach-volleyball player Alena Schurkova took the opportunity to launch a big-boob-pride campaign. "If she does this, it sends out the message that girls with big boobs can't play sports, and that is just wrong," Schurkova said. "I am 32E, and I have never found them to be a problem. I could be double what I have"—six pounds per boob!—"and I would still be okay to perform."

Maybe so, but Halep's downsizing appears to have paid off: before she went under the knife, she was ranked around 250; by 2012, she'd cracked the top 50.

When Kathrine Switzer became the first woman to don a bib at the Boston Marathon in 1967, science was unprepared to grapple with the female frame in motion. Critics warned her that the repetitive movement could cause her breasts to atrophy and her uterus to drop out of her vagina. (She ran the race in a flimsy fashion bra under a T-shirt and sweatshirt.) The sports bra wasn't even invented until 10 years later, when a group of women sewed two jock straps together and slung them over their shoulders. (An early version of the original Jogbra is now preserved behind glass at the Smithsonian.)

The advent of the sports bra "was like the birth control of the women's sports revolution," Switzer says. Still, for the next 10-plus years, scientists stayed out of athletes' efforts to make their breasts stay put. Finally, in 1990, Oregon State University researcher LaJean Lawson invited female subjects onto a treadmill and filmed the results in the first-ever study of breast movement. Today, labs have sprung up in the UK, Australia, and Hong Kong to study breast biomechanics—and deliver the results to bra manufacturers seeking to develop cutting-edge solutions.

At Britain's University of Portsmouth sits a laboratory outfitted with black floors, black curtains, and a treadmill surrounded by infrared cameras aimed directly below a subject's neck. Here, Jenny White, a lecturer in the school's sport and exercise science department, invites women to take off their shirts, outfit their breasts and torso with reflective markers, step onto the treadmill, and break into a jog. On a set of monitors, White and her group of female researchers track 3-D images of the migrating dots in an attempt to better understand how breasts move through space. Her research has confirmed that size does matter: as breasts get bigger, they accelerate quicker, move faster, and bounce higher. What she doesn't know—yet—is whether these speedy breasts really slow athletes down.

Part of the problem is that, 23 years after Lawson's seminal study, data collection is limited to relatively sluggish treadmill jaunts. "We can't take them to the park to do a decathlon," White says. It's easy to get a group of women to run at the same low speed. It's almost impossible to get them all to jump to the same height, swing a racket at the same trajectory, punch with the same power, or run at a world-record pace. And while breasts are all built from the same basic elements, the proportions and densities of the tissues vary among individuals; they fluctuate throughout the month; they transform in puberty, pregnancy, motherhood, and menopause. "It makes our job quite difficult," she says.

The research does reveal the self-selection process by which some women end up on the court while others—disproportionally, those with bigger breasts—are relegated to the stands. Hormones could play a part: "Studies suggest that curvier women may have higher estrogen levels, while higher testosterone levels are associated with more competitiveness and aggression," says Florence Williams, author of *Breasts: A Natural and Unnatural History.* "So it's possible that if you have more estrogen, you might be somewhat less inclined to compete." Other factors include the pain and embarrassment associated with larger breasts in motion. Deirdre McGhee, a senior lecturer at Breast Research Australia, has been studying breast support and bra fit for the past decade—and watching young athletes drop out as their breasts pop up. "They're embarrassed. They don't want to talk about it. And so they stop," McGhee says. "They just don't move."

McGhee counsels women to engage in physical activity that puts less of a strain on their breasts. But as the breasts get bigger, the field narrows. Busty ballet dancers are transferred to hip-hop. Postpubescent gymnasts get put on the rings. Runners are instructed to play in the water instead.

If all else fails: yoga.

The physical and social barriers that come with a larger cup size mean that the Schurkovas and Haleps of the world stand out. Nothing appears to be weighing Serena Williams down on the court, but her measurements represent such an outlier that when Caroline Wozniacki stuffed her tank top and skirt with towels at a Brazilian exhibition match last year, everyone knew which great she was ridiculing. Serena took the impression in jest, dismissing charges that it was racist. (Apparently, Wozniacki's temporary augmentation didn't weigh her down either; she won the point.)

But even when an athlete's breasts aren't notably large—and no matter how expertly she works to contain them—she still must contend with oglers who fixate on her peaks instead of her performance. When Halep announced her plans for surgery, more than 1,400 men signed a petition begging her to stay busty. Water polo matches are so notorious for nipple slips that bloggers hover over the pause button in hopes of glimpsing an areola. And in the rare case that a breast is on full display, all hell can break loose. Even as Carmouche was threatening to break her neck, Rousey felt as if her falling bra was a life-or-death situation too. If she failed to get a grip, "I'd be morbidly embarrassed," she says.

Nebiat Habtemariam can relate. At the 1997 world championships, the 18-year-old Eritrean runner suffered the longest wardrobe malfunction of all time during a qualifying heat for the women's 5,000-meter run. Lacking her own gear, Habtemariam asked to borrow another runner's red singlet for the race. What she failed to borrow was a sports bra. She spent her 18 minutes on the track with one breast perpetually in view. She didn't leave her hotel room for the rest of the week.

But the run of shame wasn't the end of Habtemariam's story. She kept running—in two more world championships, three Olympic Games, and countless other competitions. Last year she was the third woman to finish the Milano City Marathon, her lime-green and blue sports bra securely in place. It was further confirmation that the world's best athletes are those who have managed to transcend the limits—and the addendums—to the human body. Or as Rousey put it about her one-two punch of neutralizing Carmouche and her little black bra at the same time: "Multitasking!"

ELI SASLOW

"Anybody Who Thinks This Is Porn or Abuse Doesn't Know My Family"

FROM ESPN: THE MAGAZINE

THE ATHLETIC DIRECTOR walked onto the field unannounced, wearing jeans and sandals, and Todd Hoffner knew in that moment that something was terribly wrong. Nobody interrupted his football practices at Minnesota State Mankato without advance notice and permission. His success as head coach was based on maintaining total control; each practice was scripted to the minute. He believed small disruptions in preparation became big problems during games, so he sometimes asked his players to recite a motto: No mistakes. No distractions. No surprises.

Now, on August 17, 2012, his life was about to become the story of all three.

The athletic director approached Hoffner at midfield and told the coach he wanted to speak with him privately. "What's this about?" Hoffner asked, but the athletic director simply motioned for him to follow. Only a month earlier, Hoffner had earned a new four-year contract with a raise of more than 15 percent, and he had already stated his plans to stay at Mankato for the rest of his career. Hoffner and the AD walked into an adjacent building, where a woman from the university's human resources department was waiting. She handed Hoffner a typed note on university letterhead, and he hurriedly began to read, each phrase blurring into the next. Investigative leave. Effective immediately. No longer permitted on university grounds.

"Is this a joke?" Hoffner asked. "What did I do?" The woman from HR refused to answer. She told him to leave campus immediately. She said he would learn more about the university's reasoning in the next few days.

Hoffner drove back to his house in the nearby town of Eagle Lake, his hands shaking at the steering wheel, and told his wife, Melodee, who was equally at a loss. For the next three days, he barely slept. Mel vomited from stress. Todd watched game film at midnight in the living room, seeking comfort in routine. Together they made a list of potential reasons for Hoffner's banishment. He had worked his assistant coaches 70 or 80 hours a week despite their occasional complaints about long hours. He had cussed, punished players for breaking his rules, and, every once in a while, lightly grabbed a player. *Did they suddenly decide you drive people too hard?* his wife asked.

Some other colleagues saw Division II football as an obscure stopover on the way to bigger jobs, but not Hoffner, a farm boy from Esmond, North Dakota, who had started his coaching career in nine-man high school football. Now he was entering his fifth season as Mankato's head coach, earning six figures and winning division titles—by some measures the most successful coach in the school's history. Now strangers at the grocery store stopped to congratulate him and take his picture. Now he had a house in the suburbs where a motivational poster hung in the kitchen: IF YOU BELIEVE IT, YOU CAN ACHIEVE IT.

He had always wanted only one kind of life, a coach's life, and now, at age 46, he had it. There was his beautiful wife who dressed in Mankato purple, his three young kids and their tradition of Family Fun Nights on Fridays, his one free night during the off-season, when they would go to Chuck E. Cheese's, then come home to watch a movie. He was muscular, competitive, and stoic. His friends considered him the model of a football coach: beloved by some assistants, feared by some administrators, but respected by almost everyone on campus.

Now he phoned the university and heard he would receive an overnight letter, which didn't show up for days. So he began to slowly disassemble the life he had built. He wanted to prepare for the worst, in case he was suspended or demoted or even fired. He called coaches at other small colleges, asking about vacant assistant positions. He canceled his golf club membership, convinced he wouldn't be able to afford it without a job.

He was about to suspend his cable on a Tuesday morning when five police cars pulled up to his house. Two officers approached the door. Hoffner greeted them outside.

"What's all this about?" Hoffner asked.

This time he got an answer, and it only confounded him more.

He was under arrest on suspicion of producing and possessing child pornography.

By the time Blue Earth County assistant district attorney Mike Hanson sat down with two police detectives to watch the videos that would determine Todd Hoffner's guilt or innocence, half a dozen people at the university and beyond had already seen the evidence and rendered their own verdicts.

The inquiry began on August 10 because of an everyday inconvenience: Hoffner's university-owned cell phone had broken, and he brought it to the school's IT department. A technician offered a temporary replacement phone and agreed to rescue Hoffner's photos and videos. A few days later, the technician was "very shocked," he later testified, to find videos of Hoffner's naked children on his old phone—one of them 92 seconds long and the other 10, both recorded earlier in the summer.

During the previous year, the university president had sent an email to all employees telling them to report suspected sexual crimes in the wake of accusations against former Penn State assistant football coach Jerry Sandusky. "Subject: Sexual Violence Reporting," the email had read. "Importance: High." So the technician brought Hoffner's videos to a supervisor, who alerted someone in HR, who notified the police. But even the police didn't know whether what they were watching was a crime. The officers found the videos "disturbing," they said, but they also realized these were ambiguous acts by Hoffner's own children. They wanted more guidance on how to proceed, so they called Hanson.

Hanson had worked dozens of child pornography cases in his seven years as a prosecutor for Blue Earth County and had once specialized in sex crimes in Indiana. He had helped convict pedophiles, rapists, and serial sex offenders. Of all the important purposes of his job, the one he talked about most was protecting children.

He pushed Play on the first video; it showed a living room with three children standing on an ottoman in the center of the frame. There were two girls, ages four and nine, and a boy, eight. They wore towels and faced away from the camera. Around 10 seconds into the video, they dropped their towels and turned to the camera while singing in unison, "Hey, watchya doing naked!" The boy grabbed his penis as he jumped and danced. Hanson thought it looked like masturbation. The girls touched their butts and mooned the camera while they sang and giggled. Their faces sometimes cut out of the frame, but their bodies stayed in view. The children occasionally pushed each other's backs and bottoms. About halfway through the 92 seconds, they put their towels back on, climbed back onto the ottoman, and then began the naked routine again.

Hanson had seen all kinds of pornography in his years as a prosecutor. He knew the legal definitions of "lewd" and "masturbation" and "pornographic." He also believed that a good prosecutor had to trust his own eyes.

The second video, filmed only a few seconds later, showed more of the same. The girls sang and danced while naked. Then their brother ran into view wearing nothing but a football helmet. Hoffner could be heard chuckling behind the camera just before the screen went dark.

"If these videos don't cross the line, where is the line?" Hanson wrote in a court memo he later filed with the judge. (Hoffner has since had the videos sealed in court; *The Magazine* pieced together their content through court filings.)

Hanson told the police that what they were watching looked like a crime, and the police decided to pursue it.

"These videos are not the proverbial baby in the bathtub photographs," he wrote to the judge. "You'll know it when you see it."

It took four hours in jail before Hoffner was told that the charges against him related to videos of his children on his cell phone. It took a night behind bars and then another day for police to allow him to watch those videos with his lawyer. A police officer sat in the room with them to provide supervision. The lawyer took notes. Hoffner tried to pretend the children on the screen were strangers, hoping it would help him critique the videos more harshly.

They watched in silence. The police officer fidgeted in his seat.

"That was it?" Hoffner said when the second video ended. "The only thing I saw was a bunch of happy kids."

He explained to the lawyer that his children had been nearing their bedtime on a weeknight. They had just gotten out of a bubble bath, which the three kids often took together in a big banana-shaped tub upstairs because the Hoffners believed in teaching their children to be comfortable with their bodies. "There's no parenting book that says kids shouldn't be naked together," Hoffner said. He had been downstairs working while his kids took a bath. They suddenly appeared before him with their hair wet and towels wrapped around their waists. They said they had made up a skit and wanted Hoffner to film it. He had no idea what they were going to do; he didn't particularly care. He had a team to coach and a season to prepare for. Football was his obsession, and at times during the season he was home before his children's bedtime only once or twice in a week. He was a loving but distracted father, he said. And his goal in this moment was to appease them—to speed up the sometimes-interminable bedtime routine, get them to bed, and return to the TV—so he grabbed his BlackBerry and hit Record.

The kids dropped their towels. They sang and danced and shouted. His son played air guitar, and his daughters bobbed their heads to an imaginary beat. Hoffner held his phone to his chest and continued to film.

"Wow, are you guys done yet?" he said about 20 seconds into the first video.

"No," the four-year-old said.

"Let's start over, guys," the nine-year-old said.

"Guys, do the right thing!" the four-year-old said.

"Is the show over?" Hoffner asked again. And a few seconds later, just before he stopped recording, he said, "The show is over."

He had never thought about or watched the video again—until now, sitting in jail with his lawyer. Maybe here, in this space,

any video of naked children automatically looked like child porn,
Hoffner thought. But to him, it depicted a regular night at the
Hoffner house: three goofy kids, comfortable in their own skin,
trying hard to delay bedtime.

"Anybody who thinks this is porn or abuse doesn't know my
family," Hoffner told his lawyer.

He hired a publicist, who arranged a news conference. Mel agreed
to give a speech there. She never watched the videos herself, but
she had seen plenty of her children's naked dance routines. "The
charges against my husband are ridiculous and baseless," she said
during the August 27 news conference. "My family does what every
family does—we take videos and pictures of our kids in all their
craziness."

As a guidance counselor at Mankato West High, Mel knew
enough about psychology to analyze her own emotions. "Profound
sadness that manifests as anger," she said. She was angry at the
university for being "irresponsible," she said; and at the assistant
football coaches for never having the courage to support or defend her husband publicly; and at the coaches' wives, once her
closest friends, who now wouldn't even answer her calls; and at
the community as a whole for believing that her husband could be
anything other than a loving parent, a loyal employee, an unsenti-
mental farm boy, a good football coach. "I feel almost unsafe living
here, the way so many people get awkward around us and freeze us
out," she said.

She started on medication. She read books about criminology
and posted on college football message boards in support of her
husband, who had never before been arrested or suspended.

She consulted a child psychologist, who said the children would
do best in a "normal environment," so Hoffner told them he was
only on a "sabbatical" from work. Mel and the kids still went to
home football games on Saturdays because that's what they had
always done, though the games and the crowd made Mel feel even
more isolated, with no one talking to them. Hoffner was barred
from campus, so he watched on his computer at home as his former assistant coach won game after game by running Hoffner's
plays with Hoffner's players. The university forbade him from con-
tacting players. The team's new head coach, Aaron Keen, whom

Hoffner had saved in 2011 from a Division II school shuttering its football program, now preached loyalty and attentiveness. Keen had his players meet each week with a sports psychologist, who encouraged them to focus only on what they could control. Hoffner and his "situation," Keen said, were a "distraction" capable of derailing their season. The players referred to that distraction with a motto—"Flush it"—and they sometimes kept a toy toilet on the sideline to remind them to leave the past behind.

"Day by day, that team became mine a little less," Hoffner said.

Meanwhile, day by day, the prosecution's case against him was falling apart. Police seized and searched his laptop, cell phone, and a home computer and found nothing—no other images or videos that could be considered pornographic. A day care provider testified that the Hoffner children "have always exhibited appropriate social development" and "emotional competence." A certified sex therapist viewed the videos and said they consisted of "normal child's play." Blue Earth County Human Services conducted its own investigation and interviewed the Hoffner children, none of whom even remembered being videotaped naked.

"Where on your body do you not want to be touched?" an investigator asked.

"My eye," the now five-year-old responded.

"And who protects you?"

"My mom and my dad."

On November 30, a judge reviewed the evidence and ruled to dismiss Hoffner's case, concluding that the charges against him should never have been filed. "The videos under consideration here contain nude images of the defendant's minor children dancing and acting playful after a bath," the judge, Krista J. Jass, wrote in her decision. "That is all they contain."

Hanson, who had been asked by Hoffner's family and lawyer to drop the charges numerous times and always refused, said he disagreed with the judge's decision but would not appeal. Then he quickly defended his handling of the case. "No matter what the prosecutor does in a controversial case with a high-profile suspect, they will be criticized," he said before declining further comment about the case.

Hoffner and his lawyer held a news conference to address the judge's decision. He wore a purple tie, the university color, and read a prepared statement about waking from a nightmare. But as he looked around the room, he was thinking more about all the things he might never get back:

His team, which had gone 13-1 without him, earning Keen an award as regional coach of the year.

His reputation, because a Google search for his name brought up images of him in an orange jumpsuit.

His job, because the university said he was still under internal investigation and showed no signs of returning him to coaching.

After the dismissal, the Hoffner defenders came out in full force. There had been an online petition for Hoffner's reinstatement, a Facebook page, and a candlelight vigil at his house. But now donors threatened to rescind their pledges to the university. The president of the Touchdown Club, Dennis Hood, resigned. "This whole thing is nuts," Hood said. "The university made a mess of everything. They overreacted and ruined a man's life. Frankly, I'm embarrassed."

Hoffner said of the university: "They wanted to cast me as the next Jerry Sandusky. You hear my name, you see my picture, and you think, *Sick f——*. That's what I would think too. There's no coming back from that. I would have been better off if I'd shot somebody."

Hundreds of Hoffner supporters shared their outrage by forwarding a chain email that included another home video, this one shot by a Mississippi couple and submitted to *America's Funniest Home Videos* in 2008. It showed two naked boys dancing and gyrating behind their older sister—and it had aired on national TV and won the $10,000 first-place prize.

The university remained unmoved, citing the mysterious second investigation into Hoffner's conduct. It was unrelated to the initial charge of child pornography, officials said, but involved two "internal complaints" against Hoffner that the university refused to provide details about. (Despite these complaints, the school still employed Hoffner.)

Shocked by the initial charges, then by the judge's exoneration, the university community did what communities do: it ignored the awkward wreckage. Most players continued to avoid Hoffner because they had wanted to "flush it," and being around him still felt strange. The coaches' wives still left Mel's calls unreturned. The new president of the Touchdown Club said the university should move on and support a new coach. Keen and his assistants began preparations for another season, with a team that now felt wholly theirs. Hoffner was seen as both vaguely guilty and completely innocent, as an object of suspicion and a martyr, as lucky to be free and the unluckiest man in town.

About four months after his case had been dismissed, Hoffner awoke one morning in late spring to yet another day defined by his arrest. He microwaved pancakes for his daughters, then loaded the kids into a Kia minivan—"the grocery getter," he called it— and pulled out of the chalk-covered driveway. The neighborhood kids had slowly started coming back to the house to draw and play basketball, although a few parents still seemed "weird," Hoffner said.

Now he pulled up to the elementary school and watched his five-year-old walk toward the entrance. "Bye, Peanut," he shouted to her. He drove beyond the Mankato water tower, passing by his old practice field and the center of campus. He continued through a neighborhood and parked the minivan in front of a partially abandoned school building, quiet except for the hum of an industrial lawn mower.

"Welcome to my new office," he said.

The university had reassigned Hoffner during its investigation, and now he was making $101,000 for a shadow job as assistant director for facilities development. His workspace was a former storage closet, a windowless box of a room with poor cell-phone service. He had no training in facility management and no desire to learn. "I'm a football coach," he said. "That's all."

Hoffner sat in the windowless office and twirled a pen in his hand. He suspected the university would never give him his job back, but he felt trapped in a daily limbo, forced into a new kind of prison. The university refused to comment about its investigation—to anybody, about anything related to personnel. Hoffner, his lawyers, and the public could only guess as to its motives: Maybe administrators liked Keen better as head coach and wanted to "flush it." Maybe they hoped to guard against a lawsuit by finding just cause to validate Hoffner's dismissal. Maybe they were embarrassed that he'd violated policy and taken personal videos with his university-owned cell phone, whether or not those videos were illegal. Maybe they had found something unusual while analyzing years of search history on Hoffner's university-owned computers.

He had considered filing a lawsuit, but his lawyers advised him to wait until the university finished investigating and likely fired him. Then he'd appeal with help from his union and finally have grounds to sue.

He had not applied for other jobs because what other Division II school would take a risk on someone like him? Why not hire one of the 200 qualified applicants who didn't show up in an orange jumpsuit on Google?

So he sat in the windowless office and watched the clock on the wall inch toward 4:00 P.M., time for practice, the fixture of his schedule for 25 years. It happened to be the first day when coaches allowed players to put on pads and hit each other. The tradition had always been one of Hoffner's favorites—a day for the natural sorting of victims and aggressors.

He hadn't been to the football field in eight months. He wasn't sure whether he was even allowed there.

"Screw it," he said, standing up from his desk and grabbing his coat. "I'm going."

He drove the grocery getter to the practice field and parked against a fence, rolling down his window while he kept the engine running. He could sit behind the darkened windows without being noticed and listen to the familiar sound track of practice: shouting, cussing, and the shrill scream of a whistle set against the heavy bass of rap coming from a speaker.

He sunk down in the driver's seat and watched players he had recruited perform drills he had created with practice equipment he had ordered. There was number 93, the lineman he had recruited at a high school wrestling practice in Huxley, Iowa, driving roughly 200 miles back home in the dark. There was the star wide receiver who had been dismissed and was now back on the team. There barking orders in the center of the circus was his old assistant coach, Keen, whom Hoffner says he both saved from football oblivion and championed, arguing that Keen receive a salary of $60,000 instead of $50,000.

He watched in silence and timed each drill on the clock in the grocery getter. He broke down passing routes. He analyzed blocking schemes. "Good. Good," he said, talking only to himself. "Get low. Get low."

A former graduate assistant coach, helping Keen for the day, spotted Hoffner in the van, and Hoffner waved him over. The old assistant climbed into the backseat. "How you doing, Coach," he said.

"Not so good," Hoffner said.

They sat for a minute in awkward silence, watching practice unfold out the window. Hoffner had always thought football was a complicated game, one he had devoted his life's work to figuring out, but now the action on the field looked beautiful for its simplicity. Players were doing one-on-one tackling drills; each person tried to run by another without being taken to the ground. It was a game that offered the promise of self-destiny; the deserving player always won. That was the great thing about football, Hoffner thought now. It was fair and transparent. All the action unfolded out in the open for everyone to see.

In the coming weeks, the university would conclude its second investigation and dismiss Hoffner from the payroll without explanation. The union would file a grievance on his behalf. The university would again refuse to comment. Hoffner would consider signing up for unemployment insurance. More supporters would write the university in protest. A divided town would wait for the university to reveal its findings and its motives at an arbitration tentatively scheduled for late this summer, when another verdict would be rendered in the complicated, convoluted case of Todd Hoffner.

"Do I ever get to go back to my life?" Hoffner would ask. "Or have they erased it for good?"

But for a few moments inside his van, Hoffner was still just a football guy, talking to another football guy, watching a spring practice.

"That's what I miss—the idea that everything is in your control," he said, turning to the graduate assistant coach. "I got accused of something, got exonerated, and I still lost my job, my life, and my livelihood. How does that work?"

"I don't know, Coach. What can I do?"

Hoffner turned back toward the windshield. He watched a few more players go through the tackling drill.

"You can't do anything," he said. "But it's nice that you still call me Coach."

JONATHAN MAHLER

The Coach Who Exploded

FROM THE NEW YORK TIMES MAGAZINE

MIKE RICE IS COACHING AGAIN. Or rather, he's running after-school clinics for third- to sixth-graders at a vast, four-court indoor basketball facility in Neptune, New Jersey, where he also works out local high school players on Friday afternoons and coaches his son's high school team in a fall recreational league.

Considering where Rice was a year ago—preparing for his third season as head coach at Rutgers University with a guaranteed salary of $700,000—it is quite a step down. Of course, considering where Rice was seven months ago—a figure of national disgrace who was fired for mistreating his players—it's a little hard to believe he's coaching at all. "It helps when your best friend owns the place," Rice said.

We were watching his son's team, Red Bank Regional High School, warm up before a recent game against the inauspiciously named Brick Township High. Red Bank looked like your average suburban high school team, with the exception of one kid. When I asked Rice about him, he said: "The big man is terrible. Just watch."

The instant the game got under way, Rice started pacing manically up and down the floor, yelling nonstop, his raspy voice echoing across the gym. He hollered at his team after every trip down the court, invariably singling out players both for doing something right ("Are you kidding me?" he said when one of them squeezed between two defenders and laid the ball in off the glass. "You've got ballerina feet!") or wrong ("Ben, you're fighting for time! You get in the game and the first thing you do is give up an *and-1?*").

Rice wasn't berating anyone, and he definitely wasn't abusing anyone. Yet if you'd been watching him that night, you might very well have thought, *That guy is nuts.*

He was right, though: the big man had a long way to go. After he made one halfhearted attempt to stop a much smaller opponent from driving to the basket, Rice did a sideline demonstration for him: "This is a lion," he said, proceeding to roar loudly and menacingly raise both arms above his head. Then Rice lowered his arms limply by his side. "This is a wimpy little cat: *Meow.* Be a lion!"

The big surprise of the night was Rice's son, Mike III, a skinny sophomore guard who looked like a boy playing with men. He came off the bench midway through the first half and reeled off a couple of three-pointers, a reverse layup, and a teardrop shot off the dribble in the lane.

Rice and I had talked about his son's game a few times, and Rice did not always sound optimistic. "I've got to get him more into academics," he told me once, after receiving a text message from his wife informing him that Mike III had just been benched after going 0-for-3 in an AAU game.

Mike III has no shortage of ability and an excess of basketball intelligence, and Rice personally works him out in their driveway regularly. But he has a tendency to overthink things, which can be deadly for an athlete. It also makes him very different from his father, and his father's father. As Rice put it: "Rices generally go in headfirst and then think later."

Mike Rice was introduced to America last April when ESPN aired footage of him screaming at and demeaning his players, yanking them by their jerseys, shoving them, kicking them; throwing balls at their heads and groins; taunting them with homophobic slurs. Within 24 hours, millions of people had watched it, and Rice had been denounced by everyone from LeBron James to Governor Chris Christie. He was soon fired and disappeared from the public eye as abruptly as he entered it.

I first met Rice at the gym in Neptune on a hot, humid night about two months after all this happened. His daughter's under-12 AAU team, which Rice also coaches on a volunteer basis, had just annihilated an opponent, 47–11. The other team could barely keep possession of the ball, never mind get off a decent shot. I

introduced myself to Rice and told him that I felt a little sorry for
their opponents. "I don't," he said. "Tell them to work harder."

After the game, Rice invited me back to his house in nearby
Little Silver, New Jersey. Rice is frenetic on the sidelines of a basketball court, but his resting state is pretty wired to begin with, his
voice often rising to a half-yell even in casual conversation. "Have a
beer, for Christ's sake!" he shouted at me after I initially declined.

His wife, Kerry, offered to go out and get some dinner for us
but couldn't find her car key. After some searching around, Rice
produced it from his pocket. "Sorry, Pookie Bear," he said.

For the next two hours, we sat at a table on his deck, swatting
mosquitoes, drinking beer, and eating Italian takeout. His kids
were inside, watching the NBA playoffs, and Kerry eventually came
out and joined us.

It was the first time that Rice had spoken to a reporter since
delivering a brief statement of apology from his doorstep the day
he was fired, a strategic decision that was not easy for him to accept. "Everything I've ever done is fight, scratch, and claw," he told
me, "and now I have to sit back and take it, listen to people say
I was abusing my players? I was an idiot, but I never abused anybody."

From the beginning, Rice was clear he wasn't going to make
any excuses for his behavior, and he didn't. But when your life has
been reduced to a few minutes on YouTube and you've been living
under a self-imposed gag order for two months, it's impossible to
not want to explain yourself. "When you look at those moments,
they're ugly moments, there's no way of describing them any way
else," he said, adding, "Once every 20 practices doesn't make it
that way every day."

It's true that what the American public saw was a fraction of the
hundreds of hours of practices Rice conducted over the course
of his first two seasons at Rutgers. It's also true that the video was
made by a spurned ex-assistant who would end up filing a wrong-
ful termination suit against Rutgers. This was a video intended to
destroy Rice, and in some respects, it did. The question is to what
extent—and what kind of man will emerge now.

Going into the evening, I was expecting a cautious, scripted
conversation. What I got instead was my first glimpse of a man
who's not really capable of guarded moments and whose carefully
managed rollout could be managed only so carefully.

Over the course of the next few months, I would spend many hours with Rice and gradually get the feeling that he wasn't just agreeing to each of my requests for more time because I was writing "the profile," a key component of every shamed celebrity's blueprint for rehabilitation. My sense was that Rice genuinely wanted to figure out how he ended up in this position, or at least to help someone else figure it out. "It will be interesting to read how you piece this damn thing together," Rice told me during our last conversation a few weeks ago.

Rice, who is 44, was raised in a working-class suburb of Pittsburgh, where his father was the head basketball coach at Duquesne University.

The elder Rice was an honorable-mention All-American in college, a six-foot-three, 195-pound guard. ("Let's just say he wasn't the cleanest player," Rice says.) He grew up playing pickup in Detroit—his own father, Rice's grandfather, worked at a Ford factory and played semipro baseball—and he wanted to replicate that experience for his son, to instill in him the values of the streetballer. "He was a white kid playing in the middle of Detroit," Rice says of his father. "He wanted me to play the way he learned."

Rice's father refused to buy him a hoop, forcing him instead to ride his bike to a schoolyard and find some competition when he wanted to play basketball. By the time Rice was in middle school, his father was taking him along to adult pickup games. "These were some of the meanest, nastiest places in all of Pittsburgh," Rice says. "That's how I grew up, and how I was taught to play basketball, and how I was taught to handle myself."

In one conversation, Rice described his father as "the most competitive human being on the face of the earth."

"More competitive than you?" I asked.

"Oh, yeah," Rice said. "I'm calm compared with him. He's renowned."

There's some evidence to support this claim. In 1994, Mike Rice Sr. was ejected from a Portland Trail Blazers game—as a broadcaster, a first for the NBA. (Now 74, he still works as a color commentator for the Blazers.) Rice Sr. once threw his tennis racket after losing a match to one of his daughters. On the other hand, it was Rice who knocked out one of his father's teeth during a pickup game with his groomsmen on the day before his wedding.

When Rice wasn't playing basketball, he was watching it. Over the summers, while his mother took his two older sisters to tennis tournaments across the country—both became nationally ranked juniors—Rice tagged along with his father on his recruiting trips. During the school year, he spent most afternoons at his father's practices.

By age 12, Rice was barking directions at his father's players. "He'd be in their ear, saying they have to work on their jump shot or challenging them to a game of one on one," Rice Sr. says. "I'd run him off. I'd say, 'I'm not letting you come if you're going to be a distraction.' But he was always there." After practice, Rice Sr. sometimes found his son taped to the training table or stuck in the locker-room wastebasket, his hands and feet bound with athletic tape.

Rice idealizes his childhood, and his old-school basketball upbringing. "My father taught me the greatest game in the history of the world and the passion you have to have for it," he says. When I asked him if having such a hypercompetitive father might have had something to do with his behavior at Rutgers, he bristled. "Am I going to blame my father? No. That was on me. He also taught me right from wrong."

As a player, Rice did the best he could with his size and ability, earning a scholarship to Fordham University in 1987. By then, though, he had long since committed to following his father's career path. "Unfortunately, he had his mother's speed, so we ruled out the NBA early on," his father says. "His life was going to be coaching."

In early August, I was on a flight to Chicago with Rice when a woman sitting on the other side of him asked him what he did. It was her second attempt to engage him, having asked a few minutes earlier if he was a professional tennis player. (Rice was in his usual sports attire: synthetic striped polo, shorts, and sneakers.)

"I'm a college basketball coach," Rice replied.

He turned back to me. "That's always a tough one to answer. *Uh, I'm sort of between jobs right now.*"

We resumed our conversation, but the woman, whose interest in Rice was evident, soon asked him where he coached.

Rice paused. "Do you follow college basketball?"

"Not really," she said.

"Remember that coach who was fired from Rutgers? That's me."

"Shut up!"

Rice nodded. I asked if she recognized him now that she knew who he was.

"I just remember hearing the story over and over," she said. "Did you see the *Saturday Night Live* skit?" A few days after the video of Rice first aired, he was the subject of an *SNL* parody in which Melissa McCarthy played a psycho basketball coach.

"No, I still haven't seen it," Rice answered. "Everyone in my family has."

"Oh, my God," the woman said. "You have to watch it. It's hysterical!" She proceeded to recap the skit, in which McCarthy does everything from making her team serve her a meal at center court—"Where's the *bread?*"—to throwing a toaster at a player.

The woman asked if I was his lawyer, and when he told her I was a writer following him around, she asked why he waited so long to tell his side of his story. Rice said he didn't want to sound as if he were making excuses, because what he did was wrong.

"Did you not know that?"

"Oh, yeah," he said. "But you want to win. You'll do anything if you think it will help you win."

"So what have you been doing?"

"I've been doing a lot of basketball camps."

"Do you show up with a toaster?" She told him again that he had to watch the *SNL* skit. It was on YouTube; it was hilarious.

"I promise I'll eventually get to it."

Rice began working as an assistant coach at Fordham the day after he graduated from college in 1991. He spent the better part of the next 16 years bouncing between assistant jobs: Marquette, Niagara, Chicago State, Saint Joseph's, the University of Pittsburgh. In 2007, at age 38, he was named head coach of Robert Morris University in Pittsburgh, at a starting salary of $100,000, $80,000 less than he made at Pitt.

The Robert Morris team Rice inherited had just finished tied for fourth in its conference, but Rice thought he could get much more out of his players, especially because they were one of the league's worst defensive teams. He pushed his players to work harder and play more physically. "You had to give 100 percent at all times," says the captain of Rice's first Colonials team, Tony Lee, now a corrections officer in Massachusetts. "He demanded that from his players."

On the court, Rice refused to accept that his players might have limitations. Off the court, he seemed to understand that they were kids. At Robert Morris and at Rutgers, he assigned all of his players a "life coach," an assistant coach who made sure they attended classes and did their homework on time. At both schools, the team's cumulative grade point average rose considerably on Rice's watch.

Rice's Robert Morris players talk about the team ethos he built; during practice, no fallen player was allowed to get up off the floor until a few teammates had hustled over to help him. Rice basically shaped the team in his own image. "My players would rip your throat off," Rice told me. "We were an aggressive, intense team with an aggressive, intense coach. We believed in togetherness and toughness. We were old-school."

One part of coaching is pushing players to do things they don't necessarily think they can do. Another part is showing them how to lose. Not in the simple, good-sport way, but in how to take a loss and make something of it. Yet losing invariably set off feelings in Rice that he seemed constitutionally unable to process and that drove him outside the pages of the conventional coaching manual. "It was pathetic the way we defended and represented Robert Morris University," Rice said after one game. "It was an embarrassment." Rice was angry, and he wanted his players to get angry too, even to feel shame. "It's a hard paradox to explain or understand," says Andy Toole, one of his assistant coaches at Robert Morris. "He cares about you so much and he wants so much to win, he's willing to maybe go into a gray area with you to motivate you."

Still, the former Robert Morris players I spoke with said they were shocked by the Rutgers video. "Every coach yells—but throwing balls, kicking balls at players, the physical contact?" Lee said. "We had never seen that."

There are some obvious reasons that Rice might have been able to exert more self-control at Robert Morris. For starters, it's not a big-time basketball school; he was under less scrutiny there. Also, his Robert Morris team was well suited to his coaching style. The players were gritty kids at a commuter college outside Pittsburgh, not NBA prospects with a lot of other options. "Where were they going to go?" Rice says. "They were already at Robert Morris."

Rice might not have crossed the line at Robert Morris, but he also wasn't a completely different person there from the one he would become at Rutgers. When you think about it, all of the words people use to describe him at Robert Morris—"passionate," "emotional," "intense"—are not that far from "out of control." We tend to treat competitive sports, often justifiably, as a vehicle for all sorts of noble principles. But they are also, maybe more fundamentally, a realm in which men can behave like emotionally stunted rage machines. Anyone who watches college hoops is familiar with the sight of a coach in a suit and tie, neck veins bulging, screaming his head off. This may have something to do with the nature of the sport itself. Because basketball is so free-flowing, there's room for only so much strategy. A coach's ability to motivate his players—to somehow will them to play over their heads—is paramount. In this context, the raging coach seems perfectly normal. Out of context, you would be inclined to conclude the individual in question is seriously disturbed.

Maybe the biggest difference between Mike Rice at Robert Morris and Mike Rice at Rutgers is that at Robert Morris, his teams won. The Colonials ended Rice's first season in first place in their conference. In his second season, Robert Morris made it to the NCAA tournament for the first time in 17 years. They returned to the tournament the next year—Rice's last at Robert Morris—and nearly upset Villanova, a number-two seed.

Rice was developing a reputation for his success, but also for his temper. Against Villanova, a few of his players had to physically restrain him after a series of foul calls. Not long after, there was speculation in the media that Rice's courtside demeanor had prevented him from being considered for the head coaching job at Seton Hall. According to another story, even the staff pickup games at Robert Morris had to be discontinued because Rice was taking them too seriously.

On some level, Rice knew that his behavior was a problem. "The 1,500 people who came to the games at Robert Morris, I'd put on a good show for them," he told me. "If the game was boring, they could just watch me. I would watch myself and think, *Jeez, I've got to calm down.*"

In these fleeting moments Rice was capable of seeing himself as thousands, and eventually millions, of people would see him. And yet he couldn't, or wouldn't, get far enough outside himself long enough to recognize the need to change.

Rice says he stopped using the word "faggot" during his second season at Rutgers, when one of his assistant coaches pulled him aside to remind him that a student at the school had recently jumped off the George Washington Bridge after his roommate filmed him kissing another man. (I heard about this from Rice himself, who also told me that the assistant said to him, "Are you crazy?") But his homophobic slurs are still part of his lowlight reel, and he has to answer for them.

Toward that end, Rice has volunteered his services to the Gay, Lesbian & Straight Education Network. "You know how much courage it takes for a kid to come out in high school?" Rice asked me after his first meeting with a group of gay high school students in New Jersey.

In late July, the organization invited Rice to a daylong professional development seminar in Chicago. The objective was to help educators make gyms and locker rooms more inclusive. It started with the usual around-the-room introductions, only with a twist: participants were asked to give their names, their occupations, and their PGPs.

"Who can tell me what a PGP is?" asked the leader, Jenny Betz, a peppy 30-something in a necktie, blue button-down, navy trousers, and oxford shoes.

A man in a backwards baseball cap raised his hand to answer: "Your 'preferred gender pronoun.' What you like to be called."

"Exactly," Betz said, kicking things off with her own PGPs: "'She,' 'her,' 'hers,' or any combination of them will feel comfortable to me."

I had assumed that the rest of the participants would be lower-profile versions of Rice: coaches doing penance for gay slurs. As the introductions got under way, though, it became clear that the group was self-selected. They were almost all gay coaches and PE teachers from the area.

It was soon Rice's turn: "My name is Mike Rice. I am currently unemployed, but I worked as a basketball coach for 22 years. 'He,' 'him,' or 'his.'"

Over the course of the day, Rice and the rest of the participants watched videos about the experience of gay students in school sports, ran through hypothetical situations, and learned some catchphrases to help make them stronger advocates for gay students: *If you see something, say something. If it's mean, intervene. Grab a teachable moment.*

The scene bordered on comical: Mike Rice, last seen by much of America calling his players "faggots," sitting in the largest lesbian, gay, bisexual, transgender, and queer community center in the Midwest, talking about how to prevent the perpetuation of gay stereotypes. But Rice dived right into the various exercises.

At one point, Betz asked people to break into small groups and talk about a teacher or coach who made a strong impression on them. Rice told the story of his high school coach's sending him to the locker room in tears during the early minutes of an important game for yelling at his teammates to stop shooting and give him the ball.

"What the hell are you doing?" his coach asked, pulling Rice off the floor.

"What the hell are *you* doing?" Rice replied.

"That's it," the coach said. "You're done."

"It was the most embarrassing moment of my life," Rice said. "Until this happened."

Later, Betz requested two volunteers for some role-playing: what do you do when a colleague says something intolerant and offensive? "Who wants to be the PE teacher?" she asked.

Rice gamely raised his hand and went up to the front of the room with his female partner, a coach from a middle school in DeKalb, Illinois, who was supposed to ad-lib a response to his scripted lines.

"That kid has such a mouth on him," Rice read awkwardly. "He thinks he is so funny. Well, I shut him up today. I called him a little homo, and that cracked everyone up and shut him up. It's the first day we've had some peace in that class since the unit started."

His pretend colleague responded instantly: "How is that in any way appropriate?"

"What I want at Rutgers is a coach who is going to be intense, hardworking, and emotional and who is going to care every single second," the Rutgers athletic director, Tim Pernetti, said at Rice's introductory news conference in May 2010. "At the same time," Pernetti added, "I think we have a guy who understands . . . where the line is."

It would be too much to suggest that anyone could have known at that point that Rice didn't really understand where the line was. But it's easy to see that Rice and Rutgers were a bad fit from the start. This was one of the worst teams in one of the toughest basketball conferences in the country. Rebuilding the program was going to take time. Even if Rutgers improved significantly, it was not going to win a lot of games. What the team needed was not a coach single-mindedly obsessed with winning but one who knew how to lose.

The season before Rice arrived, Rutgers finished 14th out of 16 in the Big East, and then three players left the team, including the top scorer. He tried to make a virtue of their underdog status, hanging a punching bag in the locker room covered with laminated newspaper clippings about how bad Rutgers was going to be.

Rice also came up with a motto—a philosophy, really—to help guide practices: "Comfortable in Chaos." The concept was borrowed from the Navy SEALs, whose training assumes that the game plan has been scrapped and that they are in trouble. As Rice saw it, going up against teams like Georgetown and Syracuse was the basketball equivalent of a combat mission gone awry. He wanted practices to be more demanding—more hellish—than the games themselves. "Get ready for the chaos," he'd say as his players stretched out and warmed up.

Rice says he can now see that he took the idea way too far. "A good coach leads his team to water," he told me, borrowing a metaphor he picked up in anger management counseling. "A great coach leads them to water and makes them thirsty. I led them to water, put their heads in until I was satisfied with how much they drank."

It's a reality of coaching that no matter what you do, your team is not going to get better every day. During our conversations, Rice talked a lot about the ticking clock, how he felt as if he had only so much time to turn Rutgers around if he wanted to keep his job. I don't doubt that Rice felt a powerful urgency to win at Rutgers. But the pressure was only a catalyst. It was also who he was and what he did for a living that made his behavior at Rutgers seem inevitable.

"It's easy to say now, but when I was in it every day, I wanted to grab someone and just go, 'We can do this, we're going to show everybody,'" Rice told me. "Because that's who I am, and that's what I do."

By some measures, Rice's first season at Rutgers was a success. The team was projected to finish dead last in the Big East. Instead, Rutgers finished 12th, with an overall record of 15-17. As proud as he is of his Robert Morris teams, Rice considers this his greatest achievement as a coach.

His second season promised to be even better. He landed five highly rated prospects, a remarkable feat for such a weak program. Of course, five highly rated prospects also meant a lot of freshmen, all of whom had to get used to playing against bigger, stronger competition, not to mention college life. The team proved inconsistent. It showed flashes of potential, upsetting some top schools, but would then turn around and lose to schools it was expected to beat. It finished the season 14-18.

When you cut through all the mythology of the college coach as molder of young athletes, what you will find is basically a group of extremely competitive people whose livelihoods—not to mention self-images—are tied to the performance of a group of adolescent kids. This doesn't mean that coaches don't care about their players; it's just the reality of the job. "What did you think about when you were 17 to 22 years old?" Rice says, referring to some of the challenges of coaching college players. "You were out of your mind. The last thing you'd think about was jumping to the ball and making a play for your teammate and boxing out every time. You're thinking: *Where's the party going on? Who's hanging out with who that night?*"

In this sense, anyway, coaching really isn't so different from parenting. You want your kids to do better, to be better, and it can drive you crazy to watch them repeat mistakes or even just underachieve. The trick is to be able to drive down your own demons, to contain your frustration, and, more generally, to balance anger and disappointment with love and encouragement. This is what good parents and great coaches do. And it's what Rice couldn't do at Rutgers. Here's another way to look at it: college coaches often talk about saving kids from themselves; Mike Rice's problem was that he couldn't save himself—or his kids—from Mike Rice.

I've heard Rice call his behavior any number of things—"idiotic," "thoughtless," "stupid." As Rice puts it: "There's not a lot of thought that went into why you would throw a ball at somebody's feet as hard as you could. Is that going to make him rebound better? Probably not. I don't know what will, but that won't." Even as Rice acknowledges that he was wrong, he says his players understood he was just trying to motivate them. "Did any of them blink?" he asked me once. "If they were mad at me, they would have knocked the hell out of me. They're six-nine, 270 pounds."

After the video went viral, a number of Rice's players at Rutgers came to his defense on TV and in newspapers. "We always said we want to be pushed to that point where we get better," Tyree Graham, who was on the Rutgers team for Rice's first two seasons there, told me. "That's what he did."

It's not surprising that players would rally around their coach when they saw him being publicly pilloried. But not all of them agreed with what Rice was doing. The fact that Rice's players didn't fight back doesn't mean that his conduct wasn't abusive. What college athlete is going to knock the hell out of his coach? And to whom could Rice's players complain? The athletic director who hired him? The assistant coaches who were loyal to him and stood silently by while he bullied the players, or even participated in similar behavior themselves?

Rice says he wanted his players to fight back, to match his intensity. You can see how this might work as a form of motivation, but you can also see how it could easily backfire. Not all players are going to feel comfortable yelling at their coaches. And isn't it the coach's job to hold himself above and apart from his team, to be the educator, the grown-up?

One mystery of Rice's story is how his behavior went unreported in the media for so long. His practices were open to the public and regularly attended by local journalists. During Rice's first year, Jay Bilas, a college basketball analyst on ESPN and a former Duke player, watched a Rutgers practice and was so taken aback by "the volume level, the profanity, the challenging of the players," he told me, that he pulled one of Rice's assistants aside to say that someone needed to talk to him. Rutgers's new basketball coach, Eddie

Jordan, said over the summer that the school has been working with players who had some "psychological damage" from their time with Rice.

Rice's style might have worked at Robert Morris and with his first team at Rutgers—which he affectionately calls "the left-overs"—but it stopped working during his second season there. Part of the problem was that some of Rice's returning players felt that he was treating the freshmen differently, that they were being spared the worst of Coach Rice's Comfortable-in-Chaos boot camp.

Rice said one of his assistant coaches told him privately that his relentless intensity and negativity were hurting the team, and suggested he lighten up on some players. Another gave him a copy of a book called *The Positive Dog* to underscore the importance of positive feedback.

But Rice didn't listen, at least not until his second season at Rutgers was nearly over. "You're successful and now you keep building and it gets a little more out of control until it becomes a problem," he says. "And my problem became a huge problem, and I never took time out to analyze how I was going about things. Even though people would say things, I'm not hearing it. Because the intensity is what I was, the intensity is what I knew."

"You're lucky I have no more anger, buddy!" Rice joked one afternoon in June, swerving his Audi SUV to avoid a car that had just cut in front of him. We were on our way to lunch at a Ruby Tuesday near the Newark Airport. Sitting in the backseat was the man in charge of Rice's emotional and professional rehabilitation, John Lucas.

The John Lucas Athlete's Aftercare Program in Houston, where Rice has spent quite a bit of time since last spring, has become a mandatory stop on the disgraced sports figure's road to redemption. Whether you've been arrested for drunken driving (Rod Strickland) or kicked off your college football team for smoking pot (Tyrann Mathieu), John Lucas is the man to call.

"First thing I did was say you're going to have to pay for your treatment," Lucas said, recalling his initial conversation with Rice last spring. "Nobody is going to believe you're serious if you don't pay for it. And I'm not going to do insurance. When he heard the numbers—"

"Luc don't do anything cheap," Rice said.

It's hard to say what, exactly, Lucas does. He has no professional degree in psychology or social work. With his familiar recovery rhetoric, he's more AA sponsor than therapist. (Rice, he says, has to learn that he's just another "bozo on the bus.")

Lucas does, however, have the credibility of a survivor: about 30 years ago, his promising NBA career was derailed by cocaine and alcohol addiction. He also runs a lot of basketball clinics that can serve as halfway houses for a recovering Big East coach who's trying to get back into the game any way he can, even if that means spending a holiday weekend running layup drills for fifth-graders on a volunteer basis.

Between bites of his burger and fries, Lucas prodded Rice toward self-reflection. "When I was at Robert Morris having the time of my life, I wasn't having the time of my life, because I wanted more," Rice said. "When I was at Pitt, we went to the Sweet 16—but I just wanted to get a head coaching job. I always wanted more— more, more, more. I wanted to win every day. If you didn't do it, I was going to make you do it. I was going to overwhelm you with intensity, with passion, with motivation."

At the same time, Lucas also worked on the narrative of Rice's redemption. "He's going to have the gift of sensitivity now," Lucas said.

The whole conversation felt more than a little contrived, a lunchtime therapy session conducted for my benefit. Rice obviously sought out Lucas because he needed help trying to reclaim his reputation. But it would be unfair, and inaccurate, really, to say that Rice isn't going through something genuine. And if Lucas wasn't exactly offering searing psychological insights—his basic take was that Rice is no different from any other addict, only his vice is perfection—it was clear why Rice finds it comforting to be around him. Since the video, Rice has been defined, above all, by shame. (The same emotion he was often trying to get his own players to feel.) But Lucas, who during his playing days famously awoke from a bender soaked in his own urine, doesn't judge.

There's another thing too. Part of the allure of the world of competitive sports is that it doesn't require self-awareness. Your only job is to win. So when athletes and coaches find themselves in Rice's position, they often don't know how to talk about what they're going through. Lucas's vocabulary may be borrowed from a different recovery movement, but it's better than nothing.

"I make him talk to me about the fears," Lucas said.

"What are those fears?" I asked.

"I'm not good enough," Rice said.

"The fear that he won't get another job," Lucas said. "How long is everything going to be, 'Mike Rice, disgraced ex-Rutgers coach'?"

Lucas gestured at Rice, whose eyes were red and swollen with tears. "Look at the pain he's in right now. He can't forgive himself . . . If you can't see he's human and genuine, you're missing it. Here's somebody that's truly remorseful, that's trying to get everything back in a day, and I'm trying to tell him that that's gone forever. No one is ever going to forgive him. That's the good thing for Mike Rice. His self-worth will come by who he is now, not by his title."

One important distinction between Mike Rice and your average public figure looking for redemption is that Rice isn't guilty of some discreet transgression that arguably had little or nothing to do with how he did his job. His transgression *was* how he did his job. This is going to make it more challenging for Rice to get back into basketball. But he is determined to coach again.

After his son's game against Brick Township, as Rice and I drove to a pizzeria in a nearby strip mall, I asked him if he had any leads on basketball jobs. He was vague but sounded encouraged. He said that he would have to work his way back up, probably starting as a scout for an NBA team, but that he thought he would eventually get another shot.

Over the past several months, Rice told me repeatedly that he was going to emerge from this experience a better man, a better father, and a better coach. It was the sort of thing that anyone in his position would say, and I always glossed over it in our conversations. But it's actually an interesting issue. It's not, as it might seem on the surface, simply a matter of whether Mike Rice has "learned from his mistakes." It's a more universal, even philosophical question: can we really change who we are?

I was impressed by Rice's coaching during his son's game that evening, in particular how focused he was on every little thing his players were doing. This is exactly what most serious athletes want: a passionate coach who's doing everything he can to make you a better player. But I also wondered how difficult that intensity must be to corral, especially for someone with Rice's background and makeup. It's possible that Rice might be a better man and father if he could learn to harness his intensity and get past the need to always have to prove something. But that might not make him a better coach.

A lot of coaches do start their careers unable to calibrate their intensity. They gradually figure out that it doesn't much matter if this approach is successful, to say nothing of appropriate. It's not sustainable. An important part of this process is becoming self-aware, learning how to truly stand outside yourself. Another is absorbing something we were all told as kids: winning isn't everything. Or maybe it would be more precise in the context of Mike Rice to say that if winning is everything, you're probably going to wind up damaging a lot of people, yourself among them.

"I wish I would have been more thoughtful in how I went about making them forged as a team, making them tougher as a unit," Rice told me. By now, the restaurant had emptied, and our waitress was resetting the tables around us for the next day, making sure we knew that it was time to leave. Rice paused for a moment, before either saying what he knew he was supposed to say or trying on a new identity. "Or maybe just accepting that sometimes you have to accept that you are who you are. Look, we're not very good, but we're going to try every day, and we're going to do the right things."

BEN MᶜGRATH

The Art of Speed

FROM THE NEW YORKER

THE MOST ACCOMPLISHED MAN in the world's most glamorous sport stands at a drafting table all day. Using a number 2B pencil and a right-angle ruler, he produces as many as 300 drawings a week. The energy-drink company employing him dedicates another five staffers to scanning and converting his images into digital form, for analysis and manipulation on a computer-aided design (CAD) system. His name is Adrian Newey, and he is often said to perceive solid objects not by their outlines but by the flow of air currents around them. The drawings reflect this aerodynamic perversion: dense concentrations of swooping lines that flatter a rear suspension, say, and suggest something more on the order of a space shuttle. In a sense, he sketches speed itself.

Newey's sport is Formula One racing, the caviar to NASCAR's Cheetos. He is the chief technical officer for Red Bull Racing, Formula One's premier outfit, and spends most weekdays at a factory in the planned city of Milton Keynes, an hour northwest of London. "It's a bit NASA," my tour guide, Anthony Ward, said when I was granted the rare privilege of admission, last fall. We passed stereolithography machines and giant autoclaves operated by men in white lab coats, and a supercomputer with processing power equivalent to 100,000 iPads, according to Ward, who recited that last detail with a mixture of pride and chagrin. "We would be bigger if we could," he said, and began explaining the complex rules governing the ratio of resources that teams may allocate to their computational-fluid-dynamics departments and their wind tunnels, if they choose to have them. Red Bull's wind tunnel, in nearby Bedford, was originally built by England's Ministry of Defense, to test the Concorde. The rules and regulations extend for hundreds of pages, for reasons having to do with safety, politics, and whim; they amount to the "formula" that gives this billion-dollar pinewood derby its name.

Red Bull's drivers, Sebastian Vettel and Mark Webber, live in Switzerland and Buckinghamshire, respectively, and turn up in Milton Keynes only occasionally, to use the video-arcade-like simulator that mimics the track conditions of the various circuits, from the winding roads of Monte Carlo and the long straights of Monza to the steep hills of Spa-Francorchamps. "When Adrian arrived, he said that two things we should do are build a simulator and also introduce a gearbox dyno," Ward continued, referring to a dynamometer that tests the performance of transmissions under volatile, high-speed conditions. Using buttons on the steering wheel, drivers may shift as many as 3,500 times per race.

Some 550 people work at the factory, which comprises three steel-and-glass buildings, two of them linked underground. No tires are produced there; Pirelli supplies those. The engines, made by Renault, are shipped from France. The brake calipers are by Brembo, in Italy. There is a gym deep in the basement of one of the buildings, ostensibly for the pit crew to keep in shape, though I didn't see anybody working out. The Milton Keynes operation is principally about engineering and carbon composites: the chassis, or monocoque, and the odd-looking bracketing structures, called "wings," that are affixed on either end to improve the "global flow field around the car," as Newey says. The wings are tweaked throughout the season, in what's known as "bespoke customization" for each race. Everything is measured to within less than 10 microns—one-fifth the diameter of a human hair—of Newey's specifications, in the hope of shaving tenths of a second off lap times, the difference between a world champion and a 200-mile-an-hour billboard.

Newey's own office is comparatively spare and low-tech. Its distinctive feature is the drafting table—like one in an architect's studio—alongside a filing cabinet of blueprints that have inspired the fastest vehicles on wheels. "I'm probably the last dinosaur in the industry that still uses a drawing board," he said, and nearly winced, calling himself a "creature of habit." Newey is 54, just old enough (and talented enough) to have shrugged off the migration to CAD, in the 1990s, without seeming like a vain anachronism, and self-aware enough to know that this quirk has helped to elevate him in the popular conception above the rank of mere boffin. The pencil lends him a mystique. Rumors persist that he sometimes gets lost while driving home, deep in thought. Not long ago, a manufacturing trade magazine ranked him as the second-greatest corporate designer of our time, after Jonathan Ive, the creator of the iPod and the iPad, and ahead of Sir James Dyson (the inventor of the bagless vacuum cleaner), Steve Jobs, the electric-car pioneer Elon Musk, and Nintendo's Shigeru Miyamoto. A Twitter account devoted to legends about his supernatural powers of invention ("Adrian Newey designed MacGyver's Swiss Army Knife") has more than 6,000 followers. He has been called "the second-most-famous son" of his hometown, Stratford-upon-Avon, and the Michelangelo of motor racing. He is long-limbed, ever so slightly stooped, and aerodynamically bald on top, with short gray hair on the sides framing a large set of ears that interrupt his global flow field.

"Racing cars are very messy vehicles," Newey said, as if apologizing for unseen imperfections. ("He's got to dumb himself down to talk to us guys," Mark Webber warned me. "He's on another planet.") Newey continued, "If it weren't for the regulations, you certainly wouldn't design them the way they are. Having exposed wheels makes an *awful* mess. Having an open cockpit with the driver's head sticking out the top isn't great."

We sat for a while, discussing brake ducts and double diffusers and kinetic-energy-recovery systems, and then Newey invited me to join him for lunch. He unlocked a door with his fingerprint, and soon we were in the canteen with a consultant and a designer, talking about the upcoming United States Grand Prix, at the brand-new Circuit of the Americas, in Austin. It was to be the first Formula One event in the States in five years, and marked the beginning of a concerted westward push in the sport's marketing, after years of expansion to venues like Shanghai and Singapore and Mokpo, a small South Korean port known for shipbuilding and prostitution. A new street course was being planned in Weehawken, New Jersey, which would offer spectacular views of the Manhattan skyline, if the sport's promoters and Governor Chris Christie could agree on who should pay for road resurfacing. A new television contract with NBC was set to take effect in 2013, replacing the more marginalized SPEED Network. And Ron Howard was working on a movie, scheduled for wide release next fall, about the momentous 1976 Formula One season, with its fiercely contested rivalry between the carousing English lothario James Hunt and the Austrian Niki Lauda.

"Is there much talk about the Texas race in the U.S.?" Newey asked, and they all seemed vexed when I said that I hadn't heard any.

"America's got quite a lot going on there, with the election," the consultant conceded.

"For a sport outside America to break in seems to be quite difficult," Newey said.

The other designer puzzled over the matter a while longer, and asked, "So is NASCAR popular across the States, or is it just for the crazed rednecks?"

Formula One, though concentrated historically in Europe and associated with ascots and champagne, is now perhaps the only truly global sports league—a legitimate world series—with Grand Prix races staged in 19 countries across five continents. The breadth of its television audience is surpassed only by the Olympics and the World Cup, with more than half a billion viewers from nearly 200 countries tuning in each season, according to the sport's promoters. Among the competitors in 2012 were an Indian-backed team (Sahara Force India) and a Russian-backed team (Marussia), to go with the likes of Ferrari, McLaren, and Mercedes, as well as a Japanese driver (Kamui Kobayashi), a Venezuelan (Pastor Maldonado), a Mexican (Sergio Perez), and two Finns. All told, 13 nations were represented among the 25 drivers. The best of those drivers are compensated as well as A-Rod and Kobe, while the bottom half are what's known as "pay drivers"—they're expected to raise money, through independent sponsorships, to offset the privilege of wearing flame-retardant bodysuits covered in advertisements. They're like publishing interns, or the jet-set equivalent of preteen soccer players holding a bake sale to raise money for their spring tournament.

The business relationships between the racing teams and their parent companies can be dizzying to a novice. This was made especially clear to me late last year, as I watched the mostly thrilling Brazilian Grand Prix, in rainy São Paulo, on television. McLaren's

Lewis Hamilton was leading for much of the way, until he was clipped by Force India's Nico Hulkenberg in the 55th lap (of 71) and forced to withdraw because of damage to his front suspension. Force India, like the majority of Formula One teams, has no real expectation of winning races; its cars help justify the existence of a Grand Prix in New Delhi, where monkeys still outnumber luxury automobiles. It also has, as it happens, a "technology sharing" partnership with McLaren, which provided Hulkenberg and his teammate Paul Di Resta with gearboxes and hydraulics. Yet Hulkenberg's aggressive move—"That's what happens when you are racing with a less experienced driver," Hamilton later fumed—cost McLaren 24 points in the standings and, in effect, $10 million of prize money. "One can only hope that the Force India deal brings McLaren more than that because otherwise the customer programme will have been operating at a loss!" the racing journalist Joe Saward wrote on his blog. It was almost as though the Steinbrenners had lent a pitcher to the Royals to help extend the Yankees' brand awareness in Kansas City, only to watch that pitcher drill Derek Jeter in the head.

Hamilton, in any event, had already announced that he would be leaving McLaren at the end of the season to race for Mercedes—or, rather, to use the teams' more sponsor-friendly names, he was leaving Vodafone McLaren Mercedes for Mercedes AMG Petronas. This was big news. Hamilton, who is 28, is often thought of as Formula One's first black champion, and he was already the second-highest-paid driver on the circuit. But, viewed another way, you could say that he was merely expanding his commitment to Mercedes, from an outfit in which the company invests $15 million a year to one in which it sinks $70 million.

On the morning of my trip to Milton Keynes, I stopped to visit the headquarters of Formula One Management, overlooking London's Hyde Park. I was received there by the so-called F1 Supremo, Bernie Ecclestone, a self-made character who would seem to have been invented by Fleet Street to sell newspapers. Great Britain's fourth-richest man, Ecclestone is five feet three, with a white mop of hair and a perpetual squint, from being nearly blind in his right eye since birth. (A *Daily Mail* writer once called him "a tortoise in an Andy Warhol wig.") Last summer, a couple of months before his 82nd birthday, he was married for the third time, to Fabiana

Flosi, a 35-year-old Brazilian whom he met on the track in São Paulo, and who towers over him. (The joke goes that he can look her in the eye when he is standing on his wallet.) His two daughters from his previous wife Slavica, a six-foot-two Croatian who has modeled for Armani, are the Kardashians of England. Tamara, the older one, recently starred in a reality show called *Billion $$ Girl*, and Petra was married in a Roman castle before buying what had been billed as the United States' most expensive house, for $85 million, from the Hollywood widow Candy Spelling.

The son of a North Sea herring and mackerel fisherman, Ecclestone grew up in a house without plumbing, quit school at 16, and became a used-car salesman in South London, earning a reputation for "clocking" odometers, or forcibly rewinding them, in the manner of Ferris Bueller. His ruthless street savvy stood him in good stead when he got involved in racing, which had originated as a pastime for Europe's landed gentry. Racing teams traditionally negotiated with the various circuits individually. Ecclestone persuaded them to negotiate as a bloc—a sort of racing cartel. He was also quick to see the value in television for a sport in which the contestants were distinguished by degrees invisible to the naked eye, and he envisioned, in the paddock behind the teams' garages, an opportunity to cultivate an exclusive atmosphere such as you'd find at Wimbledon or Henley. By consolidating power over the sport's promotion when no one else could be bothered, he made himself indispensable, even as the cash flow that Formula One was generating, at first through tobacco sponsorships and then through exclusive television rights, attracted banks and larger financial interests. They could buy him out—and, indeed, a controlling interest in the sport is now owned by a London-based private-equity firm—but they'd still need a public face to run the show. As we spoke, in a tall, dark-glass-fronted building he'd bought nearly 30 years ago from the Saudi arms dealer Adnan Khashoggi, Ecclestone was facing the threat of indictment in Germany, on suspicion of bribery in the amount of $44 million. (He maintains that he was extorted.) But that wasn't what had him concerned. "I think Europe's a thing of the past," he said, and let out a sigh. He meant this both existentially, in the way of a right-winger who sees the welfare state choking itself to insolvency, and as a source of revenue growth for a sport that is sometimes said to thrive on cubic dollars.

"From the day you grow up and start looking at TV, all the sports you watch have an enormous number of little breaks," Ecclestone continued, addressing me as a representative American. "So you can watch any of the games—football, Lakers, whatever it is— you walk away and it's, say, 42 plays to 48, and you disappear and you come back and it's 63 versus 65. And that's how it is! It doesn't make any difference if you don't concentrate. Whereas in English football or Formula One . . . I mean, you can go to an English football match and not see a goal, which would never be acceptable in America, would it?"

The equivalent of a scoreless match in Formula One is a race in which nobody passes anyone—or, at least, in which the driver who begins in the pole position goes on to win, unchallenged from behind for 300 kilometers, or the better part of two hours. (The starting grid is determined by the fastest individual laps registered during qualifying sessions the day before the race.) After going through a "fairly dark period" a few years ago, as Martin Whitmarsh, the chairman of the Formula One Teams Association, called it, "where we weren't producing a good enough show," the sport's organizers agreed to give trailing cars an artificial boost, like a turbo button in a video game. The technology is called DRS— for drag-reduction system—and it enables drivers to maneuver an adjustable flap on their rear wings, adding about a dozen extra miles per hour on straightaways. You can activate it only on certain stretches of each track, when you're within a second of the car in front of you and hoping to slingshot past.

DRS was introduced before the start of the 2011 season, over the objection of many purists, who felt that this kind of pandering to an impatient audience was beneath the European motor-sport. Nonetheless, roughly half of all races that year consisted of Red Bull's German phenom Sebastian Vettel essentially leading from start to finish. In all but one instance, the fastest qualifying laps belonged to Vettel or to his older teammate Webber. Red Bull's cars were simply too much better, owing in large part to Adrian Newey's ingenious use of the cars' exhaust as an aerodynamic aid.

If DRS couldn't sufficiently speed the other teams up, something would need to be done to slow Red Bull down. Haggling over the "outer envelope of permissibility," as Whitmarsh put it, is the hidden essence of Formula One. "If you believe your competitors are driving a performance advantage, you've got to either duplicate it or prevent them from doing it." And so the 2012 season began with an amended set of rules in which exhaust gases could no longer be fed through the rear diffuser, as Newey had been doing, to reduce pressure underneath the car's floor. Red Bull was forced to lower the car's ride height, in compensation. The first seven races produced seven different winners. Parity restored.

Like many kids, Newey was initially drawn by the allure of stardom behind the wheel. His father was a veterinarian and a metalworking hobbyist, who tinkered with his Lotuses and Mini Coopers in the backyard while his younger son looked on. When Adrian expressed an interest in driving, his father proposed a deal. "He said, 'If you want to do it, that's great, but you're going to have to show your commitment,'" Newey recalled. "So what he offered was that for every pound I could earn he would double my money to buy a go-kart." Newey took odd jobs delivering newspapers, washing cars, and mowing lawns, and with his father's subsidy was able to buy a secondhand vehicle. "The combination of it and me was pretty uncompetitive," he said. "More and more, my interest then became modifying the car to try and make it go faster." He learned to weld, and made his own electronic ignition, scouring kits for spare parts. "I'm not sure it actually made it go any faster, but it gave me something to do," he said.

He was an indifferent student. He attended Repton, "a rather Dickensian public school," as he put it, which had been founded in 1557. "Very pretentious," he added. "It revolved around sport more than anything—depending on the term, football, cricket, or hockey." Newey was not a jock. He wore leather jackets and bell-bottoms, which were roomy enough for him to tape bottles of vodka to his shins, for use at school functions. The most memorable of those was an end-of-term concert in 1975, which the sixth-formers had organized, bringing the prog-rock band Greenslade to campus. Newey was then a fifth-former, and having doubts about proceeding to A-levels. Emboldened by the vodka, and eyeing the mixing console in the middle of the auditorium, he waited until the sound engineer was on a break and moved in. "I jumped to the controls, set them all to max, and the stained-glass walls that had survived Cromwell and God knows what . . ." With his hands, Newey pantomimed an explosion. That was the end of his time at Repton.

Newey wasted a year at the local community college, during which he mostly rode motorcycles and chased girls, before getting serious and applying to the University of Southampton. He studied aeronautics and astronautics, not because he had any particular interest in flight but because it struck him as the closest thing academia had to offer a gearhead. Race cars were like planes flying into the ground rather than above it. Instead of seeking lift, they relied on downforce, which effectively pinned them to the road as they navigated corners, but the same Bernoulli physics applied. It was all a matter of balancing downforce (good for turning) and drag (bad for straightaways). Upon graduation, in 1980, many of his classmates went to work for British Aerospace or Rolls-Royce. Newey showed up for his first job interview on a Ducati, in riding leathers. This was with a small Formula One team founded by the famous Fittipaldi brothers, Emerson and Wilson. His would-be interviewer noticed the bike and asked if he could take it out for a spin. When he returned, he offered Newey the job.

The position Newey applied for was a junior aerodynamicist, but he soon discovered that there was no senior aerodynamicist. "I was lucky in my timing," he said. Much of race car design until that point had been mechanically determined. "The aerodynamicist would give a rough idea of what he wanted, and then the mechanical designer would take it, and invariably, if things looked a little bit too difficult to package, he'd just change it and not even report back," Newey explained. "And you could see it in the cars that came out. You'd see all sorts of nasty lumps and bumps on the car where mechanical bits had got in the way of what the aerodynamicist wanted." After the late-1970s rivalry between James Hunt and Niki Lauda, which contributed to the popularity of the sport, budgets were beginning to grow, and this allowed for more research and a greater emphasis on engineering—an opportunity for Formula One teams to demonstrate their technological superiority.

Newey spent much of the 1980s working in the United States, on the IndyCar circuit. His designs twice produced Indianapolis 500 winners, and, while serving as a race engineer at the track on weekends, he impressed Mario Andretti, who immediately identified Newey as a budding genius. "We were on the grid with 10 minutes left, and he came out and changed the front springs to suit the situation," Andretti told me, recalling the Indy 500 of

1987. "As a result, I led from the get-go and had the field covered by one lap, with 20 laps to go—until the engine broke. And you know why the engine broke? Because I should've been turning 600 more revs, and I was in a bad harmonic range, vibrating. If I had been pushed more, then I would have used that shorter gear, and I probably would have finished. So, ironically, the fact that the car was so good was what killed my chances."

This tension between the abstract pursuit of excellence and realistic limits became a recurring theme in Newey's work as he returned to England and Formula One. It was the end of the turbocharged era, which had resulted in sloppy design, to Newey's eyes. The cars, relying on souped-up engine power, were often big and clumsy. Newey was relentless in his pursuit of efficiency, sometimes squeezing drivers' cockpits to the point of discomfort. Viewed from above, his cars began to look like acoustic guitars, with the chassis tapering into a needle nose. "Adrian was forever trying to find a way of making the needle nose smaller and smaller and smaller," Nigel Roebuck, the editor of *Motor Sport*, recalled. "He did actually suggest at one point arranging the pedals so that the driver's feet, instead of being side by side, were on top of one another." Roebuck added, "If you talk to any of the mechanics, Adrian's cars are always very, very difficult to work on, because they're always so tightly packaged, and everything has got to be perfect, and sometimes they're *too* tightly packaged, so things overheat and whatnot."

In November of 1996, Newey was indicted for manslaughter. He was held partly responsible for the death, nearly three years earlier, of the great Brazilian driver Ayrton Senna, at the San Marino Grand Prix, in Imola. Senna, a three-time world champion while driving for McLaren, had defected to the formidable Williams Racing Team before the start of the 1994 season. Among other reasons, he'd relished the opportunity to work with Newey, who was then Williams's chief designer. But he was having trouble adjusting to the car, and remained uncomfortable heading into his third, fatal race with the new team. A scene toward the end of the acclaimed documentary *Senna* shows the driver talking with Newey and the Williams technical director, Patrick Head (who was also charged), after one of the qualifying sessions. He complained about understeering and oversteering, an inconsistent balance from one lap to the next. As Senna approached the course's treacherous Tamburello Corner, he was fending off an aggressive pursuit from the German Michael Schumacher when he lost control, crashing head-on into a concrete barrier. He was traveling 137 miles an hour.

Fatalities were almost commonplace in Formula One in the 1960s and '70s, but Senna's was the first to be televised live, and factions within the Italian government called for banning the sport. The local magistrate, compelled by Italian law to find fault in the case of any violent death, concluded that the crash had resulted from a defective steering column, and not simply, as Newey and others believed, from a punctured rear tire caused by debris on the track. A lengthy public trial included expert testimony analyzing the angles of Senna's front wheels and changes in the car's hydraulic pressure, while the broader racing community protested that such quibbling missed the point: of course there was an element of danger, and race car drivers, like downhill skiers, were well aware of the risks. Formula One team owners, fearing further liabilities under such a precedent, threatened to boycott future races in Italy. The prosecutor, in turn, accused the sport's executives of withholding crucial seconds of footage from the race telecast. Ultimately, the judge ruled in favor of acquittal. A series of appeals, the intervention of the Italian Supreme Court, and a retrial delayed Newey's final absolution until 2005.

The incident haunted Newey—he says that what was left of his hair fell out after Senna's death—and he contemplated quitting the sport. More disillusionment followed after he left Williams for McLaren and found many of his best design efforts thwarted by the sport's sanctioning body, the Fédération Internationale de l'Automobile, for what he thought were political reasons. "The things we were coming up with Ferrari would complain about," he told me. "And anything Ferrari complained about, the FIA would appear to say, 'Yes, we'll get them banned.'" For a while, in the late 1990s and early aughts, racing insiders joked that the Paris-based agency's initials stood for Ferrari International Assistance. Newey managed to win a world championship with McLaren, in 1998, adding to the several he'd won with Williams, but Ferrari, employing Michael Schumacher as its lead driver, eventually gained the upper hand, ending what had been a decade of dominance for Newey's cars.

Alternately frustrated and bored, Newey thought about switching to designing sailboats. "I have always loved that combination of man and machine," he told me. The America's Cup challenge seemed to offer a chance to work with similar technology under different conditions. "The principles are the same," he said. "Lightweight structures. Composite structures. Simulation techniques in terms of how you operate the boat, how you tune it to maximize its performance, which is exactly the same as we do with the cars." But there were no competitive British sailing syndicates, and to learn from the best he would have had to disrupt his family (he has four children, two of them grown) and move to Geneva. What's more, the America's Cup is held at a different site every four years, depending on the preferences of the previous champion. "So you're a permanent gypsy, which is great when you're in your twenties and thirties," Newey said. "But, from a family and home-life point of view, it's about the only thing more antisocial than Formula One."

A way out of his protracted midlife crisis arrived late in 2005, when Newey got a phone call from Dietrich Mateschitz, a secretive Austrian businessman who had made billions marketing an obscure caffeinated beverage sold in Thailand as a kind of international club drink: Red Bull. As part of his lifestyle branding strategy, Mateschitz had recently branched out into sports, particularly those associated with speed. He'd bought the shell of Jaguar's Formula One team for one pound sterling, with the promise of investing at least £200 million more over the next several years. Thus far, most of the money seemed to have been put into style. Red Bull established a floating "energy station" in the Monte Carlo harbor, where the contestants in its "Formula Una" modeling competition could flaunt their bikini bodies. As part of a marketing partnership with the *Star Wars* franchise, the pit crew dressed as storm troopers. Plans were under way to host an Arabian Nights party at the Grand Prix in Abu Dhabi, with a tab running into seven figures. Mateschitz needed Newey in order to prevent his team from becoming a sideshow. His recruiting technique involved inviting Newey to Austria for a visit and flying him upside down over the mountains in an Alpha Jet.

"Once a team gets run by an accountant, it's time to move," Newey has said, and Mateschitz was offering "quite a grown-up budget," including a salary reported to be in excess of $10 million. ("Ferrari have tried to get him," Nigel Roebuck, the *Motor Sport* editor, told me. "They've offered him the earth. But he doesn't want to live outside England.") Not long before, Newey had revived his teen fantasies of glory behind the wheel and begun racing his own classic cars. In his first year in Milton Keynes, he wrecked a Ford GT40 and a Jaguar E-Type and was hospitalized overnight. "It helps to try and understand some of the pressures the drivers go through," he told me. ("I'm not sure how good his spatial awareness is when it comes to close combat," the retired Red Bull driver David Coulthard countered.) Newey later initiated a tradition of doing doughnuts on the suburban lawn of Christian Horner, the Red Bull team boss, in celebration of the victories they were amassing. "Do you know that he crashed Helmut Marko's car in his own drive?" Horner asked me, referring to the retired Austrian driver who consults for Red Bull. "Helmut lent us his car. There was a little bit of snow overnight. Adrian was keen to show off his car control and rally skills, and for some reason decided to accelerate rapidly—to do a *Starsky and Hutch* entry—and we understeered straight into a tree and took the right-hand side out of the car."

A few years ago, the makers of the Gran Turismo series of racing simulators for Sony PlayStation approached Newey about designing a pure speed-mobile with no restrictions—a kind of Formula Zero. Newey is not interested in video games, but the abstraction of the idea appealed to him, and he spent a happy weekend sketching something that looked a little like a dragonfly, with encased wheels instead of wings, as well as a vacuum pump that would suck the chassis toward the pavement when cornering. "To be perfectly honest, it would be so fast that it wouldn't really be safe," he told me. As it is, Formula One cars exert nearly 50 pounds of lateral force on the bodies of their drivers when cornering and braking at high speeds, which is why race car drivers tend to have the necks of offensive linemen. "That would certainly become one of the restrictions: at what point can a driver still hold his head up!" Newey said. Discounting human frailty, he estimated that the Red Bull X2010, as they called the fantasy car, would be about 20 seconds per lap faster than any you've seen on a track.

Designing cars that go ever faster does not, after a certain point, make for a more enjoyable spectator sport, just as the proliferation of agile seven-and-a-half-footers might render basketball claustrophobic. "Most of the regulations are to control the fact that the

car's going too *quick*," Bernie Ecclestone told me. "It's just generally the way the cars are driven that's entertaining—you know,
good for the public. 'Cause all of the drivers—well, *most* of them—
drive on the limit, and it's a case of the engineers making the limit
more difficult to reach." Circuit safety standards have evolved considerably since the death of Senna, with larger run-off areas and
more forgiving barriers, but if cars were to become much faster,
many of the venerated old tracks that lend the sport its lore would
need to be reconfigured, at a cost of millions.

Because of its direct ties to industry, Formula One is more sus-
ceptible to economic forces than most sports; after the financial
crisis of 2008, BMW, Toyota, and Honda shuttered their racing
operations, and the FIA overhauled the regulations more substantially than at any point in the previous 25 years, with an eye toward
keeping budgets under control. Broad rule changes appeal to
Newey, because they present an opportunity to reconceive the car
more or less from scratch. He'll mock up a working layout at half
scale on his drafting table, while poring over the rule book. The
2009 austerity regime inspired his rerouting of the exhaust system,
an innovation so beneficial that the team affixed decoy stickers
resembling pipes to the sides of its cars to distract spying competitors. Now, after three years of creeping restrictions against everything that had seemed to improve the cars' performance, Newey
was finding the conditions less welcome. Tens of millions of dollars were being spent in the pursuit of each last tenth of a second.
"Eventually, everybody will converge on the same solution," he
said. "Effectively, all the cars end up the same, at which point the
only differentiator is the engine and the driver." Ecclestone once
famously likened the sport's drivers to lightbulbs, in the sense that
they were interchangeable. In an overly restrictive environment,
Newey feared the same would be said of designers.

Newey is not optimistic about the next regulatory overhaul,
planned for 2014, which takes aim at the sport's carbon footprint.
It promises less powerful engines, larger batteries, and a greater
emphasis on energy renewal—in effect, hybrid race cars. "It's a
political idea," Newey said, with an engineer's disdain. Working for
Red Bull—a company that's in the business of "selling cans, not
cars," as the driver Sebastian Vettel put it—has afforded Newey the
luxury of indifference to the sport's relevance to the nonsporting
world, a point of pride for others. Newey went on, "There's always

been this notion that Formula One should be used to develop the breed—the breed being the road car—and I think if you go back into, let's say, the sixties, then there are successful examples of that. Disc brakes, fuel injection, lightweight construction—all first appeared in Formula One. But the true spin-off from Formula One into road cars now, in all reality, is somewhere between very small and zero, in terms of technology that's developed in Formula One being of real benefit to the road cars, as opposed to a salesman's dream." Any claims to the contrary by the manufacturers, he said, are "pure pretense."

There was talk of President Obama passing through Texas on the weekend of the Austin Grand Prix, and this led some Formula One insiders to wonder if he might make an appearance at the race. "Is Mr. President a big fan of the old motor-sport?" Will Buxton, the SPEED (and now NBC) broadcaster, asked, while killing time in Red Bull's makeshift hospitality suite, on the paddock. "He seems like a cool guy. That would be the best thing to make people aware that this is happening."

Obama did not turn up, though the idea was perhaps not as far-fetched as it sounds. During the next several days of walking the paddock, I spied Mexico's president, Felipe Calderón, Texas's governor, Rick Perry, and Carlos Slim, the world's richest man, among lesser dignitaries such as Ron Howard and George Lucas. The journalist Joe Saward, whose racing blog I'd taken to reading regularly, assured me that one of Princess Diana's exes was roaming about as well. Saward then began pointing out some of his fellow motor scribes: one kept a jet car in his garage, another was an uncanny juggler, and a third spoke nine languages. Saward himself is a historian of the French Resistance. "Even the motor-home girls have master's degrees," he said, referring to the hostesses at the teams' hospitality suites. "I always wanted to run off and join the circus, and in a sense I have."

Bernie Ecclestone, whom Saward described (more or less approvingly) as "stark raving bonkers," wore Texas-appropriate jeans and cowboy boots to the track, and took a break from his daily backgammon game one afternoon to speak with the local media, who wondered if he was concerned about the fact that his big event happened to fall on the same weekend as the finale of the NASCAR Sprint Cup series, in Miami. "I'll let you know on Monday," he said, and granted that the customs official who'd greeted him at the airport had never heard of Formula One. "He seemed quite reasonable," Ecclestone added.

"Away from the venue, what do you look forward to doing in Austin?" one reporter asked, in a deep Texas twang.

"I may go to LA tomorrow," Ecclestone replied.

The ace driver Sebastian Vettel, speaking with me before his first practice session, attempted to parse the differences between NASCAR and Formula One in terms that he thought I might understand. "Maybe, you know, baseball and tennis," he began. "Just because you have a racket . . ." I furrowed my brow in confusion. "Okay," he said. "Baseball, you don't have a racket. But something that's maybe similar? Doesn't mean it's the same thing. You know what I mean?" He thought for another moment, and added, "I actually wanted to say golf and baseball. Both times you have a stick, right? But you can't really compare. Obviously, Formula One is much more sophisticated. The cars are high-tech, whereas in NASCAR they are low-tech. But I don't mean there are only stupid people working there." Vettel's personal manager murmured something to him in German. "She says I'm talking too much," he said.

Vettel has curly blond hair, blue eyes, and an impish charm. He should by rights have been the media darling of this spectacle. At 25, he was already the two-time reigning world champion, and poised to become the youngest driver ever to win three titles. Scattered around the track were posters drawn up in the Wild West style. WANTED: A WORLD CHAMPION, they said, and featured mug shots of Vettel and Ferrari's Fernando Alonso, who were leading in the individual driver standings, with two races to go. Back in the summer, Vettel had visited New York and appeared as a guest on *The Late Show with David Letterman*, where he talked about the "big balls" you need as a Formula One driver. But the more success he had, it seemed, the more credit went to Newey—Alonso himself spoke of "fighting against a Newey car"—and Vettel was getting defensive. "I don't see Adrian or myself being more important than any other," he said. "I mean, when I'm on the track, I'm alone in the car, and if I steer left the car turns left, and I steer right the car turns right, so whatever I do is extremely decisive to the whole project."

I made a habit of following herds of cameras wherever they

went, and thereby learned to connect faces with some of racing's legendary names. The elfin man dressed all in plaid was Sir Jackie Stewart, a three-time world-champion driver in the 1960s and '70s. ("He's too good," Stewart said of Newey. "He's a very clever man.") The extremely tanned and perfectly coiffed fireplug who looked as if he'd just climbed off a yacht in the Mediterranean was Mario Andretti. The guy with a monocoque of a proboscis was Emerson Fittipaldi. The awesomely dressed man holding court in front of Ferrari's hospitality suite? "Oh, he's just an asshole," Saward said. "He represents what you might call the indolently wealthy."

But the real paparazzi of Formula One—the guys with the thigh-size lenses that could zoom in on an Ecclestone daughter from two blocks away—are not interested in people-watching. They stalk the pit lane, where the garages are arranged in order of success, and cluster at the front end, among the McLarens, Ferraris, and Red Bulls, hoping to catch an unobstructed view of the cars as they're reassembled each morning. A mysterious bit of film had emerged from the previous race, in Abu Dhabi. It showed Red Bull mechanics fiddling with Vettel's front wing and nose cone, which appeared supple, as if made of rubber instead of carbon. Was this another bit of Newey-inspired alchemy? Or was it a violation of the rules restricting wing flexibility, as some rivals charged? Flexing wings improve grip in high-speed corners without increasing drag on straightaways. Might it explain Red Bull's late-season surge to the front of the paddock after an inconsistent start? All I was able to discern while spying on the Red Bull garage is that its mechanics blast dance music that must be intended to drive the fussy neighbors from Ferrari mad. (You can "check out what the garage are listening to today" via the team's Spotify playlist.) Also, to judge from the open Red Bull cans in view, they may be overcaffeinated.

The course itself looked magnificent, rising out of a dusty field, southeast of the airport, that the city council had voted to annex less than two weeks before the race, in order to boost property-tax rolls. Those not arriving by helicopter had the option of taking a shuttle bus from downtown or parking in cow pastures along the access road, for $35, and using the two- or three-mile walk to get acclimated to the grinding whine of all the engine noise—the "glorious assault on the senses," the official race announcer later called it—as the 133-foot ascent to the first turn came into focus. "Turn One," I'd been told back in Milton Keynes, was "going to be epic." It was a blind hairpin to the left, and would require drivers to downshift to first gear after a furious sprint up the hill. Hermann Tilke, the Robert Trent Jones of Formula One, was the architect, and I gathered that he'd given the undiscerning American audience of 115,000 an international sampler of sorts, borrowing an S-curve and a horseshoe bend from Interlagos and Istanbul, respectively, and alluding elsewhere to the swift Becketts Corner of England's Silverstone.

Through practice and qualifying, the drivers' times steadily improved as the track was in effect rubberized when the burned residue of the tires formed a smoother surface. Because of the circuit's newness, oil was still being released by the settling asphalt, and the competitors used words like "shiny," "icy," "slippery," "wet," and "green" to describe the conditions. "Green, yeah, dirty," Newey said, sipping a cup of coffee a few hours before the race, and dismissing as an "occupational hazard" the nuisance of shutterbugs who had gathered for a shot of the wizard at rest. Newey had been vindicated in the wing-flexing controversy, which the FIA race director, in a press conference, attributed to an optical illusion, and Vettel and Webber, benefiting from still further tweaks to the front wing angles and the ride height, had secured the first and third spots on the grid.

Ferrari's Fernando Alonso, meanwhile, placed a disappointing eighth, which he deemed "logical," a result of inferior machinery. Even worse, this left him on the "dirty," or less rubberized, side of the track. Ferrari officials then made the cynical decision to sabotage their other driver, Felipe Massa, to help Alonso. With less than an hour to go before the ceremonial parade lap (in classic American muscle cars, naturally), they broke the seal on Massa's gearbox. Massa, who had actually been faster than Alonso in qualifying, was automatically penalized, and forced to drop back five spots. The newly configured grid placed Alonso in seventh, back on the clean side—and tough luck to those drivers from Force India, Lotus, and Williams who in turn were shifted from clean to dirty, as collateral damage. My Twitter feed filled with concerns from Formula One partisans that this might not sit well with an American audience obsessed by questions of fairness ("Yanks like sport over tactics"), ignoring the larger problem of widespread confusion.

Was Turn One indeed epic? There were no collisions or spin-outs, so I'd have to vote no, although I was informed, after the cars had disappeared from view, that Alonso had managed to squirt past a driver or two. A veteran race observer once described for me the conversational rhythm among spectators in terms of 90-second intervals, or roughly the amount of time it takes a car to complete a three-and-a-half-mile lap. That is, you talk for 90 seconds, and then pause out of necessity when the cars whiz by again, trying in vain to hold a thought as your teeth vibrate. I found that this held true only for the first few laps, when the cars remained bunched together, and before any drivers had stopped for a change of tires. Soon enough, the interruptions were more frequent and intermittent, and it was easier to understand the proliferation of champagne as a desensitizing device.

I was fortunate to be watching from Red Bull's section of the Paddock Club, above the pit lane, with the high rollers who had paid $5,000 each for the full experience: gnocchi, booze, and even a DJ from Miami, named Erok, whom Red Bull flies around the world to perpetuate its image as the brash upstart of the scene. Some helpful representatives of Infiniti, one of Red Bull's subsidiary sponsors, distributed handheld video screens that allowed you to shuffle between camera views from each of the cars, and after some experimentation I concluded that the best way to watch the race was from the perspective of McLaren's Lewis Hamilton, who had been made to obscure the painted letters "HAM" on his helmet after race officials learned that they were a reference not to his name but to the song by Kanye West and Jay-Z (and meant "hard as a motherfucker").

By the midpoint, it was shaping up as a two-man race between Vettel and Hamilton, with Alonso in a distant third. (Webber's alternator blew on the 17th lap, forcing his withdrawal.) Hamilton's car was faster in a straight line—by 11 kilometers per hour, the BBC commentary said—but seemed to lack the Red Bull's down-force, or grip, and he slid more in the corners. On my screen, as I pretended to be Hamilton, Vettel would appear larger and closer each time we approached a sharp turn, only to scurry away again as we accelerated out. The cat-and-mouse game continued for more than 20 minutes, as Hamilton narrowed the gap to within DRS-boosting range.

Newey stood in the pit lane with several team officials, wearing noise-canceling headphones and staring at a bank of computer screens, in a bit of pageantry for the television production. ("We could probably do a better job in the back of the garage," he confessed. "You're strung out in a line. You can't hear anything.") They monitored live data from the hundreds of sensors in Vettel's chassis and engine, advising on tire conditions, and communicated via radio and instant message with another group of technicians seated in a command center back in Milton Keynes, some of whom simulated the race in real time, forecasting when Hamilton and Alonso and the others might make a pit stop.

The ample technical support was unable to help Vettel overcome his biggest obstacle: the inconvenient slowness of Narain Karthikeyan, of the struggling Hispania Racing Team. Vettel cursed into his microphone as he downshifted into Turn Eleven on his 43rd lap and found himself momentarily impeded by Karthikeyan, bringing up the rear on his own 42nd. The brief logjam brought Hamilton to within a couple of car lengths, and gave him the window he needed on the following straight. Up went the DRS flap on Hamilton's rear wing. More cursing. The cat had overtaken the mouse.

Vettel would have to wait another week to secure his third title, but, in accordance with the complexities of Formula One, Red Bull still had cause for celebration. The second-place finish in Austin was worth enough points in the team standings to clinch the Constructors' Championship, the source of the big prize money, if not of the cork-popping glory. Few in the Paddock Club, or among the departing crowd, for that matter, seemed to notice all the Red Bull personnel assembling on the track for a team photo after Mario Andretti had welcomed the victorious Hamilton and the runners-up, Vettel and Alonso, to the podium for the ceremonial Mumm spraying. The garages were being hurriedly disassembled. On the Jumbotron above, a man in a cowboy hat sang "Margaritaville." Newey lingered a while longer, speaking politely to the remaining British TV cameras, and raised his fist and thumb in the air. Last week, a report surfaced in the Italian press that Ferrari had resumed its pursuit of his services.

NICK PAUMGARTEN

The Manic Mountain

FROM THE NEW YORKER

UELI STECK'S CLOSEST BRUSH with death, or at least the time he thought it likeliest that he was about to die, came not when he plummeted 700 feet down the south face of Annapurna, or spidered up the Eiger's fearsome North Face alone and without ropes in under three hours, or slipped on wet granite while free-climbing the Golden Gate route of El Capitan with his wife, on their honeymoon, but, rather, while he was hugging his knees in a tent on Mount Everest, hiding from a crowd of Sherpas who were angry that his climbing partner had called one of them a "mother-fucker," in Nepali. They were threatening to kill him. He had no escape. He had planned everything so scrupulously. The intended route up the mountain was sublime, the conditions perfect. He had spent years honing his body and his mind while tending to his projects and the opportunities that arose out of them. As a climber, he knew that the mountains can foil the best-laid plans, that in an instant a routine ascent can turn into a catalog of horrors. But it would be ridiculous to die like this. The expedition had hardly begun.

Steck had made his first trip to Everest in May 2011, at the age of 34. He'd built a reputation as one of the world's premier alpinists—"the Swiss Machine," some called him, to his dismay—by ascending, in record time, alone and without ropes, Europe's notorious north faces and then by taking on bold Himalayan routes, with style and speed. Everest hardly fit the pattern. In recent years, accomplished mountaineers in search of elegant, difficult, and original climbs had tended to steer clear of its crowds, expense, and relative drudgery. Still, Everest is Everest. Steck felt the pull.

That spring, 500 feet from the summit, he turned back, concerned that frostbite might claim his toes. He was also uncharacteristically spent, after climbing two other 8,000-meter peaks in previous weeks. (The goal of three in one trip was new.) But an idea had taken hold: a route that, if accomplished from beginning to end, would represent a milestone of modern mountaineering, a glorious plume. He began scheming and training for it. He returned a year later, to attain the summit via the standard route—a step toward the goal. He reached the top in the company of the lead group of Sherpas, the local people, many of whom work as porters and guides for the commercial expeditions on Everest. This was on the first day that the weather cleared for a summit push. The next day, the crowds went up—hundreds of aspirants, most of them clients of commercial companies, and their Sherpas—and, amid the traffic jam approaching the summit, four climbers died, of exposure and cerebral edema.

This year, Steck arrived in Nepal at the beginning of April. He intended to spend as long as six weeks prior to his summit push acclimatizing to Everest's high altitude, going on forays up the mountain from base camp, which is 17,600 feet above sea level. (The summit is 29,028 feet.) He'd kept his plans secret. He has long disdained revealing the details of expeditions in advance. He doesn't indulge in what he calls "tasty talking"—boasting of feats he has not yet accomplished. Also, a climber must generally be discreet about a bold route, to prevent other climbers from going there first. He was not displeased when climbing blogs reported, incorrectly, that he was going up the South Face. He had something else in mind.

His partners were Simone Moro, a 45-year-old Italian who'd been climbing in the Himalayas for more than 20 years (he'd summited Everest four times), and Jonathan Griffith, an English climber and photographer who lives in Chamonix. By the end of the month, they were established at Camp 2, at 21,300 feet, beyond the top of the Khumbu Icefall, a tumbling portion of the Khumbu Glacier mined with crevasses and seracs.

At 8:00 A.M. on April 27, they set out for Camp 3 (24,000 feet), where they planned to spend a night, to acclimatize. To get there, they had to scale the Lhotse Face, a towering slope of sheer ice and wind-battered snow. The Lhotse Face is the main ramp up to a saddle called the South Col and then on to the standard Southeast Ridge route, the one that Edmund Hillary and Tenzing Norgay ascended 60 years ago and which is now tramped by hundreds of amateur climbers a year. Every season, the commercial operators put in fixed ropes along the route up the face and the ridge—a kind of bannister to the top, which any client can clip on to and pull himself along using a clamping device called a jumar. Last week, an 80-year-old Japanese man reached the summit.

April 27 was the day that a team of Sherpas were installing the fixed rope. It is an essential and difficult job, involving heavy gear and extreme working conditions on an ice cliff riddled with crevasses. The day before, the Sherpas, with help from three Western guides, had nearly completed the job but came to an untraversable crevasse, which had forced them to take the whole rope system down and return in frustration the next day to start over along a different path.

Earlier in the month, there had been a meeting at base camp among the expedition leaders at which it was agreed that while the Sherpas were fixing the Lhotse Face, no one else would climb there. Steck and Moro, a small professional team and not part of the commercial-trip ecosystem, had not been at the meeting.

Later that morning, Steck, Moro, and Griffith reached the base of the face. A few Sherpas and an American guide asked them not to climb. "The Sherpas asked nicely," Dawa Steven Sherpa, an expedition leader who had two Sherpas on the fixing team, told me. "Sherpas are really afraid of the Lhotse Face. They really get nervous." But the Westerners felt that they could continue without interfering with the fixing crew. They climbed 150 feet to the left of the fixed ropes. They themselves had no ropes. They were climbing "alpine style"—that is, without any fixed protection, porters, or supplemental oxygen. Each had crampons over his boots and an ice ax in one hand. Unencumbered, they moved fast. Two Sherpas, annoyed, used their ice axes to knock chunks of ice down at them, until a Western guide, hearing of this over the radio, told them to stop. After an hour, Steck and the others reached the level of Camp 3, where they would have to traverse the face to get to their tent, which meant they needed to cross over the fixed line. They chose a spot where four Sherpas were at the belay, below the lead fixer, and moved slowly past them, taking care, Steck says, not to touch the ropes with their crampons or to kick chunks of ice onto the Sherpas working below. After Steck crossed the line, the leader of the fixing crew, Mingma Tenzing Sherpa, who was working 50 or so feet up the face, began yelling at Steck and banging on the ice with his ax. Mingma, a young man from the village of Phortse, then rappelled down toward Steck. Anticipating a collision, Steck raised his arms to cushion the blow and prevent himself from being knocked off the face. According to Steck, Mingma rappelled into him, then began yelling at him for having touched him. He accused Steck and his team of kicking ice chunks loose and injuring a member of his crew. Steck argued then, as he would later, that they hadn't dislodged any ice, and that they'd been climbing well out of the way. He offered to help the crew finish fixing the ropes. This seemed to anger Mingma even more. It was then that Simone Moro came along and, seeing Mingma swinging his ice ax, began yelling at him, calling him *machikne,* which translates as "motherfucker." The insult is graver in Nepali. Mingma instructed his crew to stop working. The Sherpas descended the face, leaving behind their equipment and an unfinished job. Steck and Moro, in a possibly misguided attempt at goodwill, stayed behind and finished fixing the lines themselves. The three Europeans then decided not to spend the night at Camp 3, but to head back down to Camp 2 and try to resolve the dispute.

It isn't unheard of for climbers to get into testy exchanges at high altitudes, where big egos meet thin air. One can reasonably argue over what happened on the Lhotse Face, and who deserves a greater share of the blame, even within a context of cultural, historical, and economic grievance. Many of the facts at hand — falling ice, who touched whom and in what order, the nature or validity of the prohibition against climbing that day — are in dispute, and yet may be of middling significance in light of what happened next.

When the European climbers got back to their tents, at the upper edge of Camp 2, they were greeted by an American named Melissa Arnot, who'd been sharing their camp and who was attempting a fifth conquest of the summit, more than any other woman. She warned them that the Sherpas were very angry about the incident on the Lhotse Face and that the mood in camp was volatile. She left, but after a few moments she ran back to their tent to say that a large group of Sherpas had set out from the main part of camp. She said, "I think you should run." Instead, they emerged from the tent in the hope of talking to the Sherpas. They then saw a mass of dozens of Sherpas appear on an overlooking ridge, many of them with their faces covered, some holding rocks. Steck surmised that he was in trouble.

As the Sherpas converged on the tent, a New Zealander named Marty Schmidt ran up and tried to knock a rock out of a Sherpa's hand. He was pushed and kicked, hit on the head with a rock, and punched in the eye. He too threw a punch. (The other climbers, outnumbered, chose to act submissively.) A Sherpa who had been on the fixing crew, and who was now at the head of the throng, rushed up and punched Steck in the face. Someone hit him with a rock; another threw an ice ax and crampons. Arnot got between the Sherpas and Steck, who scurried into another, smaller tent, his face bleeding. A rock bigger than a brick came through the top of the tent, and Steck crawled out. By now, Griffith and Moro had retreated a ways, and Steck went to join them. "I think this expedition is over," he said.

A group of Sherpas broke away from the pack and attacked Griffith, the photographer, kicking and punching him on the ground. A moment later, a Western guide ran up and scattered them, and Moro and Griffith ran away, but Steck went back into the tent with Schmidt. They were both bleeding. The crowd of Sherpas was outside. Melissa Arnot and the Western guide, along with a couple of Sherpas, their hands linked, blocked the way to the tent and tried to settle them down, while Steck and Schmidt cowered inside. After a while, the Sherpas demanded that Moro, who had grievously insulted their leader, appear before them, so someone fetched Moro and hustled him into the tent. Arnot told him to kneel and apologize to the Sherpas for his offensive words on the Lhotse Face, and got the Sherpas to promise that if he did so they would not attack him. Moro came out of the tent, and while he was on his knees a few Sherpas began punching and kicking him. Moro says that one swung at him with a penknife, but the blade caught the waist belt of a backpack. Moro's protectors dragged him back into the tent. Amid the chaos, the Sherpas declared that Moro and Steck did not have a permit for the Lhotse Face. Eventually, word came from base camp that they did, and the Sherpas began to retreat. Someone told Steck and Moro, through the walls of the tent, that if they weren't gone in an hour they'd all be killed.

The three Europeans packed a few things, disassembled their tent, stashed some belongings under piles of rocks, donned down parkas and helmets as armor against thrown stones, and fled. They avoided the established route, down through the heart of Camp 2, for fear of being attacked again. They could see Sherpas lining the trail. Instead, they crawled out onto the glacier, to stay out of sight, and began picking their way through the crevasses—an improvised route, undertaken without ropes, through a maze of trapdoors. No one would dare follow. After a while, they rejoined the main roped trail through the icefall, keeping an eye on the path behind them, ready to pull up ladders and cut fixed lines if there were Sherpas in pursuit. They reached base camp just before dark. None of them slept that night.

By the next day, news of a brawl had gone around the world. Conflicting accounts gave rise to a crossfire of recrimination. One opinion, widely held, especially among people far away, was that Sherpas, revered throughout the climbing world for their skill and forbearance, would not have resorted to such violence unless they'd been provoked.

In Switzerland, and in much of Europe, where alpine exploits equate roughly to playoff heroics here, Ueli Steck is a superstar. The news of the *"Krieg am Everest"* had the tabloid wattage (adjusting for Swissness) of A-Rod's affair with Madonna. Steck is a professional climber. "I'm still really impressed how this system works, to be able to make a living from climbing and not be a dirtbag for your life," he told me, before leaving for Everest. For decades, climbing was a pastime for gentlemen and vagabonds. But in recent years people have found a way to subsist at it, by guiding, or working for apparel companies, or, as in Steck's case, thriving on sponsorships and speeches and slide shows—what Steck calls "business." "To make business, you need stories," he said, by which he means amazing feats. To create stories, you need to come up with projects—bigger and bigger ones with each passing year— and then you need to succeed at them.

I first met Steck last November. He'd come to New York to run the marathon. His training regimen for each expedition is extremely meticulous, but it allows for larks, and since he runs for hours a day in the mountains, he thought he'd give the flats of the five boroughs a go. Like so many participants, he arrived in New York soon after Hurricane Sandy but before the race was canceled, at the last minute, by Mayor Bloomberg. Once it was called off, he had no reason to stay. "I would never go to a city just to go to a city," he told me. Anyway, he wanted to get back to Interlaken to spend time with his wife. In the previous two months, he'd been home only a few days, amid a whirlwind of travel around Europe and North America to give talks and to shoot promotions and advertisements for his various sponsors. Half the life of a professional climber is retelling old stories to finance the creation of new ones. Steck gives as many as 100 slide shows a year, often to corporations, who pay him well.

He was as secretive about his winter plans as he was about his intentions on Everest, but in March he agreed to see me in Switzerland, a few days before he left for Nepal. He lives in the village of Ringgenberg, next to Interlaken, which is the gateway to the valleys leading up to the Jungfrau massif, the cluster of glaciated high peaks that includes the infamous Eiger. The day I arrived, he'd been planning to spend the night in a hut on the Jungfrau's flank, to acclimatize to a higher altitude, prior to his flight to Kathmandu. But the weather was lousy, so instead he went for a jog. He ran up and down a mountain near Interlaken three times—18 miles, and 8,000 vertical feet—in three hours and 40 minutes. ("I enjoy it," he said. "I feel my legs, I see the nature.") Then, to cool down, he went to the gym and lifted weights for two hours. He explained, when I met him for coffee the next morning, that this was taking it easy: he was conserving energy for Nepal.

When you first see Steck, it is hard to believe that he can run any distance at all: he is almost comically bowlegged. He teeters on the outsides of his feet. He is lean and compact, with long muscular arms and fingers. He keeps his hair short and his face clean-shaven, and has intense blue eyes that seem to bulge and brighten when he discusses a project. He speaks with a reedy, heliated voice that suits his Swiss-German twang.

It was a day for business. Steck was wearing Levi's and a lightweight blue down jacket with his sponsors' names on it: Leki, Scarpa, Mountain Hardwear, Power Bar. He had a meeting in Bern, an hour away, with executives from another sponsor, Richner, a Swiss bathroom fixtures merchant. We drove there in his white Audi A4 wagon, with WWW.UELISTECK.CH emblazoned on both sides. (Audi, a sponsor, gives him a car every year.) He was careful to obey speed limits and to stop at crosswalks. "If I do one little thing wrong, people will make a big deal," he said. "This is Switzerland." His great fear was running over a toddler. He was anxious about his reputation—it was the distillate of all those faces and summits, his true currency—and this wasn't a country that tolerated ostentation or entitlement in its mountain athletes, he said. Though he gave liberally of himself as a pitchman, he never let reporters meet his wife or talk to his parents or see his house. He wouldn't even let me attend the bathroom fixtures meeting. But afterward he showed me around old Bern. His wife, who works for Bern's electric company, had an apartment nearby. He'd met her at an ice-climbing competition. A year later, they climbed the Eiger together and spent a night sleeping on a ledge at what is called the Death Bivouac, because of climbers who died there.

After lunch, Steck drove to the city's outskirts, to a warehouse that contained a vast climbing gym called Magnet: a Costco of climbing, with undulating pitches of varying steepness, each section a different hue, with hundreds of handholds affixed, stuck there like gobs of bubble gum, in dozens of bright colors, each denoting a particular line. Schoolkids, teens, seniors, and pros turtled in muscle: they scrambled up the walls and hung from the ceiling, belayed by companions on the ground. Steck changed into a Mountain Hardwear T-shirt and shorts and went over to a turret off to the side, a kind of pyramid stuck upside down into the ground, for bouldering—that is, scrambling without being roped. He began to maneuver around on it. A few patrons whispered and glanced in his direction—this was the equivalent of Tiger Woods showing up at the municipal driving range—but for the most part everyone left him alone. He followed a progression of blue handholds, then orange, then pink, hopping down to the mat each time, brushing the talc from his hands on his shorts and peering up at the wall, his head tilted as though the wall were a language he was trying to remember. "I can climb vertical ice—I don't even need to train for it," he said. "This is more for fun. This isn't training—just moving a little bit. I don't waste energy on climbing training. But I'm too fat now for hard rock climbing. I used to be eight kilos lighter. The weight gives me more stamina. It's less cold." After a while, he removed his T-shirt. With a woman named

Julie, the wife of a friend, on belay, he began climbing a big wall. He moved Spider-Man fast, clipping in every three feet or so, until he was hanging from the ceiling. There were strange muscles in his back. Each contortion set off a different arrangement of them.

Over lunch, he revealed his Everest plan. "The Hornbein Couloir," he whispered, eyes shining. This was a steep cleft in the rock of the North Face, on the Tibetan side. It was first climbed by an American pair 50 years ago, but Steck wanted to do it alpine style, an extremely rare feat in itself. Most years, the Hornbein holds either too much snow or too little. After ascending via the Hornbein, he planned to go down the Southeast Ridge, across the South Col, and up Lhotse, the fourth-highest mountain in the world—the Lhotse Traverse. If all went well, it would require that he and Moro spend more than three days above 8,000 meters, in the so-called death zone. No one had ever done anything like this. He had sold the exclusive Swiss rights to the story to a magazine published by Migros, the Swiss supermarket chain, for more than the trip would cost him.

Steck, a coppersmith's son, was reared in Emmental, hilly cow country, which by Swiss mountain-man standards makes him something of a flatlander. He and his two older brothers were hockey nuts; one went on to play professionally. When Ueli was 12, a friend's father took him rock climbing, and that was it for hockey. He began scaling walls in climbing gyms. Before long, he'd made the Swiss junior national sport-climbing team, but he grew restless and wanted to try his moves on the real mountains near home, chief among them the North Face of the Eiger, known as the Nordwand, the great test piece of the Alps—Europe's Everest. I drove up from Interlaken one afternoon to have a look, and seeing it for the first time, from the road leading up to Grindelwald, I found myself growling back at it. It was the bigger bear: a nasty shaded rampart of limestone and ice, nearly 6,000 vertical feet from bottom to top, bedeviled by avalanches, falling rocks, sketchy verglas (thin ice), and sudden storms that can pin a climber for days. The obsessive and often deadly attempts in the 1930s to be the first up, observed from a nearby hotel, still make for some of mountaineering's best-known tales. The first successful climb, in 1938, took four days.

Steck was 18 when he made his first ascent of the Nordwand.

It took him and a friend two days. When he was 28, he soloed the 1938 route in 10 hours. Two years later, he did it in three hours and 54 minutes, breaking the record by 46 minutes. Still, he felt he could go faster. He dedicated the next year to the task, adopting a precise (and top-secret) daily regimen to fine-tune his stamina and strength. It was a novel idea, to bring the advanced science of sport training to the imprecise art of climbing. No climber had ever done this. It hadn't seemed necessary—until Steck introduced the question of speed.

In 2008, he climbed the Nordwand in two hours and 47 minutes—less time than it takes to watch *Cloud Atlas*. The style was pure too: he waited until a storm had left fresh ice and covered old tracks, and he used no ropes or protection of any kind—just crampons and ice axes, in a technique called dry-tooling. Later, he repeated the climb for a film crew, doing pitches over and over, waiting for the setup of each shot, and the footage of him dry-tooling verglas, and running up near-vertical snowfields, where one mistake could mean a mile-long plunge, brought him international renown. Just watching on a computer screen induces vertigo, yet he says it doesn't scare him. "I'm never afraid," he said. "I wouldn't do it if I was afraid of it. I'm not an adrenaline junkie. I'm really Swiss, calculating."

On the premier mountains of the world, there is little new left to do. To achieve a notable first ascent, you'd have to climb the mountains of the moon. So it can be hard these days for a climber to distinguish himself. One can do stylish routes up obscure or remote peaks, or do several peaks in one sequence (a so-called enchainment), or else go alone and unroped up classic routes in record time. Speed became Steck's shtick. The next winter, he followed up with record ascents of the north faces of the Grandes Jorasses (he broke the speed record by four and a half hours) and the Matterhorn (the whole thing in less than two hours).

To some, all this seemed a little gimmicky or robotic. The combination of speed, which seemed an affront to the mountains' majesty, and the methodical training regimen leached alpinism of some of its romance and poetry, its shaggy rebel charm. "For this I got a lot of, how you say, flak," Steck said. "People said, 'Climbing is not a sport. A climber's not an athlete. It's about adventure, being in the mountains, going out with friends.'"

The question of purity is an old one in climbing. In the 1930s, the stodgy members of the British Alpine Club, accustomed to tramping around on Swiss glaciers with local peasants as guides, used to dismiss the young itinerant Nordwand aspirants as daredevils and glory hounds. (And lest we idealize these rebels, keep in mind that many of them were climbing for the glory, and with the backing, of the Reich, perhaps with a different idea of purity in mind.) Over time, honor and admiration have migrated toward those who ascend using fewer ropes, carrying less on their backs, stopping less often, using less in the way of human support—lighter, faster, cleaner, more self-reliant. In that respect, not many can top Steck. Still, the professional climbing game can be a mercenary one, requiring fealty to sponsors and some self-glorification, which can undercut the elegance of the feats themselves.

"The purist thing doesn't exist," Steck said. "You have to find a way to live. You're not living from eating the dirt. But you have to keep it as climbing." Steck pays for his trips himself. He is sponsored, but the expeditions are not. He doesn't want to have to factor the sponsors' interests into the calculus of risk assessment. "If someone else pays, they decide what you have to do." By the time he's on the mountain, Steck is climbing for himself and himself alone.

A climber's reputation rests not just on first ascents or flashy routes but on how he conducts himself when things go to pieces. Steck may be renowned as much for his abandoned expeditions as for the flawless ones. In May 2007, he attempted to put a new route up the south face of Annapurna, a perilous ice and rock face on the world's most lethal peak. On his first try, he got 700 feet up, and a falling rock hit him on the head, knocked him out, and off the face. He fell all the way to the bottom and regained consciousness. He was barely hurt.

Two weeks later, he met with Simon Anthamatten, an elite alpinist from Zermatt, and they agreed to give Annapurna a try. "I grew up in the guide tradition," Anthamatten told me. "You don't go alone in the mountains." The following spring, they went to Nepal. For an acclimatization climb, they achieved a first ascent of the north face of Tengkampoche, via a very technical route, which earned them a Piolet d'Or, the world's top climbing prize. Then they went back to Annapurna. They tried twice to get up the south face but were turned back each time by weather. There were two other expeditions on the mountain: a group of Russians, who had butchered a yak to eat, and whom the Swiss thought it best to avoid, and a mixed group consisting of a Russian, a Romanian, and a Basque named Iñaki Ochoa de Olza, who were attempting the east ridge. One day, as Anthamatten and Steck returned to their base camp, exhausted after a third abortive attempt, they received a call on their satellite phone from Ochoa de Olza's girlfriend at base camp, who was in touch with the Romanian climber via radio. There was a medical problem. Ochoa de Olza, stranded at 24,000 feet, was suffering, and the Russian had gone missing. They'd lost their medicine.

It was 9:00 P.M. Steck and Anthamatten had been climbing all day, and had left their high-altitude gear at the base of their route up the south face. They didn't even know the way on the east ridge. Base camp sent two Sherpas up to help them, but one was drunk and the other exhausted after a 20-mile hike up from his village. So Steck and Anthamatten turned on their headlamps and set out into the night alone, in their light climbing gear. They reached Camp 2, almost 20,000 feet above sea level, at 8:00 A.M. By now it was snowing hard, and they couldn't make out the other climbers' tracks. They came upon an avalanche-prone slope, and decided to wait until morning to cross it. The Romanian called frequently, through Ochoa de Olza's girlfriend, reporting that Ochoa de Olza's condition was getting worse. When they reached Camp 3, at noon the next day, the weather was deteriorating. The Russian had returned. He'd been on the summit and spent the night just below it. Steck and Anthamatten sent the Russian down, after Steck had swapped boots with him, and Steck proceeded up alone. In between Camp 3 and Camp 4, Steck and the Romanian met up. Steck gave him medicine and the last of his food and sent him to meet Anthamatten, who helped him down. Steck proceeded to Camp 4, at 24,000 feet, and came upon Ochoa de Olza, unconscious in a tent. Another night passed. Steck remained with Ochoa de Olza, who by the next morning was in the throes of death—unconscious, vomiting, coughing up blood. Pulmonary edema. At noon, he stopped breathing. After a while, Steck determined that he was dead. He spent the rest of the afternoon in the tent with the corpse and then decided, as night fell and the storm raged, to put the body outside. A weather report came from base camp that the next morning would be his best chance of getting off the mountain alive. Steck lay awake through the night. He was sure he heard something outside, like a man moaning. He began to wonder if Ochoa de Olza was alive. He stepped outside to see. Still dead. In the morning, Steck left the body behind, headed down, and at Camp 3 stumbled upon three rescuers, with whom he descended to base.

He and Anthamatten were hailed as heroes for abandoning their climb and risking their lives to save others. They were awarded a Prix Courage. Steck downplayed the rescue, because Ochoa de Olza had died in the end. And they'd failed to achieve what they'd come to do. "I'm done with Annapurna," he said afterward. "It gives me a funny feeling."

Eventually, he changed his mind. He had been planning to go back this fall, to have another go at the south face. But then came the *Krieg am Everest.*

Scandal is a mainstay of climbing lore, as fundamental as courage and death. Controversies swirl around every mountain, and almost every mountaineer, like so many ravens. The first great first ascent, of the Matterhorn, in 1865, by an Englishman named Edward Whymper, led to the death, on the descent, of four of his companions. Their rope snapped, and they fell 4,000 feet. Afterward, Whymper and his guide, a local Zermatter named Peter Taugwalder, were accused of having cut the rope that connected them to the others in order to save themselves. An inquiry exonerated them—the case prompted Queen Victoria to consider a ban on mountain climbing—but a whiff of dishonor, along with the timeless problem of there being no witnesses in mountain accidents except, usually, the survivors, has forever shadowed the accomplishment. Whymper later suggested that Taugwalder might have intentionally chosen a flimsy rope, a slander that stuck to the family for decades. The Wallisers, the local Swiss valley dwellers, were the Sherpas of the so-called golden age of alpinism, when wellborn Englishmen competed to knock off the high peaks of Europe. The Swiss did the work and rarely got the credit. These days, of course, the Swiss are the ones going abroad in search of glory, and Taugwalder's descendants are the wealthy owners of luxury hotels.

Now Steck has a controversy of his own. Five days after he and his companions fled Camp 2 on Everest, he was back in Switzerland. For three days, he didn't go out. He saw no friends and stayed away from town. On Tuesday, May 7, he picked me up in Interlaken in his Audi, the name on the side now like a scarlet letter. It was his first time out in the car since he'd been back. He felt people looking at him. The Swiss media had mounted a siege, albeit a polite one. *Blick*, Switzerland's version of the *Post*, ran an interview with an old Swiss mountaineer. The headline: "Stecks Ego-Trip War Eine Provokation."

Many accounts were sympathetic, but in others, and on many adventure blogs, Steck, Moro, and Griffith were being depicted as Gore-Tex imperialists, rich, arrogant European invaders of a sacred Sherpa ritual and violators of cross-cultural decorum. "For Simone, in Italy, this has not been such a problem," Steck said. "But here in Switzerland, if they can find something like this about you, they kick your ass." Many eminent climbers had spoken up in his defense, including Reinhold Messner and Chris Bonington. Still, he found himself in the unfamiliar position of being, in some quarters, the bad guy.

"I'm not really home yet," he said. "It's just too much for me. I'm totally messed up. People wanted to kill me. For me, life was over. I was sitting in the tent and I didn't see any escape. They said, 'Get that guy out here. First, we kill him and then we look for the other two.' Maybe I'm too sensitive, but I can't get over this.

"People have this understanding of the nice, good Sherpas, blah blah blah," he said. "They say, 'It was just Westerners in the wrong place. They were arrogant to be there. The Sherpas are there to do their work.' Well, I respect their work, but they should respect my work." Steck and his team had paid tens of thousands of dollars for the requisite permits, and believed that they had a right to climb on the Lhotse Face, and that the requirements of the commercial climbing operations shouldn't take precedence over those of the professional ones. If anything, their expedition, one of two professional bids that season, may have merited some deference. Their mission, from a certain vantage, was an exalted one.

For the Sherpas, and for many Westerners who have worked alongside them over the years, getting hundreds of paying clients up to the summit, Steck, Moro, and Griffith had no business being on the Lhotse Face. The Yak Route, as it's sometimes called, wasn't part of their climb, and the Sherpas' work there is vital to most of the mountain's constituents: clients, guides, porters, and the ecosystem that has sprouted up around them, from the villages on the way to base camp to the gear companies and media outlets that treat the Everest climbing season as their Super Bowl.

At any rate, the argument with the fixing team was one that Steck was willing to take some blame for. "What happened on the Lhotse Face—we can discuss this, what was wrong, what was right. No problem. But what happened at Camp 2, this was unacceptable. Even if we made a big mistake, it's no reason to try to kill three people."

Steck seemed changed from when I'd seen him in March. He was subdued, speaking almost in a whisper, with an air of bafflement. Since the Camp 2 incident, he'd had a persistent headache. He was hardly sleeping, and when he did he had nightmares, which he'd never had in the past. "I'm fucked, eh?" he said. "Now I have to fix myself. I will seek professional help."

He was surprised that several Western climbers who were friendly to him at base camp after the incident later wrote secondhand accounts on the Internet that were not only critical of him but full of what he and Moro have called false allegations and fabricated quotes.

Mike Hamill, of International Mountain Guides, the company that the fixing-crew chief worked for, wrote afterward, "The instigators were Simone and Ueli. Will these two be held accountable for inciting violence and for their cultural arrogance, or will there be a double-standard?" Garrett Madison, a guide with the commercial outfitter Alpine Ascents International, referred to an "unwritten rule" that climbers should stay off the face during the fixing day (whether this should apply to professional climbers, and not just commercial clients, for whom the ropes are intended, is arguable) and depicted the brawl as a regrettable shoving match rather than an attack by a mob. He too placed the blame for the incident on Moro and Steck. He asserted that after the confrontation on the Lhotse Face, Moro called down to Camp 2 on the radio, saying that he was ready for a "f——ing fight." Simone Moro responded, when Madison posted his account, "It makes me crying to read that false, false, false and pure invented fact. I NEVER, NEVER, NEVER, NEVER, did that radio call and provocation. (I have a lot of witness who can confirm.) Madison INVENTED those words to try to change the facts and give me responsibilities for the tension."

Hamill and Madison also repeated the crew chief's charge that Steck had kicked ice down onto the fixing team. Steck told me, "This I know: there was not a single piece of ice falling on a Sherpa." According to Moro and Griffith, a Sherpa who had been bleeding said later that he had not been hurt by falling ice; he had slipped and hit his face. Madison's account was called "the Sherpas' viewpoint"—he had talked to many of the Sherpas involved—but to some it read more like the viewpoint of someone with an interest both in placating restive employees and in reassuring future clients. "He just protects his business," Steck said.

Eric Simonson, the co-owner of IMG, said last week that he shared Hamill's and Madison's point of view. "The commercial companies will put themselves solidly behind the Sherpas," he said.

Two days after the incident, Sherpa leaders arranged a kind of peace meeting at base camp. The Western climbers and a handful of Sherpas signed a handwritten treaty stating that they'd forgiven each other and agreeing to work together in the future and abstain from violence. Its vagueness implies an equivalence between the Europeans' imprudence on the Lhotse Face and the attack in Camp 2—between name-calling, on one side, and sticks and stones, on the other. More than anything, it reflected a mutual desire, among the Sherpas and the commercial guide companies, to make the whole mess go away. Steck, Moro, and Griffith signed it, and though they did not necessarily want their attackers jailed (no one has been charged), they were pleased that several of them had been suspended from working on the mountain this season. At the base-camp meeting, Steck told me, "I saw that guy who punched me in the face, the chief from the fixing crew. I looked him in the eye and said, 'You have stolen my dream. Please don't do that to another person.'"

Not long afterward, when Steck was back in Switzerland, Moro, who is a helicopter pilot, flew his helicopter up to the Lhotse Face, to recover the body of a Sherpa who'd fallen to his death. The Sherpa who loaded the body onto the helicopter was Mingma Tenzing, the rope-fixing chief. "When he saw me, he looked at me, then looked down," Moro said.

Steck had thought his relationship with the Sherpas was a good one. Many with whom he'd summited the previous year had approached him at base camp, earlier in the expedition, to say how much they'd enjoyed climbing with him. "Some people treat the Sherpas really bad, like slaves," Steck said. "I don't want to be the face for this. I never treated a Sherpa bad in my life." After the Camp 2 incident, Denis Urobko, a Russian professional climber attempting a new route up the Southwest Face, posted his thoughts, in which he referred to some of the Sherpas as "cattle" and "pigs." "Inexperienced and self-assured, Sherpa think it's in their right to dictate the rules and God have mercy if someone decides you sent him a 'bad glance.'" Steck, whose team had been working with Urobko and his partner, Alexey Bolotov, told me that it was a great relief that Urobko hadn't been at Camp 2 the day of the attack. "It would have been a disaster," he said. "Denis was in the Kazakh army. He's not a guy who would say, 'Thank you, hit me again.'"

Steck and Moro have blamed Mingma Tenzing's initial pique on his exhaustion and frustration after working for two days in such extreme weather and his embarrassment over the fact that they were climbing so quickly, without Sherpa help. "He's a leader, he's losing face," Steck said. "It's the worst thing that can happen in Asian culture."

"The fixing team is the best of the best, the Sherpa A-team," Simonson said. "These are proud men. They see themselves as every bit as good as anyone out there. Clearly, they felt disrespected and got really worked up over it. You go to a man's house and disrespect them, and, well—this is their house."

Steck and Moro, by climbing alpine style, may appear to be self-sufficient, but they use the fixed ropes and ladders in the icefall, and they rely on porters to help establish their comfortable, well-appointed camps on the lower parts of the mountain. While they make videos for their sponsors of themselves hiking up to base camp in trail shoes and carrying only day packs, somewhere outside the frame Sherpas are lugging their batteries and cheese. This occasionally irks the Sherpas, whose indispensability is integral to their economic well-being.

Steck, like many others, has tried to view the incident in the light of the wider predicament of Everest: overcrowding, money, and, as a result, uneasy relations between Sherpas and Westerners, as well as between professionals and commercial operators. He considers himself to have been an accidental catalyst.

This year, on the Nepal side, there were almost 400 foreigners with climbing permits, and more than 400 Sherpas. An infamous photograph last year of a seemingly endless conga line of climbers trudging up the Lhotse Face via the fixed line conveyed the extent to which the mountain had become a circus. Last week, the wait to climb the Hillary Step, the last difficult pitch before the final summit ridge, was more than two hours.

Everest has evolved into a seasonal society dominated by the interests of the commercial guiding companies, which for the most part are owned and operated by foreigners. Clients pay as much as $110,000 apiece to be led up Everest. The companies in turn contract with the Sherpas, as porters, cooks, and mountain guides. A large portion of the clients' fees goes to bureaucrats in Kathmandu rather than to the Sherpas. They observe the foreigners with their luxury accommodations at base camp, their satellite phones and computers, and they know enough to wonder whether they're being gulled. If it's their house, how come they're not the ones who get to run it? The younger generation, in particular, may be less inured than their forebears to the paternalism inherent in the relationship with the *mikarus,* or "white eyes." Walter Bonatti, the great Italian alpinist, suggested that the early conquest of the Himalayas was a kind of colonialism; if so, this may be the era of postcolonial blowback.

Melissa Arnot, whom Steck credits with saving his life, called in from base camp last week. A few days before, she and Tshering Dorje Sherpa, with whom she is climbing this season, had made it to 27,000 feet before high winds turned them back. (No one summited that day.) Arnot's goal this spring had been to summit twice; she was planning to head back up after a few days of recuperating at base camp. (Three days later, she made it.)

Arnot had been staying with Steck, Moro, and Griffith at Camp 2. The day they went up the Lhotse Face, she went down to the IMG camp and listened in as tempers flared over the radio. She is certain that Simone never challenged anyone to "fucking fight." "Nothing Jon, Ueli, or Simone has said has been inaccurate," she said. "It's all really sad. They were treated like criminals for doing nothing. The apology that's owed is one for the violence. They were forced to leave, ostracized, and their reputations were battered. The commercial expeditions owe them an apology."

She went on, "These other accounts are embarrassing, claiming that Simone and Ueli and Jon are racist and classist. It's a bold and arrogant statement to make about people you don't even know."

She said that one Sherpa who had been a friend now refused to look at her. Still, she added, "I don't think this is a rift between Westerner and Sherpa, or part of an underlying racial and cultural divide. This is a fight between boys on the slope."

A few days later, I spoke on the phone with Dawa Steven Sherpa, the expedition leader for Asian Trekking, which is owned by his family and is one of just a few Nepali guiding companies. He is 29. His father is Sherpa, his mother is Belgian. He had helped arrange the base-camp meeting after the incident at Camp 2.

Dawa was in base camp on the day of the melee, but was in constant contact that day via radio with his two Sherpas on the fixing team. They too say they heard Moro say "fucking fight," but Dawa allows that their English isn't perfect.

"Simone was out of order," Dawa said. "He's a friend of mine, but he's a very fiery character. This had been building between Simone and the Sherpas for a while."

He went on, "It's embarrassing to all sides. Now my clients are getting messages from their friends back home, saying, 'I hope you're not fighting with your Sherpa.' It's very sad. For 50 years, the Sherpas have done so much for people. One small thing between a few egomaniacs, and now all the Sherpa are hurt. We feel betrayed and abandoned. The idea that Sherpas don't like Westerners? That's all bullshit."

In the background, he occasionally joined a radio conversation in Nepali with some Sherpas who were breaking camp higher on the mountain. Every now and then, a helicopter landed nearby. He didn't much want to talk about the details of the incident at Camp 2. "That was unacceptable. I can't comment any further," he said. But, he added, "I can completely understand how traumatized Ueli must've felt." About Mingma Tenzing, the head of the fixing crew, he said, "He's the most quiet guy. A shy guy, doesn't ever ask for the credit. I was in shock to hear he was the forefront of this. I wasn't so surprised that Simone was involved. There's always something happening with him. Mingma is deeply embarrassed. He's very sorry. He knows he let down his family. But it's too late."

Mingma wasn't speaking to the press. "The Sherpas are not very good at talking," Dawa said. "We're workers. We don't want to talk. The best way to repair our reputation is to work."

Steck's house is at the end of a narrow street lined with quaint Swiss homes and flower gardens, up on a slope, overlooking the village, the lake, and a broad set of cliffs that block the view of the Eiger. He built the house himself, with a crew (he is a carpenter by trade), and he and his wife moved in in January. It is spacious, by Swiss standards, with three stories and an underground garage, but it's simple and spare, a modern interpretation of a chalet, with lots of light woodwork and, on the walls, large-format photographs of famous peaks.

In his office, on the ground floor, next to a giant map of Everest, a calendar sketched out his year. The summer was empty; he'd expected to be recovering from Nepal. On a day in early September, he'd written, in tiny print, "Annapurna," with a line going down through the rest of the month.

In March, he'd talked a lot about Bonatti, whom he admired perhaps above all others. Bonatti, on a winter morning in 1965, walked up to the base of the Matterhorn's North Face and climbed it by himself, a harrowing direct route that took him five days. Steck repeated the route seven years ago in 25 hours and spoke with wonder about the experience of placing his hands and feet where Bonatti had. A pitcher playing today can never know what it was like to strike out Ted Williams, but Steck could imagine himself in Bonatti's boots—the opponent was the same. After the climb, Bonatti, 35 at the time, abruptly retired from professional climbing, and became a journalist. He lived to the age of 81. In some respects, Steck admires this more than anything.

Steck knows that to live a long time you need to quit. Before Everest, he'd figured he had two more years in him of pushing the limits. Now he wondered whether he had less. He would always climb mountains; it was a part of his personality, and his marriage. But the professional part of it, the Swiss Machine, had gone a little sour. A week after Steck got home, Alexey Bolotov, the partner of

Denis Urobko, was killed in a fall. A rope broke. They found his body on the Khumbu Glacier. He was 50 and had quit his job to devote himself to climbing. There's a part of Steck that wonders if the incident at Camp 2 wasn't in some respects a blessing. "Maybe there might have been a big accident," he said. "There are a lot of things in climbing that you can't control."

BUCKY McMAHON

Heart of Sharkness

FROM GQ

IT SEEMED SOMEHOW SIGNIFICANT, or maybe particularly
unfair, but anyhow a cold, dumb fact: Mathieu Schiller had just
paddled out. He hadn't had a chance to catch a single wave. In
a case of bad timing within worse, the 32-year-old bodyboarder,
a former French champion and the owner of a local surf school,
had launched from the beach as one of the biggest sets of the
day humped on the horizon. There'd been a month of solid swell
(which may have been significant as well), and though the wave
heights were finally beginning to decline, it was still a big day at a
surf break renowned for its powerful waves, and negotiating the
set would take Schiller a little farther out to sea than the normal
lineup. He duck-dived under the last wave, feeling the upward
surge of power as the lip of the breaking wave threw out over him.
He came up, streaming water, scanning the horizon with his char-
acteristic enthusiasm, his ever-present stoke.

Then he burst up out of the sea. The shark stood him up, his
legs in its mouth. And while he beat at its snout with the blunt end
of his boogie board, another shark leapt from the water and bit
into his torso. For one impossible, hopeful instant, while the second shark hung in the air, jaws snapping, the whole thing must've
seemed like some kind of terrible hoax, or a collective hallucina-
tion. Then the momentum of the leaping shark carried man and
beasts back down into the water, into a spreading pool of blood.

This primal scene of large wild animals hunting *us* could've
been witnessed by any number of locals and tourists sunbathing on
the beach or sipping drinks at the cafés along the promenade, for

it was three o'clock on a sunny afternoon, September 19, 2011, the
tail end of the surf season at Boucan Canot beach and a busy time
at this festive resort town on the west coast of Réunion, a French
island about 400 miles east of Madagascar. The lifeguards, surfers
themselves and friends of the victim, saw it going down right in
front of them. Vincent Rzepecki, a powerfully built 31-year-old,
was the first guard to hit the water. He couldn't believe what was
happening. He'd grown up with Schiller, had dinner with him the
night before last. Now he paddled like mad, hoping for the best.

Of the half-dozen surfers in the water, Yves Delaplin had been
closest to the accident. He remembers the fear and the shock, and
the inner conflict of fight or flight. From about 20 feet away, he
saw the slick of blood and heard Schiller call out from the middle
of it, "Shit! Yves!" Time seemed to smear into one long panicky
moment of hesitation—the sharks visible as fast-moving blurs, everyone yelling "Get out of the water!"—and then Delaplin, on a
bodyboard himself, kicked toward the accident. He was holding
Schiller in his arms when Rzepecki arrived on the paddleboard.

"Get out of here!" he ordered Delaplin. "Let me do my job!"
And with that he took custody of the victim, shifting the stricken
surfer up onto the deck of the paddleboard. Rzepecki saw at once
that the situation was hopeless. Schiller's chest was torn open;
water washed into the cavity. Still, he was determined to deliver
his friend to shore. Then the next set arrived, a series of 12-foot-
tall walls of water. Rzepecki heard the roar of whitewater behind
him, and then he and Schiller were ripped from the paddleboard,
driven down, and slammed hard on the bottom. Amid a blizzard
of turbulence, still clutching his friend to his chest, Rzepecki was
somehow aware of the sharks in the whitewater with him, gray
shapes at the edge of his vision.

He surfaced with Schiller in his arms, gulped air, and the next
wave bore down. Now his thoughts flashed back to a previous fatality at a nearby surf break, Ti Boucan. Three months earlier,
31-year-old Eddy Aubert had been killed during a late-afternoon
surf session. Not a widely popular figure like Schiller, Aubert had
been more of a soul surfer, a free spirit living with his girlfriend up
in the hills. Aubert's death had seemed an isolated tragedy rather
than part of a pattern. Now the pattern emerged. Same pattern
of bites to leg and torso. Maybe the same sharks. Sharks with no
fear of men. Rzepecki was suddenly very much afraid and close to

panicking. He was hurt and he was drowning. His friend was dead. He had to let him go.

By the time he made it back to shore, the nautical crew from the fire department was already on the beach, equipped with scuba tanks, preparing to take on the recovery of the body. According to Rzepecki and other lifeguards, the divers ran into trouble immediately. Despite employing Shark Shields (devices that emit electronic pulses to repel sharks), they were forced to retreat into caves beneath the spit of rocks that delineates the north end of Boucan Rights, while the sharks, in a highly agitated state, frisked in and out of view in the impact zone. Mathieu Schiller's body was never found.

The world-famous left point break at St. Leu is the surf spot of my dreams, and of my nightmares too. In the predawn gloom, I paddle a big red rental longboard through the chilly glass of the tranquil channel. *Sanhn-Loo!* I know the place from boyhood lore, *Endless Summer* fantasies, and surf-magazine pics. French and African. So cool. A long and leisurely paddle out, and then a fast fun ride on a perfectly peeling left-hander. Truly one of the world's great surfing waves.

Normally, on this crowded planet, I'd never get a wave at a famous break like this. I'm not good enough, not aggressive enough. But things are far from normal now on Réunion. The locals here are staying high and dry, staging a kind of informal strike. According to native wisdom, the risk of a shark attack has become intolerable. Since the death of 21-year-old Alexandre Rassiga in July, the third fatality in just over a year, there have been protest marches, a lot of shouting, and a bit of violence, with surfers demanding that the government kill the offending animals. I've arrived in the midst of a turf war between man and shark. It's Saturday morning, August 25, 2012, less than three weeks after yet *another* attack, this one not fatal but nearly so—a mauling right here at St. Leu—and there's nobody out in the water but me and Mickey Rat.

Mickey—Mick Asprey—is a white-haired 64-year-old Australian shaper who owns a shop in town. Ten years ago, he was blinded in one eye in a collision with his surfboard; that and his irascible demeanor remind me of an Aussie Rooster Cogburn. Mostly I'm watching *him* surf. He's catching four waves to my every one, and whenever he disappears behind a glassy wall, I'm left alone in the lineup, wondering if at any moment my on-site reporting, and indeed my life, will be brought to an abrupt and bloody conclusion by a streaking gray blur.

For what it's worth—and I don't suppose it's worth much in terms of safety—I have some experience with sharks. When I was field editor for a scuba-diving magazine, I sought out sharks around the world. In the lagoons of Bora-Bora, I dove with lemon sharks the size of small submarines. In Micronesia I hung out in reef passes, kicking hard against the current to watch feeding blue and whitetip sharks. And once in the Galápagos, I ascended through a veritable tornado of hundreds of circling hammerheads. I was never afraid. Always the sharks seemed oblivious to us divers, as if we existed in separate dimensions. Awesome and silent, gray against the blue, they paraded past like disciplined thespians observing the fourth wall. Yet here in the waters off Réunion, it seems that the sharks have broken through that barrier. They *see* the surfers. They seek them out.

Certainly, on that day three weeks ago here at St. Leu, a shark sought out Fabien Bujon. It was late afternoon, getting close to sundown, a bad time to be in the water, as everyone knew. The first bite took off one of Bujon's feet, and the shark—a bull shark—came at him for more. As Bujon punched at its head, the shark latched onto his hand, severing it above the wrist. He crammed his other hand into its gill slits and the shark backed off. One tough hombre, Bujon somehow managed to make the 100-yard paddle to shore unassisted.

Now the sun finally crests the 10,000-foot-tall volcano in the near distance, turning the sea a glimmering silver. I squint through the translucent water at my gloriously intact feet, wiggling my toes, and recall the warning I received from a St. Leu local. Wild-haired, eyes red-rimmed from a hard night's partying, looking like the dockside prophet Elijah in *Moby-Dick,* the man fixed me with his stare and said, "The sharks, they taste the men, and they learn to eat them."

If this is hysteria, it's highly contagious.

Surfing Réunion has never been safe—the International Shark Attack File lists 14 attacks on surfers, of which eight were fatalities, between 1989 and 2010—but the island has never experienced anything like the current spike: 10 attacks in the past two years. In February 2011, a shark tore off a surfer's lower leg at Roches

Noires, a surf break near the harbor of St. Gilles, the island's busiest resort town. A few months later, a surfer at the same break
escaped with just a chomped surfboard. Sharks also pursued a
waveski and a canoe, neither incident resulting in injury, though
in the case of the canoe, a closed-hull outrigger, the shark came
out of the water and bashed in the upper deck—an act of unprecedented aggression, or desperation. These incidents, plus
the Aubert and Schiller fatalities, all occurred within or nearby the
Marine Reserve, a 12-mile-long protected zone established on the
west coast to try to save the threatened coral of the barrier reef.

Was the Reserve itself to blame for the eightfold increase in
attacks? Some surfers and fishermen believed that it endangered
one group (the surfers) by excluding the other (the fishermen).
They felt that *la présence humaine* was needed to restore the old balance, with man at the top. Or were the attacks just a cascade of co-
incidences? Or were they due to some changes in the sea at large,
or in shark numbers or shark behavior? To begin to answer those
questions, in October 2011 the government of Réunion island
launched CHARC, an ambitious water-safety and shark-monitoring
program, the main thrust of which would be the tagging of 80
sharks by 2014. In the meantime, the popular beaches of Boucan
Canot and Roches Noires were closed to surfing and swimming for
the indefinite future.

As the CHARC scientists pursued their tagging program—catch
each shark with rod and reel, immobilize it alongside the boat, surgically implant an acoustic beacon—France's biggest dive-training
and certification organization took a more submersive approach:
they hired the world-famous Belgian breath-hold diver, Frédéric
Buyle, a kind of eco–Van Helsing of the monster-shark world, to
swim down and have a look around. A passionate shark advocate,
Buyle had won fame swimming with great whites—sans cage—and
looking at them eye to eye. Here in Réunion, Buyle was amazed by
what he saw, or failed to see. There were no sharks at all, at least
none of the smaller reef sharks found everywhere else in the tropical world. Eventually, using baits, Buyle coaxed his wary quarry
from the shadows. Moving in slo-mo and hugging close to the bottom, gray against gray, were specimens of *Carcharhinus leucas. Re-
quins bouledogues.* Bull sharks.

"Ils sont timides, très, très timides, mais present," Buyle writes in his

report of the expedition. They were there all right, but very, very wary. And very bad news.

When Buyle inspected the attack sites at Boucan Canot and Roches Noires, he concluded that both sites are ideal bull-shark habitat: sand beaches fronting ravines holding fetid streams. Roches Noires has the additional attraction of nearby St. Gilles harbor, with its murk of pollution and steady supply of fish carcasses. Buyle asserted he would never enter the water at either place without a dive mask for defense against ambush.

Nevertheless, he believed that closing the beaches had been a mistake. Who would assume the authority to reopen them? Who could decide when they would be "safe" when they never would be? Réunion island didn't have a shark problem so much as it had a people problem, peculiarly French. There was the French faith in the law, on one hand, that for every crime a criminal could be found and punished. On the other hand, just a careless plunge away, was a powerful and unpredictable species—evolving and adapting to conditions made more hostile by humans. The sea had become "a place of mass consumption," in Buyle's words—and at the same time primo bull-shark habitat. He called the situation "grotesque."

The bull shark is a species with a detestable reputation. Feared worldwide under various names—Zambezi shark, Nicaragua shark—it is perhaps the most intelligent, most adaptable, and least predictable of the large, dangerous sharks. Neither fast nor graceful like the tiger, nor majestic like the white, the bull is a bulky, round-bellied, seemingly sluggish beast, though capable of quick bursts of speed in attack. Mature females, larger than the males, attain a maximum length of about 11 feet and can weigh more than 500 pounds. Small eyes hint at the relative unimportance of sight in their hunt for prey, which they are known to pursue in coordinated attacks, often in turbid, low-visibility conditions. Through an adaptation called osmoregulation, their versatile kidneys allow them to move freely between salt water and fresh water, to enter river mouths and prowl miles upstream. On Réunion, with its steep volcanic slopes scoured by deep ravines, it had long been folk wisdom to stay out of the water after heavy rains, when fresh water laden with silt and debris sent long brown plumes into the sea. Above all, bull sharks are attracted to that turbidity, to murky waters for the cloak of invisibility. That's why bulls are rarely glimpsed until the moment of impact.

The most common explanation for why sharks attack surfers is the "mistaken identity" theory: sharks on the hunt for seals, sea lions, and turtles look up and see the silhouettes of surfers on their boards, mistake them for their natural prey, and decide to investigate with a bump or a bite. The theory helps explain both why some surfers are targeted and why so many survive their encounters with much larger, superbly evolved killing machines. As Mick Asprey points out, "We're not on the menu, mate!"

But many Réunion surfers had come to believe something different: the bulls were *learning* that surfers were easy prey. So they wait, these killer sharks. Hidden. Elsewhere. You never see them when the sea is calm. Then the waves come—a symphony to their senses, the big pounding swell. The swell churns up the bottom, the sand in solution creating that murkiness through which they navigate with the ease of the blind, like great bats. Then—voilà!— the food arrives, arranged just beyond the breakers, a dangling banquet of human limbs.

On July 23, 2012, at Trois-Bassins—traditionally the safest surf break on Réunion—a third surfer was lost. Alexandre Rassiga, a handsome 21-year-old actor-bartender, took a bite below the knee—a nonfatal injury—and then suffered a second bite to the upper thigh that severed an artery. At this point, something seemed to snap in the minds of Réunion island surfers. Aubert. Schiller. And now Rassiga. The surfers were losing their friends, losing their pastime. Boucan Canot and Trois Roches remained shut down. Now the mayor of Trois-Bassins closed *that* venerable surf spot. Robert Boulanger, president of the Ligue Réunionaise de Surf, described the mental state of his constituents as *"psychose."*

Three days after Rassiga died, some 300 surfers and fishermen marched on the capital, St. Denis. Carrying surfboards painted with slogans, they chanted "Open the Reserve now!" The protesting surfers believed that the Marine Reserve, in which commercial fishing is banned, had become like a "larder" for sharks. They were no different from criminals, these *bouledogues!*, as one furious surfer put it, except that they had the Reserve as a hideout and a refuge, a sanctuary like a medieval cathedral.

Ten days after the protest march, on August 5, Fabien Bujon was mauled at St. Leu, the island's signature break. If Rassiga's death lit the fuse, the St. Leu attack created the explosion. An angry mob of about 100 surfers and fishermen tried to break into the offices of the Marine Reserve, where they were forcibly repulsed by police.

The mayor of St. Leu, Thierry Robert, promised a shark cull. The cull would be good for business, this pro-development mayor of a tourism boomtown might have reasoned (not unlike the panicked mayor in *Jaws*). Instead the plan made international headlines, and the backlash from animal rights groups was immediate and effective. In France, Brigitte Bardot (as head of her eponymous animal welfare group) wrote a letter to the prime minister, Jean-Marc Ayrault, attacking the decision to kill the sharks. "The sea belongs first to marine life," the group announced. "We can't condemn sharks to death just to please surfers. It's ridiculous."

A minister in France bigfooted the St. Leu mayor with a compromise. Two professionals would be hired to fish the Marine Reserve for 20 sharks, bulls and tigers, which would be tested for ciguatera, a potentially deadly food-borne toxin, to see if their meat could be marketed. It was a grotesque solution, as Frédéric Buyle might've said, since the fishermen were targeting the same sharks CHARC was attempting to tag. And angry Réunion surfers were far from satisfied. But for anyone watching with dismay the endgame of the earth's last large charismatic animals—the dangerous ones, the difficult and inconvenient beasts of the shrinking wilds—Réunion island's reluctance to cull marked a long-overdue check on human arrogance.

Meanwhile, as the Réunion shark controversy boiled, signs and portents of nature's revenge—call it "bite-back"—continued to emerge around the world. Last August, scientists in the diminishing Everglades captured a record-setting 17½-foot Burmese python—an invasive species swallowing whole populations of native mammals. In southern India, the desperate poor were moving into the national parks, foraging for food, and grazing their cattle on land set aside for elephants. The elephants, tenuously confined in what one writer called "animal concentration camps," responded with rampages through towns and villages. About the same time, a lioness and her three cubs were captured in a Nairobi suburb. She was staking out her territory in backyards and vacant lots. A biologist for the Nairobi National Park said that he believed the survival of the species as a whole depended on "successful fencing."

There's a troubled history of fencing off the reefs of Réunion, where wave action makes shark netting difficult, and where the situation is further complicated by the near-invisibility of the predators. Sardon Courtois, the prophet who balefully warned me— "They taste the men, and they learn to eat them"—had gone on to say that there was no magic solution. Then he gave me his blessing to go forth and surf.

The next morning at my hotel, I can hear the rhythmic booms as waves unload on the barrier reef. The swell has begun to build. I wonder if that drumbeat is really summoning the *bouledogues* to feed. The surf is probably triple-overhead at Pointe du Diable (way too big for me), double-overhead at St. Leu (but the local surfers have posted a sign asking visitors not to surf). I decide to try my luck at L'Hermitage, a reef-pass break in the Reserve that's still open for surfing.

As I'm wading into the lagoon, about to begin the 300-yard paddle to the barrier reef, two lifeguards on a Jet Ski come blasting across the flats to confront me. "You surf alone?" one asks. "Why do you make this bad decision?" I want to answer that in a place where to surf or not to surf has become a political decision, my politics tell me to surf. But that sounds pompous, even to me. So I just shrug. One lifeguard shakes his head, glowering, dismounts from the Jet Ski, and wades ashore. The driver returns my shrug and says, "I have to apologize for my friend. He was there, you know, when Mathieu Schiller was killed."

Soon I'm out alone in the channel, watching the waves, with just a sea turtle for company. It blows its nose, cranes its neck, and regards me skeptically. We're the perfect test for the mistaken identity theory, and I'm feeling nervous. Mostly, though, I'm worried about the waves, which make a fearsome tearing sound like crashing timber as they explode onto the reef. This is no surf break for out-of-practice middle-aged men. Still, I can recall the old compulsion, the restless nights before an expected swell, the sheer joy and the camaraderie of the wave-riding tribe. I know what it must be like to have to give it up when you're in the throes of early passion for the sport—and I was just a surf-starved pup from flat-city Florida. To be a young surfer with the skill to ride *these* waves—dude, it's gotta suck.

But while many surfers are simply sitting out the crisis, a lot of others are organizing and developing tactics to get back in the water. Loris Gasbarre, a close friend of Mathieu Schiller, has started Prévention Requin Réunion, pushing for a selective culling but also fund-raising to buy Zodiacs and hire security for surf competitions. Christophe Mattei, a technologically inclined big-wave rider, is developing a smartphone app that would work in conjunction with shark-tagging data to provide real-time info on shark locations. Réunion island surfers are beginning to realize that the loss of safety is long-term and that they are going to have to adapt.

One sunny afternoon, Mat Milella dons mask and fins and slips into the water of the St. Gilles harbor, within sight of the shark warning flags flying over Trois Roches. Milella is a paid *vigie requin* (shark lookout), part of a new CHARC "securitization" program that has begun patrolling surf breaks that remain open. With a quick prayer to the surf gods and a quicker "fuck it," I splash in after him.

The 32-year-old waterman is well suited to the task: whippet-thin, with piercing eyes and golden hair, he's Rowdy Gaines reborn. We kick out of the murky harbor, heading south, away from Trois Roches, thankfully. We're within the Marine Reserve, among knobs of bleached coral. There are a few bright tropicals, various tangs and angels and parrotfish, but no sharks, no barracudas, no mackerel or grouper. Not much of a "larder," not here anyway. Milella dives down to 20, 30 feet, hanging motionless, working on his lung capacity and free-diving technique. If this were an actual lookout shift, Milella would be paired with a fellow waterman, ready at the first sign of danger to blow a whistle and clear the water. For the worst-case scenario, the *vigies* have a trauma kit and the training to use it.

With a last look around for sharks to disperse, Milella heads for shore. Though the waves are small today, they are surprisingly powerful and disorienting through a dive mask, the swirl of sand all but blinding, and I'm greatly relieved to take off my fins and wade through the shallows. As we trudge through the sand back to St. Gilles, Milella readily expounds, in fluent if heavily accented English, on the crisis. As a surf instructor and former competitive bodyboarder, he favors selective culling, but if the culling can't happen, he's still looking forward to a new era of surfing on Réunion, one that's both more careful and more hard-core.

Milella waxes persuasive about overfishing from long-liners creating starvation conditions, the local fouling of the ravines, bad water management, and faulty water-treatment plants discharging sewage into the sea. At St. Pierre, in the south of the island, there was a bad-sewage-treatment plant right in front of the break. "And *bouledogues* follow the shit," Milella says. A friend of Mat's, Vincent Motais de Narbonne, was surfing nearby when a bull grabbed his leg, dragging him down and beating him against the bottom. "He was praying his leg would go so he wouldn't drown," Milella says. Miraculously, Motais, who lost his leg at the hip, survived.

As I listen to Mat Milella, it seems to me that everything that's shitty about us *Homo sapiens*—literally and figuratively—is good for the bull sharks. And half-buried in the screed, I detect a grudging respect for the beast.

My last evening on the island, I meet with a local spearfishing legend, Guy Gazzo, at his family's *poissonerie*, their seafood shop, in a mall across the street from the beach at Boucan Canot. Gazzo, one of the world's best breath-hold divers, and still incredibly fit at age 75, has spent more time underwater with the sharks than anybody. He tells me that spear fishermen saw the problem coming—witnessing increasing numbers of bulls, which were becoming more aggressive. He recalls, back in 2006, diving off Roches Noires, when he speared a tuna and it took off, taking line. Then here it comes, back to him, with three sharks chasing it. But back then nobody took the fishermen's stories seriously.

Gazzo doesn't believe anyone really knows precisely why the sharks are attacking now, or why so aggressively. Nor why they have settled in the area. "When you choose a neighborhood," Gazzo reasons, "you a want a *boulangerie*, a charcuterie, a chemist, bus stops. Many factors make for a good home. It is the same for the *bouledogues*."

Guy Gazzo's surprising anthropomorphizing harks back to Buyle's most empathic speculations. Buyle believes that the bull sharks' social units are complex enough that the loss of a single individual could send a group into a tailspin of erratic behavior. It's also possible, Buyle posits, that if an influential individual were to be injured, the others might help it hunt for easy prey—and nothing could be easier prey than an oblivious land mammal on the surface. It's a leap of imagination to see the tragedy of the attacks in reverse perspective: a beloved bull (do they love one another?), suddenly wrenched from the water, vanishing into the sky; the grieving survivors (do they grieve for one another?) rallying together, making a necessary change.

It's a tragic change of behavior, for man and shark. Gazzo is pro-cull, but he doesn't want to see a shark massacre. And he believes CHARC had better hurry up with its study, or the surfers and fishermen will take out the sharks, poaching them by night. "All species have a survival technique, whether it's speed or size or coloration," Gazzo says. "Ours is intelligence. What's incredible in this story is that we're using intelligence to protect a species that is killing us."

Alas, we are both too smart for our own good and not nearly smart enough. Our manipulations of nature are perforce shortsighted: we are blinded by both its vastness and its proximity, its constant flux amid illusory stability. As the Marine Reserve scientists have pointed out, kill the bull sharks and you might get something worse. The world as we know it—and as we have loved it—depends on its predators for balance, yet we keep choosing the unknown world without them, the brave new world with as-yet-unpredicted monsters in it.

With our own monster fleets, floating cities hauling humongous nets, we have ransacked the seas, perhaps irreparably. Enormous catches feed our growing populations, and population increase means increased pollution. Our success predestines our peril. It's a bitch. Here on Réunion island, suffering its own successes, its steep volcanic slopes draining the effluvia of a burgeoning population, all the unforeseen dangers of bad stewardship of the environment are embodied in one beady-eyed, piggish thug of a fish. Which seems to be thriving, for a time, in our shit. Or maybe our sins aren't so much good for them as *survivable*. Like a macro version of a super-virus, bull sharks are a symptom, and a consequence. They're what you get in the sea when you've lost just about everything else: the last shark swimming.

ALICE GREGORY

Mavericks

FROM N+1

THE AIR SMELLS FAINTLY of salt water, and strongly of bon-
fires, diesel fuel, and weed. Seagulls squawk, the sky on the horizon is just turning green, and the air is cold in that prankish West
Coast way that's impossible to take seriously and pointless to dress
for. Once the sun comes up and the fog burns off, it's going to be
a perfect day.

It's 6:00 A.M., high tide, and I'm a 30-minute, eucalyptus-dense
drive south of San Francisco in Princeton-by-the-Sea, a tiny village
with some of the biggest waves in the world and not much else.
Shadowy figures are perched in the beds of pickup trucks; they
speak in low voices and occasionally take sips of coffee. I'm sitting
on the ground in the near-dark, waiting for a surf contest to begin.

An unusually steep, unusually deep Pliocene-epoch sedimen-
tary reef rises half a mile offshore. This is where Mavericks breaks,
where from November to March waves can top out at 100 feet,
making them roughly 10 times the height of what most surfers
would consider "big." Sharks are common, as are riptides and exposed rocks. Accomplished big-wave surfers—famous ones—have
died here.

Some years—when tides and swells and winds and storms combine infelicitously—the waves here fail to break at anything above
20 feet, which means for Mavericks that they are hardly waves at all.
If the conditions aren't right, the contest doesn't happen. When it
does happen, the Mavericks Invitational is announced a few days
ahead of time, and even in this case the plan is provisional at best.

The inconvenience is unavoidable; one elemental change can ruin the wave.

It's Sunday, and the Mavericks Invitational was announced on Thursday, which means that 12 of the 24 competitors had to buy plane tickets—from Los Angeles, Hawaii, Brazil, and South Africa—fast. The other 12 live less than an hour's drive away, and would probably be surfing here today, contest or no contest. They all know each other, and most surf together regularly. On this winter morning, it's been three years since the last invitational.

Compared with most professional athletes, these guys are ancient. Matt Ambrose of Pacifica is 40. Shane Desmond and Ken "Skindog" Collins, both from Santa Cruz, are 42 and 43, respectively. At 31, Shawn Dollar, also from Santa Cruz, is one of the youngest competitors. He also holds the world record for the biggest wave ever paddled into (61 feet, a scale at which almost every other surfer would opt for tow-in). I ask Dollar why the surfers at Mavericks are so old. "It's scary as shit," he says, raising his eyebrows. "It takes you years and years and years to break down fear. Put a 16-year-old kid out there? He's probably going to drown."

Surfers have the odd habit of saying "I drowned" when they mean "I almost drowned." Drowning, after all, feels like almost drowning until it feels like nothing. When I ask Dollar to explain the sensation of almost drowning, his answer, and the way he holds his face as he says it, makes me feel that the question is an intrusive one. "It's just depressing and lonely," he says, not making eye contact. "The lights start turning off, literally. It blinks in your mind and goes black. Pretty soon, it's just lights-out and you're done." He pauses awkwardly. "It's really fucking weird."

Just before Christmas in 1994, Hawaiian pro surfer Mark Foo took a red-eye flight from Honolulu to California. A swell was hitting Mavericks, and he wanted to arrive in time to catch it. Stoked but sleep-deprived, Foo paddled out and took off on a relatively innocent-looking 20-foot wave. The ride was photographed from multiple angles, and pictures captured Foo wiping out near the base. He never came up. Most think his leash got tangled in the rocks, fettering him to the ocean floor as wave after wave crashed above him. Two hours later, his body was discovered in a nearby lagoon, still tied to the shattered tail section of his board. Foo's death brought nationwide attention to Mavericks, a break whose size, until then, most surfers considered a myth.

In the following years there were rough storms, triple-wave hold-downs, too many close calls to count. But true tragedy didn't strike again at Mavericks until 2011. It was late on an early-spring day when Sion Milosky, also Hawaiian, charged what many have since estimated was a 60-foot wave. Milosky—fearless, ranked, and respected—never emerged. He wiped out, was held down by two waves, and probably lost consciousness. Twenty minutes later, he was found floating in the waters of a nearby jetty. There was no contest that year; this was just a regular day—what many surfers refer to as "getting wet."

The first heat won't begin for another hour, and not all the competitors are here yet. So far, the parking lot's mostly filled with spectators, likely all surfers themselves: kindergartners sitting on skateboards, gray-haired men with ragged backpacks and promotional sweatshirts. As they arrive, the competitors are easy to spot. They're the color of terra-cotta and look as though they've never been indoors. Surfers have a kind of compromised grace. They maintain dignity in spite of ridiculous clothing and a constant low level of physical discomfort (chafing neoprene, freezing water, piss-soaked wetsuits). Their shoes are cloven-toed, they wear skintight unitards, and most of the time they are responsible for a delicate, awkwardly shaped object that can serve as entertainment, transportation, and weapon. These are the kind of men who can be sincerely described as "beautiful." To watch them as a woman isn't to desire them so much as to wish you were a man.

The defending champion, a barrel-chested, 38-year-old South African named Chris Bertish, stands next to a propped-up surfboard and makes prayer hands at everyone who takes his picture. The other guys are seated in the beds of trucks, next to their guns, which is what you call the extra-long boards needed to surf a wave like the ones that break at Mavericks. Some guys with camera gear are hanging around them, along with a few UC Santa Cruz students who blog for surfing websites. By this point, the sun is shining and everyone's smiling and making small talk. The conditions, it's agreed, are sick. Kelly Slater, the most famous surfer in the world, was supposed to compete today, but has failed to show up. "Because he's a pussy," someone matter-of-factly says.

I overhear someone claim that 87,000 people have bought tickets. This is a demented estimate. Over the course of the day, about 30,000 people will trickle in and out, but right now it's more like 1,500—max. Sierra Nevada, the unofficial beverage of Northern California, has set up a beer garden, which in this case means "fenced-off part of the parking lot with a keg in it." There's a clam chowder truck and a hot dog cart. For a $10 ticket, it's about what you'd expect.

The crowd contains a lot of stupidly handsome Australians, even more obese adults in 49ers gear, and a good number of cruel-seeming young boys. Their mothers, though irresponsibly tanned, appear attentive. They wear flared jeans, snug tank tops, and platform flip-flops. They have French manicures, puka-shell necklaces, and toe rings. Either their taste has not changed since spring break 1998 or they've just decided, dispassionately, that this is the hottest way to dress.

A lot of the people here—both men and women—possess all the features that constitute a modern, normative standard of beauty, but exaggerated to a ghoulish degree. They're so blond and so tanned and so lean that it all actually starts to look like one big mess of congenital disorders. A towheaded guy kisses his towheaded girlfriend, and it's shocking—seconds before I had assumed they were fraternal twins.

Among the surfers, there is a lot of synthetic fiber and a lot of buckles. Most of their clothing, it seems, is designed to be either aero- or hydrodynamic. The gear is only a symptom—almost every aspect of a surfer's life is functional. They know the tides and what they mean for your plans to walk the dog on the beach. They know why salmon is more expensive this winter and when there's too much plankton in the water to swim without getting sick. Their friendships are often opportunistic, but in a straightforward way: with the fishermen who can tow them out to far-off breaks, the park rangers who clear the trails that lead to the most remote reefs, the contractors who employ them when the swells are bad.

Surf contests might be the strangest of all athletic competitions. They're not fair, and they can't be. Each wave presents a different set of challenges, and depending on how many happen to break during a heat—and on a surfer's own tenacity—he might catch one or five or none. (Getting none is called "getting skunked.")

He can take off on as many or as few as he likes, and often there
are multiple men to a wave.

In any contest and on any wave, surfers must take off from a
critical spot from which they'll travel fast and perilously. They're
graded on the size of the waves they catch and on how stylishly
they ride them. Style, in the face of a rapidly moving wall of water
many times your height, means a relatively still pose. At a big-wave
contest like Mavericks, there's not a lot of need for tricks.

The waves at Mavericks break so far from shore that the whole
spectacle is nearly invisible from the beach. The waves are white
specks and the surfers are black specks. If you didn't know better,
you'd think it was a harem of seals out there. So a Jumbotron,
mounted high up on a pole in the parking lot, will broadcast the
contest. "Jumbotron" has been on the tip of every ambient tongue
all morning, as though it were some nifty new technology or the
hushed name of an undercover celebrity.

It's not even 8:00 A.M., but the concrete is already warm. Everyone's leaning back or sitting cross-legged; some have kicked off
their sandals. I root around in my purse for sunscreen, and when
I look up the contest has already begun. The entire Jumbotron is
bright with whitewater.

Skindog catches the first wave of the day, one that looks about six
times his size. When a surfer chooses his wave, the first thing he
does is paddle away from it. Then, when he feels the momentum
of the wave beneath him—his paddling aided by the energy of the
water—he determines the precise millisecond to "pop up," which
consists of grabbing the rails of his board and, in one movement,
going from prostrate to a crouch. If he miscalculates that moment,
he'll wipe out. From this crouching position, the surfer stands and
proceeds to travel along the wave—and down the wave, which
means going sideways and forward at the same time. Meanwhile
the wave will be breaking above him.

Skindog is barreled for such a triumphantly long time that it
seems like he must have gone under. Getting barreled (traveling as
the wave curls above you, creating a tunnel) is objectively the most
impressive feat in surfing, and it is always the thing that nonsurf-
ers assume must just be an optical illusion. When Skindog finally
emerges, he's still standing. The crowd cheers.

Skindog's wave is, for lack of a better word, awesome. Or insane.

Or a slow, silent *what the fuck*. Such a big wave produces such a crude reaction that there's really no need for more precise vocabulary. Maybe surfers talk the way they do because they're used to being amazed, and that carries over into their ordinary interactions. This wave does not inspire nuanced feelings in me. Basically, I'm just like, *dude*.

I feel a tap on my shoulder and look up to see a figure looming above me, completely backlit, with a sort of white halo radiating out from around his head. I squint but can't make out a single feature. "It's John!" he says. I stand up, still confused, and realize that I'm face-to-face with my former boss, one of the co-owners of the surf shop I worked at in high school, in Bolinas, about 50 miles north. He lives in Santa Cruz now, shapes surfboards, and works for Clif Bar in some graphic design capacity. He unloads 10 Clif Bars into my hands, gives me his phone number, and wanders off to liquidate the rest of his promotional stock as quickly as possible.

The job at the surf shop was one of the better ones I've had. Usually, it was just me there. The store-approved music collection included an unlabeled, Pixies-heavy mix, a few scratched Bob Marley CDs, and something horrible-sounding that I think was Sum 41. One of my few responsibilities was to make sure a surf video was always playing on the overhead monitor. Hypothetically, I was supposed to change it, but I just played the same one on muted repeat from open to close and nobody ever said anything. For lunch, my parents or a friend brought me a sandwich. It was a great gig.

In the wintertime it was very slow. A local might run in to replace a just-broken leash or pick up a bar of wax, but otherwise I did my homework in peace. I'd sit tucked into a ball on a stool behind the counter with a sweatshirt stretched over my knees. I crammed a miniature space heater underneath my seat and let it run until the safety feature set in and automatically turned the thing off. There was no Internet and I didn't get cell-phone service. I read a lot of books and tried on a lot of flip-flops.

In the summer, things picked up. I took a plastic lawn chair out to the parking lot and moved it throughout the day so I was always in the sun. Being inside, ready to greet customers, was not a requirement. I could just chase after them at the last minute. People would drive in from San Francisco to take surf lessons—when I started, with one of the two owners, but after a few years it seemed like every boy I knew was giving lessons. Silicon Valley companies were sending their employees to us on weekends for expensed team-building exercises. These were the people who went surfing once and dropped $1,500 the following weekend on all the equipment. It was understood that we were not to make fun of them. For the renters, I took credit card deposits, selected foam boards and wetsuits, and gave directions to the beach. A few hours later, they'd return, shivering, starving, caked in sand, either humiliated or ecstatic. The chief perk of the job was the key to the shop, which meant it never mattered if I forgot my own wetsuit at home on my way to the beach. Rather than drive the five minutes back up the hill to retrieve it, I could just grab a rental suit instead.

I haven't been on a surfboard in years, and until coming out here I had forgotten that I know something about it. I know that certain numbers—degrees of water temperature, knots of wind speed, seconds of swell interval—are, for surfers, indicators of happiness. I know what the horizon looks like when a set of waves is coming in and to expect a terrible ice cream headache after a wipeout. I know what a surfer's truck smells like (mildewed neoprene and coconut wax), and that there is no greater feeling than being cold and then peeing in your wetsuit.

The first heat ends a little after 9:30 A.M., and I only have a half-hour to get down to Dock H, where I'm supposed to go out on a boat that will get as close as it can to the break. I eat two Clif Bars and half-run down the hill to where about 25 other passengers are boarding the *El Dorado*. They include one extremely intoxicated couple, multiple people in those slip-on checkered Vans bassists in ska bands wear, and two French children who become ill within minutes and retreat below deck, where they remain for the next four hours.

As we motor out of the harbor, the wake created by the boats ahead of us—*Rip Tide, New Seeker, Pale Horse, Lovely Martha*—is enough to pitch us substantially and often. Jellyfish float by, and some forlorn strands of kelp. When the water splashes against the bow, a feathery spray shoots up and produces a very brief rainbow. We pass some outcropping rocks: huge, dark brown, like half-submerged dinosaurs. They're the kind of rocks that surfers always describe as "spooky."

The white, fuzzy patch of sea that the surfers take off from is coming into focus. For now, they just sit there, saddling their boards, maybe even talking to one another. They're eyeing the horizon, looking for the next surf-worthy waves. When a set comes, the surfers will make their way to a location that to a viewer will seem mysteriously precise but to them intuitively obvious. Then they will paddle with all their might.

The San Mateo County sheriff has a boat out here, and so do the Coast Guard and the local harbor patrol. There are guys on paddleboards and motorized rubber rafts and guys zooming around on Jet Skis, here in case probability strikes and someone goes under. They occasionally stop, idle their engines, and pound a bag of trail mix. The water we're floating in is a sort of blue-green that's so pigmented it's actually tacky, like the color of a cartoon girlfriend's eyes. But just yards away it's frothy and white— what surfers call "soup."

Zach Wormhoudt, in green, is confidently zooming left on a wave when a mantle of foam suddenly obscures him. The wave he's taken off on has collapsed, going from a dark, coherent form to chaos—messier and whiter and maybe even bigger than a cloud. We all gasp. About 20 seconds later, he bobs up like a rubber ball. I can't make out his features from here, but I wouldn't be surprised if he was grinning.

Peter Mel, known as "the Condor," takes off behind two other competitors. Within moments, it's obvious that the wave is his. He is the one who has chosen the perfect starting spot, the place from which he'll acquire maximum stability and speed. He drops in at what must be an 87-degree angle. A slight frizz of white appears at the top of the wave and he cuts down—plummeting tens of feet in a matter of milliseconds. By the time he's at the midway point of the wave, the white frizz has grown to an anarchic mess of bright foam. It looks like a horizontal avalanche, and Mel, a man escaping it.

Mel remains a few feet in front of the white for an improbably long time. He traverses the wave vertically, maneuvering up the face and back down again, over and over again, crouching down, holding the rail of his board, sometimes grazing the wave lightly with his right hand—it's affectionate, almost romantic, but also possibly a little hostile. Surfers have complicated relations with the waves they ride, somehow both adversarial and amorous.

Finally, when the force of the wave has receded, Mel shoots his board over its face and down its back. The ride is over.

Sitting here on a plastic bucket that's probably a motion sickness receptacle, I'm struggling to remember the last time I had fun. People who do karaoke probably have fun in the way I'm imagining. As do, maybe, skeet shooters. Surfers definitely have fun in that way, the way going down a slide is fun when you're a kid: anticipatory, goal-oriented, breath-altering. Some crude calculations reveal that I haven't felt anything like that in at least six years, not since the last time I went surfing.

For a sporting event whose dramatic stakes easily outweigh those of any other—the Super Bowl may feel like life-or-death, but it's not—Mavericks is anticlimactic. While we wait for the closing ceremony to begin, the stage is occupied by a band that mostly plays Sublime songs for close to an hour. Much of the crowd clears out before the ceremony even starts. The parking lot looks and feels like Sunday afternoon on a college campus after a Spring Fling weekend: the sun is low, boyfriends are offering up their jackets, everyone has mild heat stroke. I smell terrible and feel like I've been slowly drinking vodka out of a water bottle for hours. It's nice. The beer garden is shutting down, and the surfers are nowhere to be seen. They're probably eating between four and five thousand calories and hopefully taking a hot shower.

Finally Jeff Clark, who runs the local surf shop and began the contest in 1999, takes the mic, smiles, and recounts some of the day's highlights. "We saw these guys do things like pulling into the barrel, just getting blown up, milking it to the inside, trying to do floaters on 15-foot elevator drops," he says. "It was fun." Clark calls the finalists up to the stage one by one: Peter Mel, Alex Martins, Greg Long, Zach Wormhoudt, Mark Healy, Shawn Dollar. Their faces, which nobody's seen all day, have a blue cast to them. It's hard to imagine them truly warming up for at least another 24 hours.

Peter Mel is the winner. When his name is announced, the audience goes benevolently wild. Clark puts a kelp lei over Mel's head and gestures generously to the award board. The prize is $50,000. Mel, who sports a full mustache, looks like the man on the Brawny paper towels logo, but swarthier and even more handsome. He takes the mic from Clark, grins, and looks at his fellow competitors. "We do the mutual thing, you know, as a brotherhood," Mel explains. "We decided to split the cash." At this, all six guys embrace in a rowdy group hug.

I come back the next day for another look. It's achingly perfect out, even more so now that the Jumbotron has been dismantled and the road is clear. The surfers are already gone; most just drove home after dinner and went to bed. It might be one of the only mornings that these guys have slept in.

There is no place more beautiful than where I am right now, and nobody cooler than the people who surf here. I am made aware of these kinds of superlatives every time I come back to California, and I luxuriate for a few minutes in the experience of knowing something for sure without having to think about it at all. And then I drive away.

RAFFI KHATCHADOURIAN

The Chaos of the Dice

FROM THE NEW YORKER

IN ORDER TO MEET FALAFEL, the highest-ranked backgammon player in the world, I took a Greyhound bus to Atlantic City, and then hopped a jitney to the Borgata Hotel. Falafel's real name is Matvey Natanzon, but no one calls him that, not even his mother, who calls him Mike, the name that he adopted when they emigrated from Israel to Buffalo—one leg in a long journey that began in Soviet Russia. Now even Falafel calls himself Falafel.

Falafel was in Atlantic City to support a friend he calls The Bone, a professional poker player who was registered in a tournament at the Borgata. The Bone, who is from Ukraine by way of Brooklyn, used to play backgammon, but he switched to poker because there is more money in it. Falafel is either a purist, or unable to master poker, or too lazy to really try, or all of the above. He is committed to backgammon, which is his main source of income—to the extent that he can find wealthy people who want to lose to him in cash-only private games. There are more of these than one might expect, but not a lot. Finding them and hanging on to them is a skill.

The jitney that travels between the Atlantic City hotels is rundown and slow, a horrible way to travel. Falafel would never take it. He can make $10,000 in half an hour playing backgammon; he can make many times that in an evening—and he can lose it all just as easily. The money comes and goes. Currently, he has no home. He has no driver's license. Until just a few months ago, he had no cell phone, no bank account, and no credit card. Pretty much everything that he owns can fit into a large black suitcase.

Still, he allows himself certain luxuries, and one of them is to hire a car rather than sit in a jitney.

Falafel had promised that he would be in the Borgata's poker ballroom, and when I arrived, at four-thirty on a gray January afternoon, the ballroom was half empty. To the nongambler, the interior of an Atlantic City casino is in no way a place of obvious joy. For Falafel, who wanted to dabble in a few quick hands while he waited for The Bone, the atmosphere was energizing. He is a big man, both in the tall way and in the overweight way, and he was dressed to relax: a soccer jersey with the logo of a Turkish cell-phone company on the front, and on the back the number 7 and FALAFEL. Propped up on his head was a yellow knitted cap, giving him the appearance of an oversized garden gnome. Nylon shorts extended below his knees. Fiddling with a dumpy black cell phone, he looked up, smiling, and asked, "How did you recognize me?"

Falafel is typically unshaven, but the stubble is not forbidding, and his face easily fills with warmth. In 2005, an Israeli filmmaker made a documentary about him, called *Falafel's Game*. In a scene filmed late one night in his hotel, Falafel says, "I'm like a kid inside. I feel like a kid—in my principles, the way I think about things." He is 44. He has known hardship: he once lived on a park bench. Pickpockets have stolen from him. Lowlifes have taken advantage of him. He has learned to be streetwise, but something kidlike remains. He lives life as if it were a game.

Falafel bought $300 in chips and sat at a table. Soon the piles before him were getting taller. He attributed this not to his skill at poker but to his gambling instincts, which are formidable in some circumstances (backgammon, mainly) and horrendous in others (sports betting, mainly). As he played, he glanced at the cards occasionally, but mostly he jabbered. When an elderly man in a leather jacket sat down and, by coincidence, began to talk about backgammon, Falafel could not contain himself. "Oh, you play?" he said. "I like to play too." The man nodded. A round of cards was dealt. "You know," Falafel said, "I'm the number-one backgammon player in the world." He glanced at a card. "None of you could beat me."

A skeptical player wearing a Miami Dolphins cap picked up his smartphone to verify. To his left, another old man asked, "Is it in the Google?"

"I'm checking," the skeptic said. "I'm just getting a lot of restaurants."

The dealer slowed play, so that the matter could be resolved—which it quickly was, generating a wave of smiles. Suddenly, a celebrity was among them. "Okay, Mr. Falafel," the dealer said. "What will it be?"

In two hours, Falafel was sitting behind $500. Things were looking up. "A year ago, if you found me then, my life would have been so much different," he said. For a time, Falafel was living in Las Vegas, with a roommate—a young backgammon whiz whom he calls Genius or Lobster, depending on his mood—but he rarely left the couch, where he watched sports, and watched the money that he bet on sports disappear. Now he saw opportunity. "This year, I am traveling a lot, playing more backgammon," he said. From Atlantic City, Falafel was planning to go to a tournament in San Antonio, and then there were trips to Los Angeles, Israel, Denmark, and, in August, Monte Carlo, for the world championships. In each place, the prospect of cash side games lay in wait. An Internet gaming site was interested in cooperating with him. He had taken on a student. Falafel was filled with a sense of purpose. He was ready, he told his friends, to turn his fortunes around.

"We should go now," Falafel said, as he cashed out; he needed to find The Bone, who was finishing a round in his tournament. The two men met in the mid-1990s, when Falafel was in New York, living in Washington Square Park, and playing chess. The Bone, whose real name is Arkadiy Tsinis, is tall and thin. He is a disciplined gambler; recruiters from Wall Street have tried to bring him into their game. "That's him," Falafel said, pointing to a man wearing a floppy leather hat and sunglasses perched on an aquiline nose. The Bone was locked in a stare-down with another player. The visible portions of his face were impassive. Eventually, with only a few chips left, he folded. Falafel tried to cheer him up as they walked over to an all-you-can-eat buffet.

Falafel's homelessness was of his own making. In 1972, when he was four, his mother, Larissa, fled Soviet Russia (and Falafel's father), moving to the Israeli town of Azor, near Tel Aviv. In Falafel's memory, Azor is ever warm and sunlit, filled with soccer matches and schoolyard friends. Larissa worked long hours at the airport, and so Falafel was often free to do as he liked—until he was 14, when she told him that she was marrying an Israeli American biophysicist, and that they were moving to Buffalo, to live with him. Falafel resented the move. Buffalo was cold and foreign. He didn't know the language. His stepfather, a Holocaust survivor, was caring but stern, and pushed him to think of life in pragmatic terms. Falafel rebelled. He did little but play chess; he drank, and even went to school a little tipsy. He went to college halfheartedly, and after graduating he lost his savings by betting on sports. Larissa refused to help him unless he found a job, and so, instead, in the winter of 1994, he hitched a ride with a friend to Manhattan, to hustle chess. "I just went through the motions," Falafel says. "My only thing was to make a bit of money so that I could survive."

Falafel knew little about Washington Square Park—a Hobbesian gaming arena in the center of Greenwich Village. "I called it Jurassic Park," The Bone said. Some of the chess players were fast-talking charmers; some had learned the game in prison. There was Sweet Pea, Elementary, the Terminator. When well-known fish—players of middling skill with money to lose—would turn up, a frenzy would erupt to vie for their action. Falafel became friendly with a wizard at blitz chess named Russian Paul, who adopted a half-mentoring attitude, involving avuncular insults about Falafel's game or his laziness or his self-destructive habits.

"I can tell you how I discovered him," Russian Paul says. "I used to play at my favorite table, and one weekend morning I came, and there was somebody snoring, sleeping under it." He hired Falafel—two dollars every morning—to hold his table for him. Before long, Falafel was playing too. By the standards of the park, where grandmasters sometimes stopped by, Falafel was in no way exceptional—"Stupid, stupid, that's stupid," Paul would mutter as he played him—but he enjoyed the camaraderie of the hustlers. Two dollars was enough to get him a falafel, which he ate every day, often for every meal. One night, Russian Paul found him passed out with patches of deep-fried chickpeas stuck to his face, and the park's newest hustler earned his street name.

H. G. Wells once said of chess, "It annihilates a man." But Falafel wasn't seeking annihilation; he wanted a way out of his self-made chaos. On a good day, he might win $30, but he lacked the easy duplicity of the more ruthless hustlers. "He does not like deception," Peter Mikulas, a former NYU employee who used to play in the park, says. "He's a Big Daddy, from *Cat on a Hot Tin Roof.* Mendacity, falseness—it bothers him."

Some of the men in the park played backgammon, which, Falafel noticed, could be far more lucrative than chess. He once watched Russian Paul beat an NYU student out of $100. Falafel had no real understanding of the game, but he was cocky and insistent, and so he sat down to play Russian Paul, who told me, "I learned how to play backgammon two weeks before him, so I took all his money." With other players, Falafel lost relentlessly. One told him, "Listen, you just don't know stuff. For $30 an hour, I'll teach you." Falafel insisted on playing him for 50 cents a point. Soon he was 140 points behind.

Backgammon is sometimes called the cruelest game. In 2008, during a snowy November outside Moscow, two strangers played on a board that one of them had carved in a labor camp. When the match ended, the winner got up, walked out of the room to get a knife, and then made good on their wager: "We had agreed to play backgammon—whoever loses dies," he explained at the time of his arrest. He was drunk-seeming, and probably a psychopath, but the story has come to serve as a parable in extremis of fortunes lost and won over the board. People have made hundreds of thousands of dollars in single sessions; one expert player lost his home. Bruegel painted the game into his apocalyptic panorama *The Triumph of Death.*

Unlike chess, backgammon is tactile, fast-moving, even loud, with checkers slammed down and tiny dice sounding like rattlesnakes as they traverse the board. Casual players who believe that they are good persist in the illusion because the element of chance obscures their deficits. At its heart, backgammon's cruelty resides in the dramatic volatility of the dice. Even a player who builds flawless structures on the board can lose to a novice. The good players simply win more often. As a result, backgammon is often played in marathon sessions that reward physical stamina, patience, and emotional equilibrium. One notable match lasted five days, with both players getting up only for bathroom breaks. The loser fell to the floor.

Like many who have become hooked on the game, Falafel found the omnipresent possibility of winning seductive. After living in the park for half a year, he moved into a tumbledown gaming club near Wall Street, a no-name place run by a gambler called Fat Nick. Stock traders would come. An associate of Vinny "the Chin" Gigante would come. Falafel slept on a recliner, and played whoever would sit with him. He also began turning up at the New York Chess and Backgammon Club, in midtown, where hard men from the Colombo crime family mixed with working stiffs and professional gamblers, and a caged white dove called Squeeze Bird watched over them all. He kibbitzed and tried to hustle opponents into playing "propositions"—arrangements on the board that contain a hidden advantage. When he was not playing, he would collapse into sleep wherever he was, and snore loudly. "You couldn't tell him, 'It's time to go home,' because he didn't have one," a player told me. Falafel lost a lot, but he also improved, and began making a few hundred dollars here and there. When Fat Nick's shut down, he returned to the street, or he slept at the White House, the last of the Bowery flophouses. One night, he recalled, "I was asleep, and a guy next to me was able to reach into my pocket. He took $1,500, and left me two $50 bills. Maybe he missed it."

Falafel's friends urged him to get off the street. One found him a room, but he could barely pay the rent. Then fortune turned his way, with the arrival of one of the game's most famous fish, a wealthy French philatelist, Internet entrepreneur, and fraudster known as Marc Armand Rousso, or, in the world of backgammon, as "the Croc." He was an eccentric—at the board, he would sometimes mutter, "Yum, yum, yum, yum, my little crocodiles," Falafel recalled—and, more significant, he was a terrible player with satchels of money to lose. "He comes in, and he loses $150,000 cash in half an hour," one opponent told me. "Then he leaves and comes back two hours later for more—but now, instead of money, he's come in with 50 pounds of gold!"

Falafel played the Croc a little, but mostly he bet on the Croc's opponents, including a skilled player named Abe the Snake. In a few months, Falafel won enough money to buy a small apartment, had he desired one. "I picked up some pants—I wanted to put something in the pocket—and I reach in and I find $4,000," he told me. "I didn't even know it existed. That's how good it was."

When he was homeless, Falafel had promised himself that if he ever made enough money he would return to Israel. "I wanted to get back and feel some love and warmth and affection and some closeness," he told me. He yearned to be married. But ever since his arrival in Buffalo he had been shy with girls, and while he was living on the street relationships were no easier. For several years, he rented a place in central Tel Aviv, and in 2001 he got in touch with a girl he had known in middle school. But things didn't work out. Relocating the warmth was not so easy.

Falafel took to spending 15 hours a day online, playing backgammon, with the shades drawn, determined to master the game. Clothes and trash piled up. He ate and ate and gained weight. Sometimes he played at a dingy backgammon club nearby. "I saw Falafel there, this big fat guy with his baseball hat backwards, playing this big, dark-skinned Israeli guy," a friend says. "They were playing high stakes, $100 a point, and the room was packed with people. It was a gladiator fight, you know, just alive, in a place you would least expect it. Falafel, with his special looks—he just looks like an idiot, and everybody here was thinking that he's just a rich American dumbass who is going to donate. And Falafel was teasing everybody. He told them that they are all idiots, and he is going to take all their money. And, the thing is, Falafel cleaned up the club. He just cleaned everybody up, and people were going insane, and the stakes got higher. He had everybody play against him. He said, 'You can consult, because you're so bad it doesn't matter. I want to hear all the stupidity.' And they would basically want to kill him, because he took their money, he took their pride, and he was really, really cocky."

Every two years, the top backgammon players around the world vote to pick the best of their peers, for a roster called the Giants of Backgammon. In 2007, Falafel was number one. "At some point, he woke up and became the best player in the world," Elliott Winslow, a top player, told me. The title is unscientific, and often debated, but no one could contest that Falafel had achieved greatness. "We can never know for certain who is the best player in a given year, but we can confidently eliminate 99.99 percent," Jake Jacobs, the roster's auditor, says. "Falafel survived the cut."

Falafel reacted to the news humbly, citing other players he thought were more deserving. "I didn't end up making a living as a backgammon player by accident," he said at the time. "I couldn't function properly in the 'normal' world."

*

Falafel is intensely loyal to the people who befriended him in Jurassic Park, and at the Borgata he decided to stay in Atlantic City for as long as The Bone could keep up his run—even if it meant delaying his trip to the backgammon tournament in San Antonio, which was about to begin. When I called Falafel to see if he was going to make it to Texas, the best he could say was, "I rate it a favorite." Backgammon is a highly probabilistic game, and Falafel's world is rarely defined by certainties. I booked a ticket not knowing for sure that he would show.

The tournament was held in the Menger Hotel, a dusty old building just opposite the Alamo. When I arrived, after 11:00 P.M. on the first day of play, Falafel had not yet turned up. In a small conference room, a couple of dozen people were milling about, and a few matches were still under way. One was between a Bulgarian man from South Carolina, Petko Kostadinov, and Ed O'Laughlin, an older player from Virginia. Kostadinov—compact, with neatly parted graying hair—was intently focused on the board. O'Laughlin, a wiry man, was dressed all in black, and his legs were folded up in his chair like crushed origami. He moved his checkers in abrupt jabs, then touched the pieces as if to confirm their solidity.

In the past half-century, backgammon tournaments—like backgammon itself—have undergone a profound transformation. The game, which has been around in some form since the time of the Pharaohs, is most popular in the Near East, and in the 1920s it became a popular club game in the West. In the sixties, the game acquired a certain glamour. Lucille Ball played, and so did Paul Newman. The world championships were black-tie—though many competitors were mediocre, a condition that soon attracted the attention of genuine gamblers, who set out to unlock the game's moneymaking potential. Backgammon is far more mathematical than chess, but, while chess has a literature that dates back centuries, backgammon had no real theory until the 1970s, when gamblers at New York's Mayfair Club began to take the game apart systematically. Chess players can visualize what the board might look like 20 moves ahead, but in backgammon the dice offer 21 random possibilities at each turn. The game must be encountered frame by frame. The players at the Mayfair drew up tables: *If one checker is 12 slots from another, there are three ways to attack, and an 8 percent chance of doing so successfully.* They rolled out positions, playing every permutation to identify the best move. Rollouts could take hundreds of hours. Players attempted to calculate, at each position, their game "equity"—the more the better. By shaving off any trace of error, they could hedge against the chaos of the dice. To the uninitiated, they undoubtedly seemed astoundingly lucky. The Mayfair denizens won a lot of money, until their skill became too conspicuous.

For players of Falafel's generation, the early theories were given a tremendous advance in the 1990s, when an engineer at IBM figured out how to apply neural-network computing to the game. The laborious rollouts were no longer necessary. One of the old Mayfair hands, Jersey Jim Pasko, a bodybuilder with a math degree, told me, "I'm spoiled. I want to do a lot of mathematical analysis, and I don't want to allow anybody else to do any." He said that many new players came into the game with a single-minded desire to make money, and lacked any sense of style and social grace, so he had dropped out of the circuit.

In San Antonio, while Kostadinov and O'Laughlin played, an official observer with a laptop computer entered their moves into a program that can roll out thousands of possibilities in seconds and calculate errors to three decimal points. Many younger players assume that its judgment is close enough to perfect. Michihito Kageyama, a former McDonald's employee from Japan who is now fourth on the Giants of Backgammon list, told me that he had created a database of 10,000 positions. He reviews 30 a day on his Kindle, as a morning exercise.

Falafel has no patience for memorization. Because he is undisciplined, he regularly makes small mistakes early on, but in the complex middle game—where checkers are spread out in ambiguous arrangements, and the differences between plays can be hard to measure—he excels. "He's very special," Kageyama told me. "He doesn't calculate equity. He's just seeing it." Perry Gartner, the president of the United States Backgammon Federation, put it this way: "Truthfully, out of the top 64 players that I know, there isn't anyone who has his intuitive understanding of the game."

I should have bet on Falafel: by the time the main tournament in San Antonio began, he and The Bone had arrived. The event was held in the Menger's Grand Ballroom, though most of the attendees—130 people—were middle-aged men in T-shirts or casual wear. "Backgammon used to be a lot more glamorous," one of the few women there told me. Falafel was wearing red Air Jordan sweatpants, a black-and-white plaid shirt, a green hoodie, and his yellow cap. His first opponent was Carter Mattig, a sound engineer from Chicago and a jocular trash-talker. Looking at Falafel, he said, "That's quite a color combination he's got today," and that afternoon he posted a photograph online of Falafel in the ensemble, titled "The Angriest Elf." Falafel was sore about it for days.

The two men found an empty spot at one of the folding tables that filled the room. When Falafel plays, his manner is casual but focused—unless he is losing, in which case his head droops as if it were filled with sand, and his body curls over the board. If an inferior player beats him, he might say, "He played horribly." When Falafel wins, he is not always gracious, and he often seems unaware of his lack of tact. Once, on a backgammon forum, Mattig wrote, "I do vomit a little in my mouth when he speaks of his 'modesty.'"

As a few spectators looked on, Falafel played Mattig, who put in earbuds and listened to music—to block out Falafel's "crying," he said. The play was brisk, and with each move Falafel, like all the Giants, was looking for fractional advantages. For most people, it is difficult to see the difference between a superlative player and a very good one. Later in the tournament, Jeremy Bagai, who is number 40 on the Giants list, pulled me aside during a game between two competitors who were playing at an exceptionally high level. "I haven't seen anything like this," he said. As a computer made clear, each move was just marginally better than the one Bagai would have made, but the aggregate effect was undeniable. Backgammon is a game of nano-distinctions.

Falafel beat Mattig, but afterward a debate arose over one of his moves: was it mathematically correct, or had luck aided him?

"I would be happy to bet on this, Falafel," Mattig said.

The stakes were set at $50. The position was entered into a computer, and players crowded around the screen.

"Oh, the move is right!" Falafel called out. "You owe me!"

"Wait, where is the move right?" Mattig said.

"Right here," Falafel said. "It's significant. It's like *1 percent.*"

Falafel called Kageyama over, showed him the position, and

asked him what he would do. Kageyama gave the same answer that Mattig had, and Falafel nodded, smiled, and told him, "That's a mistake."

Falafel was slowly making his way upward in the brackets. He had an easy time against Gary Oleson, a Walgreens pharmacist, who had come dressed in a black nylon shirt featuring a dragon strangling a tiger. While Falafel was up, 2–1, it was announced that the tournament would break for dinner. He stood and stretched, which emphasized his hemispherical belly.

"So is it true you have a bet to lose weight?" O'Laughlin asked him.

"Yeah," Falafel said.

At any given time, Falafel has more bets going than he can keep track of. He has bet on his abilities at tennis, on his dancing skills, on whether he can win an argument about Islam. (Many bets are for $1,000 — a "ruble," in Falafel's lexicon — or much more.) When he was 38, Falafel bet five rubles that he would be married in two years. (He lost.) In San Antonio, he told Perry Gartner that he had a long-standing bet: for every day he did not have a child before turning 50 he owed someone $5. Gartner, perplexed, asked how that was even a bet. "Right," Falafel said. "My downside is unlimited. But it is going to happen." Lately, it seems, Falafel has been trying to bend a vice into a virtue — and no bet has more potential in this regard than his weight bet.

"So what is it?" O'Laughlin asked. "A lot of money?"

A woman walking by answered: "It's for a *ton* of money!"

"Thanks," Falafel said.

"Well, what is it?" O'Laughlin said. "A thousand? Ten thousand? A hundred thousand?"

Falafel, who has a gambler's habit of speaking evasively, cradled his belly. "It's for money," he said.

The weight bet originated last October, when Falafel flew to Tokyo to play in the Japanese Open. One night, he and several other backgammon players were crammed into Sushi Saito, a three-star Michelin restaurant that seats only seven people. A question was posed: could Falafel and his ex-roommate Genius achieve the same weight in a year's time? By then, Falafel, who was enduring a difficult stretch of sports betting, had reached 310 pounds. Genius, who has a slight frame and is four inches shorter, weighed only 138. The question began to take on the contours of a wager, and the next day a taker emerged willing to give them 50-to-1 odds. The taker is a legendary backgammon hustler, perhaps the must successful in the game's history. He hustled me into referring to him only as Mr. Joseph—even though anyone on the backgammon circuit will immediately recognize him. He has played Saudi royalty, and he claims to have won as much as $300,000 in a match. He once told another gambler, "I used to say I'd like to have a $100,000 day. I've had those, both winning and losing, many times since then. Now I say I want a million-dollar *losing* day, which means I am wealthy enough to have a million-dollar winning day." His bet with Falafel might help him lose tremendously. No one involved is keen to see its magnitude documented, so just imagine the contents of a large armored suitcase in a James Bond movie.

Mr. Joseph was in San Antonio too. An enormous man, he was dressed in a black T-shirt and shorts, and, when Falafel and The Bone walked over, he and Genius were playing a variant of backgammon involving only three checkers, for $500 a point. He told Falafel, "You never win in tournaments. The Bone wins. He knows how to win. You find a way to lose to the worst players."

"I want to win too," Falafel said. "But sometimes I get into a spot."

The Bone interjected, "It's going to change now that he is losing weight."

"I play better if I am in better shape," Falafel said. Since Sushi Saito, he had lost about 60 pounds, and Genius had gained 20. Just about any time I ran into Genius, he was eating a J.J. Gargantuan Unwich sandwich (739 calories), from Jimmy John's. Mr. Joseph was unconcerned; he seemed to take pleasure in the bet's manipulative aspects. In 1996, he told another player, Brian Zembic, that he would give him $100,000 if he got breast implants and kept them in for a year. Months later, Zembic got them, size 38C, and, to everyone's surprise, he liked them. They helped him meet women, and he ended up marrying one of them. A year came and went—and $100,000 was wired to a Swiss bank account—but still he kept the implants in. Once, when Falafel came to visit, Zembic unbuttoned his shirt and danced. Falafel smiled and blushed.

In his own way, Falafel wanted to be transformed too. He wanted to be healthier, more mindful, more purposeful. "My life, I just got into a situation," he said. "Some of the hardships I endured, I did so without realizing that they were hardships. I should have a family. That is a big missing part of my own puzzle."

Once, in an airport, Falafel sat next to a rabbi, and asked him for his thoughts about gambling. The rabbi said that it was not prohibited, but that a life of gambling was unsanctioned by God. Falafel told me, "I see religion for what it really is: just a bluff," but he couldn't get the interpretation out of his head. One evening, outside a casino bathroom, I saw him stop a young bearded man in a yarmulke and say, "I have a question for you: do you know what Jewish law says about gambling?" The man was taken aback. It didn't matter—Falafel was already answering. "I think it is that you can gamble, but that you can't earn a living from gambling. Is that it?"

At the Menger, Mr. Joseph had rented the Presidential Suite, and on Super Bowl Sunday he filled it with food and with backgammon players. By then, the tournament was over. The mood was relaxed. Falafel had lost in the semifinals, to a longtime player from Texas, and he had been upset. But now, in Mr. Joseph's suite, the loss was easily forgotten. There was the Super Bowl to distract him—he had bet many rubles on the Baltimore Ravens. And there was his weight. He stood near an elaborate buffet that Mr. Joseph had arranged. "You can eat this," a player from Germany said, pointing to a tin of celery. Falafel already had a stalk in his mouth. He took a few carrots and a bottle of mineral water and walked over to a couch. A plate of cheesecakes was set down in front of him. "Those pies," Mr. Joseph said, casually. "Have one of those pies."

"No," Falafel said, cradling his belly. "I can't."

"I'll give you 50 bucks right now to eat one of those pies," Mr. Joseph said, pulling out a crisp bill.

"How many calories?" Falafel said.

"Thirty," Mr. Joseph said.

"Bullshit!" The Bone said.

Falafel looked at the money and hesitated. "Jeez," he said. "You're giving me a 50?" But he held his ground.

It used to be that tournaments were the center of big-money side games, but these days the few players who make their living from backgammon must look in deeper waters for big fish. Before leaving the Menger, one top player told me in hushed tones that he was going to see a billionaire who puts him up in a hotel near his house so that they can play all-night games for $1,000 a point. The billionaire is so obsessive that he can play for 15 hours uninterrupted; the player told me he had to bring a friend to cover for him during bathroom breaks.

From Texas, Falafel and The Bone headed for Los Angeles, where they rented a business suite at a Manhattan Beach hotel. Word had been quietly circulating about a group of wealthy amateurs playing for enormous stakes. Not merely fish—a pod of whales. Who would they be? Ted Turner? Carl Icahn? George and Barbara Bush host a private tournament at Kennebunkport. One of the most-read books in the Bush family is *Backgammon for Blood*, a handbook from the 1970s. ("Unfortunately, that's one of the worst books," a mathematician told me. "It was written under a pseudonym, and some people say it was intentionally bad so that people reading it would play worse.") Falafel thought he could find a way into the action from the West Coast, but he was fanatically secretive about what he knew. The money was too big—too important to his future. "This is a fantasy," he told me, by which he meant that the games were just an ephemeral opportunity, a blinding spark.

Falafel's hotel was a favorite of Jersey Jim's, who had also come, with his wife, Patty. Every day, they went across the street to a gym the size of an LAX hangar. Falafel was relying on them to help him lose weight. But he did not want to lift, or run, or exert himself intensively. Instead, he decided to restrict his diet to 1,000 calories per day, and to walk. Jersey Jim and Patty worked on him until he agreed, at least, to climb the Manhattan Beach dune: a steep, 270-foot incline near an Army Reserve facility, where athletes like Kobe Bryant come to work out.

On the morning that Falafel and The Bone arrived, a lean man with bleached dreadlocks, shirtless and deeply tanned, was doing yoga on a blanket at the base of the dune. Falafel looked a little intimidated. He watched as The Bone began striding up the incline and then slowed down. "Gee," he said. "The Bone, he's realizing that it takes a lot of energy."

Patty turned to Falafel. "This is how you lose weight," she said.

"Yeah, for sure," Falafel said. He gazed at the hill uncertainly. At his last weigh-in, he was 245 pounds. But things were looking up. He had won on the Super Bowl. He was flying back to Israel to attend a wedding, and to spend some time near his childhood home. Then he was off to Copenhagen, for the Nordic Open, to participate in a tournament known as "Denmark vs. the World." Falafel, who was captaining "the World," was putting together an international team, and hoped to bring in Genius and Abe the Snake. The whales seemed increasingly within reach. Squinting in the bright Los Angeles sun, Falafel pushed his feet into the hot sand. Slowly, he began to climb.

KATHY DOBIE

Raider. QB Crusher. Murderer?

FROM GQ

ON A COOL, DRIZZLY February night in 2003, at one-thirty or so in the morning, a police officer cruising down Lincoln Boulevard in Santa Monica spotted flames shooting horizontally out a window of the Simply Sofas furniture showroom. From overhead he could hear popping sounds as the fire leapt up to eat at the power lines in the street outside. Inside, the blaze spread quickly, engulfing upholstery and wood, roaring up through the roof and melting the metal skin right off the loading dock door.

The fire was almost immediately deemed suspicious. Firefighters reported the strong smell of gasoline, and when investigators were able to get inside the building the next day, they found three "firebombs"—five-gallon plastic water jugs cut off at the neck, stuffed with paper and filled with gasoline. The evidence was gathered and sent to the lab.

Five months later, Sergeant Robert Almada, the police investigator for Santa Monica's Arson Squad Task Force, walked into the interview room at the police station on Main Street with every reason to believe things were going his way. He had motive—revenge—and he had the kind of physical evidence almost never left behind in a fire: 30 pieces of gasoline-soaked mail, each addressed to the suspect or his wife. (In the heat of the blaze, the firebombs had caved in on themselves, preserving the magazines and catalogs and envelopes inside.) That suspect, one Anthony Smith, six feet four inches and over 320 pounds, a 36-year-old former defensive end for the LA/Oakland Raiders, dwarfed the little table in the room.

"Okeydoke," Almada said as he settled himself into a chair and opened his case file. Almada was blue-eyed and brown-haired, with bland, boyish good looks. His eagerness (the whole case was ready to tumble into place; it was *right there* at his fingertips) and the slight discomfort he felt in the presence of Smith were camouflaged by an overly casual manner. He confirmed some phone numbers he had for Smith; he asked if he preferred the interview-room door open or closed. It was all cordial enough, Almada in control . . . so how did it happen that within minutes the sergeant was floundering, struggling for a foothold while his suspect was coldly telling him his case was a pile of shit?

"You know how stupid this is. This is stupid, this is stupid," Smith said. How would he even have the time to set a fire? "I'm a very busy man. I don't have time for that crap."

Who the hell was *this* guy? A half-hour earlier, Almada would testify, while both men were sitting in the kitchen of Smith's condo in Marina del Rey, the sergeant had confronted him with the phys-ical evidence and Smith had broken down and cried. "I'm sorry, I'm so sorry," he'd said, weeping with his head in his hands. As Almada saw it, Smith was more or less confessing to the arson. (He and the store's owner had argued over money two weeks before the fire.) When Smith's wife, Teresa, had hurried into the kitchen, asking what was wrong, Smith had wrapped his arms around her and buried his face in her body.

Now *that* broken guy, whoever he was, had morphed into this deadpan, assured guy . . . whoever *he* was.

Almada thought he'd try a side attack. He took a paper from his file—a record of Smith's gun ownership. "It says you own a .45 pistol, a .22 pistol, a .357 revolver, .44 revolver, .44 Desert Eagle, .44 Colt, Olympic .223, another .223 pistol from Rocky Mountain Arms, and a .22 derringer," Almada said.

"That's it?" Smith asked.

"What do you mean, 'That's it'? That's a lot of guns for one guy."

"You ran that list and that's what you came up with?"

"That's what's listed in the Automated Firearms System, yes," Almada said.

"I only own shotguns," Smith stated flatly.

"Who bought all these guns?"

"You go back into your records and you'll see."

"These aren't my records," Almada said. "This is the Department of Justice."

"I couldn't care less whose records they are," Smith retorted.
"You go back and you check those records and you will find I was
charged with domestic violence. You know when you are charged
with domestic violence, you can't own any guns. I got rid of 'em
. . . Don't own the guns. What I do every year, I go every year to
Argentina, Uruguay, Paraguay, and Chile to go shoot. I'm a wing
shooter. That's it. Don't need pistols. I don't own guns like that. I
sold my guns."

"Okay, great," Almada said briskly. "Now back to the fire."

"Not a problem." And it really wasn't, as time would tell.

From a prosecutor's point of view, Anthony Smith is a dangerous, lucky person. Mesmerizing, seemingly untouchable. Absorbing and self-absorbed. He can do wrecking ball; he can do teddy
bear. He's a man with a temper who believes in his own victim-
hood. And he's smart . . . enough. Any slipups, and there have
been some whoppers, are countered by mind-numbing obfusca-
tion during police interviews and charismatic appearances on the
witness stand. ("He's a pretty good witness," one judge remarked.
"The DA didn't shake him. He is able to handle pressure, possibly from playing sports.") To friends and family, he's sociable and
generous, a family man with a dazzling smile and a loving heart.
A man whose talent bought him a dream life—multimillion-dollar
NFL contract, mansion on a hill, marriage to Denise Matthews,
aka Vanity, the former lead singer of Prince's eponymous all-girl
group—that somehow bled into the nightmare he now faces: a
looming trial for the brutal murders of four men.

Certainly, Smith has always been ready to bewilder. During one
of the many police searches done on his vehicles and residences
over the years, detectives found badges and numerous identification cards—two were for Anthony Smith, "Intelligence Officer,"
one for Anthony Smith of "The Organized Crime Bureau," and
the fourth was an American Press Association ID with Smith's address but bearing the slightly ridiculous name "Wayne Peartree,"
suggesting how he felt about reporters. Early on in his career,
Smith told sportswriters incredible stories about his childhood. He
said he'd been raised in New York and belonged to a street gang
called the Black Spades. When he was eight, he said, he and three

friends stole a car and crashed it, killing two of them. When it came to drug use, he really piled it on, telling a reporter that he'd started using heroin, cocaine, PCP, LSD, and speed when he was nine years old and that his brother had died of a heroin overdose.

In fact, Anthony was raised in Elizabeth City, North Carolina, a small coastal and river town surrounded by farm- and swampland, a place with the comforting or claustrophobic feel of everyone knowing you and your cousin's cousin. His mother, Naomi—a beautiful woman who drank too much, according to the old men in the neighborhood—died when he was about three years old. It's not clear who his father was. Naomi was living with a man named James Gallop at the time, who has been referred to as either his father or his stepfather. Gallop was a mean man, says a close family friend who has known Anthony since childhood; "he'd smile at you and cut you at the same time." (The family friend has requested anonymity; we will call him Bryan.) Once, when Gallop thought Naomi was stepping out on him, Bryan says, he decided to brand her by picking her up and setting her down on her wood-burning stove.

When Naomi died (they say her liver gave out), Anthony's much older half-brother Donald took over his care—after kicking James Gallop out of the house. Donald was in his early twenties at the time, so it says something about the will of the man, the cold hard certainty of him, that he could kick his mother's partner, and a violent man, to the curb. Hot-tempered and ill-humored, Donald was also industrious and respectable, Bryan says. He worked for UPS. He became a deputy sheriff, then a magistrate. Years later, Anthony told a friend that Donald used to hit him, but as Bryan puts it, they all did back then.

"That whole generation of men, they were all angry," he says. "For them, it was better to be mad than happy. They couldn't communicate, and they didn't know how to fix problems in a simple, civilized way. Oh, they liked to shine on each other, that's what we call it down south, acting like the good guy, like everything in their life was going well, even if they were coming home and beating their kids, which they were." Shining was an art, and one Anthony was learning at home.

Anthony's ticket out was football, though it took him a while to see it. He was the biggest kid at Northeastern High, but he wore glasses and was a bit of a nerd, and it was almost funny, the way he ran around with the other boys, eager to be just like them, Bryan says, not even aware that he was 10 times more athletic than anyone else, whether he was wrestling or shooting hoops or playing football. He had no ego. He wasn't even that interested in football until his junior year, when he began to work out obsessively. Anthony was always fast, but now the coaches watched him get bigger and stronger and finally committed to playing.

All of his high school coaches use the same words to describe Anthony: enthusiastic, courteous, earnest, voluble. "I don't want to say the wrong thing. He was a super good guy," says David Brinson, his defensive line coach. "He just did things a little differently. He did things Anthony Smith's way." He didn't really have any close friends, Brinson adds, but "I don't remember him not getting along with anyone. I mean, he'd walk up to you and start talking to you about anything. He just . . . he liked to be where he was."

And that seemed to be it, really, the standout quality about Anthony Smith at that point in his life—he was just glad to *be there*, out from under Donald's heavy hand and whatever loneliness lay at home. Anthony once told *Sports Illustrated* that his brother Donald "had his own life to live, but what I needed was to be a son to somebody." (Donald could not be reached for an interview.)

He found that figure in Alabama head coach Ray Perkins, who recruited Anthony to join the Crimson Tide. He kept mostly to himself at Alabama, not hanging around much with other players. He had better manners than the average 18-year-old, teammate and friend John Cassimus remembers, but some of the other guys found him intimidating, and it was hard to put a finger on exactly why. "If you looked at him, there was just something which didn't click right," Cassimus says. He would crack one of his dark little jokes that only a couple of guys found funny, and then he would fall silent. "He would create a significant amount of angst just sitting there and not saying anything. It was like going up to a dog and the dog is super beautiful, sweet-looking, wagging its tail, and it's acting really friendly, but there's something about that dog . . . You worry one day he's gonna bite your hand."

When Perkins left to coach the Tampa Bay Buccaneers after Anthony's junior year, Anthony transferred to the University of Arizona. He majored in social and behavioral sciences, won first-team All-Pac-10 honors, and was an unexpected first-round draft pick of the Los Angeles Raiders. Anthony was surprised to be taken so

early, but not that he went to the Raiders. "The team fits my personality and fits my style of play," he said. "I like sort of roaming
around in the field like a free spirit, sort of with a hard-core hell-
bent-for-leather attitude."

It was 1990, the height of gangsta rap and crack cocaine, and
the Raiders had become the beloved team of N.W.A and Ice
Cube (who would later make an ESPN documentary on the team,
Straight Outta L.A.) and every Blood and Crip who claimed the City
of Angelz as his own. Anthony landed in LA as a kind of minor
deity—to rich white sports fans and gangbangers alike—and still
with everything to prove.

At first he seemed to thrive, despite missing his entire rookie year
because of knee surgery. He spent some time volunteering for a
mentors program with the mayor's office, heading into South Central LA, often staying overnight in Compton. "I was lonely, away
from home, didn't have anybody to look after me," he told *Sports
Illustrated.* "So maybe if I'm tired or don't feel well, I stay the night
with a kid's family. Next day, I wake up, my car's washed . . . and
my laundry's done."

Over the next three seasons, he missed only one game, racking up 36 sacks, and in 1994 the Raiders rewarded him with a
four-year $7.6 million contract. He'd been enjoying his paychecks
since the moment he entered the league, but now the money was
really flowing. He bought Donald a new Corvette every year, according to Bryan; he bought several houses for himself, including a five-bedroom white-brick palace on a hill overlooking the
Pacific in Playa del Rey. But something angry and aggrieved had
started ticking in his brain. "The way I've seen people react to me,
Anthony Smith the Raider, has been sickening," he told the *Los
Angeles Times,* going on to complain about the women who loved
his money and his fame, not him, and the friends who always had
their hands out.

"He used to talk about his family asking for $30,000 like it was
$300," says former running back Harvey Williams, Anthony's team-
mate and close friend. "Anthony always said he didn't want to be
broke after football. He'd say, 'When I'm done, I want to be able
to relax and chill for the rest of my life.'"

After reading an article about the young Raider, Denise Matthews, aka Vanity, now a born-again Christian, arranged a meeting with Anthony, eight years her junior. Three days later she proposed to him, and one month after they met, he made her his second wife. (He'd had a brief marriage to a young actress a few years earlier.) But this new marriage too quickly turned to dust, recalls Dwayne Simon, a friend of Anthony's from that time. Dwayne remembers one uncomfortable team-family breakfast before a Raiders game when Denise said or did something that made Anthony furious. "He grabbed her by the arm, made her sit down," says Dwayne, a producer with the L.A. Posse and Def Jam who arranged music for Raiders games. "She tried to get up, but he snatched her back down: 'Get down!' I was really scared for Vanity. I thought he was going to break her friggin' arm."

At the same time, Smith was telling one of his rich-white-businessman friends that he had helped Denise get a kidney. (Her body was hard hit from years of drug use before she swore off that life and turned to God.) What a good guy. What an angry one. Was one of those Anthonys more true than the other? Or had he just become a violent man who knew how to shine?

A year and a half after they married, Anthony and Denise were done. (Shortly after they separated, in 1997, Anthony was arrested for domestic violence involving another woman and sentenced to anger management classes.) Finally, sometime in 1997 or '98, he started a relationship that would last. His third and current wife, Teresa Obello White, is a graduate of Stanford University and Pepperdine law school. She was working for a personal-injury firm when they met, and he told friends she would make a wonderful mother to their children.

He brought her to Elizabeth City to introduce her to his family, Bryan recalls. But what started as a Fourth of July barbecue quickly turned into a confrontation between Donald and Anthony, according to Bryan, with Donald becoming threatening enough that Anthony grabbed Teresa and they left for the airport. Anthony and Donald never talked again. "Anthony felt abandoned," Bryan says. "And that's his biggest issue."

After a mediocre 1997 season, he parted ways with the Raiders, spinning him into a panic until he signed with the Broncos in July 1998. But then, abruptly, he let it all go. While at training camp in Denver that August, Anthony called his personal assistant back in

LA. "Get the Hummer and come get me," he said. He had decided he was done with football. On the way back home, they stopped in Las Vegas, where Anthony and Teresa tied the knot.

So at 31 years old, Anthony Smith was retired. He had busted-up fingers and bad knees. He was newly married for the third time, but this time he felt he'd found the right woman. Soon he would be a father. There was plenty of adoration and goodwill out there still, though a lot less money. He stood at that cliff's edge familiar to every newly retired pro athlete.

When an athlete leaves the game, he goes from always being told what to do to free-falling through a world without structure. Now he has to find a way to survive. How does he put food on the table? His athletic talent, his pro experience, is not translatable to the civilian world. It's a terrifying moment. How does he find a new skill? Learning one takes time, patience, faith. For those who are used to making things happen by sheer will and force and power . . . how do they channel their frustration at this slower, craftier world? Those short on patience might object to starting at the bottom of the learning curve; they might start to look for shortcuts.

Soon after retiring from football, Anthony invested in at least one shady business—an online medical-billing scam that was later investigated by the Federal Trade Commission—and started spending more and more time with gangbangers and thugs. "He was bringing the edge around, and I didn't like it," Bryan says. When he asked Anthony why, Anthony told him, "These guys care about me. They're genuine dudes."

"I couldn't understand it," Bryan says. "You're married to a lawyer. You're living in Playa del Rey. Why would you be involved with these kinds of people?" He began to back away, unhappily, because he felt like now *he* was abandoning Anthony too. Dwayne Simon didn't like Anthony's new friends either. "That's when I stopped hanging around," he says. "That's when he started to change. He got that scowl, that ugly look."

By March of 2003, Anthony had become the prime suspect in the Simply Sofas arson. After speaking to Marilyn Nelson, the owner of the store, Sergeant Almada discovered that two weeks before the fire, she and Anthony had argued over some items he had left on consignment. Anthony had come to the store to pick up a check for the items that had sold and to retrieve a few unsold things, including some framed swords and a marble obelisk. When Anthony noticed that the stand on the obelisk was broken, he insisted Marilyn pay for it. They argued a bit (she believed it was broken when he brought it in), but he was adamant: "You are going to pay for it." After years of dealing with customers, Marilyn knew when to hang tough, and this didn't seem like one of those times, so she agreed. She'd already given Anthony a $615 check for the items that had sold. He said he'd come back to pick up the unsold items and told her she should have another check ready for the broken obelisk.

But before he returned, according to Marilyn, a woman identifying herself as Anthony's personal assistant called Marilyn to say that Anthony had lost the $615 check and needed a replacement. Later, Anthony showed up at the store, and while he and two of Marilyn's workers loaded his unsold items into his truck, Marilyn made out a second check, left it on the counter, and returned to her desk. She was glad to be seeing the back of this particular customer, and she didn't even bother to look up when he came back into the store. But he didn't pick up the check and leave. He stood there at the counter waiting. She busied herself with paperwork, but she could feel his eyes on her. Finally she looked up at him and asked, *"What?"* According to Marilyn, he stared her down and then pointed a finger at her, shook it slowly, turned, and left.

A few days later, Marilyn discovered that the check that was supposedly lost had been cashed. She testified that when Wells Fargo called the store to say Anthony was in the branch trying to cash the second check, her daughter told them not to. Two weeks later, Simply Sofas was torched.

On July 7, Sergeant Almada headed over to the Smiths' condominium in Marina del Rey. He described the Simply Sofas fire to Anthony, how fiercely it raged, exaggerating how firefighters had to leap from one roof to the other to save their lives. Anthony asked him what Marilyn Nelson had said about him, and Almada replied that Marilyn hadn't pointed the finger at anybody. It was the 30 pieces of mail shoved inside the firebombs that had led him to Anthony.

"If there was a fire, how was anything left?" Anthony asked, according to Almada, who says that's when he began to cry. Almada suggested they go down to the police station and continue to talk there. Anthony asked for a few minutes alone with his wife, the lawyer, and then rode down to the precinct house with the sergeant. It was a quiet ride, Almada later testified. But when they got to the station, Almada felt a change had come over Anthony.

The sergeant laid out the evidence once again, asking Anthony to look at things from his point of view. Don't you think it's odd that all the mail in the firebombs is addressed to you? Almada asked. "Can you help me out on this?"

"Well, I'm not dumb enough I'm going to firebomb a place and put my stuff in it. Help me with that. Help me with that."

"Who set you up?" Almada said. "Tell me who set you up so we can go get them."

Anthony replied sarcastically, "*Oh, it's the guy in there. I'm telling you right now, bring him in, I think it's him.* That's how foolish that question is. I'm a professional—ex-professional—athlete. How would I know? I'm not sitting here trying to insult your intelligence any more than I want my intelligence insulted. But the thing I am asking you is, go do your homework. You haven't done your homework, man."

In frustration, Almada hit him with the fact that he had just wept and apologized when confronted with the evidence; he had even asked Almada to tell Marilyn Nelson he was sorry. But Smith had an answer for that too. He had "shed a tear" because Almada had said some firemen got hurt fighting the fire. "You tell me someone got hurt, I'm gonna respond," Anthony said. "Somebody try to do something to me, someone try to do something to someone else, that still gonna hurt me. That's not right, man. You don't solve problems that way, and no $1,200 check is serious to Anthony Smith. It ain't worth it. You walk away. Situation like that, walk away. She'll get hers. Walk away. She'll get it."

A week later, Anthony returned for another go-round with Almada, at the end of which he was arrested and jailed.

At the arson trial, four gang members wearing Raiders jackets sat in the courtroom, staring down prosecution witnesses and staking out the corridors during breaks, according to the prosecutor, Jean Daly. Almada never left Daly's side, escorting her to her car at the end of each day. During the trial, the defense took Daly by surprise when they offered a whole new explanation for Anthony's tears in the condo. He was upset, he testified, because he had lost family members in a fire in Elizabeth City. (In 1996, James Gallop's longtime girlfriend, whom Anthony knew well, and her grown daughter were killed when their house burned down.) He testified that he told Almada about that fire during the drive to the police station—the ride Almada had described as virtually silent. And he offered a theory for how his mail ended up in the firebombs: He had boxes of old mail in his truck that day because he was emptying out a storage locker. He had hired a couple of day laborers to help him move his things from Simply Sofas. The workers must've put his mail in the Dumpsters behind Marilyn's store, and whoever made the firebombs found his mail and used it to set the fire. No one saw these day laborers, including Marilyn's employees who helped Anthony load his truck that day. Still, the jury deadlocked: seven to five in Smith's favor.

The DA took another crack at it, but the jury deadlocked again, this time even more weighted in Smith's favor: 11 to 1. Anthony was, by all accounts, dynamite on the witness stand. He wept, he smiled; he radiated strength and humility; the jurors loved him. By the time the case was dismissed in December 2004, he had spent 17 months in jail.

Many of his supporters attended both trials, including members of his Episcopalian church and a business consultant, Vito Rotunno, who is godfather to one of Anthony's three children. Vito visited him after the trials were over and he says he found a changed man.

"He was very paranoid," Vito says. "He was not reading things correctly. He thought I was talking to the police." Anthony would say and do strange things, Vito says, but didn't seem to realize they were strange. "I think he has a multifaceted personality," Vito says. "He's been in some really tough places, and he's been on the top of the food chain."

Vito says he ended the relationship. "Finally I said, 'If you can't talk straight to me, there's no reason for us to talk.' I guess I was around him during a good time, and then I saw his descent into not having fun."

In the early-morning hours of October 7, 2008, Sergeants Marty Rodriguez and Robert Gray of the Los Angeles County Sheriff's Department found themselves driving north on the Antelope Valley Freeway to Lancaster, a city they had no fondness for because they only knew it through their jobs. They saw the streets of Lancaster as a series of murder scenes: this shooting, that witness, this meth deal gone wrong. Besides murder, it was sand. Miles and miles of sand and scrub, broken up by houses and little shops where people killed each other.

There, on an empty stretch of road outside the city limits, Rodriguez and Gray examined the body of a thirtyish Hispanic man slumped into a pool of his own blood. He had a black eye and bruises and cuts on his back, as if he had been punched and savagely kicked before being shot to death. (The murder weapon was later determined to be a nine-millimeter.) The identification in his pocket showed the man to be Maurilio Ponce, and soon the detectives were sitting with his widow, Angie, who told them he had left the night before, driving her white Lincoln Navigator, and that yes, of course he had his cell phone with him. The police had found no cell phone and no Navigator. But it didn't take long for them to get hold of Maurilio's phone records, which showed a series of calls to Anthony Smith in the hours before his death.

The week before Maurilio was murdered, he took off work from his diesel-mechanic business. He stayed home and played with the kids, reading them stories by the fireplace and dancing with the three of them in the living room of the ranch house he and Angie had just bought. *It was almost like he knew* . . . Angie says. Maurilio was 31 years old, with a wry sense of humor. Restless. A pusher and a driver. He and Angie had met when they were teenagers, both working at McDonald's, only Maurilio was also holding down jobs at Taco Bell and a little Mexican restaurant in town, sending money back to his family in Mexico, putting his younger brother through college and graduate school. After they married, they set up shop, starting the business in 2001 with one used tire. Now Piki's Truck Repair had three employees and contracts with national trucking companies like Mayflower and U-Haul.

Two nights before his murder, Maurilio woke abruptly, his heart careening inside his chest, frightened, though he couldn't remember his dream. "Just hold me," he said to Angie. On Monday evening, October 6, Maurilio told Angie he might have to go out that night. He had business with a buddy named Tony.

It was 9:30 P.M., and down in LA, according to law enforcement officers, Maurilio's death was already in motion. Through phone records, the detectives identified calls made between Maurilio, Anthony Smith, and two other men, Charles "Chucky Cheese" Honest and Dewann White, that enabled them to track their movements that night. Each time any of these men used his phone, the officers could see where he was, as the call bounced off nearby cell towers. It's not a precise homing technique—the activated phone could be down the block from the tower or a few miles away—but it puts the phone in an area. So at 9:14, there was Dewann's phone pinging off a tower near Cheese's place in south LA. Thirty minutes later, that phone was moving west toward Marina del Rey, where Anthony lived. At 10:20, Maurilio called Anthony; both men seemed to be in or near their homes. Thirty-six minutes later, Maurilio called again, but now Anthony's phone was on the move—30 miles north, using a tower alongside the 405.

Shortly after 11:00, Maurilio's cell rang at his home in Lancaster. "Hey, Tony," Angie heard him say before he walked the phone into their bedroom. When he came out, he had changed out of his shorts and T-shirt and into a brown sweater and jeans. These were not the clothes he wore when he was going out to change a trucker's flat, but Angie didn't ask any questions. He kissed Angie, said, "Wait up for me," and left.

At 11:44, Maurilio and Anthony spoke again. By now Anthony was in Santa Clarita, pinging off a tower at the Sand Canyon exit off the Antelope Valley Freeway; Maurilio was driving south on the same road. A little over an hour later, Maurilio made a call that showed he was heading back up the Antelope Freeway, north toward Lancaster. That call, the last one made from Maurilio's phone while he was still alive, went out to A&R Diesel Parts & Service, a business that closes at 5:00 P.M. Angie will always think he was trying to reach her, hitting the wrong entry in his contacts, A&R instead of Angie. "I picture him trying to get ahold of me," she says. "He was probably trying to scroll down his phone. That was really hard for me, just to keep thinking what did he feel right then."

At 1:03 A.M., Dewann called Cheese. Both men were in or near Lancaster. And then, for 57 minutes, from 1:05 until 2:02 on the morning of October 7, all the phones went silent. What detectives believe happened during that hour would be pieced together from the crime scene evidence, the autopsy report, and interviews with two security guards who heard a series of gunshots while making their rounds at a SoCal Edison substation nearby.

Out in the western, unincorporated area of Lancaster, along a

lonely span of road surrounded by fields of electrical towers, Maurilio Ponce is forced to his knees. The wind is flowing from the
distant mountains, rustling the creosote, whistling in the electrical
wires high overhead. Maurilio's looking up now. He's not the wryly
funny man, not the shrewd, self-starting immigrant. He's without
anything but his fear and his desire not to leave his wife and three
kids—without anything, finally, but his life, felt like a bright, stut-
tering flame. And then—he is shot twice in the head and, as he
flops to the ground, three more times in the chest and back—that
too is gone.

Then the phones move south, out and away from the desert.
Down the Antelope Valley Freeway, through Acton and Canyon
Country, over to the 405, south to LA . . .

In the days after Maurilio's murder, Sergeants Rodriguez and Gray
began to stake out Smith's address at the Marina City Club, a bal-
conied condominium complex facing the harbor. On November
6, Maurilio Ponce's white Navigator appeared in one of Anthony
Smith's allotted spaces in the condo garage. Parked next to it:
Smith's green pickup truck and a stolen Nissan Xterra. One of the
Xterra's plates had been transferred to the Navigator.

A search warrant was issued for Anthony's condo and his cars,
including the Navigator, and he was taken in for questioning. Police found an AR-15 with a flash suppressor and nine-millimeter
ammunition in his condo, but no nine-millimeter weapon. In the
trunk of the stolen Xterra, there were multiple California license
plates, the kind used on government vehicles, a replica semiau-
tomatic handgun that was actually a pellet gun, two sets of yellow rubber gloves, some rope that had been cut, zip ties or cable
ties like the type used by police, four flex-cuffs, and several books,
including one entitled *Make 'Em Pay! Ultimate Revenge Techniques
from the Master Trickster.* There were also six baseball caps stamped
BAIL ENFORCEMENT or FUGITIVE RECOVERY AGENT. Searches
of Cheese's and Dewann's residences and vehicles turned up more
weapons, but again no nine-millimeter gun.

During questioning, Anthony admitted to having Maurilio's
cell phone. He handed over the keys to the Navigator. Then he
told the detectives that Maurilio was behind on his car payments
and had asked Anthony to chop the vehicle up and sell it so that
Maurilio could report it stolen. Maurilio met him at a tire yard on

Redondo Beach Boulevard, Anthony said, where he handed over the Navigator and the keys. He wasn't sure of the day. And no, he wasn't anywhere near Lancaster on the night of October 6.

As the sergeants pressed and cajoled ("I like you, Tony, but you're a liar," Gray told him conversationally), Anthony changed his story. Okay, Maurilio wasn't there in person to hand over the Navigator; the vehicle was left at the tire yard (with Maurilio's cell phone, child's car seat, and wife's pocketbook still inside) for Anthony to pick up on the seventh. And then Anthony remembered . . . that's right, yeah, he was up north on the night of the sixth. Maurilio had a job for him, so Anthony drove up to the Sand Canyon exit, where Maurilio told him to wait for instructions. But then Maurilio never showed.

The most fascinating aspect of Anthony's interview was his habit of sidestepping questions with long-winded descriptions, his tendency to prattle tediously on. This was a different Anthony from the bulletproof man aggressively facing down Sergeant Almada five years earlier. This Anthony was humble and trying hard, he insisted, to help out the detectives. He even cried a couple of times.

But he was remarkably forthcoming about his business with Maurilio. The two men, he said, dealt in stolen freight. Anthony said he didn't know how Maurilio came by the stolen truckloads of merchandise, but that Maurilio paid him to unload the goods. Ten thousand dollars a job, Anthony said, adding that they fenced everything from electronic equipment to asthma inhalers, energy drinks to fireworks. Maurilio often carried a lot of cash on him, Anthony said. Tens of thousands, sometimes more than $100,000. The night of Maurilio's murder, he had called Anthony about a new load, Anthony said.

He was, in his own way, endearing. Unfailingly polite, calling the sergeants "sir" throughout, expressing his gratitude to the detectives for "trying to work this thing out," even praising his friend Maurilio: "He doesn't play games with people's money. He, he's a good guy," he stammered. At one point in the interview, Smith even hugged Rodriguez. "I appreciate you being honest and keeping it real with me 100 percent, I really do."

When the three men went on trial before three separate juries in the spring of 2012, their defense attorneys attacked different aspects of the prosecution's case. They brought in a bank loan officer to show that Angie had often missed payments on the Navigator, suggesting that maybe Maurilio did indeed want to get rid of the vehicle in an insurance scam. Smith's lawyer Michael Evans pressed home the point that while phone records put Cheese and Dewann near the murder scene, the last transmission from Anthony's cell was down in Sand Canyon, 45 miles south of Lancaster. Evans also pointed the jury to the five calls Anthony made to Maurilio's phone on the morning after the murder. Why would he call a man he had allegedly murdered?

Still, the defense didn't seem to raise enough smoke to obscure the fact that Smith had traveled north toward Lancaster that night, speaking with Maurilio all the while, had possession of the murdered man's SUV and cell phone, and changed his story for how that came to be, offering two explanations, neither of them plausible. A dead man can't deliver a truck, after all, and if someone else killed Maurilio, he would have had to have known about Maurilio's insurance scam with Anthony and, after the murder, obligingly driven the Navigator down to LA. Even without a weapon, it seemed like the prosecution made a pretty solid case.

And yet. Cheese and Dewann were found guilty; Cheese is now serving 35 years to life and Dewann is awaiting sentencing. Smith's jury deadlocked, eight to four in the prosecution's favor. Mistrial. Anthony remains incarcerated as the prosecution prepares for a retrial, scheduled to begin sometime this summer.

On October 12, 2012, after a pretrial hearing in Lancaster—which Anthony Smith sat through expressionless in his jailhouse blues, his myopic gaze giving him a naked, just-roused-from-bed look— the man who had been described as both a "big old teddy bear" (by his friend Harvey Williams) and a guy who would "choke you out over 50 cents" (by his former friend Dwayne Simon) was ordered to stand trial again for the Maurilio Ponce murder—plus three more killings that took place all the way back in 1999 and 2001, barely after he'd hung up his cleats. Anthony has pled not guilty to all counts, and Evans characterizes the prosecution's case as having no DNA evidence or fingerprints, no murder weapons, and eyewitness testimony that is anywhere from five to 14 years old.

Dennis "Denny Ray" Henderson's body was found in the backseat of his red Chevy Impala on June 25, 2001. His head appeared to have been stomped on—he had a heel mark on his cheek, a fractured cheekbone, and a dislocated jaw. He was stabbed in his left eye, in his ear, and 11 times in his back. A cable tie encircled one wrist. It was his brother, Barry Henderson, who pointed police in Anthony's direction. Barry was Anthony's neighbor in Marina del Rey, and a friend. At the pretrial hearing, Detective Jay Moberly testified that Barry told him he'd introduced Anthony to his younger brother when Anthony wanted to buy some Ecstasy and weed. Anthony and Denny Ray started hanging out.

Barry knew Anthony as a man with a short fuse, according to Moberly, especially when it came to people owing him money. One day when the two men were heading out to lunch, Anthony made a stop at his storage locker and invited Barry to come in and take a look. Barry told Moberly he saw knives and bundles of zip ties there, police-raid jackets, machine guns, silencers, hand grenades, tons of ammunition, and a "book on how to assassinate someone." According to Moberly's testimony, Anthony told Barry that he and his associates used the police-raid jackets during robberies. He showed Barry some license plates and explained that they would rent Crown Victorias (the car of choice for police detectives at the time), exchanging the plates for these "cold" or untraceable ones. Finally, Moberly testified, Barry told him that Anthony had bragged about kidnapping and killing two brothers who ran a car wash.

Moberly dug around until he found a case matching the description—the Nettles brothers. On November 11, 1999, Ricky Nettles's body was found on a street in Compton, and his brother Kevin's body was found dumped eight miles away. Their heads were wrapped in duct tape, and they had been shot multiple times. Among other signs of torture, Ricky had a burn on his stomach in the triangular shape of a clothing iron. Both had been handcuffed.

The evening before, according to police, Ricky and Kevin were closing up their businesses on Vernon Avenue—an auto repair shop, a hand car wash, a cellular and beeper store, and a barbershop. Kevin was sitting in the small front office of the auto repair shop with a friend, watching the Lakers game. A tall black man wearing a green police jacket, a metal badge clipped to his belt, came in the shop, gun drawn. He ordered Kevin outside.

Meanwhile, Ricky and an employee named Manny were across the street, closing up the barbershop. Ricky left the shop while

Manny stayed behind to lock up. When Manny was through, he testified, he headed over to the auto shop. That's when he says he saw a large man dressed in a dark suit, with a badge fixed to his belt and a gun in a shoulder holster, putting Ricky into the back-seat of the car. Ricky's hands were pulled behind him as if he'd been cuffed. Kevin was already in the back of the vehicle, a dark-color four-door sedan. "What are you guys doing?" Manny yelled.

"We're taking him down for questioning," the big man in the suit said. Then he got into the car on the passenger side, and the car slid out of the lot and down Vernon. The next time anyone saw the Nettles brothers, they were dead, and Ricky's apartment had been ransacked.

In the weeks following Denny Ray's murder, the police suspected Anthony Smith was involved in all three killings, but the cases went cold—and stayed that way until Detectives Martin Mojarro and Jeffrey Allen from the LAPD's cold-case unit revived the investigation in 2011.

At the pretrial hearing, Manny, now a wiry 68-year-old man with a few teeth left in his mouth, took the stand and said fiercely, "Ricky never made it to the garage. He was stopped by the so-called police. He was stopped by that guy right there—" And he pointed across the room at Anthony Smith. The DA showed him Ricky's autopsy photos. Tears flooded Manny's eyes. Looking straight at Anthony, he muttered, "You son of a bitch."

During the hearing, Anthony seemed particularly vulnerable. He sat close to his lawyer, tilted toward him, occasionally scanning Evans's profile as if he might read his fortune there. Whenever evidence was passed to the defense table, mostly photographs of crime scenes, Anthony would lean forward with squinted eyes and seem to be studying them. Except for his lawyer, no one was there for him in the courtroom. His wife, now a district attorney for San Bernardino County, was absent. (During his arson trials, she'd appeared almost every day.) When family members have tried to visit him in jail, he has refused them.

"I spoke with him a few times in 2008," says Bryan. "He had changed his personality entirely." This wasn't the Anthony he'd grown up with, not even the Anthony he had known through his NFL years. "The dude is gone. I don't know who that dude is."

After Maurilio's murder, Angie lost their home and business. She went on public assistance for the first time in her life and got a job working as a cashier. Her youngest son's birthday falls on the day of Maurilio's death, and of all the children, this six-year-old has had the most difficulty grappling with his father's death. She bears no hatred toward his murderers, she says. God has allowed her to forgive them. But she is haunted by knowing how afraid Maurilio must have been that night. She doesn't know that one theory of the case is that the killers expected Maurilio to have a wad of cash with him that night, and when he didn't, they tried to get him to lead them to his home in Lancaster. Thus the phones moving back north from Sand Canyon. Thus the kicks and the punches. When Maurilio refused, the theory goes, he was taken to the outskirts of the city and killed.

Family members of Denny Ray Henderson and the Nettles brothers were in the courtroom in October too. Several of Ricky's relatives showed up each day of the hearing, including two of his children. They'd waited 13 years to find out what had happened to their father. Ricky's son Dashan had the satisfaction of watching Anthony look straight across the courtroom at him—and wince. "He looked like he'd seen a ghost," Dashan said, adding proudly, "I look just like my dad." But Anthony Smith is nearsighted. It's doubtful he saw Ricky's son at all.

CHRISTOPHER SOLOMON

The Last Man Up

FROM RUNNER'S WORLD

FOR THE PAST 16 years Tom Walsh has spent every Independence Day on a mountaintop above Seward, Alaska, tallying the agony. Walsh is the lead midcourse timekeeper for the Mount Marathon Race, the second-oldest mountain footrace in the world and, after the Iditarod sled-dog race, the most famous race in the 49th State.

Contrary to its name, the Mount Marathon Race isn't a legend for how far it stretches through the vastness of Alaska, but rather for how much unpleasantness it crams into so small a package. Starting in downtown Seward, racers run a half-mile to the foot of Mount Marathon, then scrabble about 2,900 vertical feet straight up cliffs and mud and shale before finally staggering to Race Point. There, Walsh and others note their time and bib number, hand them water, and send them hurtling back downhill in what more resembles free fall than running—over snowfields and rock fields and waterfalls and crags—until they reach the finish line back on the streets of Seward.

All of this occurs in 3.1 to 3.5 miles, depending on your route, and on trails so close to town that spectators waiting at the finish line can follow nearly every tortured step high on the mountain. By yardstick the contest is briefer than a postwork jog around Central Park. By every other count—sheer adrenaline, lung-bleeding exhaustion, potential for disaster per mile—there may be no other run like it in the world. Blood flows freely. Bones break frequently—arms, shoulders, cheekbones, legs. Sometimes, worse happens. The race has been run 85 times, and it is wildly popular.

As an isolated people who long ago learned to make their own fun, Alaskans will tell you without much hyperbole that Mount Marathon is their Olympics.

Independence Day under the undying Arctic sun can be warm and lingering and nectarine-sweet. Last July 4 wasn't one of those days. By afternoon the weather was as bad as Walsh could ever recall—windy and rainy, high 40s. He and coworkers had been on the mountain since morning, first to work the women's race, then the men's race that began at three o'clock.

A bit after five o'clock a longtime racer straggled to Race Point, a false summit marked by a large rock. The racer said he was the last guy. Walsh and his shivering comrades waited about 45 more minutes, then headed down the empty peak.

The Mount Marathon course roughly describes a treble clef—runners don't descend the same route they ascend—and as Walsh hiked down that afternoon, he saw another man slowly climbing, about 100 yards away, and dressed lightly as racers do, in black shorts, black T-shirt, black headband. It was more than two hours since the winner had broken the tape down in town. "How far am I from the top?" the racer called out.

"About 200 feet," Walsh yelled back.

The man asked if he could still "get a finish." Walsh told him to loop the rock atop Race Point and go down via the descent trail. Scarves of fog slid past them. But Race Point was still visible just above, as was Seward below, so close-seeming that the music and firecrackers of the impending party drifted up on the winds.

What happened next Walsh has replayed untold times in his head. Did he miss something? Was the man sick? Was he injured? Should he have made him turn around immediately on the sketchy up-trail? "There didn't seem to be any red flags," Walsh told me weeks later. The man was plodding, sure—but otherwise he seemed fine. So Walsh let him go.

"What's your bib number?" Walsh called out before they parted.

"Five-four-eight," the man said, and he immediately started upward.

Walsh headed down, but first texted race officials: bib number 548 would be home in about an hour and a half.

But the man wearing bib number 548 didn't return in an hour and a half. Michael LeMaitre has never come down the mountain. Mountain rescue experts, firemen, state troopers, search dogs, he-

licopter pilots, volunteers, and LeMaitre's family spent thousands
of hours scouring the mountain for him. They have yet to find
even a single clue to his fate.

Think about that for a moment: 1.5 miles up. Roughly 1.6 miles
down. Hundreds of runners within view of thousands of fans, and
a man simply vanished. How the hell is that even possible?

It is as if, one exasperated relative told me, "the mountain swallowed this man."

Seward is a town unburdened by stoplights at road's end 126 miles
southeast of Anchorage, its 2,700 year-rounders residing on a neat
thatch of rectilinear streets named for presidents everyone can still
agree on: Washington, Adams, Madison. Founded to be Alaska's
railroad gateway, today it is a town of lesser ambitions—a fish-pro-
cessing hub turned tourist burg at the head of mountain-ringed
Resurrection Bay, an inlet of the Gulf of Alaska that can glow the
unreal green of Immodium A-D, thanks to the glaciers that are
patiently grinding the surrounding peaks to flour and shipping
them to sea on muscling rivers. When the sun shines, this place is a
calendar shot of Alaska's greatest hits: Ocean. Mountains. Wildlife.
Ice. Often all in one frame.

After Labor Day, when I arrived, nearly the last of the wedding-
cake cruise ships had scooped up its Sansabelt-slacks'ed passengers and sailed south for Seattle. The herd of RVs that migrate
here each July and August had drifted north to rental lots in Anchorage. The brief, frenetic, moneymaking Alaskan summer was
over, and an autumnal drowsiness had taken hold of town. Locals
had already tugged on their winter "Seward Slippers"—tall Xtratuf
rubber boots. At gewgaw shops like Once in a Blue Moose, with its
Bear Poo Chocolate Peanut Clusters and ALASKA: JUST FOR THE
HALIBUT T-shirts, the discounts had begun.

It was from downtown where I first looked up and saw Mount
Marathon—a great green pyramid, fat at the base and tapering
with geometric precision for 3,022 feet to a rocky point. (Out
of sight it climbs more than 1,500 feet higher.) In a land of big
peaks, what makes Mount Marathon remarkable isn't that symme-
try or height, however, but sheer insistence: as it stretches north
for nearly a mile, the mountain forms almost the entire western
border of town. It is literally Seward's backdrop and backyard, its

playground, constant neighbor, and companion. When you look to the western sky, it fills the eye. It refuses to be ignored.

Like many contests of dubious judgment, the race started with a bar bet: Who could run up the big peak behind town and back in under an hour? On Independence Day 1909, Seward was a six-year-old pioneer village full of miners and other hard men. Al Taylor, a dog musher and one of those strong fathers of Alaska, reportedly took the wager. Dressed in wool pants, leather boots, and his Sunday-best white shirt, Taylor pounded up the dirt streets and into the woods. He reappeared just over an hour later and bought a round for the house, according to Millie Spezialy's history of the race. In 1915, the race up Mount Marathon—the peak was soon named for the punishing run—became an annual July 4 event. Since then, only capitalized calamity—World War, Great Depression—has canceled the contest, and then only temporarily.

One morning I headed to the trailhead with Sam Young. Young is 58, with a long upper lip, a high forehead that slopes to neatly combed-back hair, and the flatness of a Nebraska upbringing still in his voice; in another era he could have been a Dust Bowl preacher. Only his battered running shoes hint that Young is a two-and-a-half-time Mount Marathon winner. (The "half" is race lore: in 1986, after a spicy back-and-forth duel, Young and Bill Spencer, who holds the course record of 43:21, agreed to cross the finish line hand in hand.) Young has run it more than 20 times, and when he speaks of the race, his soft voice seems to cradle it like something of great value.

We stepped into the forest on a scratch of a trail. Suddenly there was mountain. No warning, no foothills—just 50 feet of rude geology. The course at times isn't one trail, but a veinwork of paths—and Young started up one called the Roots. Soon I was 40 feet up a slick wall of mud, clinging to the bones of hemlock and spruce, wishing I had a belay. Gravity tugged patiently, waiting for its chance. "You slip here, your ass is grass," Young shouted. "Now imagine doing this while buzzing with fear, adrenaline, and oxygen debt."

For decades, fewer than 10 runners competed, and it was a free-for-all—any way up and back was fair game. Men sprinted down alleys, clambered over cars, sabotaged each other's shortcuts; the night before, fences sprung up in yards that had never before boasted one. Winners won fat purses, their fame carried across the state by bush plane. (By 1950 the prize was $2,500—about a year's pay at the time. Now, instead of cash, winners get a trophy and free entry into future races.) The race's popularity swelled with the running boom of the '70s. Today, a cap of 1,000 men, women, and children as young as seven turn out, from housewives to elite athletes ($65 entry for adults, $25 for kids). About 90 percent of the adults are returnees; until a recent rule change, all finishers gained entry into the next year's race. Few relinquish their spot— and lottery bids are coveted. The only thing harder than running Mount Marathon, the saying here goes, is getting the chance to run.

"Harder" seemed unlikely. After the Roots, we plunged into the Alaskan bush, which in summer is a rioting jungleland—five-foot pushki with its blistering burn, hypodermic devil's club, alder as tight as prison bars. This "Little Shop of Horrors" crowded the trail, grabbing, stinging, thickening the air with humidity. At one point Young took a step off the track and nearly vanished into the green.

The path itself averages 38 degrees, or roughly the equivalent of one of those eastern ski runs with a name like "Widowmaker" or "Paul's Plunge." Frost it with mud that goes snot-slick after every frequent Alaskan rain, and it becomes a gruesome alpine Slip 'N Slide. Don't wear your tennis whites. "You've got to put your hands on that mountain," Brad Precosky, a six-time men's winner, had told me about certain parts of the ascent. Now put yourself nose-to-butt on this greased 3,000-foot ladder with 175 others. Seen from downtown, the up-trail is a grim, slobbering conga line of humanity.

Not for the best racers, though. Moving high above Young, I asked to see his competition form. He Gollum'd past me, his back bent and breath measured—a simian out for a postbanana stroll. A decently fit guy, I tried to keep Young's pace for 50 yards and nearly upchucked my breakfast frittata. Not even halfway up, sweat already spilled from my chin, and each calf was asking what the hell was going on. I slipped. Slid. Took a step. Slipped again. Ahead, Young kept moving higher. He fed off the altitude, growing more talkative as he climbed, casually mentioning how he used to roll rocks down on the competition to distract them. "Small stuff, nothing that would hurt anybody," he said. "There's a lot of trash going on up there."

If it seems strange that anyone could embrace such suffering, Alaskans show no such dissonance. Each Fourth of July holiday more than 25,000 people descend on little Seward to drink beer, squint at the lame fireworks that fizz in the twilight of an Alaskan summer midnight, and watch the race. Proportionately speaking, in unpeopled Alaska, that's close to all of Pennsylvania turning out to cheer a Punxsutawney turkey trot. Fans jostle five-deep behind the barricades at the finish line and pool at the mountain's base like NASCAR fans bunching at turns in hopes of witnessing mayhem. The *Anchorage Daily News*, the state's largest newspaper, covers the race as if it were the Kentucky Derby—dissecting course conditions, handicapping the top runners.

One beautiful ex-racer with the wonderfully Pynchonesque name of Cedar Bourgeois told me with damp eyes how the race had taught her skills she'd never had before—drive and mental discipline. Bourgeois is a local celebrity, a Seward-raised girl who won the women's title seven times in a row. Today, she owns Nature's Nectars, a coffee shop in the harbor that pours some of the state's best espresso to groggy fishermen. The Mount Marathon Race, she said, had done nothing less than change her life. "I would have to equate it to motherhood."

Young and I hit the halfway point, where jungle yielded to tundra. Above us a dim trail zippered up a hard gray forehead of shale to Race Point. The day blossomed around us—the Kenai Mountains pinned up a mouthwash-blue sky. Tour boats bound for Kenai Fjords National Park dragged their wakes up the bay.

On race day, there's no time to sightsee. After Race Point comes a caveman's steeplechase. Runners hurl themselves down the mountain at a full sprint. (After ascending in about 33 minutes, elite downhillers like Precosky will plunge from the top to the finish line in less than 11 minutes. The fastest on record is 10:08.) First they scramble down a long, steep snowfield at highway speeds, then run through shin-deep beds of loose shale that feel like sandboxes of shattered glass. Young flew down it with the poise of a mogul skier.

It's a helluva staircase. Just as heart and quads are redlining, runners then hit the Chute, halfway down the mountain. It's a tilted gun barrel filled with scree or snow that funnels down to a small gulley called the Gut. The Gut's centerpiece: a pretty creek dotted with yellow monkey flower and three small waterfalls. Runners have to gallop down this creek, which is strewn with what feels underfoot like wet kitty litter. At one point I slipped, lunged for a lifeline, and grabbed a fistful of devil's club, a feeling not unlike squeezing your mother's pincushion.

By this point, "people don't know their names," Young said. "They are unconscious, the walking dead." Now appeared the final obstacle between racers and the crowd's embrace: the Cliffs, several nasty crags, perhaps 25 feet high and sometimes glazed with rain or dust. Young picked an easier line for us. I was so tweaked, I nearly crab-walked down it.

Even so, the worst part of the race is yet to come. After so much up and down, the final 1,000-meter sprint to the finish line on nearly flat asphalt is excruciating, race veterans told me. "Everybody knows how to run on the street," Young said, "but not after you've been through a blender."

Why would anyone do this? you ask. The answer is that the peril of the Mount Marathon Race and the pain it inflicts are the very things that give the event its enduring allure; you could even say they are essential. Decades before Tough Mudder began roughing up paying customers, people were slapping down their money, then falling down—hard—at the Mount Marathon Race. On the flying descent, runners have fallen and had to have six-inch spear points of shale extracted from their hindquarters. Seward fire chief Dave Squires, who has aided injured racers for 26 years, told me he has seen everything from dislocations and neck injuries to angry tattoos from sliding down snowfields. A woman once rolled her ankle while evading a pissed-off bear. Another year a man was impaled by a tree branch. One roasting July 4 in the 1980s, 53 people were treated for heat illness. Squires has seen racers suffering from compound fractures—bones actually jutting from their bodies—still running toward the finish line. "Sometimes not very good," he said, "but they're still running." Among three serious injuries in last year's race, an experienced mountain runner from Anchorage chose an unusual line above the Cliffs, tripped, fell—and suffered lasting brain trauma. A pilot from Utah slid 30 feet down a muddy ramp and off the Cliffs, lacerated her liver, and was hospitalized for five days—saved only from graver injury by a quick-thinking EMT who broke her fall.

In 2009, U.S. Ski Team member Holly Brooks was leading when she collapsed in front of Seward's emergency room, not far from the finish line. She had acute exertional rhabdomyolysis—her muscles literally shredding themselves. It took doctors an hour to find a noncollapsed vein in which to insert an IV. Soon after, Brooks checked herself out against their orders and limped to a 212th-place finish so she could run again. Last year, she won.

"Many people say that if you're not bleeding from at least one spot when you get down, you didn't try hard enough," Lori Draper, a longtime member of the race committee, told me with a smile. Organizers proudly say that the race is never canceled due to adverse conditions.

Even on a normal day, the mountain can be unforgiving. Every year hikers must be rescued. A decade ago some Navy SEALs, the service's hardmen, went for a hike, worked their way onto cliffs with no exit—and had to be plucked to safety by helicopter. Over the last 25 years, the mountain has killed three hikers, though previously never during the race.

Earlier, when we finally had reached the trailhead where we'd begun, Young had taken my hand. "Did I see blood?" he had asked, examining a sliced finger. "This mountain gets a piece of you, every time," he'd said.

And here you, the reader from the Lower 48, must understand something: this is how Alaskans like their home.

Alaska is different from any place you have ever seen. Everything is bigger here: The animals. The weather. The man-eating topography. In Alaska humans still don't matter for much. "Out of the car, into the food chain," locals like to say. Wilderness? It's not some abstraction; it lives at the end of Washington Street. Go on a hike among the bears and cracking ice; feel the unease at your own contingence in the face of so much Bigness—the flip side of which is an almost electric thrill. This is why Alaskans love this country, and why they stay: to feel the surer pulse that thrums closer to the sharp edge of the blade.

Here you can test yourself daily against the country's harshness. And if you measure up, life feels that much fuller, the pulse that much more vibrant. "There's something beautiful," Bourgeois said of the best downhillers, "to see a dance made out of chaos." And if it sometimes draws a little blood? Well, that's just the world telling you that you're still alive.

There's just one caveat that comes with loving a place like this — with loving its fractured glaciers and its posing moose and the wisps of the northern lights on blue-cold nights when the mercury pools in the bulb, and with loving its mountains so much you will heave yourself against them in a muddy embrace: you must never forget that Alaska doesn't love you back. The moment you forget that, the moment you let down your guard, this place will kill you.

The crazy Frenchman loved Alaska. He loved its overflowing wildness, its bear-filled forests, its fat halibut that sulked deep in its lightless ice water, waiting to be suckered topside by a flashy jig to a hot grill and a cold lemon wedge. After high school Michael LeMaitre could have gone to Syracuse University to run track. But eventually the tall, blue-eyed New Yorker made it to the far north and enrolled at the University of Alaska Fairbanks. There he met Peggy, his wife.

Alaska in the early '70s was filled with young people eager to explore a state that was even younger than they were. Michael and Peggy took their growing family everywhere: Camping. Hiking. Fishing in Seward. Many summer Fridays after work they trooped their three young kids into the RV and pointed it toward Homer, on the Kenai Peninsula, where they'd fish all day, pull up their crab pots, and, in the dusky Alaskan midnight, light a bonfire on shore and gorge on the world's best king crab and shrimp. "We had no idea how good we had it," said Peggy, today a tough, blond grandmother of three.

It was two months after Michael's disappearance. Peggy stood and left the dining room of her Anchorage home where we were seated. She'd been describing a man who was always in motion, and now she returned with the evidence: a stack of frames bearing his PhD in business administration; a dozen training certificates; his accreditation as a grief counselor. (Frequently helping others, he volunteered at a hospice program and counseled children orphaned by the 9/11 attacks.) For the last 18 years he had worked at the local Air Force base, most recently writing résumés for colonels and privates alike as they transitioned out of the service. At home Michael, fit and younger-looking than his 65 years, was the grandfather you always wanted—a big kid who was the first into, and the last out of, Big Lake's icy waters, or the only one to take granddaughter Abby on the Apollo, the scariest ride at the Alaska State Fair.

That enthusiasm reached beyond the LeMaitre family room and into the outdoors. And here a pattern continued: Michael never let the details complicate what he wanted to do. In the '80s when he wanted to learn to cross-country ski, he didn't take lessons but signed up for the Iditaski (now the Iditarod Trail Invitational), a 210-mile wilderness race in which entrants drag their own supplies on sledges. Twice he won the "red lantern" award that's given to the last-place finisher (the second time because he stopped to help a fellow skier). As LeMaitre saw it, grit and determination—let's call it stubbornness—could see a man through a lot, and he had buckets of both.

Another time LeMaitre and his best friend, Rich Ansley, installed an overpowering motor onto LeMaitre's dory in Anchorage and sailed toward Homer, more than 120 nautical miles away. The boat's fiberglass bottom literally began peeling apart in the middle of the treacherous Kenai Narrows. They siphoned water out of the leaking boat, stopped to make some temporary repairs, and puttered on to Homer. The next morning, they took the boat fishing on Kachemak Bay.

"We've had a lot of outings," Ansley recalled, "where we said the only reason we're alive is that we entertained God."

LeMaitre more or less subscribed to "the duct-tape answer to life," his eldest daughter, MaryAnne, told me from her Utah home. "He wanted to have fun." For her father the journey was the adventure—and if you map every moment, "you're taking away the spontaneity, the come-what-may feeling."

Back in Peggy's dining room, her son-in-law, Curtis Lynn, looked at me across the dining table and asked, "Are you familiar with the military term FIDO?" I gave him a blank look. "Fuck It. Drive On," Lynn explained. That was Michael.

And the thing is, he always made it work. There were a score of dodged bullets—the dead engines, the hunting trips that went sideways. But those just became good stories. That's why, when the

CB radio craze hit in the mid-'70s, Peggy's handle became Lucky Swede, MaryAnne was TwinkleToes. And Michael? He became the Crazy Frenchman.

It wasn't out of character, then, when LeMaitre last winter applied for—and won—one of 60 men's lottery spots in the Mount Marathon Race. Soon the rookie letter arrived, with its bald admonition: "Do NOT make the July 4th race your first trip up Mount Marathon!" Peggy and youngest child Michelle, a nurse, tried to talk him out of it. He waved them off.

The night before the race, the LeMaitres and hundreds of fellow racers gathered at Seward Middle School. Outside, it was already raining—had been for days. After the annual raffle and auctions, the doors of the gymnasium were ceremonially closed for the mandatory rookie safety meeting. The gym was so packed that Michael and Peggy sat on the floor.

"If you have not been up that mountain before, you should consider going home right now, and you should not be in the race," Tim Lebling, who gave the prerace safety talk, told the crowd. LeMaitre had always been in good shape—he lifted weights and ran at the gym regularly and had finished a 12-K a month earlier—but the weeks leading up to the race had been busy. He'd run few hills, and he'd never gone to Seward to scout the course. But now, if he heard the warning (Peggy doesn't remember it, though several others who were in attendance do), he didn't move.

"No one's gotten up, so I'm assuming everybody's done it," Lebling continued. He then showed a short video and a slide show of the cavalcade of hazards—bears, falling rocks—and important landmarks, including the "turnaround rock." Lebling talked about how slick the course was this year, and about the winter's record snowfall that had left crumbling snow bridges high above rumbling creeks. "Remember—you can't beat the mountain," the safety video concluded, "but the mountain can beat you." Yet even the video seemed to capture this race's schizophrenic relationship with danger: some of those images of injuries and flying bodies were set to an adrenal-squeezing speed-metal sound track.

The next day was a pluperfect small-town Independence Day. Local guys sang the national anthem. Sacred Heart Catholic Church hawked drumsticks at its annual chicken barbecue. A parade celebrating "100 Years of City Government" marched down Fourth

Avenue with kids dressed as future city council members. And all day long, people in waves ran up and down Mount Marathon, to crazed cheers—first the shortened kids' race, then the women's race.

After the women ran, spectators at Fourth and Adams crowded in front of the bronze bust of eponymous William H. Seward, negotiator of the purchase of Alaska from Russia in 1867, who cast his jowly gaze over the men's starting line. The mood was expectant, but the weather wasn't great—chilly, the pigeon-colored skies threatening rain.

"Are you sure you want to do this?" Peggy asked her husband.

"I'm going to be fine," he replied. "I'm going to take it slow."

"Honey, you come back to me."

He kissed her.

"I will. Don't worry. I'll be back."

When the gun sounded for the second wave of the men's race at 3:10 P.M., LeMaitre and about 175 others charged through a tunnel of noise up Fourth Avenue. They ran past the fire hall, past the Chinese restaurant, past the other Chinese restaurant, past the United Methodist Church that advertised WORSHIP AT MOOSE PASS, 9 A.M. After two blocks the runners took a hard left on Jefferson Street and ran beneath the large mural of the Mount Marathon Race, painted on the side of the senior center and bearing a list of past winners in the way another small town might celebrate its prized graduates or war dead. They passed a low-slung building with a large red cross—the hospital. The road kept rising. In another block the asphalt turned to gravel. LeMaitre and the others ran past a warning sign at the foot of the mountain that read, GOING DOWN IS EVEN MORE DANGEROUS THAN GOING UP. Then the runners ran out of road entirely and faced the great green bulk of the mountain. They started to climb.

In Peggy's dining room stood a large photograph, the last ever taken of her husband, shot by a photographer on the course at about 4:30 that day. In it, Michael is just emerging from the thick brush midway up the mountain. Seward lies below, a toy landscape of streets and yards as neat as an ice tray. There is no one behind him. His knees are dirty, his gloves are soiled. He is completely soaked through by rain and sweat—shorts, shirt, headband. What you keep returning to, though, is his face. It isn't a face of misery, or complaint. The blue eyes are wide. The grin is gritted but large, even a little wild. Last place doesn't faze this face at all; it has been there before. You realize then that you know this grin: it is the grin of the Crazy Frenchman.

Fuck it, the grin says. Drive on.

Peggy shivered alone in the rain, honking her car's horn and screaming her husband's name at the base of the mountain to guide him home.

By eight o'clock when he had not appeared through the spruce—two hours after Tom Walsh had radioed to race officials that LeMaitre would soon be on his way down—the family notified authorities. Hasty searches turned up nothing. The temperature was dropping, the rain increasing. By two in the morning, an Alaska State Troopers helicopter equipped with infrared radar sensitive enough to see footprints left in snow arrived and scanned the mountain through the dusky night. Searchers landed and blew whistles—still nothing. Had anyone looked up from town in the late afternoon, he might have watched LeMaitre, seen exactly where he'd gone—he was that close. But the race was long over; everyone had turned his back on the mountain, toward cold beers, hot showers. The evening ahead. Now it was sleeting at Race Point. LeMaitre had been on the mountain for 12 hours dressed only in a T-shirt and shorts. Searchers feared that if he wasn't already injured, he was almost surely suffering from hypothermia.

The next morning the 210th Rescue Squadron of the Alaska Air National Guard, which specializes in searching for downed pilots and missing hikers, arrived with its HH-60 Pave Hawk helicopter for another infrared scan. The two choppers stalked the mountain all day. On the ground a team of 40 searchers, which soon ballooned to 60 or more, canvassed the mountain. They tried to think like the lost man: Did LeMaitre hike right past Race Point and continue up a goat path toward the true summit—only to slip down treacherous cliffs beside the path? Did he fall through a melting snow bridge created by the streams that run beneath the lingering snowfields on the racecourse and now lie, injured, out of sight? Desperate, did he beeline straight for Seward through the impossible jungle of alders and devil's club? In the following days they checked everything, to no avail—even tying strips of pink and orange surveyor's tape to branches to mark the places searched. Weeks later when I climbed it, the mountain remained tinseled with hundreds of poignant Day-Glo ribbons, each one a hope un-fulfilled.

Days passed. Rescue quietly became recovery. The bar-stool sages jawed that LeMaitre had pulled a fast one on everybody. "He's in Cabo," they said, "nursing a frosty margarita." But for many Sewardites the hurt was personal. "This is our mountain," Sam Young told me. "We can't have someone up there suffering." He and others took days off to search the mountain—some with teams, some on their own.

But where did LeMaitre go? The high tundra and rock slopes were easily enough searched. Soon the snow tunnels also had melted out, revealing nothing. Only one general scenario seemed to fit: Something sudden and drastic happened to LeMaitre—a fall? A broken ankle in the scree? A heart attack? He managed to reach the worst of the brush, or else wandered into some of Mount Marathon's frightening, unseeable cliffs—dense and difficult ar-eas where searchers might have missed him. Shock and hypother-mia took hold. And he died there.

But the mountain, so much larger than it looks from town, was loath to return what it had taken. Its rocky slopes ripped spiked crampons from searchers' feet. Its muddy slopes twisted their an-kles. And it kept raining. Four days after LeMaitre disappeared, the state troopers, who'd spearheaded the search, ended their effort. The Seward Volunteer Fire Department kept looking. A cadaver dog arrived from Oregon. Friends pored over high-res-olution photographs. The LeMaitres' son, Jon, came to Seward from Anchorage to comfort Peggy during the search. Daughter MaryAnne flew up from Utah and stayed for six weeks, climbing the mountain's gullies with volunteers. Once, she steeled herself to poke through fresh bear scat on the trail, looking for a bone, a scrap of clothing, any grisly hint of her father's whereabouts. "If it would've been me on that mountain—I know my dad. He'd be doing the same thing," she told me later as she fought back tears. "I know he wouldn't give up on me."

Finally even Chief Squires reluctantly called off the fire depart-ment's effort, hoping that when autumn stripped the jungle, a clue would appear. But soon the autumn too would pass, and then the snow would fall, and still, nothing.

In mid-August, before MaryAnne returned home, she headed up the mountain one last time. She left at three o'clock, arriving at Race Point nearly exactly when her father did. She sat by the turnaround rock and wept. Then she pulled a Dremel tool from her knapsack and carved I LOVE YOU DAD into the rock. Having experienced the mountain and Seward for these weeks, she wrote friends afterward, "If this ends up being my dad's final resting place, he is happy here."

Volunteers were still on the mountain when the soul-searching, and the questions, and the finger-pointing started. Should the race timekeepers have left LeMaitre? Shouldn't he have been stopped? Why didn't officials know who remained on the mountain? Who is responsible?

Two months before the race, former race director Chuck Echard had warned in the *Seward Phoenix Log* that race directors were asking for trouble by boosting the cap on adult racers by another five entrants last year. More bodies on the mountain meant more flying rocks, more unprepared racers. "Take care of the runners and the mountain," Echard cautioned. "Not everyone can run the race." Women's champ Holly Brooks caught the thoughts of several people I spoke with when she said, "I'm kind of surprised that something like this didn't happen sooner."

"Do we need to change some things? Of course we do," said Flip Foldager. Foldager is the 55-year-old member of the race committee with a push-broom mustache who is patriarch of one of the first families of the Mount Marathon Race. Officials, for instance, recently put a new rule in place to turn back slowpokes if they don't reach the mountain's midpoint within an hour.

But many Alaskans—organizers, runners, even the editorial writers at the *Anchorage Daily News*—reacted to LeMaitre's death with a lionlike protectiveness toward the race. They sniffed talk of any big changes suspiciously. When I was in Alaska, the adjective that modified the Mount Marathon Race the most—it dangled from the name proudly, a little provokingly—was "dangerous." It was this event's red badge of honor. Without danger, there was no race.

"It's not a safe race," Foldager told me flatly over beers one evening. "We have to manage that as well as we can."

But don't misunderstand: you can't put bumpers on a race like this, he said. The mountain won't allow it. Helmets? Ropes? Cover up one danger, another still lurks. Just as important, Alaskans won't abide it. Danger is in the very marrow of this contest. You cannot separate the two. It is part of its deep mystique. Cancel the race? Ha. People will run it anyway, guerrilla-style.

"The only way you'll ever make the Mount Marathon Race safe," Foldager told me, before finishing his beer, "is by not doing it."

And time and again during my visit, people inevitably turned the blame back on the missing man. "We were unprepared for someone being that unprepared," Draper, the race committee member, told me. Many locals see Alaska as the ultimate non-nanny state. Yes, there is community, the kind that emerges when people must rally against outside forces. But at the same time, there's still a frontier attitude, and the elbow room to go with it; you can have all the rope you want to lasso your big dreams and adventures— or all you need to hang yourself. The lesson: don't look to anyone else for help when the grizzly charges and the rifle jams. You made your bet against this country. It's your fault if you come up short.

There's a brutal fairness to this sentiment, but I left these conversations feeling that it's too easy to write off Michael LeMaitre as careless, reckless. How many of us have had near misses—the somersault over the handlebars 10 miles from the trailhead, or the mini-avalanche deep in the backcountry—and then laughed about those epics around the campfire later on when all was well? Have you ever thought how close you've come to disaster? We all have a strange friendship with risk. We crave its thrill—who doesn't want to edge a little closer to the redline where the adrenal gland squeezes and the colors grow brighter? Yet we rarely understand how close we've skirted that line, or what's on the other side. Accidents? Those happen to the other guy. Nobody ever laces up his shoes thinking he'll lead off the 10 o'clock news.

Does that make us all irresponsible?

So now you're Michael LeMaitre, toeing the starting line last July 4. You haven't been up the mountain, and you're a little nervous. Then you look up and you see the peak, so close you can almost reach and tap its summit. It's just three measly miles, round-trip! Straight up and down again, with hundreds of new best friends! You've been through so much more than this. *Take it slow,* you think, *and you'll be fine.*

Honestly—if you were Michael LeMaitre at the starting line, what would you do?

*

The morning I left Seward, I dragged my luggage into the hotel parking lot. The previous day's bright, smiling sun was gone. The rain had returned, and with it a shivery dishrag bleakness. In the harbor the season's last tourists milled about wearing crabbing gear, waiting for their tour boat to depart.

As I opened the trunk, the skies across Resurrection Bay split open. Bars of Annunciation light burst across glaciers and water and shabby hotel parking lot—the kind of unrestrained, overspilling Alaskan beauty that swells your heart and also breaks it a little bit for its fleetingness, and that makes every other soggy, frigid moment here in the far north worth it.

I turned with the light and faced Mount Marathon. The mountain stood as it always did, its Egyptian bulk leaning over town—not glowering, not protective, just . . . indifferent. With the sunlight a clear rainbow had appeared, arcing out of dark skies and landing clearly in the thick brush a few hundred feet up its face. It was silly and maudlin to think anything of it and I knew it, and I turned away. Then I turned back and spent a long time memorizing the location, though unsure who I would tell, or what I would say.

Eventually my eyes drifted down the long, meandering ridgeline. A second rainbow had appeared, falling to earth in the undergrowth some distance away from the first. And now an unlikely third rainbow tumbled from the sky and rooted itself, bright and promising, in still another place. Then, one by one, they disappeared.

CHARLES P. PIERCE

The Marathon

FROM GRANTLAND.COM

IT WAS WHAT was left behind that wrung the heart as you walked through Copley Square in Boston while the sun fell at the end of a very bad day. Tables full of unopened bottled water. Piles of those strange silver thermal blankets that have become as much a part of the annual event as spaghetti suppers and lost Scandinavians trying to find their way to Fenways Park. Bags of street clothes, waiting in great lines along Berkeley Street for owners who were god knows where. The Common. The Public Garden. Locked down in a restaurant into which they might have wandered to use the facilities. One solitary fireman, slumped on the bumper of a truck, eyes to the sky, without the energy to reach down and pick up a bottle of water at his feet, and then the shadows lengthening down Boylston Street again, and sirens and sirens, and then silence, and sirens some more. This is the tableau that's left when you take out the joy.

Nobody loves the Boston Marathon as much as the people who make fun of it year after year. This was the race that previously offered as a prize a not particularly expensive medal, a laurel wreath, and a bowl of beef stew. This was the race that, on one memorable occasion, nobody knew who actually won. I don't know anyone who loved the race that didn't mock it for its monumental inconvenience, its occasionally towering self-regard, and the annual attempts by Boston-area television stations to use it to win another shelf full of local Emmys. This includes me, and I've been around 25 or 30 of them, more or less, in one way or another, watching from the press truck, from the firehouse in Newton, from some-

body's roof, and very often from just barely inside the front door
of the late, lamented Eliot Lounge. The Marathon was the old,
drunk uncle of Boston sports, the last of the true festival events.
Every other one of our major sporting rodeos is locked down, and
tightened up, and Fail-Safed until the Super Bowl now is little
more than NORAD with bad rock music and offensive tackles. You
can't do that to the Marathon. There was no way to do it. There
was no way to lock down, or tighten up, or Fail-Safe into Security
Theater a race that covers 26.2 miles, a race that travels from town
to town, a race that travels past people's houses. There was no way
to garrison the Boston Marathon. Now there will be. Someone will
find a way to do it. And I do not know what the race will be now. I
literally haven't the vaguest clue.

　　At around three on Monday afternoon, Back Bay gradually grew
grimmer as you walked east toward Copley Square. At Kenmore,
it was actually still something of a party. People were streaming up
Commonwealth Avenue in the general direction of Boston University and, while there were still a few tearful hugs here and there,
most people seemed to feel themselves entering something of a
zone of safety as they walked by Fenway and off toward BU. Kathy
Hynes and Harry Smith, who ran together for almost the entire
race, were standing in front of the BU School of Management,
wrapped in their silver blankets. They'd made it as far as Kenmore
Square. Then, all around them, the iPhones of their fellow runners began to ring furiously, and a police officer told them to execute an immediate right-face and stop. "You could hear people
talking about 'something happening' at the finish line," Hynes
said. "And then they told us that the race had been canceled because of 'an incident.'" And that is how the news spreads today,
when two bombs go off at the finish line of the Boston Marathon,
and at least three people die and north of 100 are injured, some
brutally. The shock is sudden but its ripples fade quickly as the
knowledge of what happened goes out into the ether and then
back through thousands of personal mobile devices. Horror has
no shelf life anymore. Everybody knows already. Everybody's a
newsman. Everybody's in showbiz.

　　The longer you walked down toward the Public Garden, east
on Commonwealth, past all the stern iron and stone monuments
to great departed Bostonians, the more you saw the faces change.

People were staring now, past their friends and their families, off toward some spot in the far distance that only they could see. There were more people crying. There were even more simply wandering, dazed but unhurt, and then you realized these people were traveling through shock after they'd already traumatized their bodies over 26 miles. They were husks, some of them. They had very little left at all. Not far from Public Alley 436, just off Clarendon Street, about three blocks from what some people already were calling ground zero, Joe Nuccio hung out of the window of his apartment, recording video on his iPhone of the slowly untangling crowd on the sidewalk. Joe had heard the first explosion, then he'd heard the second, which he described as more of a blast than a bang. He felt his building shake a little. Then he threw open his window, and he saw people running past.

"The first thing you thought of was 9/11," Nuccio said. "You know, all those people running up the middle of the street. People were running, just running. They only stopped for a minute to cry and then they'd run again, and I looked out the window and I saw this white smoke rising up past the [Hotel] Lenox sign."

Ultimately, many of the lost and the confused and the separated found themselves and their loved ones at the Boylston Street end of the Public Garden. There was a general milling about and, for a moment, it almost seemed as though the spirit of the day had been recaptured, until you realized that a lot of this joy was about finding out your wife or your son wasn't maimed, and until you saw the people sitting alone, their backs against the trees, staring up through the branches as if they were hanging prayers on every one of them.

The Kings were gathered at one corner of the Garden, next to an old stone fountain. Vicky King had been running the race, and her husband and son had been waiting along Boylston Street not far from the Marathon Sports store, which had been a great place to watch the race until, in a flash of an instant, it had become the worst place to be in the world. "I don't know if you've ever been in a reenactment," said Ben King, Vicky's son. "But what the first bomb sounded like was a cannon going off, like, *Boom.* I wasn't really sure what it was. Then came the second one from up the street, and I saw the police and the EMTs just ripping the barricades away." Out on the course, Vicky was running with her friend

Nancy Breeden from Seattle. They'd just turned onto Boylston Street when they saw the commotion erupt in front of them. "A policeman came up to us," Breeden said, "and he said, 'Now, you have to run that way,' and pointed back the way we came, so we did." And that was how their Boston Marathon ended. In reverse. And, all around them in the Public Garden, what seemed to be forming itself was something that was not quite a party, but not quite a wake either. It was something solemn and celebratory all at once, like Easter morning, like a late-coming early spring.

By now, they'd cleared out the long white medical tent in the middle of Copley Square across from the Boston Public Library, over whose doors are carved the words FREE TO ALL, as though that was something permanent about the society we create among ourselves. Earlier that day, the runners who were recovering in that tent from the pain they'd voluntarily inflicted upon themselves were told, in a fashion both chilling and swift, to move to the back, and then the people who had been injured were brought in, and the exhausted, the sunstruck, and the dehydrated moved away, shuffling and stumbling in their bright silver blankets, because the medical tent now had a trauma ward and three people were dead. Now, the tent was quiet and, not far down the street, the fireman sagged on the fender of the truck and stared at the bottle of water at his feet.

I do not know what happens now. I know the event will never be the same. It is marked now, and it will be marked in the future, by what happened on the afternoon of April 15, 2013. Some of it will be locked down. Some of it will be tightened up. I walked back down to the Public Garden again, because Copley Square was growing dark and exhausted as the night began to fall. Back by the stone fountain, a woman in a silver blanket told a Providence TV station that she'd been unable to find a ladies' room after the race because all the restaurants and hotels had been locked down and she had to come all the way down to Park Square to find facilities that would deign to accommodate her. She was not happy at all, and she was telling greater Providence about it. "And I needed *to pee!*" she told some undoubtedly astounded Rhode Islanders.

There was something comfortingly mundane in how truly angry she was. The best example of this came from my friend, Steve Brown, a reporter for WBUR, one of the local Boston NPR stations. Brown swore he heard one person say, "Damn it, this is the first time I ever got DNF'd." Goddamn runners. I swear, one day, I promise, I'll laugh about them again. The Marathon will be worth mocking again. But that will not be today. It will not be any time soon. I sat down near the stone fountain, and wished all of us could wash the day away.

Contributors' Notes

Notable Sports Writing of 2013

Contributors' Notes

Award-winning sportswriter RON BORGES is a columnist for the *Boston Herald*. Before joining the *Herald* in 2007, he wrote for the *Boston Globe*, primarily covering football and boxing.

FLINDER BOYD is a California native and freelance writer. A former professional basketball player who lived in France, Spain, the United Kingdom, Slovakia, and Greece during a 10-year career, he now resides in New York. He also holds degrees from Dartmouth College and Queen Mary, University of London.

TIMOTHY BURKE has served as Deadspin's video/assignment editor since 2011. He previously spent 10 years in higher education teaching communication, rhetoric, and media courses. He lives in St. Petersburg, Florida.

JACK DICKEY is a writer for *Time* and *Sports Illustrated*. He previously wrote for Deadspin. Originally from Guilford, Connecticut, he now lives in New York.

KATHY DOBIE is a freelance writer who lives in Brooklyn and writes for *GQ, Harper's Magazine,* and *O Magazine.* She is the author of the memoir *The Only Girl in the Car.*

IAN FRAZIER is a staff writer for *The New Yorker* and the author of many books, including *Great Plains, On the Rez, The Cursing Mommy's Book of Days,* and *Travels in Siberia.* A native of Cleveland and a graduate of Harvard, he lives in New Jersey.

Originally from Northern California, ALICE GREGORY is a writer living in New York. Her work has appeared in publications including the *New York Times, GQ, Harper's Magazine, New York,* and newyorker.com.

AMANDA HESS is a *Slate* staff writer, a cofounder of *Tomorrow* magazine, and a contributor to *The Book of Jezebel*. Her work has appeared in *ESPN: The Magazine, Wired, Elle,* the *Los Angeles Times, T: The New York Times Style Magazine, Pacific Standard,* and the *Village Voice*. She has lived in Wisconsin, Nevada, Washington, Arizona, and California but now resides begrudgingly in Brooklyn.

PATRICK HRUBY is a writer for Sports on Earth and a contributor to *Washingtonian* magazine and elsewhere. He has worked for ESPN.com and the *Washington Times* and taught journalism at Georgetown University. He holds degrees from Georgetown and Northwestern and lives in Washington, DC, with his wife, Saphira. This is his fifth appearance in *The Best American Sports Writing*.

CHRIS JONES is a writer-at-large for *Esquire* and a senior writer for *ESPN: The Magazine*. He has won two National Magazine Awards for his feature writing and two National Headliner Awards for his columns. This is his fourth appearance in *The Best American Sports Writing*. He lives in Port Hope, Ontario, with his wife and two boys.

JAY CASPIAN KANG is the author of the novel *The Dead Do Not Improve*. His journalism has appeared in the *New York Times Magazine* and Grantland .com.

RAFFI KHATCHADOURIAN is a staff writer for *The New Yorker*. His work has been shortlisted for two National Magazine Awards: one in profile writing, and the other—in conjunction with the magazine's digital team—for multimedia. In 2008, his feature on the Sea Shepherd Conservation Society was included in *The Best American Nonrequired Reading*.

BROOK LARMER is a contributing writer for the *New York Times Magazine* and *National Geographic* and the author of *Operation Yao Ming*, a tale of China's global emergence told through the prism of sports. An award-winning foreign correspondent, Larmer covered Mexico and Central America for the *Christian Science Monitor* and worked for more than a decade at *Newsweek* as the bureau chief in Buenos Aires, Miami, Hong Kong, and Shanghai. From his current base in Asia, he travels widely on assignment, occasionally indulging his interest in sports stories that illuminate the societies around them. A graduate of Williams College, Larmer lives in Beijing with his wife and two sons.

JONATHAN MAHLER is a reporter at the *New York Times* and a longtime contributing writer to the *New York Times Magazine*. He is the author of the bestselling *Ladies and Gentlemen, the Bronx Is Burning, The Challenge: How a Maverick Navy Officer and a Young Law Professor Risked Their Careers to De-*

fend the Constitution—and Won, and *Death Comes to Happy Valley.* He lives in Brooklyn.

JEREMY MARKOVICH is an Emmy Award–winning producer with WCNC-TV, a columnist at *Charlotte* magazine, and a contributor to *Our State Magazine* and SBNation.com. A graduate of Ohio University, he lives in Charlotte, North Carolina, with his wife, Kelsey, their newborn son, Charlie, and their dog, Lucy. His website is www.jeremymarkovich.com.

BEN MCGRATH has been a staff writer for *The New Yorker* since 2003. He lives in the lower Hudson Valley.

Floridian freelancer BUCKY MCMAHON is a writer, painter, and sculptor—as well as a tennis enthusiast, barefoot runner, and stand-up paddle surfer. He's currently at work on a play about William Butler Yeats and the supernatural, while pitching stories about extreme sports, wildlife, the environment, and the arts.

DAVID MERRILL is a psychiatrist, psychoanalyst, and former high school wrestler. He lives with his wife and two children in New York City.

NICK PAUMGARTEN is a staff writer at *The New Yorker.*

CHARLES P. PIERCE is a staff writer for Grantland.com and the author of *Idiot America.* He writes regularly for *Esquire,* is the lead writer for Esquire.com's The Politics Blog, and is a frequent guest on National Public Radio. This is his ninth appearance in *The Best American Sports Writing.*

MARY PILON is an award-winning sports reporter at the *New York Times* and author of *The Monopolists,* a book that chronicles the secret history of the world-famous board game. She previously worked as a staff reporter at the *Wall Street Journal,* where she wrote about various aspects of economics and the financial crisis. She has worked at *Gawker, USA Today,* and *New York* magazine and is an honors graduate of New York University. She made *Forbes* magazine's first-ever "30 Under 30" list for media. A native Oregonian and fledgling marathoner, she lives in New York City. Visit her website at marypilon.com and find her on Twitter @marypilon.

AMANDA RIPLEY is an investigative journalist for *Time, The Atlantic,* and other magazines. She is the author, most recently, of *The Smartest Kids in the World—and How They Got That Way,* a *New York Times* bestseller. Her first book, *The Unthinkable: Who Survives When Disaster Strikes—and Why,* was published in 15 countries and turned into a PBS documentary. Before joining *Time* as a writer in 2000, Ripley covered the DC courts for *Washington City Paper* and Capitol Hill for *Congressional Quarterly.* A graduate of

Cornell University, she lives in Washington, DC, where she is an Emerson Senior Fellow.

STEPHEN RODRICK is a contributing editor at *Rolling Stone* and *Men's Journal.* He is also a contributing writer for the *New York Times Magazine.* This is his fifth appearance in *The Best American Sports Writing.* His book *The Magical Stranger,* a reported memoir on the death of his pilot father, Commander Peter Rodrick, off the USS *Kitty Hawk,* was recently released in paperback. He lives in Los Angeles.

ELI SASLOW is a staff writer for the *Washington Post* and a contributor to *ESPN: The Magazine.* He has won a Polk Award for national reporting and been a finalist for the Pulitzer Prize in feature writing. His first book, *Ten Letters: The Stories Americans Tell Their President,* was published in 2012. He lives in Takoma Park, Maryland, with his wife and two daughters.

When he was growing up, CHRISTOPHER SOLOMON cared so little about following organized sports, or running footraces, that his father called his statistics-obsessed older sister "the son I never had." Today he's the one who writes frequently about athletes and the outdoors for *Runner's World,* the *New York Times Magazine* and the *New York Times* Sunday travel section, *Outside* magazine, and other publications. His writing has also appeared in *The Best American Travel Writing.* He lives in Seattle, and his writing lives at www.chrissolomon.net. His dad has come around and now claims him.

PAUL SOLOTAROFF is a contributing editor for *Men's Journal* and the author of *The Group* and *The House of Purple Hearts.* This is his eighth appearance in *The Best American Sports Writing.*

DON VAN NATTA JR. is a senior writer for *ESPN: The Magazine* and ESPN .com. He joined ESPN in January 2012 after 16 years as a *New York Times* correspondent based in Washington, London, Miami, and New York. Prior to that, he worked for eight years at the *Miami Herald.* A member of three Pulitzer Prize–winning teams, Van Natta is the author of *First Off the Tee* and the coauthor of *Her Way,* both *New York Times* bestsellers, and *Wonder Girl.* He lives in Miami with his wife, Lizette Alvarez, who is a *Times* correspondent, and their two daughters.

Notable Sports Writing of 2013

SELECTED BY GLENN STOUT

THE BEST AMERICAN SERIES®

FIRST, BEST, AND BEST-SELLING

The Best American series is the premier annual showcase for the country's finest short fiction and nonfiction. Each volume's series editor selects notable works from hundreds of magazines, journals, and websites. A special guest editor, a leading writer in the field, then chooses the best twenty or so pieces to publish. This unique system has made the Best American series the most respected—and most popular—of its kind.

Look for these best-selling titles in the Best American series:

The Best American Comics

The Best American Essays

The Best American Infographics

The Best American Mystery Stories

The Best American Nonrequired Reading

The Best American Science and Nature Writing

The Best American Short Stories

The Best American Sports Writing

The Best American Travel Writing

Available in print and e-book wherever books are sold.
Visit our website: *www.hmhbooks.com/hmh/site/bas*